. . . .

Sultanistic Regimes

Sultanistic Regimes

· · · · · · · · · · · · ·

EDITED BY

*H. E. Chehabi
and Juan J. Linz*

The Johns Hopkins University Press
Baltimore and London

9 8 7 6 5 4 3 2 1

The Johns Hopkins University Press
2715 North Charles Street
Baltimore, Maryland 21218-4363
The Johns Hopkins Press Ltd., London

A catalog record for this book is available from the British Library.

Library of Congress Cataloging-in-Publication Data
Sultanistic regimes / edited by H. E. Chehabi and Juan J. Linz.
   p.   cm.
   "Based on a workshop held at the Center for International
Affairs of Harvard University in June 1990"—Acknowledgments.
   Includes bibliographical references (p.   ) and index.
   ISBN 0-8018-5693-0 (acid-free paper). — ISBN 0-8018-5694-9
(pbk. acid-free paper)
     1. Authoritarianism—Congresses.   2. Totalitarianism—
Congresses.   3. Comparative government—Congresses.
4. Developing countries—Politics and government—Case
studies—Congresses.   I. Chehabi, H. E.   II. Linz, Juan J.
(Juan José), 1926– .
JC480.S85   1998
321.9′09′045—dc21   97-41153
                                        CIP

· · · ·

In memory of David Nicholls

CONTENTS

. . . .

List of Contributors   *ix*

Acknowledgments   *xi*

PART ONE: COMPARATIVE STUDIES

1   *A Theory of Sultanism 1: A Type of Nondemocratic Rule*   *3*
    H. E. Chehabi and Juan J. Linz

2   *A Theory of Sultanism 2: Genesis and Demise of Sultanistic Regimes*   *26*
    H. E. Chehabi and Juan J. Linz

3   *Paths out of Sultanistic Regimes: Combining Structural and Voluntarist Perspectives*   *49*
    Richard Snyder

PART TWO: COUNTRY STUDIES

4   *The Trujillo Regime in the Dominican Republic*   *85*
    Jonathan Hartlyn

5   *The Batista Regime in Cuba*   *113*
    Jorge I. Domínguez

6   *The Somoza Regime in Nicaragua*   *132*
    John A. Booth

7   *The Duvalier Regime in Haiti*   *153*
    David Nicholls

8   *The Pahlavi Regime in Iran*   *182*
    Homa Katouzian

9   *The Marcos Regime in the Philippines*   *206*
    Mark R. Thompson

Notes   *231*

Index   *277*

CONTRIBUTORS

. . . .

John Booth is Regents' Professor of Political Science at the University of North Texas. He is the author of *The End and the Beginning: The Nicaraguan Revolution*, co-author of *Understanding Central America* and *Costa Rica: Quest for Democracy*, and co-editor of and a contributor to *Political Participation in Latin America* and *Elections and Democracy in Latin America*. He has published widely on political participation, political culture, and political change in Latin America, and on U.S. policy in Central America.

H. E. Chehabi is a visiting scholar at the Woodrow Wilson International Center. He is the author of *Iranian Politics and Religious Modernism: The Liberation Movement of Iran under the Shah and Khomeini*, co-editor, with Alfred Stepan, of *Politics, Society, and Democracy: Comparative Studies*, and has written numerous articles on Iranian politics and social history as well as the politics of small islands, which are his main research interest.

Jorge I. Domínguez is the Clarence Dillon Professor of International Affairs and director of the Center of International Affairs at Harvard University. The author of numerous books on Latin American history and politics, he has most recently been co-author of *Democratizing Mexico: Public Opinion and Electoral Choices* and co-editor and co-author of *Constructing Democratic Governance: Latin America and the Caribbean in the 1990s*.

Jonathan Hartlyn is professor of political science at the University of North Carolina, Chapel Hill. He is the author of *The Struggle for Democratic Politics in the Dominican Republic* and *The Politics of Coalition Rule in Colombia*. He is also co-editor, with Lars Schoultz and Augusto Varas, of *The United States and Latin America in the 1990s* and, with Samuel Morley, of *Latin American Political Economy*. He has published numerous articles on democracy and state-society relations in Latin America, which continue to be his main research interests.

Homa Katouzian is honorary research fellow in politics at the University of Exeter, and retired senior lecturer in economics at the University of Kent, United Kingdom. His books include *Ideology and Method in Economics, The*

Political Economy of Iran, and *Sadeq Hedayat: The Life and Legend of an Iranian Writer.* His current research interests are in Iranian state and society as well as modern Persian literature.

Juan J. Linz is the Sterling Professor of Political and Social Science at Yale University. Among his many publications are *The Breakdown of Democratic Regimes: Crisis, Breakdown, and Reequilibration* and, with Alfred Stepan, *Problems of Democratic Transition and Consolidation: Southern Europe, South America and Post-Communist Europe.* He is also co-editor and co-author, with Arturo Valenzuela, of *The Failure of Presidential Democracy.* He is the recipient of the Principe de Asturias Prize and was awarded the Johan Skytte Prize in political science in 1996.

The Reverend Dr. David Nicholls, theologian and political scientist, was the vicar of Littlemore, Oxford. Among his many publications are *From Dessalines to Duvalier, The Pluralist State, Deity and Domination, God and Government in an "Age of Enlightenment"* as well as controversial writings on politics, theology, and Caribbean studies.

Richard Snyder is assistant professor of political science at the University of Illinois, Urbana-Champaign and an academy scholar at the Harvard Academy for International and Area Studies. He is the editor and co-author of *Institutional Adaptation and Innovation in Rural Mexico* and of several articles on regime change, which is, together with comparative political economy, his major research interest. He is currently completing a book titled *After the State Withdraws: Neoliberalism and the Politics of Reregulation in Mexico.*

Mark R. Thompson is professor of politics at the University of Erlangen-Nürnberg, Germany. He is the author of *The Anti-Marcos Struggle: Personalistic Rule and Democratic Transition in the Philippines* and has published on the politics of the Asia-Pacific region, on the East German revolution, and on regime types and regime change.

ACKNOWLEDGMENTS

. . . .

This book is based on a workshop held at the Center for International Affairs of Harvard University in June 1990. The editors thank Samuel P. Huntington, the Center's director at that time, for making its resources available for the workshop. In addition to those contributing chapters to this volume, several scholars participated in the intense two-day discussions, and we are grateful to them for sharing their time and insights with us: Don Babai, Mary Ellen Fischer, Robert Fishman, Jeff Goodwin, Robert O. Keohane, and Theda Skocpol.

Ideally we would have liked to include chapters both on the Ceauşescu regime and on sultanistic rulers of sub-Saharan Africa. By the time the other chapters of this book were ready, however, the Romanian case had been covered in another recent work by Juan Linz in collaboration with Alfred Stepan, so we omitted it here.[1] Our efforts to include Africanists in our comparative project came to naught when none of the scholars we approached found time to write a contribution. We nevertheless draw readers' attention to the work of Michael Bratton and Nicolas van de Walle, whose analyses are congruent with ours.[2]

This book's coauthored first two chapters served as the basis for the discussions at the workshop. H. E. Chehabi prepared the first draft in the spring of 1989, while a faculty affiliate of Harvard University's Center for International Affairs, and produced the second, expanded version while he was the visiting Iranian fellow at St. Antony's College, Oxford, in 1995–96. He would like to thank the CFIA and St. Antony's College, especially its Middle East Center, for generously sponsoring his work. In Oxford he frequently enjoyed the cheerful hospitality of David and Gillian Nicholls at the Littlemore vicarage, for which he is profoundly grateful. It is with sadness that we note the Rev. David Nicholls's sudden death in June 1996, before he could see his last essay in print; his colleagues in this project dedicate this book to his memory.

PART ONE

· · · ·

Comparative Studies

1

. . . .

A Theory of Sultanism 1

A Type of Nondemocratic Rule

H. E. Chehabi and Juan J. Linz

The concept of "sultanistic regime" emerged from Juan Linz's comparative analysis of nondemocratic regimes, which systematically developed the differences between totalitarian and authoritarian forms of rule.[1] At the time Linz developed this distinction in the early 1970s, political democracies were few, whereas the range of nondemocratic regimes was enormous. Since totalitarian regimes were rare and limited to the communist world,[2] it was tempting to group all other nondemocratic regimes in the residual category "authoritarian," which denotes a wide range of governments with distinctive characteristics that allow their societies a limited pluralism short of genuine democracy. Authoritarian regimes can thus be mostly civilian one-party states, ranging from a highly institutionalized authoritarian regime such as Franco's Spain to the ephemeral single-party regimes of Africa in the very early days of independence; nonhierarchical or hierarchical military regimes like the bureaucratic-authoritarian regimes of the Southern Cone of South America;[3] or even royal dictatorships like those in the Balkans in the interwar years (as opposed to traditionally legitimated monarchies).

The structural differences among them are therefore vast.[4] But as vast as they are, some regimes appeared distinct on all the major dimensions used in the conceptualization of nondemocratic rule; Linz called them "sultanistic." The differences between these and authoritarian or totalitarian regimes are not merely a matter of degree but lie in their rulers' overall conception of politics, the structure of power, and the relation to the social structure, the economy, and ultimately the subjects of such rule. But before analyzing "sultanistic" regimes, the use of the term should be explained.

Excursus on "Sultanism"

The term "sultanism" was originally coined by Max Weber, who used it to refer to an extreme case of patrimonialism, which in his tripartite classification of the forms of legitimate authority is a form of traditional authority:

> *Patrimonialism* and, in the extreme case, *sultanism* tend to arise whenever traditional domination develops an administration and a military force which are purely personal instruments of the master. . . . Where domination is primarily traditional, even though it is exercised by virtue of the ruler's personal autonomy, it will be called *patrimonial authority;* where indeed it operates primarily on the basis of discretion, it will be called *sultanism.* . . . Sometimes it appears that sultanism is completely unrestrained by tradition, but this is never in fact the case. The non-traditional element is not, however, rationalized in impersonal terms, but consists only in an extreme development of the ruler's discretion. It is this which distinguishes it from every form of rational authority.[5]

Weber's notion of patrimonialism caught on and was used extensively, and in an influential article Guenther Roth applied it to Third World politics.[6] Given the differences between the modern states in which the patrimonial logic operates and the traditional patrimonial systems Weber had in mind, the term "neopatrimonialism" came to be widely used.[7] But Weber's formulation of patrimonialism's extreme form, "sultanism," was neglected by scholars.[8]

The term was adopted by Juan Linz in his classification of nondemocratic governments. When he began working on Spain's Franco regime in the late 1950s, he soon realized that the model of "totalitarianism" then current, based on the Stalinist and Nazi experience, did not fit. The result was the conceptualization of the "authoritarian" regime, whose different aspects he explored in a series of essays.[9] A meeting with a Spanish exile was to convince him that the authoritarian/totalitarian dichotomy did not exhaust the range of nondemocratic regimes either. In the early 1950s Linz met his Spanish compatriot Jesús de Galíndez, a representative of the exiled Basque government, who had taught international law in the Dominican Republic. Although a republican émigré, Galíndez was treated courteously by Spanish diplomats in New York. But when he wrote a doctoral dissertation at Columbia University revealing some of the inside workings of the Trujillo regime, he confided to Juan Linz in 1955 that he feared for his life, and that he had deposited his manuscript in a safe place in case something happened to him. Soon afterward the dictator had Galíndez abducted in New York and taken to the Dominican Republic, where he was tortured to death.[10] The contrast between Franco's nondemocratic regime and Trujillo's rule led to the conceptualization of a regime type for which Linz borrowed Weber's term "sultanism," since it too rested on the extreme development of the ruler's discretion. Moreover, Weber, although constructing the ideal type of sultanism in a section on traditional authority, explicitly contrasted the traditional basis of patrimonialism with the discretionary aspect of sultanism (see quotation above), implying that tradition played little role in the latter. Just as Franco's rule became the archetype of an authoritarian regime, Trujillo's became that of a sultanistic regime in Linz's 1973 classification of nondemocratic regimes.[11]

Subsequently a number of scholars confirmed the applicability of Linz's paradigm to a number of regimes not mentioned in the 1975 article. Crawford Young and Thomas Turner wrote about Mobutu's regime in Zaire that "in the personalist patrimonial state fashioned by Mobutu, we may discern much that resembles what Linz, borrowing a Weberian term, has labelled 'sultanism.' "[12] Terry Karl characterized the regimes of Juan Vicente Gómez and Marcos Pérez Jiménez in Venezuela as sultanistic, and H. E. Chehabi explored how the Shah of Iran's sultanism contributed to the Islamic revolution. For the Philippines, John Thayer Sidel applied it to local politics, and Mark Thompson to Marcos's rule. Finally, Samuel Huntington wrote that "some personal dictatorships, such as those of Marcos and Ceauşescu, like those of Somoza, Duvalier, Mobutu, and the Shah, exemplified Weber's model of sultanistic regime characterized by patronage, nepotism, cronyism, and corruption."[13] The criticism so often leveled against inductively derived theoretical concepts—that since, in Pareto's words, they lead "from facts to concepts, and from concepts back to facts,"[14] they produce circular argument—does not apply to sultanism as a concept, since it has fruitfully been applied to a *different set* of facts.

Independently of Linz's revival of the term, Richard Sandbrook called Weber's notion of sultanism "more relevant to the circumstances of contemporary Africa." He added that it flourished "under a number of guises: civilian, quasi-military or military forms of government, one-party or competitive-party systems or even under the socialist veneer of Guinea, Benin, and the Republic of Congo."[15]

At the 1990 conference on which this book is based, the late David Nicholls pointed out that whereas Weber's sultanism was a subtype of traditional authority, our cases were characterized by the decay or incomplete development of modern legal-rational authority rather than by the disappearance of all

TABLE 1.1
Types of Patrimonial Rule

	Type of Authority	Extreme Form
Traditional form	Patrimonialism	Sultanism
Modern form	Neopatrimonialism	Neosultanism

remnants of traditional authority. It is indeed true that the regimes we studied relate to Weber's sultanistic regimes just as neopatrimonial regimes relate to Weber's patrimonial type of traditional authority; therefore to be precise one should refer to them as "neosultanistic" regimes. This usage would have the advantage of not only distinguishing them from the Weberian use of the term "sultanism," but also maintaining the logic of Weber's terminology; as we shall see, just as for Weber the transition between patrimonialism and sultanism is "definitely continuous,"[16] neosultanistic regimes are an extreme version of neo-patrimonial forms of governance. The scheme shown in table 1.1 obtains.

Also, the etymology of the term "sultanism" strikes some as "orientalist." At the conference, Jonathan Hartlyn suggested the term "discretionary neopatri-monialism" to replace "sultanism." For Weber, the Near East was the "classical location of 'sultanism,' "[17] which is presumably why he chose a term derived from the Arabic language. Weber's study of the Islamic world was less thorough than his systematic explorations of Christianity, ancient Judaism, and even Confucianism, and it is not for us to pass judgment on the accuracy of his analyses,[18] more particularly on whether traditional regimes headed by a sultan were in fact "sultanistic" in the sense defined by Weber: recent scholarship tends to refute this view in the case of the Ottoman Empire.[19] Our distinction between the theoretical concept and the empirical reality that led to its initial formulation is congruent with Weber's own methodology, since he wrote else-where that "the concept of 'Kadi-justice' has [little] to do with the actual legal principles whereby the *kadi* renders legal decisions."[20] Furthermore, Weber does apply the term to other societies, such as China,[21] and the doyen of Ottoman historians, Halil Inalcik, has applied Weber's concepts to the Ottoman Empire without ascribing negative connotations to the term "sultanism."[22] Nor does the term have an anti-Islamic tinge, since, unlike the caliphate, the sultan-ate was a secular office.[23] Moreover, even the original pre-Ottoman caliphate, though endowed with a religious aura, derived in its actual organization from nonreligious models. As Inalcik puts it:

> What Max Weber meant by *sultanism* was originally derived not from Islamic precepts but from the caliphal state organization, which owed its basic philoso-phy and structure to the Byzantine and Sassanian heritage. This Iranian state

tradition was transmitted to the Ottomans through native bureaucrats and the literary activity of the Iranian converts who translated Sassanian advice literature into Arabic.[24]

To summarize, although the etymological objection to "sultanism" seems untenable, that the term belongs to the world of traditional forms of authority poses a real problem. Our approach to the social sciences is nominalist rather than essentialist, however, and since "sultanism" has already achieved some recognition among political scientists, we retain the term even though "neo-sultanism" would be more accurate, so as not to add to the terminological confusion that is already too prevalent in the social sciences. Let us now turn to the definition of sultanistic rule.

Definition and Prevalence of Sultanistic Regimes

> No king was despotic of right, not even in Persia; but every bold and dissembling prince who amasses money, becomes despotic in little time.   VOLTAIRE,
> *Philosophical Dictionary*

The ideal type of a contemporary sultanistic regime can be constructed as follows: It is based on personal rulership, but loyalty to the ruler is motivated not by his embodying or articulating an ideology, nor by a unique personal mission, nor by any charismatic qualities, but by a mixture of fear and rewards to his collaborators. The ruler exercises his power without restraint, at his own discretion and above all unencumbered by rules or by any commitment to an ideology or value system. The binding norms and relations of bureaucratic administration are constantly subverted by arbitrary personal decisions of the ruler, which he does not feel constrained to justify in ideological terms. As a result corruption reigns supreme at all levels of society. The staff of such a ruler is constituted not by an establishment with distinctive career lines, like a bureaucratic army or a civil service, recruited based on more or less universal criteria, but largely by people chosen directly by the ruler. Among them we very often find members of his family, friends, business associates, or individuals directly involved in using violence to sustain the regime. Their position derives from their purely personal submission to the ruler, and their position of authority in society derives merely from this relation. The ruler and his associates do not represent any class or corporate interests. Although such regimes can in many ways be modern, what characterizes them is the weakness of traditional and legal-rational legitimation and the lack of ideological justification.[25]

No regime fits this ideal type perfectly. Paraphrasing Weber, one might even say that although (neo)sultanism may appear to be completely unrestrained by legal-rational norms, this is never in fact the case. Regimes approximating this ideal type can be found all over the world. The regime of Rafael Leónidas Trujillo Molina in the Dominican Republic, Jean-Claude Duvalier's rule in Haiti, Fulgencio Batista's dictatorship in Cuba, the rule of the Somoza family in Nicaragua, the later stages of both Pahlavi shahs' reign in Iran, Ferdinand Marcos's presidency after his declaration of martial law in 1972, and Manuel Noriega's dictatorship in Panama come closest, as do many of the personalistic dictatorships in sub-Saharan Africa.[26]

As in any typology, there are of course borderline cases that the comparativist has difficulty assigning to one category or another. Alfredo Stroessner's rule in Paraguay is one such case. Although many comparative studies of Latin American military dictatorships include his regime as a case of sultanism, we decided against doing so, for our analysis convinced us that, as Alain Rouquié put it,

> Paraguay has not been transformed into a Nicaraguan-style Stroessner fiefdom. . . . The Paraguayan state has a tangible existence, and the army is not the personal property of the president. It is unlikely that a Stroessner dynasty will be established. The oldest son, an aviation officer, has no military base, and the marriage of the youngest son to the daughter of a powerful general, Andrés Rodríguez, did not produce the results that had been anticipated.[27]

But a few years after this was written, "the powerful general" overthrew his daughter's father-in-law and became president himself before handing power to an elected civilian head of state. To complicate matters further, a Paraguayan political scientist's systematic attempt to characterize "Stronismo" typologically yielded the result that Juan Linz's notion of "sultanism" fit it best, with the proviso that it should be called "neosultanism."[28] We have decided to stick by our original choice, however, a decision that was confirmed by the Colorado Party's retention of power after the first free elections in Paraguay, which is unique in Latin American transitions and shows to what extent Paraguay's ruling party had an identity independent of Stroessner. A similar outcome obtained in Bulgaria, where the Bulgarian Socialist Party in 1990, alone among Eastern Europe's postcommunist parties, won the first free elections, in contrast to the muddle that resulted from the overthrow of Ceaușescu in neighboring Romania.[29]

The African states present a similar dilemma. Personalism is present in most of them, but it comes in several varieties that Africanists designate in different ways. Whereas Richard Sandbrook found "sultanism" almost everywhere, Robert H. Jackson and Carl G. Rosberg divided personalist rulers into "prince," "autocrat," "prophet," and "tyrant."[30] Another team of Africanists classified Africa's regimes as administrative-hegemonial, pluralist, party-mobilizing, party-centralist, personal coercive, populist, and ambiguous.[31] Michael Bratton and Nicolas van de Walle designated almost all regimes neopatrimonial but further divided them into personal dictatorships, plebiscitary one-party systems, military oligarchies, and competitive one-party systems.[32]

Although the "tyrants," "personal-coercive" rulers, and "neopatrimonial personal dictatorships" do not totally coincide, by and large they correspond to what Linz called "sultanism" two decades ago. And here the clearest cases are Jean Bédel Bokassa in the Central African Republic, Mobutu Sese Seko in Zaire, Francisco Macías Nguema in Equatorial Guinea, and Idi Amin in Uganda.[33] In the last two cases, however, the typical enrichment of the ruler and his family was not so significant, while arbitrary rule and destruction of society were.[34]

Under communism both Nicolae Ceauşescu's rule in Romania and the regime of Kim Il-sung and his son, Kim Jong-il, in North Korea show clear sultanistic tendencies. And among democracies, the rule of Eric Gairy in Grenada (1974–79) and that of the Bird family in Antigua and Barbuda evince some sultanistic traits.[35]

Yet even in the regimes we call sultanistic, elements of a legal-rational order or of a legitimizing ideology are not totally absent. The concept of "sultanistic regime" is not a genetic but an evolutionary one, in the sense that most such regimes develop out of other forms of rule. Jean-Claude Duvalier owed his presidency to his being the son of the champion of *noirisme*. François Duvalier initially came to power through democratic elections in 1957, as did Ferdinand Marcos in 1965, Eric Gairy in 1967, Macías Nguema in 1968, and V. C. ("Papa") Bird Sr. in 1976. The Shah never abrogated the 1906 constitution. Batista in the 1950s ruled under an amended constitution and tolerated a Congress and courts. Ceauşescu came to power through the normal functioning of the Romanian Communist Party. And yet other political regimes that also had despotic and arbitrary dimensions did not develop into sultanism.

As is the case with all ideal-typical concepts, no empirical reality fully matches all characteristics of a sultanistic regime. It could be argued that it would be preferable to talk about "sultanistic tendencies," indicating a development in the direction of the ideal-typical sultanistic regime.[36] We could then speak of sultanistic tendencies that can occur in different kinds of regimes, can be stronger or weaker at different moments, and can coexist with other aspects and dimensions of governance. For simplicity, however, we will use the term "sultanistic regime" most of the time.

A regime in which some sultanistic tendencies are present, but where the circle of clients is wider and the discretion of the ruler less extensive, should be called neopatrimonial. Personalist rulers whose regimes penetrate society by means of a political party, such as the Colorado Party in General Alfredo Stroessner's Paraguay, or who represent a certain segment in society, like François Duvalier, who based his rule on the black middle classes in opposition to Haiti's mulatto elite, do not fit the pure type of sultanistic regime. Of course if the circle of people included in the ruler's patron-client relationships narrows, the regime can become sultanistic: such was the transition from François Duvalier's rule in Haiti to Jean-Claude Duvalier's. Let us now turn to a detailed analysis of this type of regime.

Characteristics of Sultanistic Regimes

In the course of this analysis we will illuminate these regimes' distinctiveness by constantly referring to other types of nondemocratic regimes around the following themes: the state over which they preside, their personalism, their constitutional hypocrisy, their social base, and their political economy.

The Blurring of the Line between Regime and State

By "regime" we mean the patterns of allocation, use, and abuse of power in a polity. This encompasses more than the political institutions in a democracy and less than the comprehensive structures of domination in totalitarian systems. Robert Fishman has noted that for understanding authoritarian regimes (and more specifically transitions to democracy) it is useful to distinguish between regime and state.[37] Under authoritarian regimes the more limited politicization of society makes it possible to discriminate between those who hold political power in the government, in the party, or in the military and those who exercise functions normally associated with a modern state in a professional bureaucracy, in the armed forces, or in the judiciary. Therefore the state apparatus is likely to persist with only limited modification in many regime changes, except when they are revolutionary.[38]

Under sultanistic rule the distinction between regime and state is much more blurred, and in very advanced cases of sultanism one can even speak of a fusion between regime and state.[39] Bureaucratic structures persist and may even be streamlined and rendered more efficient, especially at the local level where extractive opportunities are not always present, but the ruler and his associates directly intervene in the structures of governance, disregarding their internal norms, professional standards, and ethos. As we shall see, this renders the "state structures" less serviceable after a regime change.

Trujillo, Reza Shah, Somoza García, and Mobutu all began by strengthening the state after a period of institutional decay; furthermore, all subdued regional challenges to the hegemony of the center over the periphery in the early phases of their rule. It is this initial centralization of power, accompanied as it is by a strengthening of the military and other state institutions, that makes sultanistic control over society possible.

As the founders' power increases, sultanistic tendencies appear. Beyond the ruler himself, his immediate relatives, and his close associates or "cronies," the sultanistic state is characterized by an absence or perversion of legal-rational norms that is unrelated to an ideological project, and by rampant corruption and venality. In the state administration and the army such features of modern bureaucracies as areas of official jurisdiction, an office hierarchy with channels of appeal that stipulate a clearly established system of super- and subordination, the separation of official activity from the sphere of private life, and finally the management of offices according to general rules may exist on paper and, depending on the country's level of development, even in reality, but they are under constant attack by the sultanistic practice of regulating all relationships through individual privileges and bestowals of favor.[40]

At some point in their autocratic rule, the dictators often bring technocrats into the regime—both to please their American patrons and to propose to the country an apolitical and competent alternative to the political chaos that would ensue in the absence of the ruler. In Iran the last shah brought in a number of well-trained bureaucrats after the White Revolution of 1963, in the course of which he eliminated big landowners as the politically dominant social class. In what was then Congo-Kinshasa, Mobutu very early "established numerous public and semipublic agencies headed by young technocrats and former politicians concerned with the Congo's social and economic development" and relied increasingly "on the talent and expertise of such social groups as university and technical school students and former civil servants."[41] In the Philippines Marcos "brought a corps of technocrats into his government," announced in mid-1981 that he would "sit back and let the technocrats run things," and favorably impressed both U.S. officials and International Monetary Fund-World Bank officials.[42] In fact, however, the

> technocrats were given the prerogative to formulate and rhetorize the public agenda in the form of economic and development plans which formed the basis for foreign loans. The political leadership then allowed the unconstrained introduction of exceptions that made complete mockery of the spirit and letter of the plans.[43]

In Haiti, Jean-Claude Duvalier "fired his ministers and brought in a number of well-regarded young technocrats to clean up the government and impress the United States," but within "a short time . . . he had dismissed a number of them, some due to his wife's objections, and others because they actually intended to fulfill the assignment."[44]

Clearly, sultanistic rule is not incompatible with a certain rationalization of the administration, as long as this rationalization enhances the ability of the ruler and his cronies to extract resources from society. If the technocrats try to resist the regime's dominant ethos, however, they are marginalized, for even when an official is not a personal dependent of the ruler, the ruler demands compliance. In his view the official's loyalty is not an impersonal commitment to impersonal tasks that define the extent and content of his office, but rather a servant's loyalty based on a strictly personal relationship to the ruler and an obligation that in principle permits no limitation.

These officials enjoy little security: they are promoted and dismissed at will and enjoy no independent status. In Haiti, President Jean-Claude Duvalier "often dismissed and replaced cabinet members on the advice of his wife or counsel of some trusted minister. These shake-ups occurred twice a year on average . . . and ministers operated in a climate of insecurity and paranoia."[45] In extreme cases, ministers may even be subject to dishonor and persecution one day and return to the graces of the ruler next, as exemplified by the Zairian politician Nguza Karl-I-Bond, who was foreign minister, broke with Mobutu, went into Belgian exile, was condemned to death, and later repented, returned, and became prime minister. It bears emphasizing again that most modern sultanistic states do have pockets of bureaucratic organization, but the more these come under attack, the more we can say that the sultanization of the regime is advanced.

Of particular importance is the organization of the armed forces and their relation to the rest of the state apparatus. Sultanistic rulers typically maintain an atmosphere of distrust among various branches of the military and encourage mutual espionage to protect themselves from a military coup; some even use private militias to sustain their control of society, such as the Duvaliers' Tonton Macoutes or Eric Gairy's "mongoose men." Intricate structures are maintained to make each branch help control the others. Often there is no unified command, and the commanders of each force report directly to the rulers. The normal criteria for promotion are disregarded or subverted, creating resentment. The armed forces are thus deprofessionalized as the rulers aim at converting them into their private instruments for power.[46] In the Philippines Marcos made his driver, Fabian Ver, chief of staff, and in the Central African Republic Bokassa named Sublieutenant Bozize air force general after the man slapped a Frenchman who had treated Bokassa disrespectfully.[47] As the rulers' men in the military gain access to patronage, the gap between them and their less fortunate colleagues grows. In Iran, the Shah's multibillion-dollar arms purchases in the 1970s enriched those generals who dealt with procurements and thereby alienated many others.[48]

In discussing the armed forces of sultanistic regimes, it is useful to distinguish analytically between their *autonomy* and their *professionalism*. The Iranian army was highly professional, but at the same time closely related to the Shah. Likewise, Nicaragua's National Guard was loyal to Somoza and fought well in the civil war. In a country like Paraguay, it is perhaps the armed forces' relative professionalism, the outcome of the many wars the country was forced to fight against its neighbors, that has prevented the state's neopatrimonialism from degenerating into outright sultanism. The position of the armed forces vis-à-vis the ruler is crucial when the regime undergoes a crisis and may indeed determine the outcome, a theme analyzed in detail in Richard Snyder's contribution to this volume.

Sultanistic rulers sometimes create single parties. When they do, these parties' very names bespeak the rulers' efforts to make them look like "revolutionary" movements, destined to be the link between the leader and the people he guides toward new horizons: Kilusang Bagong Lipunan (New Society Movement) in the Philippines, Mouvement Populaire de la Révolution in Zaire, Comité National d'Action Jean-Claudiste in Haiti, and Rastakhiz (Resurgence) in Iran. In the Central African Republic Bokassa used the preexisting Mouvement pour l'Evolution Sociale en Afrique Noire (MESAN) for this purpose. Yet in reality the revolutionary quality of these parties is like the charisma of its leaders—mostly declarative. Nor do they fulfill the functions assigned to parties in established single-party states: the legitimation of the political system, political recruitment, and policy formulation.[49] The nature of the sultanistic regime militates against such a role.

Personalism

Paradoxically enough, whether or not their official position in the state corresponds to their actual power, sultanistic leaders do not conceal the highly personalistic nature of their rule. Outwardly this personalism has two facets: a pronounced cult of personality around the leader and a tendency toward dynasticism.

Sultanistic leaders crave charisma and surround themselves with the trappings of charismatic leadership precisely because they know they lack it.[50] They invent new titles for themselves: Trujillo called himself *generalísimo* and *benefactor de la patria;* the Shah became Aryamehr ("Light of the Aryans"). Mobutu changed his name from Joseph-Désiré Mobutu to Mobutu Sese Seko Kuku Ngbendu Wa Za Banga, meaning "The all-powerful warrior who will go from conquest to conquest, leaving fire in his wake," and he was called, among other things, "savior."[51] The dictator of the Central African Republic assumed the title of emperor, and Ceauşescu revived General Ion Antonescu's title of *conducător* in addition to being described as "architect of world peace" and "hero among the nation's heroes."[52] Amin styled himself field marshal and CBE (conqueror of the British Empire), and Macías Nguema topped all others by claiming divinity.

Sultanistic rulers also like to be thought of as great thinkers and fill many beautifully bound volumes with their speeches, declarations, and proclamations in addition to their numerous (mostly ghostwritten) books. Frequently, feeling the need to legitimize their regime ideologically, they come up with an ideology that, reflecting the regime's personalism, often bears the ruler's name. In Haiti "Jean-Claudism" became official state ideology in 1978, Ferdinand Marcos wrote a book called *An Ideology for Filipinos,*[53] the Shah published a book under his name titled *The White Revolution,* which was taught as a subject in Iranian high schools in ninth and eleventh grades, and Mobutu's works were collected in *Les grands textes du Mobutisme,*[54] Mobutuism having become official state ideology in 1974. The implementation of this ideology is sometimes accompanied by a "revolution," such as the Shah's "White Revolution" of 1963 (later renamed "Revolution of the Shah and the People") or Marcos's "Revolution from the Center,"[55] but the main function of these revolutions seems to be eliminating political opponents.

The sultanist ideology often exalts the nation's ancient glories and draws on an "invented tradition"[56] to demarcate the nation from its neighbors ethnically and even racially. The Pahlavi shahs' implicitly anti-Arab emphasis on Iran's ancient Persian heritage, discussed by Homa Katouzian, Trujillo's anti-Haitianism, discussed by Jonathan Hartlyn, François Duvalier's *noirisme,* Ceauşescu's insistence that Romanians are descendants of the ancient Dacians,[57] and Mobutu's cult of African "authenticity" are cases in point. One who truly believed in this return to the roots was Macías Nguema, who purged his country of all Western influence, even modern medicine.[58]

However, the function of this ideology is different from that of totalitarian systems, where "leaders, individuals or groups . . . derive much of their sense of mission, their legitimation, and often very specific policies from their commitment to some holistic conception of man and society."[59] The purer a regime's sultanism, the more its ideology is likely to be mere window dressing, elaborated after the onset of the ruler's regime to justify it. In Iran, Reza Shah was to some extent motivated by an ideology of Persian nationalism, and in Haiti François Duvalier was inspired by the old tradition of *noirisme* and used it to his advantage.[60] And in Romania, which, unlike all other East European states except Albania, never experienced a transition to posttotalitarianism, Ceauşescu's rule was an aberration of the Marxism-Leninism prevalent in that part of the world at the time and thus a survival of Stalinism. It is reminiscent of Stalin's personality cult that the entry on Ceauşescu in the Romanian encyclopedia was longer than those on Marx, Engels, and Lenin combined.[61]

The cult of the personality also leaves geographic traces, since sultanistic rulers like to name cities and even natural features after themselves. Orumieh and Anzali became Reza'ieh and Bandar Pahlavi in honor of Reza Shah, Santo Domingo was renamed Ciudad Trujillo, and in Haiti the town of Cabaret became Duvalierville. In Africa Lake Albert and Lake Edward were renamed Lake Mobutu Sese Seko and Lake Idi Amin, and the island of Fernando Póo became Macías Nguema Island. Only in Nicaragua did the dictator have the modesty to give his name just to a new port established on the Atlantic coast: it became Puerto Somoza (and was renamed Puerto Cabezas after his ouster).

The second aspect of personalism is the prominent role of family members in these regimes, which has led many analysts to speak of "dynasties."[62] In Haiti and Nicaragua sons "inherited" the presidency from their fathers, and in Nicaragua and the Dominican Republic family members occupied important commands in the armed forces: in the latter the dictator's son Ramfis was a brigadier general at the tender age of nine. Wives play an important role too. In Haiti both first ladies of the Duvalier regime wielded considerable influence and were involved in corruption.[63] In the Philippines, Imelda Marcos held a number of cabinet-rank positions and was named mayor of Metro-Manila, while her husband's sister was governor of the Marcoses' native Ilocos Norte province, with her nephew Ferdinand Marcos Jr. as vice-governor at age twenty-one.[64] In Romania, Ceauşescu's accession to the newly created post of "president of the republic" in 1974 was marked by ceremonies closely patterned after coronations.[65] His wife was the Communist Party's second in command by the early 1980s, his four brothers all held key levers of power, and their son Nicu was groomed to succeed his father until his constant brawling, gambling, and philandering turned party leaders (including other relatives) against the succession.[66] In Iran, of course, the old monarchical tradition was there for the Shah and his relatives to use. When he celebrated twenty-five hundred years of that tradition in 1971, one of his guests, Imelda Marcos, was so impressed that she is said to have suggested to her husband that they become emperor and empress of the Philippines (see chapter 9 below). In Equatorial Guinea, the dictator filled all major positions with members of his Esengui clan. Although he himself was ousted and executed by his nephew, his dynasty endures to this day and governs in a manner only slightly less repressive than Macías Nguema's rule.[67] In Antigua and Barbuda, Vere Bird's two eldest sons, Vere Jr. and Lester, were cabinet members, and in March 1994 the younger of the two, Lester Bird, succeeded his father by leading the Antigua Labor Party to yet another election victory. He did not include his older brother in the cabinet, perhaps because a 1990 inquiry into his alleged involvement in transporting Israeli arms to Colombian drug traffickers had recommended that he be barred from public office.[68] The only ruler who went so far as to abolish the republic and found a monarchy was Jean Bédel Bokassa, who proclaimed himself emperor in 1976 and proceeded to crown himself in 1977. The idea originated with Mobutu, who had planned to declare himself "emperor of the Bantus" but was beaten to it by Bokassa.[69]

It is the combination of personalism and dynasticism that is specific to sultanism. Other personalistic regimes, such as those of Stalin and Tito, did not elevate the rulers' relatives to political prominence, and dynasties can also appear in nonsultanistic settings. In such relatively stable democracies as Sri Lanka, India, and Jamaica, successive members of the Bandaranaike-Kumaratunga, Nehru-Gandhi, and Manley families have been democratically elected heads of government; in Pakistan, Bangladesh, and Burma daughters or widows of politicians have been the people's choice to replace authoritarian regimes. The difference is that in most cases they were not designated by their predecessors but inherited their charisma.[70] But in Texas and Alabama state governors have had their wives run for the governorship when they could not, practicing in effect the "politics of understudy" described below.[71]

The reason for the dynasticism of sultanistic regimes is perhaps that the rulers feel that they can trust only their kith and kin. Most often the sultanistic rulers come from humble origins and are looked down upon by the traditional elite. The first Somoza, Anastasio Somoza García, had spent some time in the United States as a used-car salesman.[72] The first Pahlavi shah began his military career as a soldier in the Russian-officered Cossack Brigade. Trujillo grew up in very poor circumstances and as a young man was employed as security chief for a sugar mill.[73] Batista was a mulatto who had worked as a sergeant stenographer in the Cuban army, after stints as a cane cutter, carpenter, and railway worker.[74] Ceauşescu was of peasant origin, which, though not astonishing for a communist leader, contrasted with other Romanian communist leaders like Ana Pauker, who belonged to the intelligentsia. Finally, Amin, Bokassa, and Macías

Nguema "all possessed low traditional status," and "their ethnic and socio-economic backgrounds directly conditioned their behavior while in power."[75]

Given their lowly origins and the tenuous social base of their regimes, sultanistic rulers often attempt to create family alliances with the old elite, so as to co-opt at least part of it. Reza Shah thus took a Qajar princess as his second wife, the first Somoza married into the powerful Debayle-Sacasa family, Batista divorced his first wife and married "up," and Jean-Claude Duvalier chose his wife from the light-skinned Bennett family, which, though not part of the old mulatto elite his father had eliminated from political power, was nonetheless rich.

The importance of family members is not limited to the political realm and often carries over into economic life, as different family members carve out bailiwicks for themselves. It is even possible that pressures toward sultanization of the regime come from the family of an authoritarian ruler rather than from the ruler himself.

Constitutional Hypocrisy

Rulers who destroy men's freedom commonly begin by trying to retain its forms.   ALEXIS DE TOCQUEVILLE,
The Old Régime and the French Revolution

Patrimonial rulers who claim traditional authority preside over political systems based on historically enacted rules, above all customary law, but they generally have ignored modern constitutions.[76] Sultanistic regimes, lacking an ideological basis for their institutions, often govern with constitutions inherited from a previous democratic regime or enacted to give a legitimate appearance to their rule. However, the sultanistic ruler does not necessarily occupy the position that is constitutionally the most powerful, a policy called *politique de doublure*, or "politics of understudy," in Haiti. The Somozas occasionally put a puppet in charge of the presidency; in the course of his long rule Trujillo left it to four different men, one of whom was his brother; in Iran the Pahlavi shahs always retained prime ministers who, according to the constitution, were in charge of governing the country; and in Panama Manuel Noriega continued the habit of his predecessor, General Omar Torrijos Herrera, of ruling as head of the military with a nominal president as head of state. In the African cases this practice does not obtain, except to some extent in the "imperial" phase of Bokassa's rule, when the constitution designated the prime minister as the effective ruler of the Central African Empire.

The constitutional façade of sultanistic regimes means that they pay lip service to constitutions that provide for elected chief executives and parliaments, and in some cases even multiparty systems. The leaders often make a point of extolling democracy in their country while redefining it.[77] This made it easier for conservative anticommunists in the United States and other Western countries to back them. The sultanistic rulers therefore organized elections and maintained a nominally multiparty polity, but somehow the government always won.[78] Furthermore, the defeated "minority" was not granted a secure status or an institutional role of any sort. The civil liberties of the opposition were severely restricted and arbitrarily violated.

The manipulation of the electoral process can take various forms. Trujillo held elections throughout his rule. In Nicaragua, the Somoza family gained control of the Liberal Party in the 1930s and from then on would split the opposition Conservative Party before each scheduled election by making deals with some of its leaders, then prevent the electoral success of the others by fraud.[79] Nonetheless, new opposition parties were allowed to operate in the 1970s. In Cuba, Batista held presidential elections in 1954, but under conditions that, in the end, left him as the only candidate. In the Philippines, Marcos encouraged (and perhaps paid) a candidate to run against him in the 1981 presidential elections but let him carry only his hometown. Even about Romania, which was by definition a "people's democracy" and therefore did not pretend to have competitive elections, one observer wrote that "in no other East European regime [was] the chasm between rhetoric and reality so painfully experienced as in Ceauşescu's Romania."[80]

The most extreme situation obtained in Iran, where until 1975 the Shah maintained the fiction of a two-party system. The opposition Mardom, or "People's" Party existed on paper only; one can call it a "pseudo-opposition."[81] In its decorative function this pseudo-opposition bore some superficial resemblance to the bloc parties of communist Eastern Europe,[82] in that it too lacked any social base independent of the regime and was controlled by it. In both cases party leaders were in and of the regime rather than oppositionists who had been co-opted. However, the Shah's loyal pseudo-opposition differed from the bloc parties in that unlike these it officially competed with the ruling Iran-e Novin, or New Iran Party.[83] In 1974 it briefly seemed as though the Mardom Party could play an autonomous role when it was allowed to campaign freely in a by-election, but although it won handily, the results were rigged to deny the party the seat. Soon afterward the Shah instituted a one-party system.

Sultanistic rulers also often turn to plebiscites to prove their democratic legitimacy; needless to say, they never lose one. Plebiscites are part of the democratic façade that sultanistic rulers like to erect, but they also create the image of a charismatic leader who rules by popular acclamation. In the communist world plebiscites were not customary, but Ceauşescu held one, on the pretext of wanting to legitimize a reduction in his country's military spending.[84] As Tocqueville put it, these leaders "cherish the illusion that they can combine the prerogatives of absolute power with the moral authority that comes from popular assent. Almost all have failed in this endeavor and learned to their cost that it is impossible to keep up such appearances for long when there is no reality behind them."[85] The longtime manipulation of the constitutional arrangements and the cynical acting out of electoral procedures have nefarious consequences for a hypothetical transition to democracy, as we shall see later.

The Narrow Social Bases of Sultanism

Very often sultanistic rulers originally come to power with the support of clearly recognizable groups—sometimes even, as in the case of Marcos, through fair elections. In Iran, Reza Shah's gradual seizure of power in the 1920s had the support of a sizable segment of politically articulate Iranians, including the Left.[86] In Romania, Ceauşescu came to power through the workings of the Communist Party and enjoyed genuine popularity in the 1960s as a de-Stalinizer who repudiated the 1968 Soviet invasion of Czechoslovakia and championed Romanian independence. In the Philippines, finally, Marcos's imposition of martial law in 1972 was greeted with relief by significant sectors of the Filipino population. In Central America regimes that later degenerate into sultanism often start with a certain antioligarchic dimension. The Somozas and Batista had some backing from the hitherto somewhat excluded mestizos and mulattoes, respectively, while François Duvalier and Eric Gairy in the beginning championed the cause of the blacks in relation to their countries' socially dominant mulattoes. In Panama, finally, Omar Torrijos's dictatorship, the forerunner of Noriega's sultanistic rule, improved the lot of the blacks and mestizos.

As the regimes become sultanistic, however, they lose much of their initial social support and begin to rely increasingly on a mixture of fear and rewards. The beginning of the sultanistic phase can usually be dated with the benefit of hindsight. In Iran, Reza Shah's dismissal of most of his early modernist collaborators in 1933, and Mohammad Reza Shah's "White Revolution" of 1963 heralded the two shahs' sultanistic period. In the Philippines the declaration of martial law in 1972 was a crucial turning point.

The ability of sultanistic rulers to stay in power depends on their freedom from the need to forge alliances with civil society and to build coalitions. This freedom increases, as we will see later, if they can monopolize certain economic resources. Given the weakness of the regime's links with civil society, crucial social strata that might support a capitalist authoritarian regime because of its pro-business and anticommunist policies are alienated from the sultanistic regime. In Romania, by subverting the hierarchy of the Communist Party Ceaușescu alienated the *nomenklatura,* and in the end it was elements of the old party apparatus that ousted him: Ceaușescu's successor, President Ion Iliescu, had once been the old dictator's protégé but was later purged for "liberalism" and "intellectualism." In the end the social bases of a sultanistic regime are restricted to its clients: family members of the rulers and their cronies. For these, however, loyalty to the ruler derives only from their own interests rather than from any impersonal principles, for which reason they do not constitute a distinct stratum, group, or social class. Nonetheless they do exist, and through their own clients they create a multiplier effect that links enough people to the regime so that it can function. Although a lot of people may benefit from a sultanistic regime, therefore, they do not really constitute a broad social base.

There are, of course, exceptions. A dictator may enjoy genuine support in his home region or from his own ethnic segment because he favors it. Marcos favored the Ilocos Norte province in the Philippines, and in Uganda Idi Amin's fellow northerners benefited, relatively speaking, from his rule.[87] Occasionally the ruler will combine his rule through patrimonial officials with populist gestures: this seems to have been the pattern of the first Duvalier, who exploited the tensions between Haiti's blacks and mulattoes.

A puzzling feature of some sultanistic regimes is the success of public figures identified with them in free elections after the overthrow of the regime. Joaquín Balaguer's repeated victories in the Dominican Republic's presidential elections, even though not always obtained through honest means, testify to a certain popularity. In Nicaragua, Arnoldo Alemán handsomely won the presidential election of 1996, beating Daniel Ortega and relegating the candidate of the center to a distant third place. It is important to remember that these victories are not belated vindications of the sultanistic rules of Trujillo and Somoza: they reflect the candidates' personal popularity and do not mean that most of the population wants to return to the old days, just as the victories of former communists in Eastern Europe do not mean that Eastern Europeans yearn for a return to pre-Gorbachev communism. In all these cases public figures associated with the old regime run for office under the rules of the new regime, and their electoral platforms do not include the reestablishment of the old regime.

It is often alleged that sultanistic leaders substitute superpower patronage for a domestic power base. The close association of most sultanistic leaders with the United States is beyond doubt, but one should not deduce from this that they are American puppets: at times, during more populist interludes, they may even temporarily assume anti-American positions. These dictators are adroit at making friends in the United States, and they lavish important sums on lobbying. Often congressmen and even senators become their defenders in the United States; it is therefore by no means clear who manipulates whom to whose greater advantage. The recently published diaries of the Shah's longtime minister of court and boon companion, Amir Asadollah Alam, make it quite clear that not only did the Shah not take any orders from the United States in his heyday, he even maintained a network of powerful supporters in Washington's inner circle to influence U.S. policy.[88] Likewise, Marcos "knew that neocolonial manipulation can be a two-way street," and both he and his wife maneuvered adroitly in Washington circles.[89] Somoza too was able to mobilize influential friends in Washington,[90] and before them Trujillo had retained the services of lobbyists in the U.S. capital.

Distorted Capitalism

A prince must abstain from the property of others; because men sooner forget the death of their father than the loss of their patrimony. NICCOLÒ MACHIAVELLI,
The Prince

Although some sultanistic regimes have presided over considerable economic growth, in the long run the personalism and corruption of the political system negatively affects economic development. To some extent these distortions are adumbrated by Weber's analysis of the economics of patrimonialism. Under patrimonialism, he wrote, "there is wide scope for actual arbitrariness and the expression of purely personal whims on the part of the ruler and the members of his administrative staff. The opening for bribery and corruption . . . tends to be a matter which is settled from case to case with every individual official and thus highly variable." This means that "two bases of the rationalization of activity are entirely lacking; namely, a basis for the calculability of obligations and of the extent of freedom which will be allowed to private enterprise." Given the absence of procedural predictability, "under the dominance of a patrimonial regime only certain types of capitalism are able to develop," and he lists capitalist trading, capitalist tax farming, capitalist provision of supplies for the state, and capitalist plantations and other colonial enterprises. But a patrimonial system can also be conducive to the establishment of monopolies,[91] an option contemporary sultanist rulers have often taken.

True patrimonial systems are limited by tradition, whereas in modern sultanistic ones the scope for arbitrariness is much wider, while the greater development of the state apparatus means that bureaucratization is more advanced. The personalistic use of power for the essentially private ends of the ruler and his collaborators means that the country is run like a huge domain. The boundaries between the public treasury and the private wealth of the ruler become blurred. He and his collaborators, with his consent, freely appropriate public funds, establish profit-oriented monopolies, and demand gifts and payoffs from business for which no public accounting is given. Often the privileged are thus exploited, as landowners, merchants, and foreign capitalists buy their peace by making payments to the regime.

The ruler's enterprises contract with the state, and the ruler often shows generosity to his followers and to his subjects in a particularistic way. His family most often shares in the spoils. The economy is subject to considerable government interference, but this interference is rarely tied to any grand project of sustainable accumulation: the main aim is to extract resources. This "kleptocratic state"[92] operates by control over essential services, monopoly ownership of critical commodities, kickbacks on contracts, and plain confiscation of property. This monopoly ownership can take the form of state-owned industries (such as oil in Iran, copper in Zaire, or diamonds in the Central African Republic/Empire) whose revenues can be to a smaller (Iran) or larger (Africa) extent appropriated by the rulers. Or rulers can set up monopolies as private persons. Examples of the latter include Batista's lottery scheme or Empress Catherine's monopoly on the sale of school uniforms in the Central African Empire, uniforms whose manufacture was a monopoly of one of Bokassa's mistresses.[93]

The constant patrimonial interference in economic life leads to distorted market economies that, though embedded in the sphere of capitalism, cannot truly be called capitalistic. Whereas capitalism is based on the "sacredness of private property" and on the working of the market in allocating resources, opportunities, and profits, sultanism often involves arbitrary takeover of property, directly or indirectly, by coercion and without compensation. Also, individual entrepreneurs' opportunities in the market are distorted by the ruler's intervention in economic life: he has the power to deny access, he can allocate public funds to private enterprises linked with himself or with his cronies, and he can eliminate from the market competitors not ready to abide by his demands. Mafia economics is not market economics. Nonetheless, to maximize the benefits the regime derives from the economy, a certain rationalization of activity can take place in the more economically advanced countries, leading to the appearance of pockets of rationality. But the absence of secure property rights inhibits long-term productive investment, since sultanistic regimes are unable to develop the institutions necessary for a dynamic and complex economy. Given the personalism that pervades institutions, the institutional and legal framework necessary for resolving conflicts and enforcing contracts cannot be set up.

This said, there are periods in the life span of a sultanistic regime when it may preside over quite respectable growth rates. Given how it is managed, however, this growth tends not to add to the ruler's legitimacy. Moreover, given that sultanism subverts accountability and predictability, it thwarts sustainable accumulation.

The characteristics of sultanistic regimes can further be grasped if we compare them with the other types of nondemocratic systems.

Sultanism and Other Types of Nondemocratic Rule

Since so many of our cases are in Latin America, it is important to define the difference between sultanistic rulers and the traditional caudillos of that continent. Caudillos were a product of the nineteenth century. In the wake of independence, as state authority disintegrated, military leaders based in the rural areas seized power at the head of armed bands of loyal followers and thus filled the vacuum of authority.[94] Some became state builders: Uruguay owes its existence to General José Gervasio Artigas. Unlike modern sultanistic rulers, whose power derives from existing structures at the center of the polity, the caudillos had a more local base, possessed genuine leadership qualities, and at least initially, inspired personal loyalty.[95] Although there is some resemblance between caudillism and sultanism, and though such sultanistic dictators as Rafael Trujillo and the first Somoza perhaps evinced some continuity with the caudillos of an earlier age, the typical sultanistic ruler does not partake of the heroic world of the traditional caudillo; the sort of mythology and folklore that caudillism begot is unlikely to be engendered by sultanism.

Sultanism differs from totalitarianism in that, like authoritarianism, it lacks a genuine ideology, articulated by pro-regime intellectuals, to legitimize it and guide its policy formulation. Romania and North Korea, where Ceauşescu and Kim Il-sung did take Marxism-Leninism seriously, are obvious exceptions here, but in the Dominican Republic too, ideologues such as Joaquín Balaguer elaborated a detailed ideology that claimed to guide Dominicans toward democracy but was honest enough not to call the regime democratic.[96] As we have seen, some sultanistic rulers produce (or have ghostwriters produce) something they like to call "ideology." But we have only to think of the appeal totalitarian ideologies have for intellectuals not subject to their rule, for young people, and for students to perceive the absence of anything remotely similar under sultanism. No one not subject to their rule, not even most of their supporters and probably not even the rulers themselves, takes these ideological efforts seriously: they are pseudo-ideologies.

Another major difference from totalitarian regimes is the fusion between the private and the public roles of the ruler and the lack of commitment to impersonal purposes. Totalitarian dictators such as Stalin, Hitler, Mao, and Castro believe in their own mission, and so do their followers. There is a purpose to their rule other than personal enrichment, and for this cause they succeed in mobilizing intellectuals not only in their own societies but also outside. In addition, they cultivate an ascetic image (which may or may not reflect their true nature) that is quite at variance with the undisguised hedonism of most (but not all) sultanistic rulers and especially their relatives and cronies.

A third difference with totalitarian regimes, and a consequence of the previous two, is the absence not only of a single party but also of the ancillary organizations such as women's groups and youth groups that were so essential to Nazism and communism. Related to this is the absence of continuous political mobilization for a variety of tasks that provide a sense of participation in social and political life. As in authoritarian systems, passivity and apathy characterize sultanistic regimes, which offer few, if any, channels for participation, even to their supporters.

The final difference from totalitarianism is that sultanistic regimes penetrate their societies very unevenly. Those areas of public life that threaten the ruling group's extraction of resources, such as the press, may be controlled to a degree approximating totalitarianism, while others are left alone. Somoza's acquiescence to de facto autonomy for the Indians of the Atlantic coast is an example.[97] Even in tightly centralized Pahlavi Iran, the state's penetration of distant Baluchistan province was less thorough than elsewhere.

As in all regimes, the specific traits of a sultanistic regime are most developed at the top, elite level. In a modern society, the post office and certain administrations like the judiciary (political cases excepted) will work in similar ways for most people no matter what the political regime. In rural areas village life may go on relatively untouched by the changes at the center.

Sultanistic regimes differ from authoritarian regimes in a number of ways.

Authoritarian regimes are more institutionalized, and the limited political, and even more important, social pluralism they tolerate creates a variety of structures that support the regime, which recruits its elites from them. The much simpler clientelist structures, the absence of predictable paths of career advancement in the bureaucracy and the army, the arbitrary recruitment by the ruler of his lieutenants thus contrast with authoritarian regimes, although in this case the contrast is less sharp than with totalitarianism.

The second difference is the absence of the rule of law, be it a repressive one: sultanistic regimes constantly violate their own norms. Moreover, in line with the constitutional façade they maintain, sultanistic regimes often privatize repression, in the sense that it is carried out by informal groups in the service of the ruler as well as by formally constituted state agencies implementing explicitly repressive legislation.[98] Under sultanistic rule even the violation of people's basic human rights is arbitrary and may strike supporters and opponents of the regime alike, giving rise to pervasive fear and suspicion in society.[99] In any event, sultanistic regimes can exercise degrees of repression ranging from the relatively benign reign of Batista[100] to the demented paranoia of Macías Nguema, who is estimated to have been responsible for a minimum of fifty thousand deaths, drove a third of his country's population into exile, and eliminated its intelligentsia on a scale comparable only to the Khmer Rouge.[101] Regimes that act illegally according to their own laws create uncertainty and unpredictability in public life. This capriciousness has an adverse effect on economic development, among other things, since entrepreneurs who lack connections to the ruler cannot plan ahead rationally, a point we will come back to.

Oppositional activity against sultanistic regimes often concentrates abroad as sultanistic domination drives many citizens, especially intellectuals, into exile. These exiles can be a fertile base for oppositional undertakings, since they deeply resent not only the corruption and repression at home, but also the ideological vacuum behind it. Intellectuals are more likely to excuse repression when it is carried out in the name of a transformational ideology ("You can't make an omelette without breaking eggs") than when it is exercised for private gain. This resentment is heightened by the tendency in many sultanistic regimes to expand the repressive activities of the state abroad: opponents in exile are often kidnapped or killed. The existence of an opposition in exile complicates political life in the event of an overthrow of the sultanistic regime.[102]

2

. . . .

A Theory of Sultanism 2

Genesis and Demise of Sultanistic Regimes

H. E. Chehabi and Juan J. Linz

The Genesis of Sultanism

Sultanistic regimes have been relatively few in number, and almost all have by now disappeared. However, the appearance of new sultanism cannot be excluded. Sultanistic regimes are unlikely to be established in advanced industrial societies, yet an underdeveloped economy is not a sufficient precondition for the emergence of sultanism. The factors favoring the emergence of sultanism are both macrostructural and institutional, but these variables do not explain everything: the presence or absence in a given society of individuals who are willing to become sultanistic rulers matters as well.[1]

Macrostructural Factors

Two sets of factors stand out: economic conditions and the international environment.

Socioeconomic Conditions

About patrimonial structures Weber wrote that "little can be said about purely economic preconditions for [their] rise."[2] Matters are slightly different for modern sultanistic regimes: although there are no necessary and sufficient conditions for their emergence, it is nonetheless possible to identify certain factors that help bring them about.

The stabilization and continuity of sultanistic regimes require a certain modernization of transportation and communications as well as of the military and police organizations and some civilian administrations, to provide funds to sustain the rule and prevent threats to it. The isolation of the rural masses, their lack of education, and their poverty are probably necessary to ensure their passive submission out of fear combined with gratitude for occasional paternalistic welfare measures made possible by a modicum of development.

Since some of the classic sultanistic regimes of the Caribbean and Central America appeared in small countries, one might speculate whether size was a factor. Small internal markets mean that where customs fees are an important source of funds, political control can be extended through customs, whose revenues are easily appropriated. In more complex societies, sultanistic regimes have a chance of survival only when they can dispose of considerable resources produced by sectors that do not require a large modern industrial labor force and entrepreneurial class, a modern administration, urbanization, expansion of education, and so forth. Rentier states in which the regime is not bound by tradition (unlike the oil monarchies of the Arabian peninsula) are thus more vulnerable to sultanization. Easily exploitable natural resources whose production is in the hands of one or only a few enterprises with high profits can provide the resources for such a regime, especially when elites are weak. Sugar, oil, and copper exemplify this, each in a different way.

Sugarcane cannot be sold without industrial processing. Even independent farmers are thus dependent on the sugar mills, which are capital intensive. And since the market for sugar is mostly international, the product has to go through customs. This constellation of factors allows for the political-economic symbiosis that lends itself to sultanism, as Cuba and the Dominican Republic illustrate.

In Venezuela the discovery and initial exploitation of oil by foreign companies coincided with the rule of Juan Vicente Gómez (1908–35), and an oil-led boom also provided the basis for the rule of Marcos Pérez Jiménez (1948–58); both dictatorships displayed marked sultanistic traits.[3] Oil also made possible Iran's "petrolic despotism" in the latter years of the last shah's reign, from 1963 to 1979.[4] And in Zaire "the copper industry [was] the declining treasure trove of Mobutu's corrupted state; Mobutu survive[d] politically and enriche[d] himself primarily by taking a percentage off the top of copper export sales."[5]

Finally, massive doses of foreign aid or loans can encourage corruption, especially if the aid is unconditional. In the Philippines the enormous borrowing of the years 1979–84 made it possible for crony capitalism to thrive.[6] In Haiti, U.S. aid grew tremendously after Papa Doc's death,[7] but much of the money was diverted into the pockets of both Haitian and American officials. As one observer put it, "the principal recipient of foreign aid was Jean-Claude Duvalier."[8] After the 1972 Managua earthquake, Somoza bought cheap land outside the city, then sold it at a hundred times the original price to the National Housing Institute to build new housing. A U.S. relief grant paid for the purchase, but not a single house was built.[9] Foreign aid also helped enrich Mobutu;[10] in Equatorial Guinea "the Nguema dictatorship in its last years was largely sustained by the fiscal infusions of the United Nations Development Program into the country";[11] and Antigua and Barbuda, whose population is about seventy thousand, has received about $200 million in various kinds of U.S. aid since the late 1970s.[12]

It would be a mistake to consider sultanistic regimes an inevitable outcome of socioeconomic structures, however, although there are certain structures that facilitate the emergence of sultanistic tendencies. One cannot ignore many other factors contributing to the emergence and stability of such regimes—including the interest in "order" of foreign investors who have established stable "business relations" with the ruler. In many cases the rulers owe their rule to foreign intervention in the first place.

Crisis of Sovereignty

> I will take advantage of your generosity to express the
> doubts which . . . we moderns have about such things as . . .
> the Nicaraguan independence.   G. K. CHESTERTON,
> *The Napoleon of Notting Hill*

One feature most of our cases have in common is that throughout their contemporary history their independence was ambiguous and often not respected by more powerful neighbors. In terms of political development, therefore, these polities have suffered persistent crises of sovereignty.[13] This pattern is most striking for Central America and the Caribbean.[14] It can be no coincidence that an international law textbook published in 1922 lists in its chapter on "dependent states" Cuba, Panama, the Dominican Republic, Haiti, and Nicaragua—all nominally sovereign at the time but precisely those states that later fell victim to sultanism.[15]

Perhaps the most striking example is the Dominican Republic. After gaining independence from Spain in 1821, the country was annexed by neighboring Haiti in 1822, only to recover its independence in 1844. By 1861 the ongoing civil, political, and international strife impelled the authorities to request the return of Spanish colonial rule. The Spaniards stayed until 1865. Once it regained its independence, the country's president sold his country to the United States, but the U.S. Senate refused to give its consent to the ratification of the treaty. In 1903 the United States took over the customs receivership and occupied the country from 1916 to 1924, actually administering it between 1916 and 1922. Trujillo came to power in 1930, and four years after his overthrow the United States again invaded the country in 1965.[16]

In Nicaragua foreign powers constantly intervened in civil wars of the nineteenth century, until in 1855 an American adventurer, William Walker, invaded the country with fifty-eight fellow Americans and declared himself president. From 1912 to 1933 Nicaragua was constantly occupied by U.S. troops, against which Augusto Sandino waged the struggle that made him the lodestar of Nicaraguan nationalism.[17] This era ended only when Somoza García took power in 1934. After his family's overthrow in 1979, the United States again meddled heavily in Nicaraguan affairs by arming rebels and mining the country's harbors.

The annexation of Cuba either by purchase or by outright seizure had been openly discussed in the United States during the nineteenth century.[18] When the country finally became independent in 1902, U.S. influence and interference were legally guaranteed by an amendment to the Cuban constitution that Cuba's constitutional assembly had approved at the insistence of the United States. The "Platt Amendment" granted the United States access to bases and coaling stations and constrained Cuba's sovereignty in financial and territorial matters. Its crucial third article stated that the United States could "exercise the right to intervene for the preservation of Cuban independence [and] for the maintenance of a government adequate for the protection of life, property, and individual liberty."[19] Although the clause was abrogated in 1934 by mutual agreement, the United States remained an interested actor in Cuban politics until 1959,[20] occupied the island between 1906 and 1909, and sponsored an invasion of it 1961. To this day the United States leases Cuban territory for a military base at Guantánamo Bay.

Panama owed its independence from Colombia in 1903 to U.S. intervention, motivated by interest in constructing a canal linking the Pacific and Atlantic Oceans. By a treaty signed in 1903 the young republic granted the United States the use, occupation, and control of parts of its territory (what became the Canal Zone) and the right to deploy military forces to defend the canal and shipping. Of all the countries of Central America, Panama remained most closely tied to the United States. It never had its own currency, and its use of the U.S. dollar led to the development of a sophisticated banking sector that was used for both legitimate and criminal purposes (laundering drug money).[21] In 1941 the United States promoted the ouster of elected president Arnulfo Arías, who was suspected of fascist sympathies. A U.S. exclave cut Panama in half until President Carter signed a treaty in 1977 gradually turning over administration of the Canal to the Panamanians. And in the end it was by an invasion that Manuel Noriega was toppled in 1989.[22]

Haiti, the second oldest independent republic of the Western Hemisphere, suffered American intervention several times in the nineteenth century and was occupied by American troops from 1915 to 1934. François Duvalier's rule (1957–71) contained a strong element of black nationalism and was at times tinged with anti-American rhetoric. But in 1986 Americans played a decisive role in organizing his son's departure, and they invaded again in 1994, this time to help reestablish democracy.

The crises of sovereignty of the five nations are well described in the aforementioned textbook of international law, which concludes that "in proportion as the United States by virtue of these conventions exercises rights which they confer as a privilege peculiarly its own, and in which no foreign State is permitted to participate, it appears to assume internationally a certain responsibility for conditions of government within the territories concerned."[23]

In the Philippines the American withdrawal after World War II was fraught with ambiguities, as David Steinberg explains: "Monetary arrangements, trade issues, access to natural resources, and land ownership were all decided in ways that were favorable to American interests, and the decision to retain vast territories as military bases shattered the illusion that independence would usher in a golden era of Philippine-American partnership based on mutual respect."[24] The infatuation of many Filipinos with the United States was such that at times there have been movements advocating U.S. statehood for the islands.

Iran was never a colony in the formal sense of the word, but its independence was heavily impinged upon in the heyday of European imperialism, a status Lenin termed "semi-colony."[25] By 1907 the United Kingdom and Russia had divided the country into zones of influence; during World War I the belligerent states did not respect Iran's proclaimed neutrality; in 1919 Britain tried to force a protectorate on it; in 1941 the Allies again invaded Iran in disregard of its neutrality; and in 1953 the United States and Great Britain engineered the overthrow of the Nationalist government and enabled the late Shah to rule as an absolute monarch until his overthrow in 1979.[26]

In other cases foreign intervention is more circumscribed. An example of more limited intervention is Venezuela, where Gómez's coup of 1908 was directly aided by the United States.

In this context one might also note that when the provinces that later became Romania received autonomy under the Ottoman Empire, they were ruled until 1877 by Greek phanariots rather than by indigenous elites concerned with emancipating their country, as was the case, for instance, when Bulgaria was an Ottoman vassal state from 1878 to 1908. Ottoman suzerainty over Romania ended as a result of the Russo-Turkish War of 1877; the country's "independence and existence as a national state were thus externally determined."[27]

The newly independent Third World states whose political regimes are more or less sultanistic also show strong foreign impact. In Zaire the country's very independence in 1960 sparked an international crisis that led to United Nations intervention, and when Mobutu staged a coup in 1965, he was helped by the U.S. Central Intelligence Agency.[28] Among those British colonies that hosted U.S. bases as a result of the 1940 agreement between Churchill and Roosevelt, Antigua was the only island that kept its American bases after independence,[29] and the agreement granting the U.S. military access to V. C. Bird International Airport is described by the U.S. State Department as "one of [the most] if not the most, generous arrangements with a foreign government anywhere in the world."[30]

What accounts for these infringements on the sovereignty of these countries? One factor that immediately comes to mind is that all lie in strategically sensitive areas. Hispaniola and Cuba are very close to the United States, Nicaragua and Panama were possible sites for a canal linking the Pacific and Atlantic Oceans, the Philippines hosted America's most important bases in Asia, and Iran occupies the land between Russia on the one side and India and the Near East on the other. Zaire is in the heart of Africa, and Antigua was home to important U.S. military installations during the Cold War.[31] The domestic situation in these countries has therefore been of interest to foreign powers, chiefly the United States.[32]

A second factor at work in the Caribbean was that chronically unstable governments were unable to repay their debts, which would then lead to foreign intervention to secure payments. In Nicaragua, Haiti, and the Dominican Republic this would be done by taking over customs.

The fact remains that not all countries that have experienced long crises of sovereignty have developed along sultanistic lines: Egypt and China come readily to mind. Prolonged crises therefore seem to be a favorable but not sufficient precondition for the appearance of sultanism. How, then, can we elucidate the link between foreign intervention and sultanism? It seems that sultanistic tendencies arise when a foreign power seeks some control over a country but wants to retreat from direct occupation. The sultanistic ruler then becomes the guarantor of the external power's interests. Therefore it is in some sense the very retreat of the foreign power that favors sultanism, since the foreign power leaves behind a partially modernized administrative and especially military apparatus that enables the ruler to concentrate power in his hands. This situation applies to the Nicaraguan and Dominican National Guards, Haiti's Garde d'Haïti, and the Panamanian Defense Forces, which were strengthened by the United States after the 1977 treaty so as to provide security for the Canal and which after Omar Torrijos's death in 1981 enabled his eventual successor, Manuel Noriega, to rule in a more and more sultanistic way after he took power in 1984.[33] In the African cases the rise of the intellectually mediocre Macías Nguema was engineered by the Spanish so as to neutralize more educated nationalists, and the British in Uganda constantly promoted Idi Amin in disregard of all criteria for advancement, so that a man who had enlisted in the King's African Rifles as a cook and remained functionally illiterate all his life was rewarded for his services (including those against the Mau Mau rebellion in neighboring Kenya) by being given the highest rank open to an African in 1960, just before independence.[34]

In the American sphere of influence, the sultanistic rulers have U.S. support for most of their tenure. Trujillo enjoyed it until Batista was overthrown, and when François Duvalier died in 1971 the United States deployed two warships between Haiti and the American mainland to prevent the return of exiles, thus aiding the transfer of power from father to son. The Shah was called by Henry Kissinger "that rarest of leaders, an unconditional ally";[35] Ferdinand Marcos enjoyed the support of five U.S. presidents; and Mobutu's rule was twice rescued by Western intervention when rebel forces invaded Shaba province in 1977 and 1978. But we should also point out that America was interested not in perpetuating sultanistic rulers per se, but in maintaining stability and a general pro-American stance under strong states. Democratic regimes fulfilling these conditions were also supported,[36] as was communist Yugoslavia.

Thus domestic instability first creates the conditions that make it easier for foreign powers to intervene, then foreign intervention leads to regimes that substitute foreign support for domestic coalition building and may become sultanistic. The foreign aid that flows into these countries can further deepen sultanism. Finally, note that the very fact that all these regimes (with the exception of Romania, which is a borderline case) have appeared in the Western sphere of interest is perhaps no coincidence, since their lack of identification with a genuine ideology is more compatible with dominant Western views of politics. In those Third World regimes that were in the communist sphere of influence, such as certain *socialisant* regimes in Africa, or influenced by fascism, such as Getúlio Vargas's in Brazil or Juan Domingo Perón's in Argentina, the self-conscious imitation of the ideological models in the developed countries probably acted as a brake on sultanistic tendencies. Romania of course does not fit this pattern, but even here the appearance of sultanistic traits in Ceauşescu's regime more or less coincided with his rapprochement with the West, where he always had a better press than many less brutal communist dictators.

Political Institutional Factors

As we saw earlier, sultanistic regimes do not have a specific set of institutions; sultanistic tendencies appear under various constitutional arrangements. Two sets of paths to sultanism can be empirically observed: the breakdown of clientelist democracy and the decay of nondemocratic regimes.

Breakdown of Clientelistic Democracy

Some sultanistic regimes have come to power in countries with at least some previous history of democratic politics. We know that certain features of a democratic regime can survive the breakdown of democracy and resurface under the changed conditions of the successor dictatorship. Similarly, it seems that dictatorships arising after the breakdown of clientelistic democracies will sometimes display sultanistic tendencies: one could say that the number of patrons has been reduced to one.[37] In a clientelistic democracy, patronage, and favors have to be widely distributed to win elections, but the alternation of parties in power keeps one party from monopolizing the pork barrel indefinitely. The electoral competition thus favors a wider distribution in society of the benefits of patron-client relationships. Batista's regime after his coup of 1952 and Marcos's after 1972 fit this pattern most clearly, but elements of it are present also in Nicaragua, where, as John Booth shows in his chapter, the Somozas' rule began with the first Somoza's taking over the Liberal Party, one of the country's two traditional clientelism-based parties. But Nicaragua is different in that the Liberals and Conservatives had deep class and regional roots in the country and in fact represented two camps in Nicaraguan politics, somewhat as happened in Colombia.[38]

Cuba enjoyed a constitutional government between 1939 and 1952, but "clientelistic politics that revolved around personal attachments rather than doctrinal commitments made the system vulnerable to shifting partisan arrangements and manipulation from above."[39] The widespread corruption that accompanied democratic government led to considerable initial support for Batista's coup of 1952 and little overt opposition to it.

In the Philippines, pre-1972 democracy had been marked by competition between the Liberal and Nationalist Parties.[40] Party labels did not denote ideological differences, however, and candidates would often switch affiliation before elections. Pork barrel was the principal method of gaining votes. The system remained competitive because those who lost, or believed they did not benefit sufficiently, switched to the other party. After his election in 1965, Ferdinand Marcos used this system to a greater extent than all his predecessors—so much so that in 1969 he became the first sitting president to be elected to a second term.[41]

Decay of Authoritarian and Totalitarian Regimes

In a traditional polity like premodern China, the harem and the eunuchs associated with it would often wield power after an emperor died, while his underage successor was under the tutelage of women.[42] In the West, the principle of primogeniture prevented the emergence of court parties that put rulers on thrones, whose occupants would then trust nobody and perpetuate a climate of insecurity. In Iran, as Homa Katouzian shows in his chapter, the sultanism of the two Pahlavi shahs derived in part from the old patrimonial monarchy that had been in place until the constitutional revolution of 1906–7. But that revolution, although ultimately unsuccessful in installing a stable liberal regime, did prepare for the creation of a centralized state with a modern bureaucracy, a state Reza Shah inherited and developed further. He and his son first established authoritarian regimes (1921–33 and 1953–63, respectively) and then proceeded to govern sultanistically after eliminating their erstwhile allies from all positions of influence (1933–41 and 1963–79). The development of sultanism in Iran therefore combines elements of both its traditional and modern varieties.

Modern authoritarian regimes sometimes become deinstitutionalized as time passes and the rulers become more mercurial and corrupt. Batista's second presidency (1952–58) had strong sultanistic tendencies, whereas in his first term (1940–44) he had ruled constitutionally.[43] Jean-Claude Duvalier's rule (1971–86) was more sultanistic than his father's (1957–71), since he neglected to maintain the patronage network his father had built. Noriega's sultanism followed the mild and rather progressive authoritarianism of Omar Torrijos, who had made great efforts to extend the social bases of his regime by reaching beyond Panama's traditional white elite.

African sultanism also results from a degeneration of authoritarianism, but of a different kind. The colonial legacy in the sub-Saharan states had two consequences that favored personalism. First, these states' arbitrary borders meant that each state's population was a culturally heterogeneous mix of peoples with no common precolonial traditions, and so at independence the young states started out with no remnant of traditional legitimacy. Second, colonial government was by definition authoritarian government, and it was under this form of rule that the new states' elites were socialized into politics.[44] When, after independence, the new elites took over the administrative bureaucracies bequeathed by the Europeans, these bureaucracies were transformed from instruments of policy to "patrimonial administrations in which staff were less agents of state policy (civil servants) than proprietors, distributors, and even major consumers of the authority and resources of government."[45] This development is in contrast to the experience in the other two main areas of post–World War II decolonization—the Caribbean, where responsible self-government preceded independence by many years, and Asia, where precolonial state traditions survived European imperialism.[46] Personalism is thus rampant in Africa, although as we saw earlier it has many guises, and only a few regimes in fact fit our model of sultanism.

Totalitarian regimes can also at times be vulnerable to institutional decay leading to sultanization. Ceaușescu's regime is the best example of this, although strong sultanistic tendencies can also be observed in Saddam Hussein's Iraq. Here the Baath Party's 1968 coup d'état created a one-party regime endowed with a distinct ideology that can in many ways be called totalitarian.[47] Yet by the 1990s Saddam Hussein's relatives occupied many vital positions in the state, some of them being heavily involved in corruption; a personality cult had developed around Hussein that even grew after his defeat in the Gulf War; and a cult of ancient Babylonia appeared alongside the Baath's Arab nationalism.[48]

One pattern of arrested sultanization deserves particular notice. In modern authoritarian regimes, sultanistic tendencies, especially those associated with family-related corruption, sometimes appear toward the end of a ruler's tenure in office. One of the biggest problems facing any nondemocratic regime is succession, since very few have any fixed and accepted rules to regulate the passing of power from one ruler to another.[49] Authoritarian leaders thus often stay in office well beyond the point where they can effectively exercise power. Within the regime the lack of a widely accepted successor can then lead to an inertia where all involved agree to postpone the inevitable as long as possible. At this point those who enjoy the closest personal access to the aging ruler, often family members, can wield great influence behind the scenes, since they are in a position to manipulate him in ways that further their own interests. One might call this phenomenon *fin-de-règne* sultanism. Some of the hierarchical military regimes in Latin America—Argentina, Brazil, and Uruguay—avoided this eventuality by insisting on collective rather than personal leadership and on limited mandates with presidential elections among the military.

In Spain, the aging Franco was subject to considerable pressures from family members (most notably his son-in-law the marquis of Villaverde) and persons in his entourage to tamper with the rules of succession so as to replace Prince Juan Carlos with his cousin Alfonso de Borbón-Dampierre, who was married to Franco's granddaughter. Don Alfonso was made duke of Cádiz, but Franco ultimately resisted these pressures. The emerging camarilla was also suspected of corrupt dealings.

In the Soviet Union, the last years of Leonid Brezhnev's tenure as secretary-general of the Communist Party were marked by increased political clout and self-enrichment by his family members.[50] In Tunisia sultanistic tendencies went beyond family corruption in the last years of President Habib Bourguiba's long rule. Tunisia's postindependence political system was in many ways a classic authoritarian regime in which a single party, the Parti Socialiste Destourien, provided the backbone of the institutional structure.[51] In 1974 Bourguiba, who had reached the end of his constitutionally allotted three terms, was "elected" president for life. At the same time, seven high-ranking signatories of a declaration deploring arbitrary decision making were expelled from the party.[52] By June 1986 institutional decay had reached the point where the president could suspend the election of the members of the PSD's central committee by a party congress and instead name them himself. His niece, who had managed to drive the president's wife into American exile, was now his closest aide and screened all his visitors. She, his *chef de cabinet*, and the president's personal physician became Bourguiba's closest advisers and opposed the prime minister, Mohammed Mzali, who had tried to reach an accommodation with the opposition.[53]

The state of affairs in Spain in the very last stage of Franco's rule, the Soviet Union in the last years of Brezhnev, and Tunisia in the last years of Bourguiba were a departure from previous norms and tended toward what might be called a "sultanistic situation."[54] In Spain and the USSR the death of the ruler set in motion institutional mechanisms that in the first case led to a legally regulated establishment of the monarchy that later eased the transition to democracy,[55] and in the second resulted in the reformist rule of Yuri Andropov, whose brief tenure in office in 1982–83 prepared the ground for Mikhail Gorbachev's reforms. In Tunisia Bourguiba's hand-picked security chief Zine El Abidine Ben

Ali ousted the president for life in a palace coup and inaugurated a period of liberalization that for a while seemed to lead to democratization but instead ended in a reconsolidation of the authoritarian regime.[56] In authoritarian regimes, therefore, sultanistic pressures face obstacles that diminish the likelihood of a sultanistic situation's leading to a sultanistic regime. However, the possibility always exists.

Leadership Factors: The Ruler's Personality

There is no simple biographical and psychological portrait of the ideal-typical sultanistic ruler, but certain traits are found with some frequency in these dictators, although of course none can be found in all. Founders of sultanistic regimes tend to have limited education and come from socially marginal backgrounds, and their upward mobility tends to have gone come through accidental channels. They tend to be shrewd but morally unscrupulous, distrustful, and vindictive, and they often show an amazing capacity to lie and womanize. In addition to their hedonism, they often betray a streak of personal cruelty.[57] Some of them, like François Duvalier, Macías Nguema, Gairy, Bokassa, and Amin, dabble in the occult.[58]

Given that sultanism is an extreme form of personalism, it is almost tautological to point out that the personality of the ruler is a key element in understanding a sultanistic regime. But whether a leader with a good number of these traits appears on the scene is not structurally determined, and thus one cannot rule out an element of chance. An interesting feature of some sultanistic regimes is that the founder is often more politically savvy than his son (and somtime heir): examples are Reza Shah and his son Mohammad Reza Shah, Trujillo and his son Ramfis, Papa Doc and Baby Doc, Somoza García and Somoza Debayle, Nicolae and Nicu Ceaușescu, and perhaps Kim Il-sung and Kim Jong-il.

The Transformation, Breakdown, and Legacy of Sultanism

A sultanistic regime can endure a long time, but experience shows that most end in a more or less chaotic way. When they do come to an end, they are less likely than other types of nondemocratic regimes to be replaced by democracies.[59] Even in Africa, where personalism is rampant, the record of the early 1990s shows that democracy was least likely in those regimes we would call sultanistic.[60]

The specific patterns of regime breakdown and transition are dealt with by Richard Snyder in the next chapter. In the following sections we will merely discuss some general themes that often inform the end of these regimes.

The Difficulty of Political Liberalization

> The most perilous moment for a bad government is one when it seeks to mend its ways.   ALEXIS DE TOCQUEVILLE,
> *The Old Régime*

The weakness of institutions and the manipulation of democratic procedures make the establishment and consolidation of democratic politics very difficult. If the sultanistic leader or his successors in an interim regime decide to begin to liberalize, the chances that the attempt might succeed and pave the way for a genuine democracy are slim.

An established one-party state can democratize itself by allowing one or more opposition parties to contest elections: Turkey in 1945, Senegal in 1976, South Korea in 1988, Eastern Europe after 1989, the two island states of Cape Verde and São Tomé e Principe in 1991, and Taiwan in 1989 are examples of this scenario.[61] In bureaucratic-authoritarian regimes, which more often than not present themselves as temporary solutions with no claim to permanent legitimacy, the ruling military can decide to extricate itself from the exercise of power by holding elections and handing over control to the winners of these elections. That the military ruled as an institution usually means that the extrication of the military is not contested.[62]

In either case, the "first free elections," often "stunning elections" in which the opposition wins unexpectedly for the rulers,[63] are a clear break with the past and are likely to provide subsequent politics with considerable legitimacy. At the same time, the institutional continuity with the predemocratic regime means that elements more or less connected with the authoritarian regime have a role to play in the new democracy, which weakens opposition to it: examples are Hernán Büchi in Chile, Manuel Fraga Iribarne in Spain, and the renamed "socialist" parties in Eastern Europe. The institutional continuity also means that former single parties can come to power again, as happened in Turkey, Lithuania, Hungary, Bulgaria, and Albania. The relative strength of the state of law under the predemocratic regime also allowed the constitution of opposition groups in the crucial period before and during the transition.

Another factor favoring the establishment of democracy is that in non-sultanistic regimes pockets of legal-rational authority remain, such as capitalist enterprises, the judiciary, and the armed forces. Entrepreneurs are interested in predictability for their planning and thus prefer democracy to political upheavals,[64] judges jealous of their independence can provide legal protection to critics of the regime, and the military is interested in maintaining its institutional integrity.[65] The spread of legal-rational authority in society is crucial, for without it there can be no stable liberal politics.

Under sultanistic regimes the situation is different. If, for whatever reason (foreign pressure, attempt to defuse mounting opposition by providing a safety valve), the sultanistic ruler decides to liberalize his regime, the chances that this might lead to democracy are limited. Given the prior history of fear and suspicion, the democratic opposition is unlikely to trust the change. In addition, various actors are likely to accuse each other of past collaboration with the regime or of readiness to be co-opted by it. Since the regime is extremely personalistic, the ruler himself is the target of the opposition: compromise between the regime and the opposition becomes well-nigh impossible, since there is no neutral force to which both could appeal as an arbiter. The opposition demands nothing less than the ouster of the ruler and often his trial, for it cannot lend credence to his promises to lead democratically henceforth or to abandon power peacefully, given his record of deceit and manipulation. Although there may be groups within the regime willing to defect from it, there are no trusted moderates in the regime to negotiate with, since everybody is tainted by association with the ruler. All of this means that the ruler cannot look forward to a peaceful life after his ouster.[66] The cost of tolerating an opposition is therefore high, and this makes liberalization problematic.

In the period after he promises liberalization, the emperor's nakedness becomes apparent to all: as the crisis drags on, the probability of the regime's weathering it diminishes. Given its lack of links with civil society and its narrow social base, the regime's capacity for countermobilization is severely limited, which encourages maximalist tendencies in the opposition.

It is during the crisis following the initial promise of liberalization that the regime loses whatever vestiges of legitimacy it may have retained with at least some citizens. Natural calamities, which are "unique historical events" and therefore not integrated in theoretical constructs,[67] seem to come into play with striking regularity in sultanistic regimes. By demonstrating the regimes' inability to provide adequate relief and giving them an opportunity to pocket aid coming from abroad, natural disasters delegitimize them. In Iran, the two earthquakes of 1962 and 1978 (claiming twenty-five thousand and twelve thousand victims, respectively) preceded the uprising of June 1963 and the 1979 revolution. In Nicaragua, the Managua earthquake of 1972 (five thousand victims) led to greater corruption and deepened the citizenry's outrage. In the Philippines, the 1976 earthquake (eight thousand victims) destroyed the church in which President Marcos's daughter had been married amid great pomp and circumstance, a symbol not lost on the population. Finally, a series of natural disasters characterized the early 1980s: in Haiti swine fever broke out in 1981 and led to a government-ordered slaughter of pigs, the peasants' traditional source of wealth; Hurricane Allen destroyed much of the coffee culture; the identification of AIDS and its discovery there hurt the tourist industry; and in 1985 a drought led to a 20 percent fall in food production and dried up the hydroelectric capacity of Lake Péligre, leading to widespread rural flight, transportation difficulties, and hunger. The blatant inability of Duvalier to respond worsened the situation and helped undermined his regime.[68] The special vulnerability of sultanistic regimes to natural disasters is demonstrated by the relative ease with which the Mexican regime coped with the 1985 earthquake in that country: in spite of Mexico's endemic corruption the political system was institutionalized enough to cope with the crisis.[69]

The basic illegitimacy of the sultanistic regime has yet another dimension in the case of the pseudodemocracies, since here "free elections" are not a clear break with the past, because the government claims that elections have always been free. This is precisely what arouses the suspicion of the opposition, which denies that the government has the will and the moral caliber to organize genuine elections. It also strengthens the hand of the nondemocratic opposition in its competition with the democratic opposition, for it can accuse the latter of being what we would call a pseudo-opposition, opportunistic or, at best, hopelessly naïve. The manipulation of democratic procedures by the sultanistic regime thus weakens the appeal of democracy itself. A corollary of this is that sultanism begets a political atmosphere in which scheming, conspiracies, betrayals, secretiveness, and rumor mongering flourish. And these are not ingredients of a political culture conducive to democracy.

The contrast with the people's democracies of Eastern Europe is telling: the bloc parties never pretended to rival the ruling Communist parties and consequently were able to play a role during the transition to democracy, either as autonomous parties or, in the case of East Germany, as regional organizations of the established West German parties. It seems that only if a sultanistically ruled country has a history of democratic politics can democracy be revived in the course of an election: the Philippines is the pertinent case.

Faced with a serious challenge, the sultanistic regime disintegrates rapidly. When Batista was faced with Castro's rebels, the Shah with essentially unarmed demonstrators, Idi Amin with an invasion force consisting of exiles and Tanzanian troops, Jean-Claude Duvalier with widespread demonstrations, and Mobutu with a strong rebel force, their regimes collapsed. It is a sign of these regimes' close links with foreign powers that the latter are closely involved in the final transfer of power. Both the dictators and their opponents believe that foreigners make and unmake governments, and this itself can draw in outside powers. Given mounting opposition, the rulers' foreign allies abandon them and often try to look for a "third force" that can stave off a revolution; occasionally, as in the Philippines and Haiti, they even find one and arrange for the dictator to leave. If no third force is found, the ruler and his cronies flee abroad at the last moment, as they are abandoned by everybody.[70] The least lucky ones are ousted by their former patrons once they are no longer useful: the U.S. invasion of Panama and the subsequent arrest of Manuel Noriega, which cost the lives of five thousand Panamanians, is the most glaring example, although France also aided militarily in toppling Emperor Bokassa in 1979—after it had paid for his coronation.

Sultanism and Mass Movements

> Men trust a great man because they do not trust themselves.
> And hence the worship of great men always appears in time
> of weakness and cowardice; we never hear of great men until
> the time when all other men are small.
>
> G. K. CHESTERTON,
> *Heretics*

As Jeff Goodwin and Theda Skocpol have argued, sultanistic regimes are more vulnerable to revolutionary overthrow than liberal democracies or inclusionary authoritarian regimes:[71] recent examples include Cuba, Iran, Nicaragua, and Grenada.[72] Sultanistic dictators are more likely to generate elite and middle-class opposition from landlords, businessmen, clerics, and professionals, who resent their monopolization of key sectors of the economy, their heavy-handed control of the flow of ideas and information in schools and the press, their subservience to foreign powers, and the general climate of corruption.

In certain circumstances, analyzed by Richard Snyder in the next chapter, sultanistic rulers come to face a genuine revolutionary movement. In a vacuum of authority and with increasing delegitimation of existing institutions, there arises the need for someone to assume leadership. A full-blown societal crisis favors the emergence of charismatic authority or, as Weber put it, "the 'natural' leaders in moments of distress—whether psychic, physical, economic, ethical, religious, or political—[are] neither appointed officeholders nor . . . persons performing against compensation a 'profession' based on training and special expertise . . . but rather the bearers of specific gifts of body and mind," that is, charismatic leaders.[73] Of course one must concede an element of chance here, since the presence or absence of a leader able to catch the imagination of the masses is not determined structurally: Cuba, Iran, and the Philippines found such leaders in Fidel Castro, Ayatollah Ruhollah Khomeini, and Corazon Aquino (none of them officeholders or endowed with special training or expertise in statecraft); in Nicaragua someone like Edén Pastora, who had marched into the capital after Somoza's flight, might have emerged as a charismatic leader, but he decided to break with the Sandinistas; in the end the *comandantes* collectively derived some charismatic authority from the myth of Sandino. In Haiti it took a few years for the charismatic leadership of Father Jean-Bertrand Aristide to emerge.

Religion plays an important part in the opposition to sultanistic rulers, at least in the last stage of the regime. To some extent this is due to the weakness of civil society under sultanism, which, almost by default, confers great importance on those few institutions that maintain a presence in society. Religious organizations and in the end organized religion become a major locus of oppositional activity as they provide support, resources, and leadership.

But there is more to the role of religion than its organizational resources. The ubiquity of sin and the general degeneration of mores under high sultanism (the last years of Somoza's, the Shah's and Jean-Claude Duvalier's regimes), combined with the unrestrained nouveau-riche lifestyle of the elites, breed resentment. This resentment leads to a "religious ethic of the disprivileged which . . . teaches that the unequal distribution of goods is caused by the sinfulness and the illegality of the privileged, and that sooner or later God's wrath will overtake them."[74] This explains why religious opposition typically begins not among the hierarchy, but among the laity or lower-ranking priesthood. In the days before Vatican II and the Latin American bishops' conference of Medellín in 1968, Catholic bishops could still support Trujillo during most of his rule,[75] or be divided in their attitude toward them (Batista),[76] but in the 1970s Latin America's Catholic Church became more critical. In Nicaragua, Christian base communities that started in the mid-1960s and increased in numbers after the 1972 earthquake opposed Somoza's dictatorship.[77] In Haiti the Catholic base communities (*ti legliz*) organized opposition among the peasantry and were initially regarded with suspicion by the hierarchy.[78] In the Philippines a number of priests were active in the poorest regions of the country at a time when a considerable sector of the bishops was still apolitical or discreetly pro-Marcos.[79] In Iran, finally, religious agitation in the 1970s was mainly inspired by Ali Shariati, whose teachings were frowned upon by the ulema.[80]

This antidictatorial stance of lower-ranking clerics or even laypeople initially contrasts with that of the hierarchies, and it is only gradually that the latter come to join the active opposition.[81] Nicaragua's bishops, all of whom had been critical of Somoza, and the ayatollahs residing in Iran, who had spoken against the Shah, joined the struggle openly only a few months before the overthrow of the dictators. In the Philippines and Haiti it was visits by the pope himself, in 1981 and in 1983, that put the church on record being critical of those regimes.[82] In Nicaragua and the Philippines the two events that gave the conservative hierarchy the final push were the assassinations of Pedro Joaquín Chamorro in 1978 and Benigno Aquino in 1983. Both men were moderate opponents of the sultanistic dictators, and their deaths signaled to the clergy that repression had reached an intolerable level—especially since the Chamorros were friends of Archbishop Miguel Obando y Bravo and the Aquinos of Archbishop Jaime Sin.

In the Catholic countries the switch in the attitudes of the clergy stripped the dictators, who liked to present themselves as champions in the struggle against atheistic communism, of any shred of legitimacy. An almost mystical atmosphere pervades the change of power, which has aspects of what Victor Turner called "liminality":[83] In Cuba a dove's landing on Castro's shoulder at a mass rally on 8 January 1959 was interpreted by some Catholics as a sign of the Holy Spirit,[84] and in the Philippines on Easter Sunday 1986 Cardinal Sin drew a parallel between the resurrection of Christ and the redemption of the Philippine nation.[85]

Contemporary Catholic doctrine frowns on the clergy's direct participation in partisan politics, and so relations between the hierarchy and such activist priests as Miguel d'Escoto and Ernesto Cardenal in Nicaragua, or Jean-Bertrand Aristide in Haiti, soon cool down, to the point where by now the last two have left the priesthood. The politicized part of the Shi'ite ulema in Iran, unbridled by the principle of rendering to Caesar the things that are Caesar's and to God the things that are God's,[86] took power soon after the Shah's overthrow and neutralized both the politicized laity and the quietist ulema opposed to the exercise of direct power.[87]

The sultanistic regime's inability to find a political solution to the political crisis has already been shown, yet when confronted with a military challenge, it does not fare much better. The armed forces are particularly corrupt and at times even inefficient, in part because the dictator has been more concerned with preventing his own overthrow by military coup than with establishing an effective fighting force. The very fact that they are a praetorian guard in the end promotes the defection of many members from the sultanistic ruler. The Cuban military's dealings with Fidel Castro, discussed by Jorge Domínguez in his chapter, are the best example of the unreliability of a sultanistic army, a pattern confirmed by the performance of Mobutu's troops in 1997, but such a fighting force can also be quite willing to fight, as was the case in Nicaragua, where Somoza's National Guard fought the revolutionaries and was defeated in a civil war. When the rulers finally decide to step down, their armies, given their organizational incoherence, often disintegrate, opening the way for a guerrilla army (Cuba) or countergovernment supported by mass movements (Iran, the Philippines) to take power.

After the installation of a revolutionary government, prospects for democracy are bleak. If a charismatic leader emerges who is committed to democracy, it has a chance, as the Philippines show; but even here that nation's long history of democratic governance before 1972 helped too. Where the charismatic leaders are not democrats, the mass movements they lead will drown the democratic forces, which are weak for reasons already discussed. Even if the postsultanistic regime lacks a charismatic leader, the absence of strong and independent state institutions makes the functioning of democracy very difficult: Nicaragua, Haiti, and Romania illustrate this problem. The flight of the ruler and the delegitimation of his regime lead to a genuine break with the past and the installation of a provisional government, which is composed of ideologically heterogeneous people who have no electoral mandate but who face enormous societal expectations.[88] The moderates in such governments are sooner or later pushed aside either by radicals (Cuba, Nicaragua, Iran) or by remnants of the old regime (Dominican Republic, Haiti, Romania). If the regimes thus constituted are more authoritarian than sultanistic, a transition to democracy may still come about, but not without international pressure: in the Dominican Republic the United States was involved in the assassination of Trujillo and insisted in 1978 that the incumbent regime accept the electoral victory of the opposition. In Haiti and the Philippines the United States actively sought to remove Jean-Claude Duvalier and Ferdinand Marcos from office after widespread demonstrations led the Reagan administration to fear another "Iran." In Panama Americans removed the dictator themselves. In Nicaragua American assistance to the contras resulted in a stalemated civil war, then international pressures and assistance led to an agreement that made free and fair elections possible. Thus Violeta Barrios de Chamorro acceded to the presidency in 1990.[89] Finally, outside assistance was also required in Haiti to reinstate the democratically elected president, who had been ousted by a coup.[90]

In the revolutionary cases, the crises of sovereignty that the sultanistic rulers never resolved come to haunt their former foreign patrons after the revolution. The postsultanistic regimes are more likely than not to blame their countries' travails on foreign powers, and since the new powerholders share the view that their predecessors were foreign puppets, they interpret their victory as a victory over imperialism, leading to hubris that results in confrontational policies toward the United States. The Cuban, Iranian, and Nicaraguan revolutions were all anti-American.[91]

After Sultanism

> Liberty is a food that is good to taste but hard to digest: it
> sets well only on a good stomach. I laugh at those debased
> peoples that let themselves be stirred up by agitators and
> dare to speak of liberty without so much as having the idea
> of it; with their hearts still heavy with the vices of slaves,
> they imagine that they have only to be mutinous in order to
> be free.   JEAN-JACQUES ROUSSEAU,
> *The Government of Poland*

Whether a sultanistic regime's overthrow results in another dictatorship or a democracy, traces of it can often be found in the successor regime; the scars it leaves in a nation's polity are deep. If the sultanistic regime is replaced by a democracy, chances are this new democracy will display strong clientelist tendencies, with the democratically elected leaders using the resources of their office to build nationwide patron-client relationships. Joaquín Balaguer is the best example; his last reelection in 1994 was riddled with irregularities. Even Corazon Aquino was accused of favoring her relatives after she took office.[92]

If the sultanistic regime is replaced by a revolutionary one, institution building in the new regime can be very slow, as is shown by the initial difficulties in Romania, contrasting with more successful democratization elsewhere in Eastern Europe (Yugoslavia excepted).[93] Moreover, the new system tends to pivot around the founder as long as he is alive, which means that personalism remains a feature of the system. Castro's Cuba and Khomeini's Iran illustrate Weber's insight that "charisma knows no formal and regulated appointment or dismissal, no career, advancement or salary, no supervisory or appeals body, no local or purely technical jurisdiction, and no permanent institutions in the manner of bureaucratic agencies, which are independent of the incumbents and their personal charisma."[94] In Cuba, after a period lasting roughly from the mid-1970s to the mid-1980s in which a halfhearted attempt was made to copy Eastern Europe's institutional structure, Castro once again rules in a manner that one observer has called "socialist caudillism."[95] Iran's political institutional structure is riddled with inconsistencies, and corruption and arbitrary government prevail.[96] In Cuba as in Nicaragua, the Castro and Ortega brothers divided the presidency and the leadership of the armed forces between them, just as the Somozas and Trujillos had done before. And when the Sandinistas transferred the nationalized industries to the army after their election loss in 1990, the Ortega brothers, by maintaining their control of the army, in fact lined their pockets handsomely. Under their successors, the politics of understudy continued, with President Chamorro allowing her son-in-law, Antonio Lacayo, to run the country.[97]

In terms of the rationalization and institutionalization of government, therefore, the situation in Cuba, Iran, and Nicaragua is quite reminiscent of the sultanistic regimes that were to be replaced. This is not to suggest that the revolutions made no difference: the masses probably benefited from the overthrow of the dictators, but we must also remember that Cuba's and Iran's revolutionary regimes have jailed, killed, and driven into exile far more citizens than Batista or the Shah.[98] Like the regimes they replaced, these revolutionary regimes present unfavorable preconditions for a transition to democracy,[99] as is shown by the fact that Cuba followed neither other Latin American states nor the Soviet bloc on the path to democracy.

The "loss" of American clients in revolutions that ousted sultanistic rulers has not been easily digested by the U.S. government. Repeatedly the new regimes had to face American interference in their internal affairs, as old habits died hard: the Bay of Pigs invasion in Cuba, the Dominican intervention in 1965, and the support for the contras in Nicaragua have been cases in point, as was, in a different way, the invasion of Panama in 1989 after the local client was no longer acceptable.

The main conclusion to be drawn from a comparative analysis of sultanistic regimes is that, if overthrown, they are more likely to be replaced by a revolutionary or an authoritarian regime than by a democracy. To the extent that some of the sultanistic rulers could play on the West's interest in stability and on Western support during the Cold War era, they might become more vulnerable now that global competition between the superpowers has ended. However, a greater U.S. desire to avoid any foreign intervention and similar reluctance by other industrial democracies to get involved might allow the survival of the few sultanistic rulers that remain or even the establishment of new sultanistic regimes.

Most of the regimes analyzed in these introductory chapters belong to the past. This poses the question whether sultanism is still relevant to an understanding of today's world. Sadly, the answer is yes. Some sultanistic regimes in

Africa, such as those ruling Zaire and Equatorial Guinea, have shown considerable resilience, and in those unfortunate countries where the state has ceased to exist, such as Somalia and Liberia, the various petty warlords that have replaced the state display many sultanistic traits.[100] But subnational sultanisms are not confined to territories where the central state authority has broken down; they can also come about and persist in countries where the state is not strong enough to penetrate the nation. John Thayer Sidel has argued that although pre-Marcos national Philippine politics was dominated by bifactional competition, at the regional level many "local kingpins" monopolized political power in a quintessentially sultanistic way through "guns, goons, and gold."

What is more, this pattern of "petty or local sultanism" persisted under Marcos, even surviving the demise of his regime.[101] Similarly, Guillermo O'Donnell has warned that in the aftermath of democratization and economic restructuring in such countries as Argentina, Brazil, and Peru, attempts to reduce the size and deficits of the state bureaucracy have weakened the government's ideological legitimation and its ability to uphold legality equally in different parts of the national territory. "Provinces or districts peripheral to the national center (which are usually hardest hit by economic crises and are already endowed with weaker bureaucracies than the center) create (or reinforce) systems of local power which tend to reach extremes of violent, personalistic rule—patrimonial, even sultanistic—open to all sorts of violent and arbitrary practices."[102] Similar developments may be taking place in some Mexican states. Since it is at the local level that state policies are carried out, contested, reshaped, resisted, or revised,[103] the spreading of sultanistic practices at the local level bodes ill for the emerging democracies. Parts of the former Soviet Union could conceivably fall victim to sultanistic tendencies. The persistence of *nomenklatura* control, coupled with the absence of an entrepreneurial class, has engendered an intertwining of political and economic power that could well lead to sultanism if a leader emerges who has the requisite qualities to raise himself above the party apparatus. Belarus's president Alexander Lukashenko seems to be on the way to becoming such a dictator, as is Turmenistan's Saparmurad Niyazov.[104] On the other hand, the higher density of international exchanges, the emergence of a transnational civil society, and the end of the Cold War, which has left some sort of democracy as the only internationally legitimate form of government, may signify that the sort of sultanistic regime we have described is a thing of the past, at best viable in a few out of the way places, like Equatorial Guinea, that the world overlooks.

We close by stressing again the destructive legacy of sultanism at the national level. The corruption of society and the illegitimacy of individuals and institutions mean that these countries lack the bureaucracies, police, and armies that a state of law and a democracy need. Because habits of violence, distrust, and lack of social solidarity pervade these unhappy nations, the transition to democracy or even to stable authoritarianism will not be easy. There lies the biggest challenge both to democrats in these countries and to outside forces that want to encourage democracy in the Third World.

3
. . . .

Paths out of Sultanistic Regimes

Combining Structural and Voluntarist Perspectives

Richard Snyder

Sultanistic regimes command great interest both in the literature on social revolutions and in the literature on regime transitions. Students of revolutionary change are interested in sultanistic regimes because so many are linked to the rare phenomenon of social revolution. For example, the sultanistic regimes of Shah Mohammad Reza Pahlavi in Iran, Anastasio Somoza Debayle in Nicaragua, and Fulgencio Batista in Cuba, all of which were toppled by revolutionaries, have been analyzed comparatively by numerous scholars seeking to specify the causes of revolution. These three cases have led students of revolution to identify sultanistic dictatorships as one of the regime types most vulnerable to revolution.[1]

Students of regime transitions, on the other hand, have been drawn to the set of sultanistic regimes because it contains numerous nondemocratic holdouts—regimes that have resisted the wave of democratization that has swept the globe during the past two decades.[2] Cases such as Haiti and Zaire, where democratization has stalled or been stillborn, are of interest because studying them can shed light on factors at work in failed transitions.

Successful transitions to democracy such as occurred in the Philippines after Marcos pose puzzles for students of both revolutions and transitions. The combined presence of a sultanistic regime and a powerful revolutionary opposition in the Philippines under Marcos make it a "most likely" case of revolution and a "least likely" case of democratization. Hence the absence of revolution and the presence of a moderately successful transition to democracy are equally surprising.

The location of the set of sultanistic regimes at the intersection of these literatures is especially intriguing given the starkly different analytic goals and explanatory modes characteristic of the two. Much of the recent literature on social revolutions has sought to identify types of states or social formations vulnerable to revolutionary collapse, typically employing *structural* explanations that focus on the causal role of impersonal, objective social relationships.[3] Much of the recent literature on regime transitions, by contrast, has sought to identify types of nondemocratic regimes susceptible to democratization, usually relying on *voluntarist* explanations that emphasize the contingent choices of elite actors during processes of regime change.[4]

In response to criticisms that the emphasis on structural explanations understates the role of political action in making (or failing to make) revolutions, students of revolutionary change have recently sought to incorporate the efficacy of human action into their analyses alongside structural causal factors.[5] Similarly, in response to criticisms that the emphasis on voluntarist explanations understates the causal role of structural factors, students of transitions have been seeking to link political action to structural constraints in analyses of regime change.[6] Thus the two literatures appear to be moving toward each other as they both search for explanations that integrate human agency and social structure. Unfortunately, scholarly recognition of this convergence has been obscured in part by disciplinary boundaries, which tend to insulate students of states and revolutions from students of regimes and transitions.[7]

The intersection of the two literatures in their shared focus on sultanistic regimes offers an opportunity to transcend disciplinary partitions and bridge these two literatures.[8] To this end I introduce a framework for analyzing the dynamics of sultanistic regimes that seeks to combine the strengths of both literatures by uniting a focus on structural factors with a focus on political action and historical contingency. I then use this integrative framework to account for the varied paths of political development traversed by sultanistic regimes.

The cases chosen for analysis exemplify a variety of possible trajectories for sultanistic regimes: revolution, as in the cases of Somoza Debayle in Nicaragua, Mohammad Reza Shah in Iran, and Batista in Cuba; nonrevolutionary transition to civilian rule, as in the cases of Ferdinand Marcos in the Philippines and Nicolae Ceauşescu in Romania[9]; and transition to military dictatorship, as in the case of Jean-Claude Duvalier in Haiti. The cases of Mobutu Sese Seko in

Zaire until 1991 and François Duvalier in Haiti exemplify the remarkable longevity and stability of some sultanistic regimes.[10]

A Framework for Explaining Paths out of Sultanistic Regimes

I take two steps to construct an integrative framework that combines structural and voluntarist perspectives in the analysis of transitions from sultanistic regimes. First, to overcome the structural determinism for which the literature on revolutions has been criticized, I define the actors relevant to the transformation of sultanistic regimes in a manner that does not reduce them to passive carriers of fixed interests and identities derived from positions in institutional or social structures. Since political actors are not automatons who mechanically play parts demanded of them by structures, the groups who participate in the transformation of sultanistic regimes must be defined in a way that is sensitive to actors' abilities to shift strategic postures and take advantage of margins of maneuverability within structural constraints. To meet this challenge, I define the actors relevant to transitions from sultanistic regimes according to strategic postures rather than by institutional or structural roles.[11]

Second, to overcome the extreme voluntarism for which the regime transitions literature has been criticized, I do not assume that regime change is always a fluid process in which actors have broad discretion. Instead, for each case I map the institutional and social structures that are the strategic contexts in which these actors operate in order to pinpoint precisely how much room, if any, exists for strategic maneuvering.[12]

Defining the Actors Who Make Transitions

Four domestic groups are relevant for analyzing the dynamics of sultanistic regimes: regime hard-liners, regime soft-liners, the moderate opposition, and the maximalist opposition.[13] Regime hard-liners are unconditionally committed to perpetuating the dictator's rule. They prefer to go down with the ship rather than exit gracefully and therefore must be forced to give up power. This group typically includes the ruling clique—that is, the dictator and his immediate circle of cronies—but may extend to other actors within the state who are not part of this ruling inner circle.

Soft-liners are the other main actors within the regime. They perceive their survival to be separable from the dictator's and, especially during times of crisis, may come to view their association with him as more a liability than a benefit. Hence they may seek to sever their ties with the dictator, perhaps turning against him in hopes that they themselves may seize power. This group often includes factions of the military or members of the state's administrative bureaucracy alienated by the dictator's interference with their autonomy and professionalism.[14]

Two categories are also relevant for analyzing opposition to sultanistic regimes. The maximalist opposition abhors allying with any regime incumbents and is committed to goals that extend far beyond simply removing the dictator. Maximalists seek to overthrow the existing regime and seize control of the state. Their agenda often involves radically transforming state and society as well as restructuring the nation's links with the international system. This group typically consists of revolutionary organizations.[15]

The moderate opposition, on the other hand, is committed to the limited goal of ousting the dictator and his ruling clique. Members typically will ally with whichever group can forward this objective. Thus, in contrast to maximalists, they are willing to support or join regime soft-liners seeking to overthrow the dictator. Since moderates prefer groups that share their minimal agenda of removing the dictator over groups with plans for radical change, regime soft-liners are usually their first-choice allies. However, if regime soft-liners are absent or are perceived to be incapable of ousting the dictator, moderates may choose to ally with maximalists, who are seen to share at least their objective of removing the dictator. Moderates are not necessarily a democratic opposition—their immediate goal is simply to replace the sultanistic dictator's arbitrary rule with a more predictable, institutionalized regime. The moderate group typically includes domestic economic elites shut out of the dictator's patronage network and alienated by the disruptive effects on their business activities of the dictator's arbitrary and unpredictable use of power. These "noncrony" elites often resent the personal enrichment of the ruler and his family and seek to dissolve the fusion of public and private created by the sultanistic regime.[16]

The presence of hard-liners, soft-liners, moderates, and maximalists cannot be assumed in all cases of sultanism.[17] Any combination of these groups may be absent or extremely weak because the varying structural characteristics of sultanistic regimes shape the political space within which they can organize and hence condition the possibilities for their very existence. Even when there is structural space for the organization of one or more of these groups, they do not necessarily form because, for a variety of reasons, actors do not always take advantage of structural opportunities.[18] And when moderates, maximalists, hard-liners, or soft-liners *do* organize, their strategies, relative strengths, and coalitional options are critically shaped by the structural context in which they operate.

Mapping the Structural Contexts of Transitions

The structural factors relevant for explaining the dynamics of sultanistic regimes can be deduced from the core defining feature of this type of regime: the ruler's maintenance of authority through personal patronage rather than through ideology, charisma, or impersonal law.[19] The central role of patronage in these regimes creates an authority structure that is radial in nature, with the dictator occupying a central hub that is linked via patronage spokes to clients both within the state and in civil society.[20] In addition, sultanistic dictators are frequently themselves clients of foreign powers, especially superpower patrons such as the United States. Thus three critical relationships capture the varied structural dynamics of sultanistic regimes: the ruler's relationship to state institutions; the ruler's relationship to domestic societal elites; and the relationship of domestic actors (that is, hard-liners, soft-liners, moderates, and maximalists) to foreign powers.

Ruler-State Relations

The degree to which the patronage network radiating from the ruler penetrates state institutions—especially the military—tends to be uneven and to fluctuate over time. There is often an ongoing struggle between the dictator, who seeks to wrest autonomy from state institutions, and incumbents of these institutions, who seek to retain autonomy. When state institutions are thoroughly penetrated by the dictator's patronage network, the political space for the emergence of regime soft-liners is minimal, and the ruling clique and the state are essentially fused into a unitary, hard-line actor. By contrast, when state institutions are insulated from the dictator's patronage network, the structural potential exists for soft-liners to organize within these institutions and oppose the dictator.

How far the ruler has undermined the autonomy of the armed forces through patronage (for example, by subverting its organizational hierarchy and replacing it with a hierarchy based on loyalty to his person, and by dividing the officer corps) is a critical variable that differentiates cases of transition from sultanism where the impetus for political change comes from above, within the incumbent regime, from cases where it originates from below, involving societal actors outside the regime. When segments of the armed forces have *not* been thoroughly divided and co-opted by the dictator and are capable of autonomous action against him—as in the Philippines, Haiti, and Romania—a military coup, with or without civilian support, may remove the dictator. Where the military lacks sufficient autonomy to act independently of the dictator—as in Iran, Nicaragua, Cuba, and Zaire—the possibility for political transformation hinges on the efforts of maximalist opposition groups with the coercive resources necessary to defeat the dictator's loyal military. Hence, in such cases political change tends to be violent and revolutionary if it occurs at all.

To assess the degree of military autonomy, we can examine whether the armed forces have control over the supply of their matériel, the ability of officers to predict their career paths and to communicate discontent with one another, how completely the officer corps is divided along ethnic or regional lines, and the dictator's capacity to purge elements of the armed forces whose loyalty he questions.[21] In Zaire, for example, Mobutu's efforts to divide the military through frequent rotation of officers, periodic purges of the officer corps, and exploitation of ethnoregional tensions minimized the space within which soft-liners could organize and consequently reduced the armed forces' capacity to turn against him.

When assessing military autonomy we must also consider whether the dictator has a paramilitary force that functions as a counterbalance to the regular armed forces and whose members infiltrate and spy on the military. In Haiti, François Duvalier's Tonton Macoutes were such a force. Their infiltration of the armed forces and Duvalier's purges of the officer corps minimized the Haitian military's capacity for autonomous action during his rule. Such institutional counterweights that limit the discretion of the regular armed forces are not always paramilitary. For example, Ceauşescu used the Romanian Communist Party in addition to the Securitate, the secret police, as an effective check against military coup d'état.

By contrast, Marcos's attempts to undermine the autonomy of the Philippine armed forces by packing the officer corps with individuals loyal to his person were less successful than the measures taken by Mobutu and François Duvalier. Pockets of institutional autonomy, clustered around career officers, remained within the Philippine military despite Marcos's efforts to subordinate it. Many of these career officers, who had worked their way up through the established hierarchy, became disgruntled by Marcos's dilution of the military's professionalism. These disenchanted officers were able to organize a movement within the armed forces to restore its integrity and discipline. This organization, the Reform the Armed Forces Now Movement (RAM), served as a cover for plotting the abortive coup that triggered Marcos's overthrow in 1986.

The dictator's discretion plays a key role in both the creation and transformation of the ruler-military relationship. Although all sultanistic rulers are compelled to devise mechanisms for securing the loyalty, or at least acquiescence, of the military, they can employ a range of strategies to achieve this objective.[22] Two alternative ruler survival strategies vis-à-vis the military warrant consideration here because they seem to have important ramifications for future processes of transition from sultanism. Anchoring the ruler-military relationship in the dictator's choices and strategies underscores the role of human agency in both the creation and the reproduction of this "objective" relationship.[23]

The first strategy, exemplified by François Duvalier's use of the Tonton Macoutes, is to transfer primary responsibility for applying state violence to a loyal paramilitary force, stripping the regular military of virtually all security functions.[24] Although this strategy can reduce the short-term possibility of challenges to the dictator from within the regime, it can paradoxically promote such challenges over the long term. Since the regular military is isolated and not a full-fledged participant in the regime, it can easily come to view its survival as independent from the dictator's, especially when, as in the case of Haiti, power is transferred to a son of the dictator whose competence to rule is perceived as questionable. And perhaps more important, because responsibility for performing the bulk of the dictator's "dirty work" rests with the paramilitary guard, *not* the regular military, in the eyes of the population the armed forces may remain relatively untarnished by the regime's abuses. Thus in Haiti, during the overthrow of the Duvalier dynasty in 1986, shouts of "long live the army" by civilian protesters against Jean-Claude Duvalier could be heard on several occasions, and some viewed the military as an ally that could help deliver the nation from the Duvalier regime.[25]

The second strategy for neutralizing the threat of a military coup is exemplified by Mobutu, who took strong measures to undermine the capacity of the Zairian armed forces to turn against him, yet continued to rely on them to maintain internal control. This strategy closely intertwines the military's survival with the dictator's, encourages predatory behavior by the armed forces against civil society, and weakens their legitimacy with the population. Consequently, the chances are slim that the military will turn against the dictator and that, if it does, it will be able to participate in a legitimate, interim "caretaker" government that oversees a smooth transition from sultanism. These two factors increase the likelihood that transitions from sultanism will be violent.[26]

Ruler-Society Relations

Sultanistic regimes vary in how far the patronage network penetrates civil society, co-opting societal elites through material rewards. The degree of inclusion of domestic elites within the patronage network influences the growth of both maximalist and moderate oppositions. When the dictator's patronage network is inclusive, penetrating deeply into society, political space for opposition groups is narrow because these vertical patron-client linkages both co-opt elites and extend the reach of the state's surveillance and control. By contrast, when the dictator excludes domestic elites from his patronage network, state penetration into society is relatively shallow, opening political space for the growth of opposition.[27]

François Duvalier in Haiti, Somoza García in Nicaragua, and Ceauşescu in Romania limited the growth of opposition by constructing extensive patronage networks that co-opted societal elites. The combination of elite inclusion and deep state penetration of society contributed to the longevity and stability of these regimes. The breakdown of sultanism in Haiti, Nicaragua, and Romania was due in large part to the prior unraveling of these patronage networks and to a corresponding increase in the exclusion of political elites.

By contrast, Mohammad Reza Shah in Iran, Somoza Debayle in Nicaragua, and Batista in Cuba unintentionally encouraged the growth of opposition by excluding domestic elites from political power and economic patronage.[28] Alienation of elites encouraged formation of broad and effective coalitions of convenience between moderates and maximalists, in part because the armed forces in these three cases had been thoroughly co-opted and divided by the ruler and consequently were incapable of autonomous action against him. The absence of military soft-liners within these regimes pushed the moderate opposition to ally with revolutionary maximalists who had the military or organizational capability to unseat the dictator and his subservient army.[29] Robert Dix has argued persuasively that the ability of maximalists to construct such broad coalitions was a key cause of revolution in Iran, Nicaragua, and Cuba. In each case the maximalists, who had coercive and organizational resources superior to those of their moderate allies, easily dominated these coalitions and used the moderates as stepping-stones to state power, turning against them after the common goal of removing the dictator had been achieved.[30]

Exclusionary sultanistic dictatorships are not always toppled by revolution.[31] First, they do not necessarily confront significant maximalist or moderate oppositions. Organizational difficulties, the absence of political cultures of opposition, the lack of effective leaders, and state repression can all hinder the emergence of potent opposition movements even in an exclusionary environment.[32] For example, would-be maximalist and moderate opponents in Jean-Claude Duvalier's Haiti were frustrated by organizational problems and by the debilitating legacy of years of repression. Second, even if maximalists have not been killed and have been able to organize, they may choose not to pursue a strategy of armed confrontation. Or they may be incapable of defeating the dictator's armed forces in battle, especially if the military has some organizational coherence. Third, if there are soft-line segments of the armed forces with the ability to act autonomously against the dictator, a coalition of moderate civilian opposition groups and disgruntled segments of the military, or elements of the military acting alone, may seize power and block revolution even when a powerful maximalist opposition does exist. Marcos's overthrow exemplifies this pattern of a military-moderate alliance blocking a powerful maximalist movement.

On the other hand, the exclusionary regimes of Somoza, Batista, and the Shah *were* toppled by revolution. This occurred because powerful revolutionary movements emerged against them, the armed forces were unable to act against the dictator, and consequently moderates lacked potential soft-line allies and chose to ally with the revolutionaries. The resulting broad coalitions dominated by the maximalists were able to seize power when these dictators fled and "their" armies unraveled.

That a sultanistic regime excludes societal elites from patronage benefits cannot by itself predict whether that regime will move toward revolution, as in Iran, Nicaragua, and Cuba; will experience a military coup, as in Haiti; or will undergo a transition to civilian rule, as in the Philippines. To explain how a highly exclusionary sultanistic regime is displaced, we must also examine the organizational capacities and strategic choices of maximalist and moderate opposition groups, the coalition options available to moderates (especially whether autonomous soft-line military factions are available as allies), and the dictator's ability to counter challenges to his control of the state.

To sum up, sultanistic regimes that effectively co-opt societal elites through patronage networks can inhibit the growth of both maximalist and moderate oppositions. Consequently, depending on the military's capacity and desire to oust the dictator, they tend to be relatively stable and long-lived. On the other hand, sultanistic regimes that exclude elites from patronage and limit it to a small clique surrounding the ruler tend to encourage the growth of opposition and are generally unstable. Revolution is the likely outcome of this instability in cases such as Iran, Nicaragua, and Cuba, where a coherent revolutionary movement challenges the dictator and where military soft-liners are absent. Military dictatorship is the probable outcome in cases like Haiti under Jean-Claude Duvalier, where no coherent maximalist or moderate oppositions organize against the exclusionary dictator and where military soft-liners have the ability to turn against him and fill the vacuum of power created by his flight into exile. Civilian rule is the likely outcome in cases such as the Philippines, where a powerful moderate opposition and a revolt by military soft-liners can dislodge the dictator and enable the civilian opposition to take control without opening the way for a seizure of power by maximalists.

Foreign Power–Domestic Actor Relations

Analyses of transitions from authoritarian rule have tended to focus on domestic, internal factors, downplaying the role of international actors in the explanation of regime change. According to O'Donnell and Schmitter, such a domestic focus is justified because "it seems fruitless to search for some international factor or context which can reliably compel authoritarian rulers to experiment with liberalization, much less which can predictably cause their regimes to collapse."[33] In the analysis of transitions from sultanistic regimes, however, a focus on international actors is crucial. As I noted earlier, sultanistic dictators are often dependent on foreign patrons, who supply critical military aid and material resources that can help fuel their domestic patronage networks.[34] Furthermore, moderate and maximalist groups opposed to these dictators frequently receive assistance from foreign actors (often from former patrons of the dictator). For these reasons, considering the role of international actors seems more essential for analyzing transitions from sultanism than for analyzing transitions from other types of nondemocratic regimes.[35]

I am not implying that international forces alone determine the developmental trajectories of sultanistic regimes. The impact of these forces is mediated by the configuration of domestic actors (for example, the presence or absence of intraregime and societal opposition groups) and by the willingness of domestic actors (especially the incumbent dictator) to participate in the schemes of foreign powers. Short of invasion, foreign powers can influence transitions from sultanism by strengthening the capacities of various domestic actors and shaping the menu of political strategies they can choose from, thus reducing or enhancing their maneuverability. Changes in international support for the dictator or opposition groups, for example, may affect the perceived costs and payoffs of particular strategies, thereby influencing the choices of actors during moments of regime change.

In Iran, Nicaragua, and Cuba, the dictator's extreme dependence on superpower patronage contributed to the success of the maximalist opposition. According to Farideh Farhi and Jack Goldstone, Batista's, Somoza's, and the Shah's extreme reliance on U.S. support encouraged revolution because this support promoted exclusionary and repressive regime behavior by providing military and economic resources, which allowed the ruler to detach his repressive state apparatus from its social base and dispense with domestic coalition building. U.S. support also frustrated the nationalist ambitions of elites and undermined the rulers' control during times of crisis because the United States insisted on liberalizing reforms and limited coercion.[36]

Although dependence on U.S. support contributed to the revolutionary overthrow of the Shah, Somoza, and Batista, the extreme dependence of a sultanistic ruler on a foreign power does not necessarily encourage revolution, and may even inhibit it. When the dictator is heavily dependent on a superpower patron that can identify and support an acceptable and cooperative alternative (usually regime soft-liners or moderate opposition groups), that patron may be able to use its leverage to remove the dictator from office in times of crisis and ease the acceptable opposition into power. In this way a superpower patron can inhibit revolution by defusing a crisis that, if allowed to continue, might strengthen the hand of maximalists and provide an opportunity for them to seize power. The United States was able to "manage" the transitions in the Philippines and in Haiti by exerting pressure on Marcos and Jean-Claude Duvalier and by switching its support to the civilian moderate opposition, led by Corazon Aquino, in the Philippines, and to military soft-liners, led by General Henri Namphy, in Haiti. Conversely, in Iran, Nicaragua, and Cuba, the United States was unable to find an acceptable, viable alternative to the incumbent dictator and contributed to its client's revolutionary overthrow by pursuing a destabilizing "human rights policy" intended to limit the dictator's use of coercion through the threat of withholding vital military and economic assistance.

How dependent sultanistic rulers are on foreign patrons varies significantly from case to case. For example, during the mid-1960s, François Duvalier received virtually no foreign assistance, and consequently outside influence on his regime was minimal. Sultanistic rulers can also limit the leverage external actors have over them by diversifying sources of foreign support to avoid overdependence on a single patron. Mobutu and Ceauşescu used this strategy and benefited from the military and economic aid of various supporters without becoming vulnerable to their policy preferences. When foreign actors have limited leverage over the dictator, their ability to influence the course of political development is restricted to supporting the dictator's opposition or to intervening directly.[37]

To sum up, the framework introduced above for explaining transitions from sultanism consists of two procedures that combine structural and voluntarist approaches to the study of regime change. First, the actors who participate in transitions from sultanistic regimes are defined in a way that highlights their ability to shift strategic postures within the margins of maneuverability allowed by structural constraints. Second, these margins of maneuverability are specified by analyzing three critical relationships—ruler-state (especially ruler-military), ruler-society, and foreign power–domestic actor—that define the structural contexts of transitions from sultanism. Taken together, these two procedures constitute an integrative framework that links structural constraints to the shaping of political action in the analysis of regime change.

Alternative Paths of Political Development for Sultanistic Regimes

In the following sections, the integrative framework is used to account for the multiple paths of political development for sultanistic regimes: political stability, revolution, military dictatorship, and civilian rule. The case analyses are organized around the structural variables that define contexts of action: the relationships of rulers to the military, of rulers to elites, and of domestic actors

TABLE 3.1
Structural Characteristics of Sultanistic Regimes

Cases	Penetration of State by Ruler's Patronage Network	Penetration of Society by Ruler's Patronage Network	Ruler's Dependence on a Single Superpower Patron	Regime Outcomes
Zaire until 1990; Haiti under François Duvalier	High	High	Low	Political stability
Nicaragua under Somoza García	High	High	High	Political stability
Iran, Cuba, Nicaragua under Somoza Debayle	High	Low	High	Revolution
Zaire after 1990; Panama prior to 1989 U.S. invasion	High	Low	Low	Civil conflict between dictator and societal opposition
Romania after 1985	Low	Low	Low	Military coup leading to rule by civilian soft-liners
Philippines; Haiti under Jean-Claude Duvalier	Low	Low	High	Military coup leading to rule by civilian moderates in Philippines; military coup leading to rule by military soft-liners in Haiti.
No cases	Low	High	Low	
No cases	Low	High	High	

TABLE 3.2

Relative Strengths of Domestic Oppositions to Sultanistic Dictators

Cases	Strength of Regime Soft-liners	Strength of Moderate Opposition	Strength of Maximalist Opposition	Regime Outcomes
Zaire until 1990; Haiti under François Duvalier; Nicaragua under Somoza García	Absent	Low	Low	Political stability
Iran, Cuba, Nicaragua under Somoza Debayle	Absent	Low	High	Revolution
Zaire 1991–95; Panama before 1989 U.S. invasion	Absent	Medium	Low	Civil conflict between dictator and moderates
Romania after 1985; Haiti under Jean-Claude Duvalier	High	Low	Low	Military coup leading to rule by civilian soft-liners in Romania and by military soft-liners in Haiti
Philippines	High	High	High	Military coup leading to rule by moderates

to foreign powers. Where these structural factors created opportunities for strategic maneuvering, the analysis probes whether and how actors took advantage of these opportunities.

An analysis of tables 3.1 and 3.2 underscores the importance of examining *both* the structural contexts of transitions *and* actors' responses to opportunities for strategic maneuvering within these contexts. Together these two perspectives are used to explain alternative paths of development for sultanistic regimes. Table 3.1 summarizes the structural characteristics of the cases and reveals that variations in structural features of sultanistic regimes cannot by themselves explain alternative paths of transition. For example, in the cases of Haiti under Jean-Claude Duvalier and the Philippines under Marcos, *similar* structural characteristics are associated with quite *different* outcomes of transitions from sultanism: Duvalier's ouster resulted in a military dictatorship, whereas that of Marcos resulted in rule by civilian moderates. And in the cases of Nicaragua under Somoza García and Haiti under François Duvalier, *different* structural characteristics are associated with the *similar* outcome of political stability.

Table 3.2 summarizes the relative strengths of domestic opposition groups. The similarities between the clustering of cases in tables 3.1 and 3.2 reveal the important influence that the structural characteristics of sultanistic regimes can have on the strength of domestic oppositions. However, a comparison of the tables also suggests that the structural characteristics of sultanistic regimes cannot fully explain the strength of opposition groups. For example, Marcos's regime in the Philippines and Jean-Claude Duvalier's in Haiti had similar structural characteristics, yet moderate and maximalist oppositions were strong in the Philippines and weak in Haiti. Likewise, Ceauşescu's regime in Romania and Jean-Claude Duvalier's in Haiti had different structural characteristics, yet the relative strengths of oppositions were similar in these cases.[38] As the case analyses will reveal, we must consider the strategies and organizational abilities of would-be regime opponents in order to account for such unpredictable responses to structural opportunities for building opposition movements.

Political Stability

The extreme personalism and low levels of institutionalization of sultanistic regimes have led some observers to conclude that these regimes are highly unstable and fragile.[39] However, the set of sultanistic regimes includes some of world's longest-lived and most resilient governments. The Duvalier dynasty lasted thirty years, and the Somoza dynasty endured more than forty, with smooth transfers of power from fathers to sons in both cases. The analysis below focuses on the regimes of François Duvalier in Haiti and Mobutu in Zaire in order to identify the factors that seem to explain the durability of some sultanistic regimes.

Based on these two cases, sultanistic regimes with ongoing stability seem characterized by extensive penetration of both state *and* society by the dictator's patronage network, allowing little space for the organization of opposition either within or outside the regime. The absence of soft-liners and civilian opposition in these cases makes regime hard-liners the sole players in the domestic political arena. In addition, the hard-liners who preside over such stable games of political solitaire tend to avoid extreme dependence on a single superpower patron.

Haiti: François Duvalier

François Duvalier consolidated his regime by decimating his opponents and constructing a patronage network based on the black, rural middle class, composed of peasants with medium-sized landholdings. According to David Nicholls, "a whole structure of dependence and patronage" had developed in the Haitian countryside, which was dominated by this black middle class.[40] By securing the backing of this key group through patronage, Duvalier took advantage of the existing power structure in the countryside, where 80 percent of the Haitian population resided, to extend the reach of his state into the interstices of Haitian society. Since the middle class was the main potential support base for would-be moderate opponents to Duvalier, its inclusion in his patronage network restricted the growth of moderate opposition.[41] By extending state penetration of civil society, furthermore, Duvalier's co-optation of black elites worked in conjunction with his personal paramilitary organization—the Tonton Macoutes (the bulk of whose leadership was drawn from the rural middle class)[42]—to prevent effective moderate or maximalist mobilization against him.

The army had dominated Haitian politics for 150 years before Duvalier's rule, and he was keenly aware that most of his predecessors had been deposed by the military. To ensure that he too would not fall victim to a military coup, Duvalier took immediate steps to undermine the autonomy of the armed forces. He purged the officer corps, unified the armed services under his personal authority, and created an elite Presidential Guard billeted at the presidential palace.[43] Duvalier also used the Tonton Macoutes as a counterweight to the military. By the time of the dictator's death in 1971, one Haitian in twenty was estimated to be affiliated with the Macoutes; by comparison, the entire armed forces numbered only seven thousand.[44] By 1964, Duvalier was able to claim with justification, "I have removed from the army its role of arbiter of national life."[45]

Duvalier also maintained significant autonomy from foreign powers. Between 1962 and 1966, foreign aid was virtually cut off in reaction to the regime's repression. Because he did not depend on foreign support, Duvalier was relatively insulated from external pressures for political reform.[46] The United States and other international actors had limited leverage over him short of direct destabilization or invasion. In any event, since Duvalier was a reliable Cold War ally, the United States was minimally concerned with influencing Haitian politics.

By the mid-1960s, Duvalier's insulation from foreign powers, his balanced use of co-optation and repression, and his subordination of the armed forces had minimized the political space for the organization of opposition. According to Nicholls, "The army officers, the Roman Catholic Hierarchy, the U.S. embassy, the business elite, the intellectuals, the trade union leadership, one by one had their wings clipped."[47] The stability of the elder Duvalier's rule and the smooth transfer of power in 1971 to his son Jean-Claude were products of this environment equally devoid of maximalists, moderates, and soft-liners. Jean-Claude's rule, which will be discussed shortly, did not enjoy such stability.

Zaire: Mobutu Sese Seko

Mobutu Sese Seko, Zaire's dictator, was in power for over thirty years. Until 1991 Mobutu's rule, like François Duvalier's, was characterized by remarkable political stability. In the middle of 1991, however, this stability gave way to conflict and stalemate between a weak moderate opposition and regime hard-liners. This discussion identifies the factors that seem to explain this prolonged stability and highlights the changes in these factors associated with its recent breakdown.

The ongoing stability of Mobutu's regime before 1990 was a consequence of the co-optation of elites, brutal repression, and the exacerbation of ethnic and regional divisions by state patronage, all of which effectively inhibited the growth of both maximalist and moderate oppositions; the undermining of the armed forces' institutional autonomy, which eliminated the political space for soft-line opposition; and Mobutu's ability to extract vital military and economic assistance from foreign patrons while limiting the leverage these patrons had over him by diversifying his sources of external support. As a result, the structural spaces within which maximalists, moderates, and soft-liners could organize were minimal: hence, *stasis.*

Like François Duvalier, Mobutu limited the growth of opposition by co-opting elites through an extensive patronage network that bound members of the dominant political-commercial class to the state. The core of his patronage system was the Popular Movement of the Revolution (MPR), Zaire's only legal political organization until 1990. Mobutu's patronage network was characterized by such frequent circulation of elites that observers have likened Zaire's politics to a "game of 'musical chairs.' "[48] This circulation atomized Zairian elites by pressuring them to focus exclusively on self-aggrandizement during the short period when they had access to state power and perquisites. Schatzberg writes that, according to the " 'rules' of Zairian politics, it [was] better to profit while possible to insure oneself and one's family a bit of security after the fall."[49]

In addition to inhibiting elite opposition, state patronage worked against the solidarity of opposition groups when they did arise by exacerbating regional and ethnic identities, thereby fragmenting civil society and impeding broad-based mobilization against Mobutu. Young and Turner describe how the patrimonial structure of Mobutu's state discouraged collective action in pursuit of state resources by reinforcing particularistic divisions within society:

> Access to the state on the part of civil society is more efficaciously secured by penetrating its softened shell by means of a patron-client net, in pursuit of immediate, particularized advantage, rather than by assaulting its bastions through formal pursuit of the general interest. Affinities of kinship and ethnicity supply the ideological cement for clientage links between state and society. . . . An "economy of affection" . . . infiltrates the state and defines the terms of its relationships with society.[50]

Limited social mobility, a consequence of economic stagnation in the 1970s, made these "economies of affection" especially important, because using kinship, ethnic, and regional affiliations to establish ties to a patron was virtually the only avenue of upward mobility. Elites encouraged and exploited regional and ethnic identities to help them construct support bases that they used to extract state resources.[51] This politicizing of ethnicity, kinship, and regionalism by Mobutu's patronage network splintered civil society and limited the possibilities for mobilizing against him.

The ethnoregional patron-client networks further hampered the organizational efforts of Mobutu's opponents by preventing the polarization of society into "haves" and "have-nots," as occurred in cases such as Iran, Nicaragua, Cuba, and the Philippines. In Zaire, in contrast to these other cases where patronage was restricted to a small group of the dictator's cronies, an important third category existed: those "have-nots" who could claim regional or kinship affiliations with the "haves." This third category significantly widened the perimeter of Mobutu's patronage circle and limited the appeal of opposition movements.

Co-optation of elites, the fragmenting effects of state patronage in civil society, and Mobutu's selective use of coercion against those who voiced dissatisfaction with his regime effectively stifled internal opposition. According to Turner, in 1987 "there was no shortage of opposition parties, but these were based outside the country and seemed unlikely to pose a significant threat to the regime."[52]

Mobutu neutralized the threat of a military coup by maintaining close personal control over the armed forces, encouraging rivalries among officer factions, and purging officers deemed untrustworthy. With these tactics he prevented formation of pockets of autonomy within the armed forces that could serve as breeding grounds for soft-line factions. Arthur House likens Mobutu to the "center of a spoked wheel" in his relations with the military. According to House, Mobutu maintained his supremacy over the military's command structure by rotating officers frequently and by encouraging them to report rumors to him personally.[53] Young and Turner observe that, in addition to creating an extensive patronage network, Mobutu controlled the military by fostering and exploiting rivalries among factions of officers, defined in terms of ethnic or regional identity, institutional affiliation, generations, and levels of training.[54] To ensure the loyalty of the military's top echelons, Mobutu packed their ranks with officers from his home region of Equateur.[55] Also, purges of the officer corps were frequent; in 1978 over two hundred of the most promising junior officers—nearly 10 percent of the officer corps—were dismissed because Mobutu doubted their reliability.[56]

Mobutu's resilience was also due to substantial military and economic assistance from an assortment of foreign patrons (including at various times China, France, Morocco, Belgium, North Korea, Egypt, Israel, South Africa, and the United States).[57] These foreign powers gave vital economic assistance, which helped fuel Mobutu's patronage network. Foreign powers even intervened militarily to prop up the Mobutu regime against armed invasion. In 1977 and again in 1978, Moroccan troops (assisted in 1978 by French and Belgian troops) came to Mobutu's aid when the Zairian Armed Forces (FAZ) proved incapable of repelling incursions of a mere 1,500 to 2,000 meagerly equipped mercenaries from Angola into the Shaba region of Zaire.[58]

Mobutu was able to take advantage of the patronage of foreign powers without incurring the "cost" of extreme vulnerability to the policy preferences of a specific backer. By diversifying his sources of external support he limited the leverage these supporters individually had over him. In an interesting role reversal (a case of the tail wagging the dog), Mobutu was able to squeeze resources out of his foreign backers with minimal reciprocal obligations by exploiting Zaire's strategic and economic importance and using the threat of chaos if his regime was to collapse.[59] As Young and Turner put it, the " 'Mobutu or chaos' formula" unfailingly brought Western powers to the dictator's rescue.[60] Mobutu was also adept at performing what Thomas Callaghy called the "ritual dance of the debt game."[61] This dance ensured continued inflow of the development loans and other economic aid Mobutu needed to maintain his patronage network.

In 1991 the ongoing political stability in Zaire was shattered by mass riots and protests against Mobutu that plunged the country into chaos, hence disproving the "Mobutu or chaos" formula. This protest was motivated both by the country's worsening economic crisis and by the emergence of an invigorated moderate opposition after Mobutu lifted a twenty-year ban on opposition parties in April 1990.[62] In September 1991 Mobutu agreed to share power with the moderate opposition, assenting to the appointment of Etienne Tshisekedi as prime minister.[63] However, Tshisekedi, a fierce Mobutu opponent since 1980 and leader of the largest opposition group, the Union for Democracy and Social Progress, was dismissed by Mobutu three weeks later, triggering another cycle of rioting.[64] Constitutional negotiations between Mobutu and the moderate opposition resumed in April 1992. Yet in spite of significant international pressure to relinquish power, as of 1994 Mobutu continued to refuse to transfer authority to a transitional government.

The following factors help account for the breakdown of stability and its replacement by a stalemate between hard-liners and a weak moderate opposition. In terms of ruler-society relations, Mobutu's patronage network penetrating civil society appears to have broken down largely because of the withdrawal of foreign assistance, opening political space for moderates to organize inside Zaire for the first time in decades. Moderates took advantage of this opening, but their organizational efforts were impeded by the fragmenting legacies of thirty years of sultanism. Internal divisions among them were common, and Mobutu was still able to use patronage to exacerbate these divisions and "drive a deep wedge into the forces of the opposition."[65]

In terms of ruler-state relations, by contrast, Mobutu's penetration and control of the state seem to have remained more solid: the Zairian military brutally harassed moderate opposition leaders and fired on anti-Mobutu protesters on several occasions.[66] Hence moderates continued to lack potential soft-line allies.

In terms of the role of foreign powers, Mobutu's outside patrons have shifted their support to the moderate opposition. The winding down of the Angolan civil war and the disappearance of Soviet influence in Africa with the end of the Cold War reduced Mobutu's usefulness as an ally, encouraging the United States, France, and Belgium collectively to end aid and lead international efforts to force his ouster.[67] This withdrawal of foreign support contributed to the breakdown of Mobutu's patronage linkages with civil society.

In sum, structural changes in ruler-society relations opened space for societal opposition, which moderates used to organize. However, maximalist groups remained weak and did not take advantage of this structural space. At the same time continuities in ruler-state relations inhibited the emergence of regime soft-liners. The resulting stalemate between regime hard-liners and opposition moderates lasted until the civil war between Hutus and Tutsis in neighboring Rwanda spilled over into Zaire.[68] When Rwandan militias active among the more than one million Hutu refugees in eastern Zaire began fighting with the Banyamulenge, Zaire's Tutsis, the latter forged an alliance with longtime Mobutu opponent Laurent Kabila that, with help from other African states, overthrew Mobutu, whose armed forces disintegrated as the rebels advanced.

Revolution

Revolution is the path away from sultanism that has received by far the most attention in comparative studies of sultanistic regimes.[69] These studies, however, have tended to focus exclusively on the revolutionary cases of Somoza Debayle in Nicaragua, Batista in Cuba, and Mohammad Reza Pahlavi in Iran to show that sultanistic regimes are more likely than other types of nondemocratic

regimes to be overthrown by revolutionaries. Consequently, the structural features of sultanistic regimes that many of these studies identify as causes of
revolution—overdependence on a superpower patron and political exclusion of
domestic elites—do not differentiate sultanistic regimes toppled by revolutionaries from those such as Marcos's and Jean-Claude Duvalier's that were not (see
table 3.1).[70] Their omission of nonrevolutionary cases of sultanism has led these
analyses to understate the critical role that variations in the ruler's relationship
with the military play in differentiating revolutionary from nonrevolutionary
cases. As the analysis of nonrevolutionary paths out of sultanism in subsequent
sections reveals, the absence of military autonomy is an additional structural
cause that seems necessary for revolutionary collapse of sultanistic regimes.

In this section I review the structural factors that are necessary, but not
sufficient, causes of the overthrow of sultanistic regimes by revolutionaries. I
emphasize that a satisfactory account of revolutionary paths out of sultanism
should look beyond these structural factors to consider maximalists' efforts and
abilities to take advantage of structural opportunities for revolution.

Structural Causes of Revolution in Iran, Nicaragua, and Cuba

The regimes of the Shah, Somoza, and Batista were all characterized by
thorough penetration of state institutions by the dictators' patronage networks.
The resulting fusion of the ruling clique with the state left little political space
within which soft-line opposition could develop and stripped the military of its
capacity for autonomous action. The undermining of the military's autonomy
by the dictator's patronage network also eroded its overall competence and
organizational coherence, making it vulnerable to disintegration when challenged in combat.

The nature of the ruler-state relationship thus had the effect of collapsing
these three regimes into unitary, hard-line actors, minimizing the possibility
that the impetus for political transformation could come "from above," from
within the regime itself. According to Midlarsky and Roberts, this absence of
potential soft-line allies may have meant that moderate opponents had no
choice but to join revolutionary forces that had the military capacity to unseat
the dictator and his subservient army.[71]

In terms of ruler-society relations, the regimes of Somoza, Batista, and the
Shah were all characterized during their final years by the narrowness of the
dictator's patronage circle and the shallowness of its penetration into civil
society. This exclusion of domestic elites from patronage and power opened
space within society for the growth of moderate and maximalist oppositions.

Finally, all three dictators were heavily dependent on U.S. support. The external military and economic resources these rulers received from the United States allowed them to dispense with domestic coalition building, which encouraged the decoupling of these regimes from their societies and the exclusion of domestic elites from patronage. Their extreme dependence on the United States also stimulated opposition by frustrating the nationalist sentiments of domestic elites. And when powerful maximalist opposition groups challenged these regimes, the United States' insistence on liberalizing reforms and limited use of coercion restricted the rulers' margins of maneuver and undermined their confidence and control.

Based on these three cases, then, the sultanistic regimes most vulnerable to revolutionary overthrow share the following structural features: extensive penetration of the state by the dictator's patronage network, which undermines military autonomy; minimal extension of patronage into civil society; and extreme dependence on one superpower patron.[72] Although these features help pinpoint which sultanistic regimes are structurally most susceptible to revolutionary overthrow, they are not by themselves sufficient causes of revolution. In addition, a revolutionary movement must take advantage of these structural opportunities by organizing against the regime, succeed in ousting the dictator, and then seize state power.

The Limits of Structural Explanations: Zaire

The case of Zaire buttresses the claim that structural variables cannot by themselves predict that a sultanistic regime will fall to revolutionaries. The domestic structural factors that contributed to revolutionary collapse in Iran, Nicaragua, and Cuba (the fusion of ruler and state and shallow patronage penetration into civil society) were also present in Zaire since at least 1991.[73] Yet until 1997 no maximalist organizations remained marginal and weak, and failed to take advantage of this "revolutionary situation."

The weakness of maximalists in Zaire may have been a partial consequence of ongoing state repression or lingering fragmentation of civil society caused by Mobutu's patronage network. However, after 1990 Zairian *moderates* were partially able to overcome these same impediments, suggesting that other factors are needed to account for the absence of maximalists until 1997. One important factor may have been the failure of Zairian maximalists to use what Foran calls "political cultures of opposition" as bases for building revolutionary ideologies and movements.[74] By contrast, maximalists effectively tapped into the "cultural idioms" of nationalism in Nicaragua and Cuba and Shi'ite Islam in Iran to forge powerful revolutionary ideologies that helped them mobilize support.[75] The global exhaustion of Marxist-Leninist ideologies, which revolutionaries had successfully combined with nationalism in several of Zaire's neighbors (e.g., Angola and Mozambique) during the 1970s, may have posed an additional impediment to the organization of maximalist opposition in contemporary Zaire. Had the structural vulnerabilities of Mobutu's regime developed a decade or two earlier, when the wave of Afrocommunism was sweeping the continent, Zairian maximalists might have been able to join their Angolan and Mozambican counterparts as leaders of revolutionary African Marxist states instead of coming to power twenty years later with the help of foreign troops.[76]

In their quest to incorporate human agency alongside state and social structures in explaining revolutionary change, students of revolution have recently reexamined the cases of Iran, Nicaragua, and Cuba to highlight the role of political action in the creation and consolidation of maximalist movements.[77] In addition to emphasizing the structural space for such movements created by exclusionary sultanistic regimes, these analyses identify the crafting of revolutionary ideologies by leaders who took advantage of political cultures of opposition as a necessary cause of revolution.

Such efforts to highlight the building of revolutionary ideologies and movements are important reminders that the negative "stimulus" of an exclusionary sultanistic regime does not automatically lead to the "response" of broad-based revolutionary mobilization. Although the catalyzing effects on opposition coalition building produced by common enmity toward a sultanistic ruler were clearly important in the revolutionary cases, the efforts of maximalist leaders to build and sustain these movements should not be overlooked.

Rather than focusing strictly on political action "from below" (the role of human agency in the creation of revolutionary oppositions), students of revolution seeking to integrate agency and structure might also benefit by widening their focus to include action "from above" (the role the choices of regime incumbents play in bringing down "their" regimes).[78] The literature on regime transitions could offer useful insights for investigating whether incumbent elites' strategies of rule, leadership, and decisions during moments of crises promote or impede revolution.

Military Dictatorship

Cases in which the breakdown of sultanism results in military rule are typically characterized by limited penetration of the state by the dictator's patronage network, which opens space for soft-line opposition within the state, especially by the military. The decisions of military soft-liners to take advantage of their autonomy and act against the dictator are often motivated by factors external to the ruler-military relationship, such as pressures from mass uprisings against the dictator or encouragement by foreign powers. In cases of transition to military rule, moderates and maximalists are often weak and disorganized, allowing soft-line military factions who succeed in ousting the dictator to seize control of the state without contest (at least in the short term).

The February 1989 ouster of Alfredo Stroessner by the Paraguayan military fits this pattern. Although Stroessner's regime had strong sultanistic tendencies, it was not strictly sultanistic because of the central role played by the Colorado Party, which functioned during his rule as a relatively institutionalized mass patronage machine.[79] The overthrow of Jean-Claude Duvalier in Haiti in 1986 better exemplifies this path out of sultanism.

Haiti: Jean-Claude Duvalier

Haiti saw two quite different transitions from the sultanistic rule of the Duvaliers: first a peaceful transfer of power from father to son in 1971 (see above) followed by a fifteen-year continuation of the dynasty, and then the replacement of sultanism by military dictatorship in 1986.[80] The breakdown of sultanism at the end of the younger Duvalier's rule after more than twenty years of stability was a consequence of changes in the ruler-state, ruler-society, and ruler-superpower relationships that encouraged societal elites to withdraw support for Duvalier and opened space within the state for organization of a soft-line opposition. This breakdown led to military dictatorship because soft-line factions of the armed forces turned against Duvalier and were able to fill the political vacuum left by his flight into exile. No coherent maximalist or moderate oppositions existed at that time that could challenge the military's seizure of power, despite the highly exclusionary character of Jean-Claude's regime.

After marrying into an affluent mulatto family in 1980, the younger Duvalier began to exclude from his patronage circle the black elites who traditionally had been the regime's core base of support. Instead, Jean-Claude favored the mulatto commercial elites, who demanded greater patronage rewards in exchange for support and whose ties to the rest of Haitian society were more limited than those of their black middle-class predecessors. As a result, the extensive patronage network constructed by François Duvalier unraveled, dissolving the key ruler-society links that had enabled the Duvalier regime to penetrate and control civil society.[81]

Significantly, Jean-Claude's exclusion of the black elite did *not* lead to the formation of a coherent opposition. Twenty-five years of Duvalierism had stifled both maximalists and moderates; potential opposition leaders had been either exiled, killed, or co-opted. Because of this dual legacy of repression and co-optation, Haitian moderates lacked the leadership and organization to challenge the dictator. Would-be revolutionaries were perhaps even less able to challenge Duvalier than were moderates. Haitian maximalists had never established a large base of popular support and had not recovered from a series of crushing defeats by the elder Duvalier's forces in the 1950s and 1960s.[82] In Haiti, in contrast to Nicaragua, Cuba, and Iran, no viable revolutionary organizations existed that could take advantage of the weakness of moderates and pull them into broad coalitions against the dictator. The legacies of co-optation and severe repression during François Duvalier's rule continued to pose insurmountable obstacles to the organization of moderate and maximalist oppositions to Jean-Claude. Thus, despite high levels of exclusion of black elites after 1980, both moderates and maximalists remained weak. As we shall see, the weakness of civilian opposition groups aided the military's seizure and monopolization of power in 1986.

By shifting the basis of his support to the mulatto elite, Jean-Claude loosened his grip on the countryside and also increased his dependence on foreign aid. The loyalty of the mulatto elite was contingent on the state's ensuring them a high standard of living, and foreign aid, primarily from the United States, was Duvalier's main source of funds to meet the high price of his new constituency's support.[83] Jean-Claude actively sought U.S. assistance to fuel his patronage network and, in doing so, eroded the autonomy from foreign powers his father had enjoyed.

A group of Haitian army officers had disapproved of the younger Duvalier from the beginning of his rule.[84] According to Abbott, as popular pressure mounted against him after 1984 (see below), these officers, led by army chief of staff Henri Namphy, "began sounding out fellow officers, so that a core of key men could be counted on to assist in a bloodless ouster and not take up arms in final defense of the President."[85] The military conspirators found a fertile field of recruits in the ranks of former officers dismissed by Jean-Claude; an important part of their strategy was to have these officers reinstated. The ability of these malcontents to communicate and to plot a coup without Duvalier's knowledge reflects the transformation of the ruler-state relationship under Jean-Claude's rule: the closing of political space for organization of soft-line opposition during the elder Duvalier's rule had been reversed. The military was now poised to reassert its traditional role as arbiter of national politics. It was able to exercise its regained autonomy and to seize power when spontaneous mass protests and pressure from the United States forced Duvalier to relinquish state control.

The unraveling of Jean-Claude Duvalier's patronage ties to the black elite, his dependence on U.S. aid, and his loosened grip on the military were structural factors that weakened his regime. However, these structural factors do not by themselves explain his overthrow. The sultanistic regime did not collapse under its own weight; a combination of internal and external actors gave a crucial push.

Continuing economic crisis sparked a series of spontaneous and church-catalyzed popular uprisings between 1984 and 1986. The Duvalier regime's ability to contain this growing unrest was diminished by the weakening of its capacity to penetrate and control civil society, resulting, as I noted above, from the disintegration of the black middle-class patronage network. The Catholic Church (especially local priests and activists called the *ti legliz,* or "little church," to distinguish them from the more conservative hierarchy)[86], which had recovered from crippling confrontations with the elder Duvalier in the 1960s, was galvanized by the pope's 1983 visit to Haiti and emerged as a potent center of opposition, organizing and channeling popular discontent.[87]

As these internal pressures against Duvalier increased, the United States used its leverage to push him out of office and clear the way for the military softliners, with whom it had been secretly negotiating, to seize power.[88] On 29 January 1986 the United States announced it was withholding $26 million in scheduled aid to protest Duvalier's brutal response to the wave of mass protests. This move was tantamount to a public withdrawal of U.S. support. The United States encouraged the military conspirators by promising concessions to those who assisted in the dictator's removal. General Namphy and his fellow conspirators used this U.S. guarantee as a bargaining chip to persuade the leaders of the Tonton Macoutes to abandon Jean-Claude. On 6 February Duvalier boarded a U.S. Air Force C-141 headed for France. In Haiti, the United States was able to find and support an acceptable replacement for the dictator and to "manage" the transition by pressuring its dependent patron out of office, thereby defusing mass mobilization against him.

The absence of both moderate and maximalist political organizations and the Macoutes' disarray after Duvalier's flight allowed the military to seize power unchallenged. It was the only force able to fill the political vacuum left in Duvalier's wake. The United States' initial willingness to support the fledgling military government by sending arms and aid helped solidify the armed forces' control.[89]

After Duvalier's ouster, the military presided over five years of political chaos during which a series of short-lived military or de facto regimes attempted to govern and one election was aborted by a polling-place massacre.[90] Democratic opposition groups remained weak and disorganized. In 1990, in response to international pressure, the military elite decided to tolerate fair elections. Father Jean-Bertrand Aristide, a Catholic priest whose support was based mainly in grassroots church and neighborhood organizations, won by a landslide, and in February 1991 he became the first freely elected president in Haiti's history.

Although Aristide's relations with the military were initially positive, they soon deteriorated. Aristide demoted and replaced many officers, made plans for a new civilian police force, and proposed a European-trained presidential guard—all of which created resentment and fear within the armed forces. Aristide's passionate commitment to liberation theology and his populist rhetoric also alienated the economic elite. With the blessing of many members of this elite, the military ousted Aristide on 30 September 1991.[91]

The continued domination of the political arena by the military and the weakness of democratic forces can both be understood as legacies of Haiti's sultanistic *and* presultanistic periods. As I noted above, the Duvaliers' long rule fragmented civil society and reinforced preexisting patterns of inequality and clientelism. However, the roots of current instability and authoritarianism reach back into Haitian history long before the Duvaliers. The military dominated Haitian politics before François Duvalier's rise to power. Hence its reemergence at the center of the political arena after Jean-Claude's overthrow can be viewed as a revival of historical political patterns after a "sultanistic interlude." Although the Duvalier dynasty certainly reinforced antidemocratic structures and traditions, it did not create them. On the contrary, these preexisting structures probably should themselves be regarded as *causes* that explain the dynasty's origins.[92] The advantages for analysis of situating sultanistic regimes in long-term trajectories of national political development will be discussed in the chapter's conclusion.

Civilian Rule

Cases in which transitions from sultanism lead directly to nonrevolutionary civilian rule are typically characterized by shallow penetration of the dictator's patronage network into state *and* civil society, creating structural space for the organization of opposition in both arenas.[93] In such cases power is transferred either to moderate opposition groups or to civilian soft-liners, usually after a revolt against the dictator by military soft-liners. A central puzzle posed by cases of direct transition from sultanism to civilian rule concerns why power is transferred to civilians rather than seized by the mutinous military soft-liners as occurred in Haiti.

This path out of sultanism is exemplified by the cases of Marcos in the

Philippines, where power was transferred to the moderate opposition, and of Ceaușescu in Romania, where power was transferred to civilian regime soft-liners. The cases of Marcos Pérez Jiménez (1948–58) in Venezuela and Rafael Trujillo (1930–61) in the Dominican Republic,[94] although not analyzed here, are also examples of nonrevolutionary transitions from sultanism to civilian rule.[95]

The Philippines: Transition to Elite Democracy

The transition from Marcos's regime in the Philippines is the only case examined here in which the full complement of hard-liners, soft-liners, moderates, and maximalists was present. As one might expect, the role of contingency and strategic interaction appears to have been especially important in this four-player transition. The presence of military soft-liners and a powerful revolutionary opposition alongside the moderate opposition raises the question, Why was power transferred to moderates and not to one of the two armed groups?[96]

Marcos's regime, like the revolutionary cases, was characterized by exclusion of traditional elites, which encouraged growth of both maximalist and moderate oppositions, and by extreme dependence on U.S. support. Despite these similarities, however, revolution did not occur, because there existed pockets of intrastate autonomy within which military soft-liners organized. Instead, the breakdown of sultanism in the Philippines led to a transition to civilian rule because a powerful moderate opposition was able to eschew alliance with maximalists and take power with the help of military soft-liners who revolted against the dictator.

In 1986, approximately 1,500 of the military's 13,500 officers were members of the Reform the Armed Forces Now Movement (RAM), which had been formed with U.S. support in 1985 by officers disturbed by the influx of Marcos's patronage appointees.[97] On 22 February 1986, in the context of widespread public outrage over Marcos's use of violence and fraud during presidential elections held earlier that month, a group of officers affiliated with the RAM launched a coup against the dictator. Although the coup itself failed, it was supported by tens of thousands of civilians, mobilized by the Catholic Church, who formed a human buffer to protect the mutinous officers. This outpouring of "people power" led to a wave of military defections and to Marcos's departure three days later.[98]

The military revolt allowed the Philippine moderates (who had coalesced into a powerful movement with broad popular support behind the leadership of Corazon Aquino and the Catholic Church)[99] to eschew alliance with the maximalist National Democratic Front (NDF).[100] Had the military not revolted, the Philippine moderates, like their Iranian, Nicaraguan, and Cuban

counterparts, would probably have had little choice but to ally with the maximalists, who were accumulating the coercive resources needed to dislodge
Marcos. In the Philippines, the key structural factors that push moderates into
alliance with maximalists were absent: an exclusionary sultanistic regime in
which the military's capacity for autonomous action has been undermined.
The coup against Marcos allowed the moderates to replace him without opening the way to a seizure of power by the revolutionary opposition.

In the Philippines, in contrast to Iran, Nicaragua, and Cuba, the dictator's
extreme dependence on U.S. support inhibited revolution. The Aquino-led
moderate opposition and the military soft-liners (the RAM) were acceptable to
the United States as replacements to Marcos. More important, the Aquino
coalition was a *viable* successor to Marcos because of its organizational coherence and broad popular support. The presence of an acceptable and viable
civilian alternative enabled the United States to influence the transition in the
Philippines by using its leverage over Marcos to usher him out of power and
to ease in the moderates. When the army officers affiliated with the RAM
launched their coup at the end of February 1986, the United States gave them
fuel and ammunition and threatened to cut off Marcos's military aid if his
troops attacked the rebels.[101] President Ronald Reagan offered Marcos asylum,
an offer the besieged dictator accepted after consulting U.S. senator Paul Laxalt.
Laxalt advised Marcos, "Cut and cut cleanly. The time has come."[102] Hours later
U.S. helicopters ferried Marcos into exile. By pressuring Marcos out of power,
the United States helped clear the way for the moderate Aquino coalition,
backed by the church and the mass mobilization of people's power, to take
control. Thus U.S. policy worked to keep state power beyond the maximalist
NDF's reach.

We have seen how the combination of a potent moderate opposition, a
mutinous military, and U.S. pressure inhibited revolution in the Philippines in
1986. A second question must also be addressed: Why didn't the Philippine
military seize power for itself, "Haitian-style," and block the civilian moderates?
The Philippines are unique among the cases of sultanism discussed here in
terms of the moderate opposition's levels of organizational coherence and popular support.[103] Challenging the broad-based, popular Aquino coalition would
have been difficult for the Philippine armed forces in 1986, especially given the
factionalism within its ranks and its low popular legitimacy stemming from its
abusiveness during Marcos's rule.[104] As for the small band of about three hundred officers that launched the 22 February coup, they surely would have been
crushed without the protection of the legions of civilians summoned to their
aid by the church. The military defectors were dependent on civilian support,

which Aquino commanded more than anyone else. For these reasons the military, having chosen to withdraw its support from Marcos, had few options but to support Aquino, at least temporarily.[105]

Significantly, the option of withdrawing support from Marcos was palatable to the military defectors precisely because there existed a viable, *moderate* civilian alternative to the dictator. Had a group unacceptable to the military, such as the maximalist NDF, dominated the civilian opposition, the RAM officers might well have postponed their coup plans until they felt capable of seizing power on their own, without civilian assistance. Alternatively, they might not have attempted to remove Marcos at all, preferring the deleterious effects on the military of a sultanistic dictator to those of a leftist government. The presence of the moderate Aquino coalition allowed the military soft-liners to turn against Marcos, secure that, if the armed forces did not take power, an acceptable civilian group would.

Romania: The Resurrection of "Presultanistic" State Institutions

The transition from Ceauşescu's regime in Romania in 1989 involved a smaller cast of actors than did the transition in the Philippines. In Romania, soft-liners, with civilian and military components, and hard-liners were the only well-organized groups during the transition. And in contrast to the Philippines, the civilian regime that succeeded the sultanistic dictator had strong authoritarian tendencies and was composed of individuals with close ties to the old regime.[106]

Ceauşescu's rule, which Linden aptly labels "socialist patrimonialism," was based on a three-way balance between the Romanian Communist Party (RCP), the army, and the secret police (Securitate).[107] Ceauşescu skillfully played these three institutions off against one another. This system of manipulated "checks and balances" combined with Ceauşescu's direct measures to undermine each institution's autonomy was the basis for his regime's stability until the late 1980s.[108]

Although Ceauşescu was able to use the RCP, the army, and the Securitate as counterweights to one another for many years, his ruling clique appears to have penetrated and transformed state institutions to a lesser degree than did those of the Shah, Mobutu, or the Somozas. In contrast to these cases, Ceauşescu's sultanistic regime was superimposed on a *preexisting* party-state apparatus. One of the most striking features of the Romanian case is the resilience of state institutions with pre-Ceauşescu roots: the Communist Party, the state administrative bureaucracy (which was closely intertwined with the RCP), and the military all emerged relatively intact after Ceauşescu's ouster. This institutional resilience and the central roles in Ceaușescu's overthrow played by military and RCP soft-liners indicate that his regime sat lightly upon the state compared with other sultanistic regimes.

By the end of 1989, Ceaușescu had alienated the armed forces, the RCP, and the international community, and his rule rested precariously on the terror created by the Securitate.[109] A wave of spontaneous mass protests, which began in the city of Timișoara on 17 December 1989 and soon swept the country, created an opportunity for army and party soft-liners to throw off the sultanistic ruling clique that had ridden piggyback on their institutions for two decades. The clash of soft-liners and hard-liners took the form of pitched battles between disloyal and loyal security forces (mainly Securitate members), which lasted until Ceaușescu's capture on 23 December by military rebels and his execution several days later. The absence of well-organized moderate or maximalist opposition groups enabled the National Salvation Front (FSN), a civilian-led coalition with close ties to both the Communist Party and the military, to take control without contest.[110]

Ceaușescu's ouster is similar in many ways to Jean-Claude Duvalier's overthrow in Haiti. In both cases organized societal opposition groups were absent during the transition, and spontaneous mass protests played central roles triggering and pushing forward the dictator's overthrow. In both Haiti and Romania, revolts by soft-liners in the regular armed forces led to the ouster of the dictators and their personal, paramilitary guards—Duvalier's Tonton Macoutes and Ceaușescu's Securitate.[111] The weakness of democratic groups in both cases cleared the way for transfers of power to successor regimes in which members of the former elite played a central role.[112]

Beyond Transitions from Sultanism

The time frames of the case analyses in this chapter are limited to the periods encompassing sultanistic rule, its breakdown, and the transition to a regime type distinct from sultanism. This time frame is adequate for explaining *short-term* outcomes. As the number of "postsultanistic" regimes grows, however, it is increasingly important to develop analytic frameworks for understanding political dynamics after sultanism. The revival of presultanistic political practices, social structures, and state institutions in Romania, Haiti, and the Philippines suggests that the key to understanding postsultanistic patterns of political development may often be found in historical events antecedent to the sultanistic episode. To comprehend political dynamics after sultanism, then, it may be fruitful to situate sultanistic regimes in long-term trajectories of national political development in order to capture foundational, presultanistic events whose resilient legacies may influence patterns of development after sultanistic episodes. Thus, paradoxically, expanding our time frame forward into the postsultanistic period may simultaneously require us to stretch it backward into the periods preceding the rise of sultanism.[113]

The historical continuities that appear especially salient for understanding political dynamics after sultanistic regimes (weak domestic classes, fragmented civil societies, "soft" state institutions, and "crises of sovereignty" associated with external intervention) may themselves have played significant roles in the origins of these very regimes. Such factors, which are constant across the presultanistic, sultanistic, and postsultanistic periods in many of the cases analyzed here, may help explain how one man was able to consolidate so much power during a specific historical juncture and shift his country temporarily onto a sultanistic path of development.

Although historical structures and practices antecedent to the sultanistic regime may be important for understanding postsultanistic political dynamics, we should not assume that the sultanistic episode itself has no autonomous influence on subsequent political trajectories. The impact of the sultanistic period on future patterns of political change is especially transparent in those cases where the dictator's style of rule and the structure of his regime led to the organization of revolutionary movements and promoted their seizure of state power. In each case, we need to investigate empirically how far the sultanistic episode eroded or reinforced antecedent political practices and structures.[114]

In addition to accounting for the varied dynamics of sultanistic regimes, a central objective of this chapter has been to show how broad programmatic guidelines for linking human agency and social structures in explaining regime change can be translated into concrete research strategies. The category of sultanistic regimes offers unusual leverage for developing such strategies because it lies at the intersection of a literature that has so clearly emphasized structural explanations (the literature on contemporary revolutions) with one that has so clearly emphasized voluntarist explanations (the literature on regime transitions). I have attempted to use this intersection as a basis for developing an integrative explanatory framework sensitive to the causal roles of both human agency and social structure in the transformation of political regimes.

Several lessons can be drawn from this analysis for those interested in constructing such integrative frameworks. First, this analysis suggests the utility of regime typologies and categories that expose the structural logics of regimes by isolating "critical relationships" linking actors within a regime to each other and to outside actors, both domestic and international. Such regime categories make it easier to map the structural contexts of regime transitions and can thus help us specify the margins of maneuverability available to actors. In the analysis above of transitions from sultanism, for example, conceptualizing sultanistic regimes in terms of three critical patronage relationships—the relationship of the ruler to state institutions, the relationship of the ruler to societal elites, and the relationship of foreign powers to domestic actors—was an effective means of specifying the varied structural contexts of such transitions. This analysis also indicates the utility of conceptual tools that disaggregate regimes and societies, enabling us to probe dynamics of conflict and coalition between multiple actors. The conceptual distinction between ruler and state, for example, proved especially helpful because it enabled us to differentiate cases where transitions from "above" were structurally possible (cases in which segments of the armed forces were autonomous from the ruler) from those where the impetus for political change could come only from "below" (from outside the regime). The distinction between government and state might offer similar explanatory leverage in cases that are not sultanistic.[115]

Second, this analysis suggests the importance of the comparative method for combining structural and voluntarist perspectives. Case studies, especially those confined to short periods, are ill suited for joining human agency and social structure in the explanation of regime change because they must rely on counterfactuals to assess the causal role of each. For example, in his case study of the breakdown of democracy in Brazil in 1964, Alfred Stepan argues that socioeconomic and institutional constraints were necessary but not sufficient causes of regime breakdown because they left a small margin of maneuverability within which incumbents' political strategies could have averted regime collapse.[116] Stepan's claim for such a margin of maneuverability is grounded in the counterfactual argument that regime breakdown would not have occurred if the incumbent president, João Goulart, had acted differently.[117] This claim would have been significantly more plausible had Stepan analyzed a *factual* case where there were structural constraints similar to those in Brazil in 1964, yet regime breakdown did *not* occur because of differences in incumbents' actions. His single case study method did not afford this opportunity.

By contrast, the analysis presented above uses comparisons of varied structural contexts of transitions from sultanism, rather than counterfactuals, to gauge the latitude for actor discretion during processes of regime change and to justify claims that in some cases actors' contingent political strategies had an important influence on the dynamics and outcomes of these processes. In cases where *similar* structural contexts led to *different* outcomes, as in Haiti under

Jean-Claude Duvalier and the Philippines under Marcos, and where *different* structural contexts led to *similar* outcomes, as in Nicaragua under Somoza García and Haiti under François Duvalier, we have a strong basis for inferring that structural factors by themselves were not sufficient causes of regime outcomes.[118] The comparative method enables us to ground such inferences in empirical regularities rather than in counterfactuals. Using the comparative method to map and juxtapose varied structural contexts of transitions should prove an indispensable tool for scholars seeking to build integrative frameworks for explaining regime change.

Finally, the integrative approach developed here, which combines structural and voluntarist perspectives by using cross-sectional mappings of the varied structural contexts of transitions, is especially suited for analyzing *short-term* outcomes of regime change. Scholars interested in exploring longer-term processes of regime change, such as political trajectories encompassing presultanistic, sultanistic, and postsultanistic periods, will need integrative frameworks that combine an appreciation for the long-term, persistent effects of past events with a sensitivity to the inherent dynamism of human agency. Path-dependent research strategies, especially those that emphasize "critical junctures," may offer fruitful tools for linking past constraints to subsequent regime outcomes in ways that highlight how these constraints were created, reproduced, and eventually transformed by human action.[119] Integrative path-dependent frameworks will need to balance the goal of capturing and accounting for continuing effects of past constraints against allowing room for actors to play autonomous causal roles in regime change. In other words, they will need to overcome the tendency, exemplified by the structuralist works of Barrington Moore and Gregory Luebbert, to treat the developmental path linking historical junctures and subsequent regime change as the "deliverer of the inevitable."[120] They will also need to overcome the tendency to treat events during historical junctures as themselves predetermined by antecedent structural factors. Rather, the creation of structures and institutions during such junctures must be characterized by choice and contingency.

Addressing issues such as these will help scholars solve the difficult problem of combining social structure and human agency in explaining regime change.

PART TWO

· · · ·

Country Studies

4
. . . .

The Trujillo Regime in the Dominican Republic

Jonathan Hartlyn

Rafael Leónidas Trujillo Molina was the key military figure behind a coup that overthrew the government of President Horacio Vásquez on 23 February 1930; after questionable elections, he assumed the presidency of the Dominican Republic on 16 August 1930. What appeared to begin as another era of caudillo rule, however, soon transformed itself into what was "probably the strongest and most absolute dictatorship ever to be established in Latin America."[1] Trujillo maintained a firm grip on power, though he was not always in the presidency, until his assassination on 30 May 1961. He was not the first strongman to dominate politics in his country, but his regime was the longest lasting of all of these and had the most profound effect on life in the Dominican Republic.

Of all the cases considered in this volume, the Trujillo regime may well be the closest approximation to the ideal type of a regime with high levels of "sultanistic tendencies."[2] The regime was based on personal rule, with loyalty grounded in a mixture of fear and rewards. Trujillo exercised power without restraint within his small republic, acting at his own discretion, unencumbered by ideology or bureaucratic norms. During his reign, as he accumulated fabulous wealth and power, the country experienced large-scale but centralized and controlled corruption, arbitrary and capricious decisions combined with scrupulous attention to legal forms, and ruthless violence.

Similar to what Chehabi and Linz indicate in their discussion of the ideal type, the Trujillo regime also differed from more classic authoritarianism by the absence of even "semioppositions," though "pseudo-oppositions" were sporadically permitted.[3] Only toward the end, though, did repression become more informal and privatized, including the establishment of "private armies." And over the three decades when Trujillo held power, the regime became substantially more bureaucratized and institutionalized. Of all the Latin American cases, Trujillo's rule may have had the most totalitarian tendencies, in terms of using technology to seek to control all aspects of the lives of Dominicans, including their private lives, and in terms of control over communications, transportation, education, and intellectual and cultural life. Except for the church, which was abjectly supportive of the regime until almost the very end (in what appeared to be a mutually beneficial arrangement), there were no independent organizations or associations in the country. Although Trujillo's regime did not have as clearly defined an ideology as the ideal type of totalitarianism specifies, it did employ ideological and mythical elements built around anti-Haitianism, Catholicism, and economic nationalism to legitimize itself and to fashion certain policies. It more clearly differed from the ideal type in that Trujillo fused his private and public roles and had no clear commitment to any impersonal purposes.

The regime marked the Dominican Republic profoundly. In spite of Trujillo's brutality and venality, his apparent commitment to order, "strong" government, state building, national integration, and economic nationalism helped to generate a degree of public acceptance among the most vulnerable elements of the population that lived under him. Indeed, in an opinion poll taken in the early 1980s, 25 percent of those surveyed said they believed that the thirty-one-year Trujillo regime had been a "good government," another 25 percent expressed no opinion, and 46 percent said they believed it had been a "bad government." Further exploration of the data shows that the favorable opinions tended to be concentrated among older, less educated, and more rural strata of the population. Similarly, in a 1994 opinion survey, 32.5 percent of a national sample stated they valued Trujillo positively, with another 11 percent saying they didn't know; 36.8 percent of the rural part of the sample saw the Trujillo regime positively, with 15.2 percent saying they didn't know.[4]

The first section below explains the emergence and initial consolidation of the Trujillo regime in light of the country's crises of sovereignty; past authoritarian regimes and clientelist protoparties and personalistic politics; centralization of repressive forces and improved transportation induced by the U.S. occupation; and Trujillo's personality and sense of social and ethnic rejection. A second section then examines the historical, state, ideological, political, economic, and international factors that were most important in explaining both the longevity of the regime and its most significant changes over time. Trujillo's remarkable centralization of power, monopolization of the economy, destruction or co-optation of enemies, and astonishing constitutional hypocrisy were combined with the forging of national integration, the establishment of state institutions, and the beginnings of industrialization, however distorted.

A third section examines the unraveling of the Trujillo regime and considers its aftermath. Regimes like Trujillo's appear incapable of legitimizing and institutionalizing themselves for the long term. They sow the seeds of their own destruction by alienating their beneficiaries and supporters and creating ever greater numbers of disgruntled former beneficiaries as well as by helping to induce societal changes that can lead to new pressures. They also face risks from changing international circumstances and the loss of support from their foreign patron. The Trujillo regime did become increasingly neosultanistic over time, as the aging leader became more erratic and repressive, which played a role in unleashing both the domestic groups and the international forces that opposed the regime. Many of the difficulties in achieving a democratic transition in the country (particularly the one of 1962–63, which ultimately failed), as well as some of the continuing problems in consolidating democracy, are attributable to political-institutional, cultural, and economic legacies of the neosultanistic Trujillo era. However, it is also evident that the nature and timing of the end of the regime and subsequent events responded to changing U.S. policy in the wake of the Cuban revolution.

This final section also supports the contention that democratic transitions from neosultanistic regimes are especially difficult, in contrast to transitions from other neopatrimonial regimes. It argues that the different treatment of the economy and the military and the political opposition by the neopatrimonial and authoritarian—but not neosultanistic—Balaguer regime of 1966–78 aided a democratic transition in the country in 1978.

The Emergence of the Trujillo Regime

The emergence and initial consolidation of the Trujillo regime bore considerable resemblance to historical patterns in the Dominican Republic and must be understood in light of the country's crises of sovereignty, past authoritarian regimes, and clientelist protoparties and personalistic politics. However, Trujillo's rule soon acquired sultanistic tendencies and characteristics that went well beyond those of previous regimes. These traits were a consequence of factors related to the centralization of repressive forces and improved transportation induced by the U.S. occupation, followed by a shift in U.S. policy toward "noninterventionism," and they also reflected Trujillo's personality, drive, desire for power, and sense of social and ethnic rejection.

The country's nineteenth-century struggle for independence and for formal sovereignty was a difficult undertaking, affecting both national integration and state building. National integration was truncated first by a Haitian invasion and then by the attempts of some Dominican elites to trade nascent Dominican sovereignty for security under foreign powers (while further enriching themselves). State building suffered under the dual impact of international vulnerability and unstable patrimonial-authoritarian politics. And national integration and state building were both also affected by bitter regional struggles based on different economic interests and desires for power that accentuated the caudillo politics of the country. Though reform efforts continually reemerged, efforts to extend liberal guarantees and citizenship rights to broader sectors of the population repeatedly failed.

Initial independence from Spain, declared in 1821, lasted only a few months in the face of a takeover by neighboring Haiti. In 1844 independence (or secession) was declared anew and successfully withstood some fifteen years of attempts by Haitian governments to reincorporate Dominican territory. Fear of Haiti, which under elite prodding evolved into a strong racist sentiment, led Dominicans to seek protection from powerful third countries, chiefly France, Spain, and the United States. Complex interactions ensued among Dominican governing groups, opposition movements, Haitian authorities, and representatives of these powers.[5] Government largely revolved around a small number of caudillo strongmen and their intrigues involving foreign powers. Spain was persuaded to reannex the country in 1861 (when the United States could do little because it was preoccupied with its own Civil War), but internal opposition finally helped restore independence in 1865. An effort was made to convince the Grant administration to take over the country, but the U.S. Senate rejected the proposal.

The century ended with the neosultanistic seventeen-year reign of Ulises Heureaux (1882–99, indirectly from 1884 to 1887), an able military leader and a shrewd, despotic political leader.[6] Ironically, the dark-skinned Heureaux, who grew up in poverty, oversaw changes in society that would make the emergence of another figure like him more difficult, except under different conditions generated by the U.S. intervention. During his rule and in the subsequent decades, the country's economic structure underwent substantial change. Modern sugar estates began to replace cattle ranches, even as exports of coffee and cacao expanded. The first railroads were completed, and other basic infrastructure was built. Heureaux made initial attempts at professionalizing the army and bureaucratizing the state, though in a deeply personalistic fashion. As the regions became more connected, however, social stratification also became clearer and more stable as "unequivocally negroid features became an obstacle for individual mobility."[7]

Two other legacies of the regime were debt and instability. Heureaux borrowed extensively from foreign bondholders as he sought to pay off an earlier loan, gain greater room to maneuver in the face of domestic creditors, enrich himself, grease his political machine, and also carry out some of the public works and other projects for which the foreign loans were ostensibly sought. The immediate aftermath of his brutal era was massive political instability: there were four revolts and five presidents over the subsequent six years. Weak protoparties and clientelist politics built around caudillo figures and regional uprisings furthered economic chaos and political instability.

Gradually, control of Dominican affairs by the country's northern neighbor grew. Pressures by European creditors on the Dominican Republic (as well as the Anglo-German blockade of Venezuela in 1902–3) led to President Theodore Roosevelt's "corollary" to the Monroe Doctrine. By 1905 Dominican customs was headed by a U.S. appointee, a relationship formalized in a 1907 treaty that also paid off all previous loans with a new one, making the United States the country's only foreign creditor. In 1916 U.S. troops landed to "protect the life and interests" of the American legation and other foreigners.[8] Dominicans expected a brief U.S. military presence that would depart after elections were held; but though U.S. officials had not planned for a lengthy occupation, it ultimately lasted until 1924.

The goals of the occupation forces were surprisingly vague and only gradually began to take shape. Eventually the military moved to implement what could be characterized as "technocratic progressive" reforms, under the assumption that certain socioeconomic, financial, and administrative changes would generate the conditions for political and constitutional stability. Programs were enacted in education, health, sanitation, agriculture, and communications, highways were built and other public works were carried out, and a census was taken.[9]

Ultimately, the most significant measure was the establishment of a new Dominican constabulary. In the Dominican Republic as elsewhere in Central America and the Caribbean, U.S. officials hoped that establishing new police forces initially under U.S. tutelage would permanently depoliticize the armies in these countries, bolstering stable, constitutional government. Following the mid-1921 announcement of a plan for withdrawal, the U.S. military government focused on creating an effective force.[10] Complex negotiations ending in

U.S. oversight of elections in 1924 and the inauguration of a new president, Horacio Vásquez, in July 1924 led to the withdrawal of all U.S. marines a few months later.

Thus the United States had helped establish a relatively effective national military institution in a country previously without one, in which traditional powerholders were weak. As Lowenthal wrote: "From the time of independence until the U.S. occupation of 1916 ended the period of *caudillo* politics . . . the Dominican Republic was not characterized by a powerful triad of oligarchy, church and military, but rather by exactly the reverse: an insecure grouping of elite families, a weak and dependent church, and no national military institution."[11] Furthermore, there were no long-standing political organizations or parties.

Then, in the 1920s, the United States began to move from military occupation, the most complete involvement in the affairs of another country possible short of formal colonization or annexation, to an opposite extreme of "nonintervention." This approach emerged in reaction to the growing Latin American and international opposition to U.S. occupations in the Caribbean and Central America and was aided by the absence of any perceived threat to continued U.S. influence in the area from an outside power. It gradually became transformed into President Franklin D. Roosevelt's "good neighbor" policy. Largely unintentional, but somewhat predictable, consequences of the occupation combined with this shift in U.S. policy toward nonintervention removed any remaining constraints on the head of the country's newly established military force from taking power and dominating his country as no ruler had before him.

The leader of the Dominican National Army, Rafael Trujillo, was born in 1891 to a family of modest means, of mixed Spanish, Creole, and Haitian background, and raised in San Cristóbal, a small town near the capital. He began his meteoric rise within the newly established Dominican Guardia Nacional in 1919. In late 1921 he entered the Haina Military Academy as a second lieutenant, and by 1924 he was a captain in the then-renamed Policía Nacional responsible for the city of Santiago. President Vásquez quickly promoted him to major and then to lieutenant colonel and chief of staff. In June 1925 Trujillo became a colonel and head of the country's police force. Two years later he was named brigadier general, a promotion linked to the transformation of the police force into the National Army, which took place in May 1928. In less than ten years, Trujillo emerged from being an obscure minor officer in a newly formed constabulary force to become head of the country's army. As was to be discovered, he harbored strong sentiments of social rejection and of animosity against the country's elite families, the so-called *gente de primera*, whom he forced to work for him and often humiliated.[12]

At the same time, the country's political patterns continued to be based on personalistic and clientelist rule, questionable constitutional maneuverings, intrigue, and occasional rebellion, all of which predated the U.S. occupation. President Vásquez, elected for a four-year term in 1924, modified the constitution four times, extending his term in office by two years; at the age of seventy, he modified the country's electoral law to make it difficult for the opposition to win as he sought reelection, in part on the urging of political associates. Ultimately this led to an uprising against the president some three months before the scheduled elections, with considerable popular acceptance. Through complex negotiations that preserved the form of constitutionalism, the presumed leader of that rebellion, Rafael Estrella Ureña, became provisional president pending the elections. But Trujillo had played a critical secret role in ensuring the success of the rebellion against Vásquez.

An elaborate, occasionally bloody charade then ensued. Two political groups emerged for the elections, one with Trujillo as presidential candidate and Estrella Ureña running for vice president. Trujillo used the army almost as a private instrument of repression, leading the Central Electoral Board to resign some nine days before the elections and the other party to withdraw the day before them. Official results gave Trujillo the victory by a 99 percent margin and admitted to a 45 percent abstention rate.[13]

Although the political events that eventually brought Trujillo to power were consistent with past political patterns in the country, several consequences of the U.S. military occupation and "lessons" Trujillo may have learned greatly strengthened his capabilities as head of the newly formed military force. The U.S. military occupation had changed the Dominican Republic. The major regions of the country were now linked to Santo Domingo, the capital city, by highways and improved communications. The population was largely disarmed, further limiting the possibility of armed uprisings such as had occurred in the country's past. In addition, the U.S. military had demonstrated efficacy in confronting a guerrilla challenge during the occupation period and in controlling the population through a variety of repressive measures.

Finally, the policy of nonintervention espoused by the U.S. State Department was to assist Trujillo. Trujillo apparently surmised (correctly, as it turned out) that the United States might accept a government he headed if it appeared to come to power through elections, even questionable ones, although an outright coup d'état would be unacceptable. In spite of opposition from the U.S.

minister at the time, it is also apparent that Trujillo's takeover of power was viewed favorably by his friends within the U.S. marines.[14] In subsequent years Trujillo would continue to sidestep U.S. diplomats in Santo Domingo when necessary, assiduously cultivating his U.S. military contacts even as he provided attention and lavish gifts to U.S. congressional representatives and hired lobby-ists he thought could gain him influence in Washington. Thus, in Trujillo's first visit ever outside of the Dominican Republic, to the United States in 1939, he was accompanied by a U.S. marine officer who had stayed on as an adviser after the occupation period. Furthermore, his warmest receptions were among the military; for example, Major General James C. Breckinridge, Trujillo's former commanding officer in the Guardia Nacional in 1924, received him with fullest honors as the commander of the marine barracks at Quantico Military Base.[15] In this way, in spite of the apparent discomfort many U.S. diplomats felt about Trujillo, he was able to portray himself within the country as having the strong support of the United States.

In sum, Trujillo's rise to power and initial consolidation built upon histor-ical patterns of caudillo rule within the country, combined with structural changes including the establishment of more professional armed forces and improved transportation and communication services in the country that were a consequence of the U.S. occupation, as well as the U.S. shift to a policy of nonintervention that promoted the success of his plotting. Improved com-munications and infrastructure in a country that was still relatively poor, unin-tegrated, and isolated meant that Trujillo had the means to put down potential regional rebellions without necessarily having to incorporate and control the entire country's population.

The role that the country's prolonged self-doubts and the actual constraints on sovereignty played in Trujillo's emergence and consolidation is complex. The country's insecurity helped generate a form of politics in which some leaders assiduously cultivated foreign incorporation; in turn this approach weakened national integration and state building and encouraged foreign inter-vention. The ruinous debt accumulated by Heureaux, the country's first neo-sultanist leader, helped set the stage for additional constraints on the country's sovereignty and eventually for the U.S. intervention of 1916. United States occupation further weakened the country's major social and political actors, led to the formation of the National Guard, and opened the way for Trujillo's emergence; in this context, expectations about U.S. involvement and a potential veto against Trujillo entered (incorrectly, as it turned out) into the calculations of domestic Dominican actors. Subsequently, Trujillo was able to articulate a vision of regaining national sovereignty as an ideological underpinning for many of his actions.

Trujillo in Power

Trujillo's rule quickly moved beyond the traditional Dominican caudillo regimes of the nineteenth century, and by the end of his first term (if not sooner) its neosultanistic tendencies were clear. By the end of his second term, it was evident that this regime's despotic and totalitarian features went beyond those of Heureaux, his historical predecessor. There would be occasional partial liberalizations in response to international pressures, particularly following the Haitian massacre of 1937 and in the immediate post–World War II era. But Trujillo's accumulation of wealth and power would continue, reaching a peak in 1955. The regime's deterioration began shortly thereafter, however, accelerating in 1958.

Evolution

Before we turn to how various factors initially sustained and then in some cases undermined Trujillo's rule, a brief chronological overview will be useful. On assuming office in 1930, Trujillo quickly began a strategy of concentration of personal power, state building, and national consolidation, while gradually enunciating a discourse of nationalism, work, order, and progress. During his first year in office he dealt with three uprisings against his government, including one led by his vice president; the deterioration of the country's financial situation; and just eighteen days after he assumed office, a devastating cyclone that swept through the capital city. In response to the cyclone, Trujillo was granted sweeping emergency powers, which he used to consolidate his control; the disaster also put Trujillo back in contact with a number of U.S. military figures who were to become his crucial allies even as various U.S. officials were impressed by his apparent administrative efficiency.[16] During the rest of his first four-year term in office, Trujillo discovered and brutally repressed several other conspiracies. In 1931 he also took the critical step of creating the Dominican Party, funded by a 10 percent deduction from its members' paychecks, with all decision making concentrated directly in his hands; for example, he held undated letters of resignation from officeholders in all three branches of government. Other parties were forced to disband.

Trujillo's megalomania and desire to accumulate wealth also became evident in this first term in office. Pico Duarte, the highest mountain in the Antilles, was renamed Pico Trujillo; and Santo Domingo, the capital city, was renamed Ciudad Trujillo. According to the *Guinness Book of World Records*, at the time of his overthrow in 1961, Trujillo had more statues of himself in public places than any other world leader. When he served as president in the 1950s, he was officially referred to as His Excellency, the Generalissimo, Doctor Rafael Leónidas Trujillo Molina, Honorable President of the Republic, Benefactor of the Nation, Restorer of the Financial Independence of the Country, and Commander-in-Chief of the Armed Forces. By 1934 Trujillo had imposed a series of monopolies on salt, meat, and rice and taken other steps that made him the country's richest man, foreshadowing the incredible concentration of wealth that he would build over the next three decades.[17]

Carefully orchestrated elections ensued. With all other parties abolished, Trujillo easily gained "reelection" in 1934. Officially, his party received 100 percent of all votes cast. However, in apparent response to the international outcry following the brutal, large-scale massacre of Haitians along the border in October 1937, Trujillo stepped aside in 1938 and allowed his vice president, Jacinto Peynado, to be "elected" president. Once again, only one party presented candidates, and it received 100 percent of the votes cast. And when Peynado died in 1940, his term was completed by the vice president, Manuel de Jesús Troncoso de la Concha.

In the 1940s, Trujillo considerably expanded his economic holdings while retaining political power. In the midst of World War II and with Trujillo actively cooperating with its war effort, the United States did not object to his holding power directly; thus Trujillo was "elected" to a third (five-year) term in 1942 as two parties went to the polls with exactly the same lists, the Dominican Party and the Trujillista Party. Brief but real pressures for democratization followed the end of World War II; Trujillo liberalized for a short period, allowing communist exiles to return, and the regime experienced its first labor strikes. But Trujillo cracked down again as international pressures for democratization eased in the context of the emerging Cold War, and he was reelected in 1947. In that year, two regime-sponsored "opposition" parties were allowed to run, and each officially received a similar vote of just under 4 percent of the total, which was carefully distributed so that each could win exactly one deputy seat. The 1940s also witnessed frustrated exile invasions against the regime, even as the country's military apparatus continued to expand considerably.

Trujillo's initial schemes to enrich himself, as I noted above, revolved around the creation of state or commercial monopolies. He then gradually moved into industry, forcing owners to allow him to buy up shares, while also enjoying healthy commissions on all public works contracts. After World War II, Trujillo expanded into the industrial production of such products as cement, chocolate, cardboard, flour, paint, and alcoholic beverages, often in collaboration with local investors or with Spanish or Syrian-Lebanese entrepreneurs who had settled in the country. From 1938 to 1960, manufacturing establishments doubled, and the number of employees increased almost two and a half times.[18] Trujillo also nationalized the electric company, and in 1941 he bought up the United States–owned National City Bank, which he renamed the Banco de Reservas.

Trujillo's largest investments were in sugar, however. As late as 1948, with the exception of a few properties owned by the Vicini family, the country's sugar industry was foreign owned. Trujillo entered the sugar industry both because he could wield additional power in that way and in order to enrich himself. He began modestly with a small mill in 1949, then began construction of a massive (and economically irrational) mill while gradually pressuring foreign companies to sell by planting stories in the press, promoting labor disturbances, and citing the companies for health and labor violations. By 1956, twelve of the sixteen mills in the country belonged to the Trujillo family, all except the country's largest one at Central Romana (whose ownership was being negotiated when he was killed) and three owned by the Vicinis. As he expanded his economic holdings, "the organized and systematic use of every State power in furtherance of Trujillo's private ends was conspicuous." This ranged from privileged access to energy and water, to free use of military labor, to the use of the state banking system for Trujillo's benefit. The planning and implementation of the entire sugar operation were so poor that except for the numerous subsidies it would have lost money.[19]

While retaining direct control over the military, in 1952 and again in 1957, Trujillo had his pliant brother, Héctor B. Trujillo, elected president. The voting "results" again demonstrated near or total unanimity for the single candidate.[20] The regime appeared to be at its apogee in 1955, when the country sponsored a massive world fair to celebrate the twenty-five years of the Trujillo era. At that point Trujillo's domination of the island appeared absolute, even as support from the United States for its staunch "anticommunist" ally was also high. Yet the fair constituted a massive drain on the country's budget, as did Trujillo's cash purchases of several sugar mills and the country's electric company, as the country entered a period of much slower growth. And the willingness of Dominicans to resist the regime more openly within the country gradually grew in the face of Trujillo's political and economic megalomania and intensifying exile operations. In 1956 the kidnapping of Jesús de Galíndez marked a turn toward a more erratic and brutal use of repression, as Trujillo's rhetoric focused less and

less on the national goals he had initially articulated and more on the "communist" threat.[21] The crisis deepened after Fidel Castro's triumph in Cuba on
1 January 1959; it ended—for Rafael Trujillo—in a blaze of bullets in May 1961.

Explanations and Characteristics

How was Trujillo able to maintain nearly total control over a country for so
long? Five sets of factors are important. First are background *historical* factors
of geographical isolation, weak traditional powerholders, lack of potential challengers from other social groups, and a more effective repressive apparatus.
Related to these are how he built on and enhanced *state structures*, especially
those related to repression. Yet his prolonged rule did not rely on repression
alone. He employed *ideological* arguments, initially revolving around economic
nationalism, anti-Haitianism, and Catholicism, to project himself domestically
and to justify his vast financial empire. Various *economic and political* means
meshed strategies of repression, co-optation, and corruption while permitting
him to enhance his personal wealth and power. Finally, *international* factors
play a central role, given the country's dependence on the United States. Trujillo
pursued an active policy toward the United States, and he was helped initially
by his strong contacts with U.S. military and by the United States' "good
neighbor" policy of nonintervention and then by the U.S. focus on anticommunism. Indeed, a dramatic shift in U.S. attitude toward Trujillo was crucial in
the denouement of his regime.

Important historical and structural factors were discussed in the previous
section. They include the country's relative socioeconomic backwardness, weak
and divided social forces and political actors, improved communications and
transportation, and better trained police and armed forces that aided Trujillo's
rise to power, in combination with the initial U.S. policy of nonintervention.

Trujillo built on these, enhancing the state's repressive features. He used all
means at his disposal to reinforce the natural isolation that was a consequence
of his subjects' living on an island. By his second term, he had started to employ
more sophisticated technological measures of control over the population,
beginning with interception of correspondence. Over time, reflecting some of
the more totalitarian features of the regime, these moved into telephone tap-
ping, surveillance of foreign diplomats and journalists, and targeted assassinations, both at home and abroad.[22] Foreign radio programs were often jammed,
foreign press reports kept out, the mail censored; enhancing isolation and
control, few Dominicans were given permission to travel abroad.

Central to Trujillo's domination of the country was control over expanding

TABLE 4.1
Growth of the Security Forces under Trujillo

Year	Army	Air Force	Navy	Police	Total	% Increase [a]
1924	na[b]	na	na	na	1,243	
1929	na	na	na	na	2,128	71
1932	na	na	na	na	2,179	2
1935	na	na	na	na	2,770	27
1938	3,081	31	100	627	3,839	38
1944	5,269	76	135	900[c]	6,380	66
1948	6,298	171	1,042	1,622	9,133	43
1955	13,500	2,000	3,000	1,500	20,000	119
1958	11,400	2,214	2,900	1,500	18,014	−10
1960	17,500	10,000[d]	3,500	see[d]	31,000	72

SOURCE: Bernardo Vega, *Trujillo y las Fuerzas Armadas Norteamericanas*, 225, 445.
[a]Percentage increase from previous total reported.
[b]na = not applicable.
[c]Figure for police taken from 1942 figures.
[d]Total for air force, police, and newly created Legion forces.

armed forces and police, which were clearly his personal instrument rather than a national institution.[23] Trujillo remained commander-in-chief of the armed forces even when he was not formally president (in 1958, in the face of U.S. pressure, Trujillo claimed to have stepped down as commander-in-chief, but the ostensible move was never publicized within the country). As table 4.1 illustrates, Trujillo expanded the size of the armed forces and police dramatically while he controlled the country. In spite of a sharp drop in the overall government budget in the 1930s owing to the effects of the depression, the military budget grew: in 1929 it was $1.5 million, 9.4 percent of the government budget; in 1938 it was $1.84 million and 16 percent of the budget. In subsequent decades, as the economy improved, the military portion expanded even more dramatically.[24] And by the mid-1950s the best-trained troops and the best military weapons, not only planes but tanks and other military hardware, had been transferred to the Dominican equivalent of the air force, known as the Dominican Military Aviation, controlled by Trujillo's son Ramfis.

Trujillo still confronted challenges within the armed forces. The role of Ramfis highlighted the fact that the morale, autonomy, and abilities of the armed forces were affected by nepotism, rotation of officers, and manipulated promotions. Ramfis was made a full colonel in the army at the age of four and a brigadier general by age nine; he resigned that rank when he was fourteen, but by the time he was twenty-three he was again a brigadier general as well as chief of staff of the air force. On at least two occasions, Trujillo simply promoted trusted civilians to high positions in the army (Anselmo Paulino Alvarez in 1949 and Johnny Abbes in 1958). Several of Trujillo's brothers entered the army after the U.S. marines had left and, through their family connections, eventually became generals; other relatives also held high posts in the military or the government. Trujillo's brothers in the military were permitted to engage in small-scale corruption, protection rackets, and contraband; generally, though, the bureaucracy operated in a reasonably honest fashion out of fear of Trujillo. After consolidating his grip on power in the 1930s, including uncovering a plot emanating from the military in 1931, Trujillo confronted renewed military plots against him that he successfully dismantled in 1939 and 1946. Trujillo's network of domestic and international spies took on an additional dimension in 1957 with the creation of the dreaded SIM (Military Intelligence Service), headed by Johnny Abbes.[25]

One of Trujillo's most brutal uses of his repressive forces was the large-scale massacre of Haitians in October 1937, resulting in an estimated five thousand to twelve thousand deaths.[26] What combination of factors ultimately led Trujillo to order this action remains unclear. After an extensive review, Vega asserts that although a desire to "whiten" the country probably played a central role, numerous other factors contributed, including an aspiration to control critical border areas more effectively in the face of growing illegal Haitian migration, the ineffectiveness of deportations, and the actions of some Dominican military officers more involved in profiting from illegal migration than in controlling it. By this massacre, Trujillo sought to assert centralized control over all Dominican territory and to prevent any potential threat to his regime that could emanate from Haiti, as so many conspiracies had done in the country's past. Before the massacre, Trujillo had also sought to influence Haitian politics and to bribe key officials (in fact a bribe helped lower the compensation he paid to Haiti after the massacre). In the 1940s, towns and military outposts were founded in the border regions, the church was encouraged to extend its missionary work into the region, new roads were constructed, and greater commercial links were established with the rest of the country.[27]

Yet Trujillo's regime was not based purely on repression, though over time it increasingly became so. With the collaboration of several leading intellectuals, Trujillo articulated certain ideological positions that resonated across different social sectors of the population. His was the first prolonged period in the country's history when the country did not experience direct intervention by Spain, the United States, or Haiti. Trujillo built on the country's antipathy to Haiti to help assert a nationalist ideology appealing to traditional Hispanic and Catholic values.[28] Especially in the 1930s, he also verbalized a vision of discipline, work, peace, order, and progress. As these ideas became embodied in a number of large-scale public works and construction projects, particularly as the economy began moving out of the depression in the late 1930s, they almost certainly gained him respect—if not support—among some elements of the population, since he also presented himself in messianic guise. By the 1950s, and particularly after signing a concordat with the Vatican in 1954, Trujillo would often attack "international communism" as a threat to the country's traditional values that he claimed he was seeking to uphold. Yet Trujillo never articulated a fully formulated ideology; indeed, even his espousal of "anticommunism" changed dramatically in his final, desperate days.

Trujillo also waved the ideological banner of economic nationalism, although it sometimes cloaked his personal accumulation of wealth. This was abetted by the country's abject dependency on the United States and by its tragic history. In fact, many of his economic measures were inferior to those taken by other Latin American states in the same period. Yet in seeking to legitimize his rule, Trujillo could argue that he ended United States administration of Dominican customs, retired the Dominican debt, and introduced a national currency to replace the dollar. The 1924 convention that paved the way for the withdrawal of U.S. troops had maintained an extensive role for the United States in Dominican internal economic affairs and in the customs house in order to ensure the prompt repayment of the country's outstanding debt and to prevent accumulation of new debt without U.S. approval. In the words of one U.S. diplomat, the country remained a "tutelary state."[29] After extensive negotiations, Trujillo signed an agreement with Cordell Hull in 1940 (ratified in 1941) ending the U.S. administration of Dominican customs. Finally, in July 1947, employing reserves built up during the war years, Trujillo completely paid off the country's foreign debt. Shortly afterward the country established a central bank and a national currency (the peso) to replace the U.S. dollar, which had been used until then in lieu of a local currency; although initially respectful of the central bank's autonomy, toward the end of his rule Trujillo openly violated it.[30]

Thus, ideologically Trujillo portrayed himself with some success as a forger of the Dominican nation, builder of the state, and defender of its economic interests. As he amassed a sizable fortune, he also built up the Dominican state, reduced direct control by foreigners over the economy, and stimulated incipient industrialization. He and his propagandists, though, exaggerated the efficacy of the measures he took and the role of his regime in restoring the country's financial independence and sovereignty while downplaying the tremendous costs his economic measures ultimately represented for the nation.

Economically, Trujillo eventually became the single dominant force in the country by combining abuse of state power, threats, and co-optation. Although certain of the country's economic elite maintained some individual autonomy, there was no possibility for independent organization. Trujillo enjoyed humiliating those who had previously enjoyed both social prestige and economic wealth; they disliked him intensely but were forced to conform. Only in his last two years did any concerted opposition emerge from within the economic elite. Indeed, Trujillo's economic holdings at the time of his death were incredibly extensive, further concentrating total control of the country in his hands. He controlled almost 80 percent of the country's industrial production. About 60 percent of the country's labor force depended on him directly or indirectly, with 45 percent employed in his firms and another 15 percent working for the state. Thus Trujillo's domination of the island was increasingly economic as well as military and political.[31]

The only organization that retained any autonomy within the country was the Catholic Church; yet until the very end of his rule it remained abjectly loyal to him. This was a church that had been decimated by the Haitian occupation of the nineteenth century, and by 1930 its position was still relatively precarious. Trujillo favored the church tremendously, subsidizing the construction of church buildings, enhancing religious education, providing stipends for clergy and ultimately providing other prerogatives to the church through a concordat with the Vatican in 1954, as the number of priests also increased dramatically. Ricardo Pittini, archbishop of Santo Domingo and leader of the church from 1936 until 1960, was an open admirer of Trujillo and provided unequivocal support for his regime. However, an open break between Trujillo and the church finally came in January 1960, in the form of a pastoral letter that was read in all the country's Roman Catholic churches. It followed the arrival of a new papal nuncio and Trujillo's brutal treatment of young guerrillas, some of whom were the children of wealthy Dominicans from prominent families. Over the next year, Trujillo sought unsuccessfully to acquire the title of "benefactor of the church" as he launched a bitter campaign against the church that drove the bishops to write him a conciliatory letter the following January.[32]

Politically, Trujillo combined guile, cynicism, ruthlessness, and co-optation. There was careful manipulation of constitutional norms and legal requirements that ostensibly were followed faithfully, a single-party apparatus totally dominated by Trujillo, and incredible manipulation of individuals, who found themselves moved and removed from public office in complex and disconcerting fashion even as personal rivalries were promoted and tested. At its apogee, the Dominican Party had branches throughout the country, helping to keep Trujillo apprised of local realities, needs, and potential threats to his rule. The party's charitable activities, homage to Trujillo, and campaign efforts were financed largely by a percentage taken from the salaries of public employees.

Although the Dominican Party played no role in either political recruitment or policy formulation, in certain periods of the Trujillo era it did help to legitimize his rule. Trujillo made voting mandatory, and not having one's identification card stamped to show one had voted could be risky.

Trujillo's political style fueled distrust and conspiracy. He was known to be generous with money as well as willing to go to elaborate lengths to plot revenge or assassination. His ruthless political abilities were particularly evident in his response to democratic pressures from the United States after World War II in the face of greater labor activism within the country. He convinced Dominican communists in their Cuban exile they could return to function openly and legally, and they did so in 1946, with the misplaced belief they would be able to act effectively. In that year the second major strike under Trujillo's reign took place (the first was in 1942). Repression increased in 1947, however, and one month after his May 1947 reelection, Trujillo had the Communist Party declared illegal. A wave of repression effectively destroyed the party as well as the nascent independent labor movement as Trujillo took advantage of the growing anticommunist attitude of the United States during the Cold War.[33]

If these various domestic factors were critical in sustaining Trujillo's grip on power, international ones were as well. Trujillo's complex web of conspiracy, intrigue, and violence extended well beyond Dominican borders, as he provided aid for various regional dictators and worked against perceived foreign enemies, some of whom supported exile groups plotting against him. The governments most hostile to Trujillo were those of Ramón Grau San Martín in Cuba (1944–48), Rómulo Betancourt in Venezuela, and Juan José Arévalo in Guatemala; Trujillo was involved in plots against the governments of the first two, as well as against other governments. As early as January 1945, Juan Bosch, in exile in Cuba, was actively seeking weapons and funds for a possible invasion and overthrow of Trujillo.

Given the Dominican Republic's history and continuing dependency, the nature of complex relations with the United States was also of central importance. Early in his rule, Trujillo found strong backing among military contacts he had forged during the U.S. occupation, which counterbalanced an often hostile State Department. Trujillo employed public relations firms and assiduously cultivated his military contacts and individual politicians in the United States to enhance his reputation and sustain U.S. endorsement. He went to elaborate lengths to demonstrate domestically that he retained support from the United States, and U.S. diplomats often expressed their frustration at being manipulated by Trujillo even as U.S. military personnel openly praised his rule. Until the final crisis years (1959–61), the most critical period for Trujillo was in the immediate post–World War II era when hostile U.S. diplomats were able to block his efforts to purchase arms and promoted a more active policy in support of democracy. As the Cold War developed, however, this policy receded. Thus an effort by Dominican exiles to launch an invasion against Trujillo's regime from Cayo Confites off Cuba in 1947 was stopped largely by the Cuban government, with U.S. pressure playing a contributory role (another invasion effort in 1949 also failed). By 1955 U.S. civilian diplomats were joining their military counterparts in praising Trujillo for his anticommunism, though this warm embrace lasted only until 1958.[34] And by 1959, as the ideological, economic, political, and international bases of the regime continued to erode, more and more domestic and international actors were asking how Trujillo was to be removed from office and who would replace him. Ultimately, then, Trujillo's power base rested on firm control of the state's repressive apparatus, on an ability to dismantle plots against him or prevent them through fear or cunning, and on United States forbearance. Shifts in the last two ultimately led to his undoing.

Trujillo's Fall and Its Aftermath

Transitions to democracy from regimes with sultanistic tendencies are fraught with extreme difficulties, not only because these regimes are commonly found in countries where democratic experience is weak or absent, but more specifically because of the features of neosultanistic rule itself.[35] Given the nature of these despotic regimes, if the dictator does not die of natural causes, he is typically removed by assassination, conspiracy within the armed forces, violent protest from civil society, revolutionary struggle, or some combination of these. Depending on how the dictator is removed, it may be possible for family members or other close associates to retain power; in the case of an armed revolt or revolution it is likely that those who eliminated or overthrew the dictator will assume power themselves in a nondemocratic fashion. An immediate transition from neosultanism to a democratically elected government is almost impossible because of the lack of moderate, somewhat autonomous forces within the regime willing to negotiate such a move and because the country has no independent societal organizations and political institutions and parties, which can emerge only after the fall of the dictator. Even if a provisional government is formed that promises democratic elections, however, ultimately these may be postponed or manipulated. Another complicating issue is commonly a legacy of conspiratorial, manipulative politics and an absence of trust. And when these dictatorships are in small, internationally vulnerable states, the actions of major powers may also be crucial.

A transition to democracy from neosultanistic or other neopatrimonial dictatorships appears most likely when the armed forces were somewhat autonomous from the despot and could eventually be purged or otherwise controlled by the new democratic leaders, and when there was a strong moderate opposition based both on independent societal economic actors and on preexisting democratic parties as well as a weak revolutionary opposition.[36] Given these conditions, it is not difficult to discern why a transition to democracy from the Trujillo dictatorship was highly problematic. Trujillo's domination of the island republic was extensive: the military was his personal instrument, no political opposition was countenanced, and no independent societal organizations existed, although this also meant there was no strong revolutionary opposition. Ultimately, a combination of economic deterioration, exile activism, and the dramatic shift in the United States' attitude toward Trujillo emboldened domestic opposition and conspirators. After Trujillo's assassination, however, only the overwhelming presence of the United States helped ensure an end to the Trujillo era, permitting the armed forces to break with the Trujillo family and letting oppositions emerge openly.

Considerable instability and uncertainty followed Trujillo's assassination in May 1961, as various family members and close regime associates sought to cling to power. It took some eight months, with considerable pressure and oversight by the United States, to move to a provisional government that represented a clear break with Trujillo. That government, dominated by anti-Trujillista but conservative and economically wealthy forces, called for elections, which it expected to win easily. But the elections were won by Juan Bosch, recently returned from exile. He campaigned successfully on the principle that the cleavage in the country was not between Trujillistas and anti-Trujillistas but between rich and poor.

Although it did not last, democracy advanced further in the Dominican Republic at this time than one would have expected given the country's history and the legacies of the Trujillo era. The risks of Trujillo *continuismo* or of a provisional government's "hijacking" democracy were both avoided, as truly democratic elections were held. However, all the powerful forces within the country—business groups, the church, and the military—united (ostensibly under the "anticommunist" banner) to overthrow Bosch only seven months into his term. And a civil-military conspiracy to try to bring him back led the United States, out of an exaggerated fear of a "second Cuba," to intervene militarily in the country in 1965. After elections held in 1966 were won by Trujillo's former collaborator Joaquín Balaguer, foreign troops left. Under Balaguer's authoritarian, neopatrimonial, but not neosultanistic rule from 1966 to 1978, the treatment of economic, military, and political power differed substantially from that under Trujillo, in part owing to changes in Dominican society and international circumstances.[37] In key respects these appear to have aided a democratic transition in 1978, though democracy in the country remains fragile and uninstitutionalized.

Trujillo's Fall

A negotiated exit from Trujillo's regime was impossible because of his intransigence, leading to the multiplication of efforts to be rid of him through other means. By the late 1950s Trujillo was facing challenges from all sides: growing domestic opposition, exile activism, and international pressure from Latin American governments, particularly Venezuela with the return to power of Betancourt. The country's economy was suffering, and an aging Trujillo showed declining mental acuity. He came to rely increasingly on a set of advisers who were strongly anti-American and more willing to use violence, including his son Ramfis, who was especially bitter after the U.S. military flunked him out of the Army War College at Fort Leavenworth. The advisers took steps that further alienated upper- and middle-class elements, such as killing the anti-Trujillista middle-class Mirabal sisters by means of a staged auto accident in November 1960. Fearing invasions by exile armies and domestic unrest, Trujillo dramatically expanded the size of the armed forces, sponsoring the creation of a number of paramilitary groups and private armies by close associates.[38]

A critical factor in explaining Trujillo's fall, however—if not the central one—was the shift in attitude of the United States. Just a few years could make a tremendous difference, as the contrasting fate of the Somozas and of the Trujillos demonstrates. In September 1956, when the Nicaraguan president Anastasio Somoza García was gunned down by an assassin, a surprised President Eisenhower instructed that a helicopter take him to a hospital in the Panama Canal Zone, where he eventually died, and the United States saw the transfer of power within the Somoza family with equanimity. But in May 1961, when Trujillo was assassinated, the Central Intelligence Agency was intimately involved in the plots leading up to his death, and the United States interfered extensively to ensure that Trujillo's family would not retain power. The change in attitude of the United States is explained by one fact: the Cuban revolution.

There were two key issues. On one hand, the Eisenhower administration and then the Kennedy administration wished to embark on a more interventionist policy against the perceived growing threat of Fidel Castro in Cuba, and Latin American support for a shift away from noninterventionism against Cuba required that the United States be willing to act against rightist dictators as well. On the other hand, after the fall of Batista, the United States also began to believe that political democracy and social reform might be stronger bulwarks against communism than dictators such as Trujillo. This too called for a more interventionist strategy.

The Cuban revolution led the United States to shift to a far more interventionist policy in the region. From 1959 to 1961, in the Dominican Republic the "United States engaged in its most massive intervention in the internal affairs of a Latin American state since the inauguration of the Good Neighbor Policy."[39] This extensive involvement continued even after the death of Trujillo, culminating with the 1965 intervention and its aftermath. A summary of U.S. policy intentions during this period is provided in President John Kennedy's dictum that in descending order the United States would prefer a democratic regime, continuation of a Trujillo regime, or a Castro regime, and that it should aim for the first but not renounce the second until it was sure the third could be avoided.

Domestic opposition, exiles' initiatives, and international pressure all expanded together. There was a failed invasion attempt from Cuba in June 1959, and a major underground movement that emerged soon thereafter was brutally crushed in January 1960. The children of the wealthy were among the victims of this repression, emboldening the economic elite in their opposition. For the first time, the Catholic Church expressed its disapproval. International pressure built inexorably. In June 1960 the Organization of American States' Inter-American Peace Committee condemned the Dominican Republic for human rights violations, the first time the OAS had criticized the internal policies of a noncommunist American state. That same month, Trujillo was linked to a failed attempt to assassinate Betancourt, leading the OAS to impose sanctions against his regime in August. Trujillo again attempted (as in 1945–47) a controlled "liberalization" for external consumption, but the United States and other international actors were now openly skeptical. Before the OAS meeting, Trujillo resigned as head of the Dominican Party, and in August his brother resigned from the presidency, to be replaced by the vice president Joaquín Balaguer. Free elections were promised, and opposition parties were asked to organize. Out of desperation, Trujillo began to turn to the Soviet bloc. The Communist Party was legalized in June 1960, but emissaries to the Soviet Union met with no success. The Eisenhower administration increased the economic pressure on Trujillo by ensuring that the Dominican Republic would not reap a bonanza from the cancellation of Cuba's sugar quota in July 1960. Toward the end of the year, under the urging of the United States and Venezuela, OAS economic sanctions were extended to include petroleum, trucks, and spare parts.[40] The country's economic situation declined, capital flight increased, particularly by Trujillo family members, and blundering repression continued.

In that context, conspirators who largely were former supporters of the regime assassinated Trujillo on 30 May 1961. They had been first vigorously and then ambivalently encouraged by the United States. However, their plot was discovered before they could move against other major members of the Trujillo clan, and the one general they had found to collaborate with them faltered. Attention immediately focused on what kind of regime would replace Trujillo. Members of the Trujillo family sought to retain power, Balaguer fought for an independent power base, multiple underground movements began to function more openly, and exile groups, including Juan Bosch's PRD (Partido Revolucionario Dominicano, Dominican Revolutionary Party), soon returned to the island. In the days after Trujillo's assassination, a U.S. Navy task force patrolled offshore, prepared to implement previously approved plans for armed intervention. Its purpose was to block any possible Cuban involvement and prevent the success of any pro-communist movement in the country.[41]

Thus a break with the Trujillos came only months later. The complex details sketched below highlight two key issues. The first included the failure of moderate forces to compromise with each other in the context of a lack of institutions; a legacy of conspiracy and intrigue; and a polarized atmosphere generated by the Cuban revolution and the defense of economic privilege. The second was the extent of U.S. involvement and its equivocal impact as it focused increasingly on preventing the emergence of a possible new "Castro regime."

After Trujillo's assassination, OAS sanctions were retained on the grounds that the extent of change represented by the new Balaguer regime was uncertain. The United States imposed additional pressure by an informal boycott of Dominican sugar. Both President Balaguer and Trujillo's son Ramfis, as commander of the armed forces, began to implement "democratization" measures, exiling some of the most visible symbols of repression and promising free elections for May 1962. Yet fearing a potential breakdown of order that could favor communist groups, the United States opted to work with Balaguer and the army while putting pressure on them to move the country toward liberalization. But this controlled liberalization confronted growing domestic opposition, fueled by the return of political exiles as well as by opposition from

Venezuela. By mid-1961 the Balaguer government faced serious domestic opposition from three primary sources: the PRD returned from exile; the National Civic Union (UCN, Unión Cívica Nacional), which was formed by some of the most prominent Dominican businessmen and was to become a conservative but anti-Trujillista movement; and the Political Group Fourteenth of June, which would become a leftist, Castro-influenced party. In spite of bitter differences, all three were united in their desire to completely rid the country of the Trujillos.

Events gradually drove the United States to take a more forceful stance. As part of the liberalization strategy, Balaguer was encouraged to incorporate the opposition groups into a coalition government, but they continued to resist his overtures. Nevertheless, after the exit of Trujillo's hated brothers, the "wicked uncles," in late October, the United States called for a partial lifting of OAS sanctions against the country. Then Trujillo's son Ramfis, still head of the armed forces, suddenly decided the pressures of office were too much for him and opted to go into gilded exile.[42] He urged his uncles to return to the island, and they did so on 15 November. The United States was determined not to allow them to return to power, however, fearing that the violence and instability that it would provoke would favor communism. Balaguer, opting to break with the Trujillos and side with the United States, refused to step aside. In the face of a threatened U.S. military intervention if they tried to reimpose themselves, Héctor B. Trujillo and José Arismendi Trujillo and a number of their close collaborators fled into exile again four days after they returned.

The country celebrated as the Trujillo period finally came to an end, ripping down statues, destroying busts, and attacking other symbols of the dictatorship.[43] A provisional government formed by members of the UCN, known as the Council of State, was finally established in January 1962, after Balaguer was removed and an attempted coup by an emerging military strongman was put down.

Nevertheless, democracy did not come quickly or easily to the Dominican Republic. With Balaguer in exile, the Council of State did oversee democratic elections, held in December 1962. The UCN and associated business and church interests were stunned when Bosch swept the elections by such a wide majority that he could even rewrite the constitution as he sought. The campaign was extremely polarizing, since Bosch was falsely accused of being a communist. After the elections, Bosch was initially conciliatory but became increasingly intransigent. Church and business elements were unhappy with parts of the new constitutional text that was eventually approved, but many in fact had begun working for Bosch's overthrow from the moment he was inaugurated.

The Dominican military had never been purged of its Trujillista elements, and though the U.S. ambassador strongly favored democracy (though with a crackdown on communists), other elements of the U.S. government were strongly anti-Bosch. Who among all these actors was "more to blame" for Bosch's overthrow in September 1963 only seven months after he was inaugurated remains a subject of considerable historical dispute. What is unquestionable, is that an important historical opportunity was lost.

Further polarization ensued. The triumvirate that eventually replaced Bosch was increasingly dominated by the conservative businessman Donald Reid Cabral. Reid Cabral sought to prolong his stay in office by elections scheduled for September 1965 that would exclude his two potentially most significant opponents, Bosch and Balaguer, who remained in exile. As a result, numerous civil-military conspiracies emerged. It was Reid Cabral's efforts on 25 April 1965 to dismantle one of these conspiracies that helped provoke a series of events leading to the "constitutionalist" uprising that sought to bring Bosch and the PRD back to power. The United States then intervened three days later when the "loyalist" Dominican military was unable to control the civil-military rebellion. Although the civil war had been confined largely to urban areas, it left some three thousand dead and produced a polarized country even more committed to conspiratorial politics. U.S. "extrication" was achieved in 1966 after complex maneuverings by means of elections, pitting a vigorous Balaguer against Bosch, who campaigned in a desultory fashion, fearing for his life. Because of the circumstances of the U.S. intervention, many in the country viewed Balaguer's electoral victory as tainted and considered his administration lacking in moral legitimacy.

Most academics would consider the twelve years of Balaguer's rule from 1966 to 1978 as a form of authoritarianism because there was an absence of free and competitive elections and of civil liberties. It was also neopatrimonial because of the way power and resources flowed directly through Balaguer's hands. But in 1978, in what may be considered a democratic transition, Balaguer lost elections and after complex maneuverings handed power over to S. Antonio Guzmán of the PRD. The Dominican case is distinct from many other Latin American instances of democratization in that the transition was from one civilian ruler to another and occurred as part of a process of elections without a formal constitutional break. Both international and domestic pressure were important to ensure that the electoral results would be respected, at least at the presidential level, and that power would devolve.

Although some scholars have sought to emphasize the similarities between Trujillo's rule and that of Balaguer, certain critical differences are apparent that reflect distinctions between the arbitrary, discretional power of sultanistic regimes and that of more clearly authoritarian regimes. Furthermore, these differences in the treatment of economic, military, and political power, which resulted in part from changes in Dominican society and in international circumstances, also played a role in facilitating a democratic transition in 1978 that the country was unable to realize in the 1960s.

Economically, under Balaguer neopatrimonialism was combined with the emergence of more clearly independent private economic groups. The period 1966–78 was one of high economic growth, averaging 7.6 percent increase in real GDP over the whole period and 11 percent from 1968 to 1974. Growth was based on increased export earnings, import substitution in consumer goods, and public investment projects. It was encouraged by the U.S. sugar quota and generous economic assistance, particularly in the early Balaguer years. Balaguer certainly governed in a patrimonial fashion, since he controlled large parts of the budget directly out of his office and sought a predominant political role by ensuring that he was the central axis around which other major political and economic forces revolved. At the same time, he eventually undermined his position by promoting the development of business groups separate from the state, even if dependent on it. In this there is a sharp contrast to the Trujillo period. Organized labor remained weak owing to a combination of repression, co-optation, and extremely restrictive labor legislation.[44]

The military was never the personal instrument of Balaguer, as it had been of Trujillo, and Balaguer was unmistakably a civilian. Balaguer had a commanding presence within the military as a result of his ties to the Trujillo period, his anticommunism, his statesmanlike caudillo image, and his acceptance of both military repression and large-scale corruption. However, he clearly was not a military figure as Trujillo had been. He sought to manage the military by playing off the ambitions of the leading generals and shifting their assigned posts. Yet Balaguer's relations with business were complicated by the growing incursions of the armed forces into business and politics, and he occasionally confronted serious challenges. In 1971 he dismantled a coup effort led by General Elías Wessin y Wessin, who was sent into exile. Throughout the 1970s, however, the economic and political ambitions of the military increased.

Politically, Balaguer never attempted the extent of control that Trujillo did. Rather, he assiduously practiced a policy of co-optation, as semioppositions flourished and eventually a real opposition emerged. Elections held in 1970 and in 1974 were boycotted by (real) opposition parties because of military harassment, in 1974 just days before the election. But the extent and nature of repression, particularly after 1976, were considerably less than in the Trujillo years.

Selected PRD representatives and other party figures were brought into his government or offered diplomatic posts after the 1966 elections and subsequent ones. Similarly, several radical opponents were given posts at the public university and granted some autonomy within that sphere. By the 1978 elections, though, Balaguer had alienated a number of his former supporters by his drive for power, reelection aspirations, and policy decisions.

This set the stage for a peaceful democratic transition through elections. In several respects, Balaguer was approaching the 1978 elections from an unfavorable perspective. An economic downturn finally affected the country about 1976, with the fading of the sugar boom that had offset oil price increases. The immediate problem the economic slowdown created for the regime was exacerbated by socioeconomic changes induced by earlier economic growth under Balaguer. The country's substantial growth, industrialization, and urbanization had expanded middle-sector and professional groups disgruntled by Balaguer's patrimonial politics, which appeared to discriminate against newer and regional groups. In the absence of any "threat" from below, they favored democratization, and a few endorsed the PRD directly. Changes within the PRD between 1974 and 1978, including more moderate programs and efforts to strengthen its international contacts, and the firm position of the Carter administration in the anxious days after the elections, were also significant in ensuring the democratic transition. Another problem was Balaguer's own physical decline, particularly his failing eyesight, which became public knowledge in January 1977. The postelection, preinauguration period was tense, and electoral results were "adjusted" to provide Balaguer with some "guarantees," namely a majority in the Senate (which appoints judges)—in essence, a "political pact." Yet the succession went through, and just as critically (from the point of view of referring to this as a democratic transition, and in contrast to several Central American cases in the 1980s), the United States supported moves by the new president to purge the Dominican military of some of its most Trujillista generals. These issues and others were certainly important. But most noteworthy for understanding the consequences for subsequent political outcomes of whether a regime was neosultanistic are the implications of the key differences in the Trujillo and Balaguer (1966–78) regimes.

Conclusions

I will resist the temptation to repeat how examining the Trujillo regime through the prism of the concept of sultanism effectively highlights its emergence, its consolidation of power, and its evolution. Rather, I will end with an etymological excursus and some related substantive points. Based on arguments presented by Max Weber, Chehabi and Linz refer to regimes like Trujillo's as sultanistic, or because in the twentieth century such regimes inevitably have had elements of legal-rational order and of a legitimizing ideology rather than being perversions of traditional rule, they call them "regimes with sultanistic tendencies." Given this move away from a simple, direct term, regimes such as Trujillo's could be called "discretional neopatrimonial regimes": "neo-" because such regimes no longer base whatever claim to legitimacy they make exclusively or even primarily on "traditional" grounds, and "discretional" to indicate the incredible autonomy the individual ruler possesses. As a shorthand, however, and analogous to the use of "neopatrimonialism" acknowledged by the editors in their introductory chapters, I have used the term "neo-sultanism" above to refer to the Trujillo regime.

A no-adjective or nondiscretional "neopatrimonial regime" would be a kind of regime in which power is centralized in the hands of the ruler, who seeks to reduce the autonomy of his followers by generating ties of loyalty and dependence, often generating complex patron-client linkages and blurring public and private interests and purposes within the administration. Neopatrimonialism can coexist not only with a variety of authoritarian regimes (though not all kinds), but also with at least somewhat democratic regimes, as has been demonstrated in the Dominican Republic with Balaguer's return to power in 1986.[45]

For the purposes of this chapter, the principal substantive point of distinguishing between these two kinds of neopatrimonial regimes (discretional and nondiscretional) is that it helps us understand the nature of and possibilities for democratic transition. The Dominican Republic suffered at least two despots with "sultanistic tendencies," Heureaux and Trujillo. The immediate consequence of each regime was a period of considerable political turmoil. Heureaux, especially by his irresponsible debt management, exacerbated foreign involvement in Dominican affairs; the subsequent creation of the Dominican constabulary by the U.S. marines during their occupation helped set the stage for Trujillo's emergence. As long-lasting as individual neosultanistic regimes might be, however, the Dominican case suggests they may be temporally based, most likely to appear under certain conditions of geographic isolation, relative economic backwardness, weak societal actors, more centralized forces of repression, and limited state rationalization and professionalization; obviously they also require a leader with the appropriate disposition.

The differences between Trujillo's neosultanistic regime (1930–61) and the subsequent regime of Balaguer (1966–78), which could both be considered neopatrimonial, are themselves in part explained by changing economic, societal, and political circumstances. In particular, by the late 1960s the country was no longer so isolated, and societal and political actors were stronger. Had Balaguer been a different sort of leader, his regime might have had more "sultanistic tendencies"; but given the development of social and political forces and the country's international relations, it could never have approximated the features of the Trujillo regime.

It is not necessarily that a democratic transition from Trujillo was impossible. Even though the Trujillo regime approximated the neosultanistic ideal type so that the country had a near institutional vacuum on Trujillo's demise and weak societal and political actors, a provisional government formed in 1962 did successfully organize democratic elections. But considerable U.S. involvement was a constant and important factor during this period. A coup overthrowing the elected president, Juan Bosch, only seven months after he assumed office in 1963 and U.S. military intervention in 1965 in the face of a civil-military uprising to return Bosch to power underscore two reasons democracy failed at this time. One reason was the inability of anti-Trujillista moderate forces to commit to an effective political pact in support of democratic rules of the game; the other was the polarized atmosphere within the country, so that the defense of economic privilege could be imbued with anticommunism even as the fear of a "second Cuba" outweighed other considerations for U.S. policymakers.

Nor was a democratic transition in 1978 inevitable. Far from it. Unlike the situation in the early 1960s, however, such a transition could now occur directly without the need for a provisional government and be aided by informal understandings among moderate forces inside and outside the regime. In 1978 the country's economy and its social forces were more developed, its opposition groupings were more sophisticated, various political and military actors had "learned" the dangers of polarization and violence from the 1963–65 debacle, and the United States was more focused on achieving democracy than on avoiding communism in the island republic. But the contrast with the Trujillo era in the politics, the economic management, and the links to the military of the neopatrimonial but not neosultanistic Balaguer regime is critical in explaining why a democratic transition (albeit to a fragile, unconsolidated regime) was easier in 1978 than it had been in the 1960s.

5

. . . .

The Batista Regime in Cuba

Jorge I. Domínguez

> The charge has been made that Batista is a usurper of
> authority. It is true that he seized power on two occasions.
> But it is also true that in each case he took the power from a
> weak, ineffective government which had shown no capacity
> for leadership.   EDMUND A. CHESTER,
> *A Sergeant Named Batista*

Fulgencio Batista was Cuba's premier political leader from 1933 to 1958, exercising de facto or de jure presidential power except between 1944 and 1952. But as reflected in the peculiar defense of Batista's rise to power made by his quasi-official biographer, Edmund Chester, Batista's claim to legitimate rule was remarkably feeble. He possessed no "traditional" authority. Nor was he a "charismatic" figure in the technical sense of that expression. Chester wrote that Batista had "a great sense of humor," and he also reported that Batista's "humor is noticed once in a while in some of his official acts."[1] In fact, though Batista was often quite charming in person, he was rather awkward and stiff in many of his speeches. Both on 4 September 1933 and on 10 March 1952, Batista rose to power as a usurper, not by winning elections or by following prescribed constitutional rules for access to power. Both times his claim to legitimacy was that his predecessors were even worse ("weak, ineffective" and lacking in "leadership")—a highly personalistic and subjective claim to the right to rule over his fellow citizens.

My task in this chapter is to characterize Batista's second regime (1952–58). In order to understand the regime from inside, whenever possible I will draw on his own writings (even if they owe much to his unacknowledged collaborators) and on the writings of authors who were associated with him in some way.

The overall argument is that the longer Batista remained in power the more he displayed sultanistic tendencies, though even in the end his regime did not quite fit the characterization sultanistic.[2] By "sultanism" I mean that this regime was personalistic, arbitrary, centralized, nonideological, distrustful, corrupt, and unprofessional. I will argue that when the regime fell it was not because Batista failed in the pursuit of his preferred policies but, on the contrary, because he had succeeded to a large measure in sultanizing the government. The regime's characteristics made for its swift disintegration in the face of a revolutionary challenge.

Biographical Note

Fulgencio Batista, a light-skinned mulatto, was born in 1901 in the small town of Banes in Oriente province (eastern Cuba), the son of poor rural folk. His father was a sugar worker; his mother died when he was fourteen. As a teenager, he was a migrant worker (with jobs as cane cutter, carpenter, and railroad worker). In 1921 he joined the Cuban army as a private; in 1928 he was promoted to sergeant-stenographer. In 1926 he married Elisa Godínez, whom he divorced in October 1945. A month later he married Martha Fernández, whose personal traits fit in much more easily with the Havana elite. He had three children from his first marriage and four from the second, and in his will he recognized an illegitimate daughter, born in 1935 when he was chief of the armed forces. The first of his four children by Martha Fernández was born in 1942 while he was president of Cuba. In part because of his social background, Batista was at first shunned by Havana "high society" after seizing power in 1933.[3]

Cuba was hit hard by the world depression. After resisting years of insurgent attempts and urban terrorism, on 12 August 1933 President Gerardo Machado's dictatorship was overthrown; though the provisional government that replaced it had U.S. government support, it could not consolidate its power. The structures of the state and of the armed forces crumbled. Massive riots broke out in Havana and other cities; mobs assaulted the officials of the old regime. In the midst of such chaos, on 4 September 1933 a ramshackle coalition of noncommissioned officers (led by Batista), university students, and others overthrew the feeble government and the equally enfeebled military high command. On 9 September Ramón Grau San Martín was installed as president of Cuba with

Batista's support. By shrewd use of politics and military force, Batista soon forced out of office many of his initial collaborators, including President Grau in January 1934.

With the support of the U.S. government, Batista established himself as Cuba's "strongman." From 1934 through 1940 he served as chief of the armed forces while various civilians occupied the presidency for short terms. These puppet presidents did not always agree with Batista, so they were successively removed from office by various means. In 1940 he was elected president of Cuba. Cuba's constitution prohibited immediate reelection; Batista thought that his coalition could win free elections and that he could revert to the role of the power behind the presidency—one of many examples of rulers who miscalculate the support they enjoy. More recent examples of this stunning mistake are Ferdinand Marcos in the Philippines, Augusto Pinochet in Chile, and a succession of communist regimes in Eastern Europe, especially in Poland. Thus in 1944 he presided over national elections, won by Ramón Grau at the head of an opposition coalition; Batista recognized the election results and peacefully turned the presidency over to his long-standing opponent.[4] In 1948 Batista was elected to the Senate from Las Villas province. He launched a campaign for the presidency in the 1952 elections—elections that were not held because Batista seized power on 10 March 1952.

The Conditions for Sultanistic Tendencies

One set of factors that would contribute to the sultanization of Cuba's political regime in the 1950s is the nature of political society before Batista's March 1952 coup. Cuban politics in the twentieth century had a strong nonideological and clientelist component. As the decades passed, to be sure, certain ideological and programmatic trends appeared, but their significance remained secondary until 1959. Batista did not invent Cuba's nonideological and clientelist politics, but he came to embody them.

In the 1930s Batista built a powerful nonideological coalition by wooing his enemies. For the 1936 presidential elections, for example, former president Mario G. Menocal, leader of Cuba's most conservative political and economic forces, opposed the Batista-backed coalition. After the elections it was discovered that the opposition had not been recognized by any victory for the Senate; the cabinet thus retroactively amended the constitution to award some Senate seats to the opposition, all Menocalistas or "Democrats." By 1940 Menocal's Democrats had joined the Batista coalition.

Similarly, Batista's armed forces severely repressed the Communist Party in the mid-1930s. By the end of the 1930s the Comintern had instructed communist parties throughout the world to seek "popular front" alliances; Cuba's communists approached Batista to make a deal. Batista was all too willing to reestablish social peace at low cost; he brought the communists into his coalition and, in 1939, permitted the founding of the communist-led Cuban Labor Confederation, Cuba's only labor confederation ever since. When Batista was inaugurated as president of Cuba in 1940, his coalition spanned Cuba's ideological spectrum; conservatives and communists served in his cabinet in the early 1940s.[5]

This nonideological trait was pervasive throughout Cuba's political society. Consider the behavior of two of Cuba's most prominent conservative politicians. Gustavo Cuervo Rubio, a Democrat, was Batista's vice-presidential candidate in 1940 against Ramón Grau and his Auténtico Party. As vice president, he defected to form the opposition Republican Party, aligned with Grau's Auténticos for the 1944 elections. For the 1948 elections he switched again to rejoin the Democrats as their vice-presidential candidate in coalition with the Liberal Party (also a conservative party) against the Auténticos. Ramón Zaydín had been Speaker of the House of Representatives as a Liberal Party member in the Machado dictatorship and, as a member of the Republican Party, an opponent of Batista in the mid-1930s. By the early 1940s Zaydín had rejoined the Liberals and become Batista's prime minister. In the late 1940s Zaydín led the Liberals into an alliance with the Auténticos—his presumed archenemies for the previous fifteen years—and entered President Carlos Prío's Auténtico-led cabinet.

These tactical shifts were evident as well on the political left. A grateful Communist Party supported the Batista coalition in the 1940 and 1944 presidential elections and in the 1942 congressional elections.[6] But communist loyalty was short-lived. In 1944 the Batista-coalition had seized control of both houses of Congress even as Grau and the Auténticos won the presidency. In December 1945 the communists crossed the aisle, joined in coalition with the Auténticos, and delivered the Senate majority to the new Auténtico president as part of a deal to retain communist control over the labor confederation. In the 1946 municipal elections the Communist Party supported 126 candidates, of whom 103 were in coalitions; the party's allies in these elections were distributed nearly randomly across the ideological spectrum.

Consider the nine congressional elections from 1936 through 1954. Never fewer than one-quarter, and as high as nine-tenths, of the members of Cuba's House of Representatives who had been reelected shifted political parties to gain reelection; they often affiliated with their former enemies who had become electorally more popular. The median proportion of reelected representatives who shifted parties was 56 percent. In the Senate the median proportion of members reelected or promoted from the House who shifted parties was 45 percent.

In such a political system, the key incentive is access to political power and its rewards, including money and status. Such a political system lacks the racial, ethnic, linguistic, cultural, regional, religious, or social class cleavages that characterize democratic or other authoritarian regimes and that might serve as bases for political coalitions on other than clientelist grounds. There were few structural impediments in Cuba's civil society and political society to the making and remaking of political coalitions. Political loyalty, not just to programs or ideas but even to political leaders, was extremely weak. Even clientelist bargains were tactical and therefore unstable over the long run. Cuban society was already too modern for the old-fashioned stable loyalties of political machines in more traditional settings, and for this reason Cuba's political system differed from regimes that were more clearly sultanistic.

These nonideological, personalistic traits of Cuban politics, however, dated to the foundation of the republic in 1902. They made Cuban politics open to sultanization but did not require it. We need to search for factors closer to the 1950s to explain the shift toward sultanization.

A second important factor that contributed to the sultanization of Cuban politics was the structure of the state itself. Two characteristics of the Cuban state encouraged sultanistic tendencies. The first was the guarantee to the owners of property that the shifting pattern of tactical alliances would not hurt them or their property. These guarantees were made necessary by the social, economic, and political upheavals in Cuba in the early 1930s: social and economic elites demanded enough order to safeguard their interests. The innovation adopted under Batista's leadership in the 1930s was the informal segregation between the making of key economic policies and the filling of public offices.

The United States' Jones-Costigan Sugar Act cartelized the U.S. sugar industry and U.S. imports from Cuba. Cuba's Sugar Coordination Act of 1937 codified the domestic side of the cartel. Decision making over sugar policies—Cuba's premier economic enterprise—was highly and closely regulated. Policy and administration were in the hands of an autonomous and powerful entity, the Sugar Stabilization Institute, run by a board of twelve sugar mill owners, six sugar growers, and three government appointees. This system institutionalized access to political power for those who owned and operated the sugar industry and agriculture; the institute conducted the international relations of the sugar industry on behalf of the public sector and the private sector. This highly stable arrangement endured until 1959. Protected property owners could let politicians personalize other aspects of Cuban politics because the relations between the state and the economy's key sector were secure.

Another feature of the structure of the state that promoted sultanization was the nature of civil-military relations. In 1944 the new Auténtico administration under President Grau purged Cuba's armed forces of those who had risen through the officer ranks during the preceding eleven years thanks mainly to their personal connections to Batista. By the end of 1944 the new government had retired some two hundred officers, including many generals. More would leave during 1945. The Auténticos also discharged the entire command of the national police. In their place, the Auténticos promoted academy-trained junior career officers. This promising policy, however, suffered from the serious malady of the Grau and Prío administrations—widespread corruption.

For many officers, the overwhelming evidence of corruption among government civilians was sufficient cause to support a coup. Moreover, a number of senior military officers themselves became corrupt, impairing the loyalty of their junior officers. As a result some junior officers began to plot the overthrow of the democratic regime and provided initial, decisive support to the Batista coup. On 10 March 1952, no regiment of the Armed Forces of the Republic took up arms to defend the constitutional order against Batista's coup.[7]

Though state and society seemed well suited for sultanistic tendencies, Batista himself bears responsibility for the regime change. Public opinion polls ranked him last of three candidates for the 1952 presidential elections. Batista's public rationale for the March 1952 coup was that President Prío was seeking to perpetuate himself in power and was possibly collaborating with the communists.[8] Batista's charges have been analyzed closely by historian Hugh Thomas, who finds them suspect and highly improbable.[9] Prío condoned gangsterism, enriched himself, and allowed others to profit from graft. But he had expelled the communists from control of the labor confederation in order to become president of Cuba and was probably one of the few political leaders in mid-twentieth-century Cuba with a genuine commitment to democratic politics. I will consider Batista's ideas in the next section.

There can be no sultanization without a would-be sultan. One difference between the highly clientelist, personalistic, and at most loosely ideological nature of politics in Brazil and in Cuba, both of which have loosely organized political parties, is that Cuba had Batista whereas Brazil had a more bureaucratized, professional state, and especially more professional armed forces. Sultanistic tendencies increased in Cuba, therefore, because this non-ideological politician took advantage of the weakly structured nature of Cuba's political society, the peculiar property guarantees embedded in the Cuban state, and the divided and decomposed features of the Cuban armed forces. There were neither structural nor ideological and moral nor leadership constraints to stand in Batista's way. That was why his 1952 coup proceeded so smoothly.

In contrast to the significance of the factors cited above, other considerations seem less important. It is difficult to specify a relation between the structure of the economy or its growth patterns and the likelihood of sultanistic tendencies. By the beginning of the twentieth century most Cuban adults were literate. The very nature of the sugar industry meant that many Cubans were directly involved in manufacturing. Cuba was a rather urbanized country; even agricultural workers often lived in towns and went out to work in the fields. Rural folk were poor, to be sure, but not isolated from national or international affairs. Since the 1860s, the very openness of economy and society had made insurrections easy and frequent. The armed forces of Spain were on the verge of defeat by Cuban rebels when the United States intervened in 1898. In 1906 the armed forces were defeated by insurrectionists, provoking another U.S. intervention. As noted, in 1933 noncommissioned officers overthrew the president and the officer corps. Cuba lacked petroleum or mineral resources that would have aided the construction of a highly centralized rentier state. The country did not receive much foreign aid, nor was it heavily indebted to foreigners (the benefits of sugar price subsidies from sales in the U.S. market were highly dispersed throughout the economy). Cuba's economy was developed enough that corrupt rulers could use the funds for sultanistic purposes, but otherwise Cuba shares no evident economic prerequisite with other apparent sultanistic situations.

There is also no clear relation between Cuba's crisis of sovereignty and sultanistic tendencies. There is no doubt that U.S. intervention in Cuba during the first third of the twentieth century contributed powerfully to creating clientelist relations and to weakening the links between state, political society, and civil society. One source of power had been access to U.S. support in clientelist fashion. The United States' presence, moreover, had weakened Cuban rulers' claim to legitimacy. Indeed, there were strong sultanistic tendencies in Cuba during those decades. Yet sultanism peaked not then but later, as U.S. power over Cuba receded. In 1934 Cuba stopped being a formal U.S. protectorate upon repeal of the so-called Platt Amendment. The U.S. military presence in Cuba was modest thereafter, and the real value and centrality of U.S. investments in Cuba's economy declined in the 1930s and 1940s. Thus the connection between Cuba's early twentieth-century crisis of sovereignty and the increased sultanization of its politics in the 1950s is somewhat remote: U.S. intervention had contributed to the foundation of a pattern of politics that leaders decades later exploited to sultanize their rule.

Anti–United States nationalist politics and anti-imperialist politics surfaced in Cuba in the 1920s and 1930s as they did in many other Latin American countries. But Cuba's nationalist effervescence was aborted by the evolution of party politics described above. By the late 1930s and early 1940s, the main anti-imperialist parties, the communists and the Auténticos, chose to ally with their presumed ideological adversaries in the contest for power. Cuba's strong anti-imperialist nationalism would resurface only after the 1959 revolution.

Batista's Rule

Consistent with the preceding analysis, an important feature of Batista's rule was its nonideological character, drawing supporters freely across the ideological and partisan spectrum. After the March 1952 coup, Batista formed a four-party coalition that included his old conservative partners, the Liberals and the Democrats, but also Rolando Masferrer's Radical Union Party. Masferrer had fought alongside the communists in Spain during the civil war. In the mid-1940s he founded the Socialist Revolutionary Movement, an "action group" or violent political gang that contributed to a marked escalation of political violence in Cuba. By the early 1950s Masferrer was a senator in the Batista coalition.

Batista's most significant new partner after the March 1952 coup, however, was Eusebio Mujal, secretary-general of the Cuban Confederation of Labor. Mujal was the Auténtico Party labor politician who, with Prío's backing, had seized control of the labor confederation from the communists five years earlier. Mujal refused to back President Prío when Batista staged his coup and, instead, became a pillar of the new order. After the 1952 coup, as before, the labor confederation secretary-general was the president's ally; no revolutionary general strike succeeded in Havana until after Batista fled the country on 31 December 1958. These political parties, and the labor confederation, provided the bases of support for the Batista regime.

Another feature of Batista's rule was that he did not alter the institutionalized protections for economic elites. The elites retained access to and control over important chunks of the state. After his 1952 coup, Batista further reassured the economic elites by creating a Consultative Council of eighty members to replace the Congress. The council's members included the presidents of the sugar mill owners' association and of the sugar growers' association; the secretaries-general of the labor confederation and of its most important federations; and members from the key professional associations (bar association, medical association, etc.).[10]

To reassure the economic elites, Batista even kept many of the same top officials in such institutions as the central bank. The bank's board of directors had three representatives of the Cuban government and one each for the Cuban and the U.S. banks. In 1952 the three government representatives on the board resigned. The representative of the Cuban bankers became bank president; the alternate representative of the Cuban bankers became a regular member; the representative of the U.S. bankers did not change. More important, the nine department heads before the coup remained in their posts; when the Batista government fell in 1958, six of the nine still served in the central bank.

This reassurance of economic elites also indicates that Batista was prepared to respect merit and civil service procedures in certain sectors of his administration. He noted this respect (especially in the strategic banking and sugar sectors) with pride in the opening sentences of his published self-defense.[11] This sets the Batista regime apart from the sort of sultanistic regimes that recruit almost exclusively through patronage appointments.

In marked contrast to these guarantees to the economic elites was Batista's relationship to the armed forces. He discharged hundreds of officers, many of them career professionals who had withheld support from the coup even if they had not rallied to the constitutional regime. As Louis Pérez has aptly written, "The lumpenproletariat in uniform returned to active duty." Batista recalled the officers personally loyal to him who had been purged in 1944–45 and entrusted to them the top commands of the armed forces.

Noteworthy was the case of the Tabernilla clan. General Francisco Tabernilla Dolz became chairman of the Joint Chiefs of Staff. His son Francisco Tabernilla Palmero, retired in 1944, was recalled to active duty in March 1952 as a lieutenant and within a month was promoted to lieutenant colonel. A second son, Carlos Tabernilla, who had retired as a lieutenant, in 1952 reached the rank of colonel within two months of his recall to active duty; in 1955 he became chief of the air force. The third son, Marcelo Tabernilla, was promoted to captain on the very day in 1952 that he was recalled to active duty and to commander two months later. Tabernilla Dolz's brother-in-law, Alberto del Río Chaviano, became military chief of Oriente province (the most important command outside Havana) as a brigadier general. Similarly, Batista's brother-in-law rose from lieutenant to brigadier general in five years. Brigadier General Rafael Salas Cañizares brought three of his brothers into the command hierarchy of the national police. It was these unprofessional, politicized officers who faced Fidel Castro's insurgency and lost.[12]

After the regime's collapse, in May 1959 General Tabernilla Dolz held Batista responsible. Tabernilla noted Batista's "centralizing urge to control everything" and charged that Batista had "sown disorder, lack of discipline, and unhappiness with his favoritism in promotions." In August 1960 an even angrier Tabernilla accused Batista of having "destroyed the morale of the armed forces by using them for electoral purposes." Batista's "lust for wealth," Tabernilla charged, also "demoralized" the military. Military promotions were awarded to those personally loyal to Batista "who lacked professional capabilities and merits." Batista "violated the promotions code and indefinitely suspended the competitive examinations for military appointments." As an example, Tabernilla recorded Batista's appointment of his personal cook as a police lieutenant. Batista permitted the growth of "illegal gambling," with the proceeds going to the presidential palace. Tabernilla did acknowledge, however, receiving from Batista an appreciable though unspecified sum of money.[13]

The highly unprofessional nature of Batista's armed forces and his arbitrary decisions are typical of sultanistic regimes. Batista's policies deprived the armed forces of autonomy, subjecting them to his whims, and weakened and impeded their professionalism. This helps to distinguish his regime from the military regimes of various kinds that came to power in South America in the 1960s and 1970s. As Alfred Stepan has argued, different in many respects as were the Brazilian and the Peruvian authoritarian regimes of those years, their armed forces were quite professional as well as generally autonomous from presidential control.[14]

Batista's ideas about ruling were especially important. As Batista's former press secretary José Suárez Núñez has shown, the Batista who came to power in 1952 was a changed man since his earlier, more active years (1933–44). He watched films until late at night and thus got up late in the mornings, neglecting presidential duties until after lunch. He read little, ate a great deal, and played canasta several hours a week, requiring such games even in military barracks.[15] Batista wanted to be president in search of private pleasure, not to use the presidency for public benefit.

Neither Batista nor any of his closest associates has subsequently denied allegations of corruption. Batista's typical response to those accusations has been to quote the remarks of others to the effect that corruption exists everywhere. He quotes the former U.S. ambassador to Cuba (and former U.S. assistant secretary of state) Spruille Braden: "Of course there was always corruption . . . but also on Manhattan island, not to say the rest of New York City, there are similar situations of . . . criminality." Batista has also cited a public letter from most of his former ministers: "We do not deny that dishonest acts committed during our administration may be identified, as could also be done with regard to previous administrations in Cuba, and as occurs everywhere. It suffices to read the world press to understand that such acts occur everywhere." As if to reinforce the justification that "everybody does it so it must be all right,"

Batista appended a note of his own to his ministers' letter to call attention to the hundreds of millions of dollars invested in Cuba in the 1950s by U.S. firms.[16] This mentality justifies corruption not by denying its existence but by asserting its normality. Moreover, continued routine behavior by others, as exemplified by foreign investments, renders everyone a tolerant accomplice.

Rulers, Batista thought, ought to get rich. But even venal rulers need political support. Batista's rule rested on three fundamental concepts: distribution, growth, and order. These are not unusual in themselves. What was peculiar to the gradual sultanization of Cuban politics is the way Batista implemented them.

Distribution and Growth

The quintessential policy of Batista's regime was managing the national lottery for distributive purposes. Established under Spanish colonial times, the lottery was at the center of a great many corrupt episodes during Cuba's independent political life in the twentieth century. Batista refined the use of the lottery to serve his purposes, however. As he has written, he removed the lottery from the national budget so none of its funds would enter the national treasury.[17] Decree Law 2185 (1954) authorized the director-general of the lottery "by means of decisions approved by the president of the republic" to make use of the lottery's profits to fund educational, social welfare, and cultural organizations.[18] In effect this institutional arrangement enabled Batista to *lawfully* distribute large sums of money to reward his friends and supporters, entirely at his own discretion, unencumbered by rules. This innovation contributed to the regime's sultanization in comparison with previous epochs by increasing the ruler's personal control over growing economic resources.

Batista has given a remarkably detailed account of his use of lottery funds from 1952 to 1958. He dwells on his gifts to journalists and to the Roman Catholic Church. Because he wanted favorable reporting, journalists and other authors received over $1.3 million (the peso was equal to the U.S. dollar). Batista's lottery funds for the Catholic Church (over $1.6 million) are broken down by diocese and parish, perhaps intending to show that the bishops who had criticized him most had also gotten his money. He gave over $1.3 million to labor unions directly and another $3.6 million to their social security funds. He reports giving away over $63 million all together to specific organizations. These funds enabled him to purchase support or at least acquiescence and thus to contribute to the stability of his regime. He appends a footnote, however, indicating that "contributions in cash or in kind to specific individuals, or confidentially to individuals acting on behalf of their organizations, made by the president or by Mrs. Martha F. de Batista, directly or through the Office of the

Presidency, are omitted from this accounting." Thus even larger sums of money were used to buttress this highly personalized and clientelist regime.[19] By previous Cuban standards, Batista weakened political institutionalization and the rule of law, thus personalizing and centralizing Cuban politics even further.

Other aspects of Cuban politics promoted corruption. There are innumerable anecdotes about corruption in Cuba, but consistent with my self-imposed limitation of not citing Batista's enemies wherever I could avoid it, noted at the outset of this chapter, let us focus on the 1956 report of the Bureau of Foreign Commerce of the U.S. Department of Commerce. This report looked favorably on U.S. investments in Cuba and in general gave good marks to the Batista administration's economic policies.

First, the report noted that corruption existed before Batista's return to the presidency. An audit of Cuba's budget accounts for 1946–50, conducted by Price, Waterhouse at the Cuban government's request, found that the Cuban government's formal receipts exceeded expenditures by $59 million; nevertheless, a deficit of $104.6 million accumulated in fact. There was an unaccounted "loss" of over $160 million. The report, then, cited Cuba's own Tribunal de Cuentas's audit for 1952–53, which found that only about 61 percent of the government's revenues and only 68 percent of its expenditures were formally a part of the national budget. On the revenue side, the tribunal, and the report, expressed concern that the state funded 243 extrabudgetary accounts that had little supervision and less accountability.[20]

The regime's distributive objectives were not limited to the personal enrichment of those it favored; its development policies fostered the use of funds earmarked for development for distributive purposes as well. For example, the U.S. Bureau of Foreign Commerce noted the allocation of funds by the Bank for Social and Economic Development (BANDES), which the regime founded in 1954: "Primary emphasis was placed on public works projects providing temporary employment but contributing little to increased national production. Less than 10 percent of the allocations could be classified in a production and development category.[21]

A similar distributive orientation was evident in the social security system. Cuba lacked a unified system, relying instead on forty-seven different social security entities, each of which administered its own funds. The existence and capacities of such funds depended on the political clout of the would-be beneficiaries; twenty-four of the agencies served the more powerful labor unions. Appointments to their boards were also linked to friendship and personal influence rather than to competence or merit.[22]

In order for funds to be distributed, the economy had to grow, and it did, especially between 1953 and 1957. In constant 1937 pesos, real per capita income rose from 123 in 1953 to 154 in 1957. A less flattering comparison matches per capita income on the eve of the 1952–53 economic recession, which was 135, to per capita income during the civil war year of 1958, which was 142.[23]

Some of this growth was financed by the state's development banks. This in turn posed another issue: the regime's use of the state's development banks, and especially of BANDES financing, to require private business firms to take on regime leaders as business partners. Many BANDES loans were contingent on accepting Batista and his family as shareholders. Consider the account of a developmentally minded business executive:

> He and his son Rubén in the latter years of my business ventures, specifically the . . . factory company, he became my "business associate." They were minority shareholders; exactly, if my memory does not fail me, their investment was $400,000 which, I will never forget, his son Rubén had in cash in a briefcase and gave them to me to buy shares of stock on a morning at his house in Primera Avenida in Miramar way back I believe around 1953 or 1954. . . . They never interfered at all with the management of our business and they always received a good return on that investment . . . I was never Batistiano by heart but due to my perhaps excessive business ambitions I must confess I was Batistiano by convenience.[24]

More generally, Batista's former press secretary, Suárez Núñez, claims that Batista was subtle in his exercise of corruption. He avoided stealing directly from the Treasury and instead relied on payments of commissions (typically 30 percent of the cost) for government contracts—contracts that were indeed honored. This helps explain Batista's devotion to public works, noted above: they created jobs and generated kickbacks. Suárez Núñez also confirms that the BANDES was Batista's preferred institution to build up his private fortune.[25]

Thus the pattern of economic growth, as much as the pattern of distribution, featured the appropriation of wealth by regime incumbents in highly personalized fashion that circumvented or broke the rule of law. Batista's innovation was not the practice of corruption but its orchestration by one man; corruption in previous administrations had been more democratic too. This shift was consistent with the regime's sultanization.

Political Order

Successor to a weakly institutionalized constitutional regime and mindful that his earlier rule had been strengthened by his sponsorship of a new constitution in 1940, Batista's regime in the 1950s rested in part on constitutional hypocrisy.

The regime formally sponsored presidential elections in 1954 and in 1958. In preparation for his presidential campaign for the 1954 elections, Batista even formally "resigned" as president (installing his long-standing associate, Andrés Domingo y Morales del Castillo as president for a few weeks). Former president Ramón Grau agreed to run as the opposition's candidate in the 1954 elections. Nonetheless, expecting massive fraud, shortly before the election Grau withdrew from the race and called for an electoral boycott. Batista was "elected" without formal opposition.

The Batista regime differed from more clearly sultanistic regimes, however, because there was an opposition operating within the permissible constitutional norms. In the 1958 presidential elections, former president Grau and Carlos Márquez Sterling ran for president as opposition candidates; their supporters ran for lesser offices. Batista's prime minister, Andrés Rivero Agüero, was the official candidate; he was proclaimed the winner by a share of the votes far greater than that allotted to the combined opposition presidential candidates. That parts of this tolerated opposition were manufactured by the regime reduced their credibility then and qualifies them conceptually for the label "pseudo-opposition."

The regime was not truly bound by its own constitutional and electoral law procedures. In the 1954 elections, the regime in fact chose eighteen members of the opposition whom it declared elected as members of the Senate (seventeen took their seats) to avoid the embarrassment of controlling every Senate seat. In 1958 the regime's electoral fraud was so massive that even U.S. ambassador Earl Smith, who had befriended Batista by this point, would write that Batista had failed to live up to "his solemn promise to me [that] he would hold free and open elections acceptable to the people."[26] Similarly, the regime canceled the constitutionally required 1956 nationwide congressional elections.

Batista believed that his tolerance of some opposition would gain him support, above all in the U.S. government. For this reason he authorized various "dialogues" with civic groups to find a solution to the problem of political legitimacy, whose only plausible outcome was his own resignation. Batista met personally with some of the leaders of these civic groups, and he deputized others to do so, in private and in public, effectively keeping the illegitimacy of his rule in the public eye. The most prominent of these "dialogues" occurred in 1955–56, led by Cosme de la Torriente and the Society of Friends of the Republic; other mediations were attempted by the Roman Catholic bishops and by the Havana Bar and the National Medical Association. Because he had no intention of resigning, the eventual failure of these negotiations further eroded his base of power. Some of the civic group leaders (especially among the lawyers and medical doctors) felt so deceived that they openly joined the opposition to the regime, thereby weakening Batista's initial coalition from 1952.

Batista's constitutionalist ambivalence is equally evident in the regime's handling of press censorship. Though the frequency and intensity of censorship increased as the regime was challenged by the insurrection, censorship remained remarkably porous. For example, from 1952 to 1958 the Cuban press published twenty-five attacks against the regime by Fidel Castro. Nine of these appeared either before Castro's 1953 attack on the Moncada military barracks or in 1955 immediately after Batista had granted him amnesty. More noteworthy is the publication of thirteen of Castro's statements while he was already a political exile dedicated to the violent overthrow of the Batista regime, as well as of two major revolutionary manifestos, in 1957 and 1958, while Castro was in the mountains fighting Batista. Castro's interview with Herbert Matthews of the *New York Times* was also published in *Bohemia,* the leading Cuban news magazine.[27]

Ted Gurr has hypothesized that a regime's coercive control varies curvilinearly with the size and resources of its repressive capacity and with the severity of its sanctions, control being least when size, resources, and severity are at intermediate levels.[28] That was an accurate characterization of the Batista regime. Or to put it more simply, Batista was an inefficient dictator. His press censorship and his constitutional manipulation were distinctly inconsistent. That inconsistency contributed directly to the regime's unraveling: there was enough constitutionalism and press freedom to expose the regime's illegitimacy but not enough repression to crush the opposition.

Much of the revulsion against the Batista regime stemmed from its acts of repression. Some of the repression was lawful: some who committed acts of violence were arrested, brought before a court of law, and sentenced to prison. Much of it, however, was unlawful because the regime's security forces, as we shall see below, were grossly unprofessional; they indulged all too readily in police brutality. This very unprofessionalism is also an important explanation of the ultimate failure of this behavior.

Batista's response to these accusations has been twofold: that the acts of his opponents were worse, and that the acts of any regime's forces are difficult to control in the midst of civil war. He claims that some of his supporters have accused him of not having been harsh enough.[29] It is untrue, however, that the regime's acts of repression occurred only during civil war. An exemplary witness is former U.S. ambassador Arthur Gardner. Gardner became Batista's personal friend. In his writings, Batista praises and quotes Gardner, calling him a credible witness to his presidency.[30] Therefore it is appropriate to quote from Ambassador Gardner's secret telegram describing killings in Havana in February 1957, far from what was still a weak insurgency in eastern Cuba:

> We here now convinced recurrent killings of persons government maintains are oppositionists and terrorists are actually work of police and army. At least three such killings have occurred Habana alone during past few days. Official explanation is that men were apparently killed by other oppositionists. However . . . Legal Attaché . . . received indirect admissions culpability within police circles . . . from other evidence police responsibility at least one case. This all part attempt (1) answer force with counterforce (2) give justification continuing suspension constitutional guarantees (3) throw fear into active insurrectionaries (4) stop terroristic activities including bombings.[31]

The reliance on repression does not mean, however, that the law and the courts did not work at all. They did, but mainly in regulating the economy and society apart from the maintenance of public order. The regime's agreements with economic elites depended in part on its general willingness to honor the independence and efficacy of the civil courts to settle social and economic disputes. The courts lacked independence in political or military spheres, however. Their capacities and constraints thus summarized the rewards the regime accorded to economic elites and the unrestrained punishment it reserved for its opponents.

The Breakdown of the Batista Regime

Studying the breakdown of the Batista regime requires more extensive treatment than can be given here; such a study also overlaps with a different topic—the outbreak of the revolution. Nonetheless, it is worth emphasizing that much about the Batista regime's collapse is best understood as derived from its essential characteristics, which made it incapable of resisting the revolutionary forces.

The regime lacked an ideology; indeed, it even lacked guiding ideas of a general sort other than the goal of generating prosperity. As economic growth faltered during the second half of 1958 and as Batista's continuation in office seemed more a liability than an asset in maintaining political order, its erstwhile supporters deserted: it lost the economic elites, the U.S. government, rank-and-file labor union leaders, and so forth. The regime's political parties failed to rally the population and neglected the tasks of political mobilization. The lack of loyalty in Cuban politics made such desertions seem not abnormal. No political, societal, or economic cleavages impeded them. Many politicians had switched allegiances again and again during the preceding twenty years. Why not do so again in order to remain, as ever, on the winning side?

The revolutionaries had put forth a program that emphasized Batista's removal from power. The ruler himself was the fundamental target of the revolution. He had to go, making impossible the sort of compromise between the armed forces and the civilian opposition evident in the 1980s in much of South and Central America. The social and economic content of the revolutionary program seemed only a variant of the ideas of Cuba's moderate left. The programs of revolutionaries denounced corruption and unconstitutionality and promised the rule of constitutional law. The puritanical streak that would appear in the 1960s was at best a flicker in the late 1950s. The Roman Catholic Church as an institution played no role in Batista's overthrow, though many individual Catholics, of course, did so on their own. Religion was a minor factor in this process.

Only landlords had to worry about a revolutionary land reform, whose terms nonetheless seemed moderate enough. The economic planks of revolutionaries seemed to emphasize economic growth from which many could profit. The demands for the expropriation of foreign property had never exceeded the realm of public utilities, and even with regard to the utilities there seemed to be some backtracking. It seemed, therefore, that the guarantees for economic elites would continue into the 1960s just as they had survived regime changes since the 1930s. In December 1958 as in March 1952, in the end organized interest groups stood aside, or even welcomed the regime's fall.[32]

The most stunning feature of the Batista regime's breakdown, however, is that it happened so suddenly and so thoroughly. In mid-1958 Fidel Castro's guerrillas numbered only about three hundred, and his brother Raúl Castro commanded another one hundred. Both groups of rebels operated mainly in the mountains of eastern Cuba in Oriente province. Six months later they marched into Havana. Why? Within the context of this chapter, one answer lies in the structure of the state, in particular the structure of the armed forces.

Batista had succeeded in deprofessionalizing the officer corps of Cuba's armed forces. When in 1956 many of the remaining professional officers, led by Colonel Ramón Barquín, sought to stage a coup, they were defeated and jailed, and the armed forces were thereby deprived of their services.

The army's military campaigns against the guerrillas were inept. Many officers simply did not know how to do their jobs. When Fidel Castro's forces landed in eastern Cuba on 2 December 1956, they were not pursued for three days, giving them a chance to learn their way around the region. After six days of active pursuit, the army declared victory and withdrew from the mountainous region of eastern Cuba, leaving the rebels with valuable time to organize, lick their wounds, plan strategy, and recruit peasants. This pattern of occasional army offensives followed by declarations of victory and military withdrawal was repeated several times throughout 1957.[33]

By early 1958 other aspects of the crisis within the army became clear: government military offensives collapsed through defections and desertions and through the simple unwillingness of many field officers and troops to fight on behalf of the Batista regime. (The army's soldiers were volunteers, not conscripts.) Afraid of conspiracies within the military, specifically in the Havana garrisons, Batista had to keep his most trusted officers, those politically loyal to him, in command in Havana. He also needed loyal troops in Havana, so that the officers dispatched to fight the rebellion in eastern Cuba were those least willing to fight on his behalf. They did not.

To protect the sugar harvest so that exports would continue and thereby to keep his pledge to the economic elites, Batista prevented the army from undertaking offensives against the guerrillas during the harvest season. The troops were committed to fixed defensive positions to protect sugar plantations and mills. This meant, for example, that the army launched its last major offensive in June 1958 as the rainy season began. Its motorized equipment soon got stuck in the mud, and the offensive failed.

By mid-1958 the army began to retreat in eastern Cuba whenever the rebels attacked. The main constraint on rebel victory became the lack of personnel to occupy the territory that the army seemed willing to yield. The rebel bands did not really beat the army; the army beat itself. Or more precisely, the capacity of the state to defend itself declined drastically as the military collapsed from within. The rebels took advantage of the structural implosion of the armed forces that occurred during the last six months of 1958.

By late 1958 the collapse of the army from within accelerated. In November Batista uncovered a coup attempt led by the general who was chief of army operations. A bit later another coup attempt was foiled, this one led by the chief of the navy air corps. In December the chairman of the Joint Chiefs, General Francisco Tabernilla Dolz, with one of his sons and his brother-in-law, visited the U.S. embassy to propose to organize a joint coup against Batista. General Eulogio Cantillo, chief of army operations in Oriente province, the man directly responsible for the conduct of the war against the guerrillas, opened direct talks with Fidel Castro.[34]

On New Year's Eve, Batista, the Tabernilla clan, and their closest civilian and military associates simply gave up and fled the country. In their absence the armed forces disintegrated. At that time no guerrilla forces threatened the capital city of Havana. The military had not been defeated in the battle of Havana—there never was any such battle, because Batista surrendered state power.

In short, it is the crisis within the state, and especially within the military, that explains why Batista fell. Batista's sultanistic tendencies were his undoing: his purge of professional officers, his distrust of his own appointees, his insistence on being his own field commander (despite his total absence of field command experience), the lack of loyalties within the structures he had created, the absence of commitment to fundamental ideas, and the low morale among the troops induced by overwhelming evidence of corruption. The state entered this crisis because it had become more sultanized than ever in the past. Batista's manner of rule, and the nature of the regime he designed, explains why and how he fell.

6
. . . .

The Somoza Regime in Nicaragua

John A. Booth

This chapter explores the development and extent of sultanism in the Somoza dynasty of Nicaragua and the rebellion against and eventual collapse of the regime of Anastasio Somoza Debayle in the late 1970s. I use both aggregate data from the 1950s through the 1970s and descriptive data to examine Nicaraguan sultanism and to reveal how the rate and nature of economic growth, income and wealth distribution, and the last Somoza regime's response to unrest may have contributed to the rebellion that ushered in the Sandinista revolution of 1979–90.

Anastasio Somoza García was appointed head of the Nicaraguan National Guard in late 1932 as U.S. occupation forces were being withdrawn after their futile attempt to defeat Augusto César Sandino's antioccupation and revolutionary guerrilla movement.[1] Breaking with the political neutrality of the officer corps enforced under U.S. tutelage, Somoza García and his uncle, President Juan Bautista Sacasa, began to appoint officers with Liberal Party loyalty. To consolidate his hold on the Guard, in early 1934 Somoza García conspired with senior officers to assassinate Sandino. He then began to maneuver to capture the presidency, which he accomplished by deposing Sacasa in 1936 and engineering an electoral victory for himself. Using the National Guard for control and the Liberal Party (which he rechristened Liberal Nationalist—PLN) as a vehicle for patronage and organization, Somoza García ruled Nicaragua until his assassination in 1956. His two sons, Luis and Anastasio Somoza Debayle, succeeded him, relying on the Guard and PLN jointly to control the Nicaraguan polity. After Luis died from a heart attack in 1967, Anastasio Somoza Debayle alone ruled Nicaragua. For analytical purposes, one may reasonably divide the dynasty into three separate regimes, each with certain distinctive characteristics despite their many common elements—rule by Somoza García (1936–56), joint rule by Luis and Anastasio Somoza Debayle with Luis ascendant (1956–67), and rule by Anastasio Somoza Debayle alone (1967–79). Based on the definition of sultanism provided by Chehabi and Linz in chapter 1, I believe one may characterize all three Somoza regimes as having sultanistic tendencies, but I consider the last, that of Anastasio Somoza Debayle, the purest example of sultanism.

Nicaragua's Liberal and Conservative Parties, clan- and region-based factions with roots in the colonial period, traditionally served as vehicles for patronage. Because dynasty founder Anastasio Somoza García relied on the rather broad clientelist network of the PLN to establish and operate his regime (and later on a co-opted Conservative Party as well), his regime should probably be viewed as having significant patrimonial traits. Somoza García used the National Guard to cow or eliminate his opponents, but the Liberal Nationalist Party was his vehicle for political and bureaucratic control and distribution of patronage. The party was eventually transformed into a tool for Somoza García's personal control of the state, lost much of its ideological distinctiveness, and came to be run by relatives and cronies of the dictator. Nevertheless, Liberalism was the more popular in the early decades of the century and enjoyed a wide clientelist base in the Nicaraguan polity. Knut Walter has shown that, despite its personalistic and corrupting features, Somoza García's regime made significant progress in modernizing the Nicaraguan state and agroexport economy, and that it definitively subordinated to the state the once powerful regional caudillos of both parties.[2] When a significant pro-democracy movement arose among urban middle sectors and some disaffected elements of his own party in the mid- and late 1940s, Somoza García turned both to organized labor and to key Conservative leaders to further broaden the base of support for the regime.[3]

The joint regime of Luis and Anastasio Somoza Debayle (1956–67), in which the older Luis was the more influential, may have developed an even broader clientelist linkage system during the 1960s than that extant under their father. In addition to relying on the PLN and Conservatives, the brothers built new links to agricultural and nascent industrial bourgeois factions.[4] This occurred especially during the period of rapid modernization, industrialization, and economic growth spawned by the Central American Common Market after 1960. During this epoch, with Luis at the helm of the PLN and usually in the presidency (Anastasio commanded the National Guard), there was sufficient political liberalization that some observers expected a transition to democracy. The political economy of Somocismo so broadened the alliance network of the regime that it produced a convergence of Nicaragua's three major bourgeois sectors. This convergence involved increasing cooperation and shared investments among the three groups of capitalists[5]—one centered in the Banco Nicaragüense, one centered in the Banco de América, and the third centered in the Somoza family. The regime itself benefited directly from the collaboration among these powerful economic sectors because they not only represented major economic interests but, through cooperation with the Somocista capital sector, also promoted tolerance of the regime.

The death of Luis Somoza brought about a rather rapid deterioration of the system into nearly pure sultanism under his younger brother Anastasio, who like his father was known by the nickname "Tacho." The new ruler's repressive and violent personality traits, lack of political skill, and worsening alcoholism, combined with institutional decay, increasing cronyism, and corruption, characterized the last Somoza's regime (1967–79).[6] It was a period particularly notorious for dictatorial caprice and excess, even given the checkered histories of Nicaragua and the dynasty. These excesses of greed, corruption, and repression broke down long-functioning systems of co-optation of other actual and potential powerholders. They also alienated many former clients and allies of the Somozas and generated many new enemies for the regime. The political economy of Somocismo changed rapidly in these circumstances. The convergence of the three great sectors of the bourgeoisie stalled and then began to reverse in the 1970s. Anastasio Jr.'s greed and economic mismanagement became too much for the other capitalist factions to tolerate, so that they began to reject the Somoza regime.[7]

Characteristics of the Three Somoza Regimes

Although all three regimes shared certain characteristics, there were also significant differences between them.

Genesis

Because of both internal and geopolitical traits, the Somoza dynasty developed in a society that had suffered repeated crises of sovereignty throughout its national history. Liberal-Conservative conflict led to repeated civil wars, often with external involvement. Geography proved to be Nicaragua's destiny in that the United States, Britain, and other powers were attracted by the ease of transit across the Central American isthmus there and particularly by prospects for constructing an interoceanic waterway. After the United States arranged in 1903 to build a canal in Panama instead, protecting the monopoly of that facility became a primary motor for U.S. intervention in Nicaragua. Foreign meddling in Nicaraguan politics after 1900 was extensive, especially by the United States, whose troops occupied the country for most of the period from 1912 until 1933 in an effort to maintain its canal monopoly in Panama and contain what were believed to be threatening leftist and nationalistic elements in the Nicaraguan polity.

In only a minor way, if at all, may we attribute the onset of sultanism with the regime of Anastasio Somoza García in Nicaragua to the decay of authoritarian rule. The Liberal regime of modernizing dictator José Santos Zelaya had been ended by U.S. intervention in 1909. The political climate in Nicaragua for the next quarter century before Anastasio Somoza García seized power in 1936 was extraordinarily unstable politically. Before 1936 there took place repeated brief rebellions (by both Conservatives and Liberals), two civil wars started by the Liberals (who had been frozen out of power by U.S. intervention on behalf of the Conservatives), U.S. occupation and manipulation of domestic politics, significant decay of the Nicaraguan state and its infrastructure and fiscal resources, the six-year guerrilla rebellion against U.S. occupation by Sandino, and the U.S.-backed and -directed counterinsurgency war against the rebels. During the last several years of this political chaos Nicaragua also experienced severe economic difficulties because of the Great Depression.

Nicaragua's populace in the 1930s consisted substantially of illiterate peasants, mostly either small-scale subsistence farmers or tenants, sharecroppers, or wage laborers on the large coffee and cattle estates. The level of modernization of the Nicaraguan state and society had advanced substantially during the Zelaya period (1893–1909) but was badly eroded by ensuing wars, the U.S. occupation and U.S. financial receivership of key state revenue sources, and the depression. One of the few modern institutions left in Nicaragua by the time of Somoza García's ascent to power was the U.S.-trained and battle-hardened National Guard. Somoza and his son Anastasio Somoza Debayle, who succeeded him as Guard commander in 1956, used the Guard's institutional capability as their central instrument of political control. They took periodic, if not continuous, pains to keep the Guard modernizing and technically capable in many respects. The Somozas also manipulated the Guard's officer corps and the institution as a whole in ways that undermined professionalism but strengthened their personal control over it. The Guard operated Nicaragua's telegraph, radio, telephone, mail, police, customs, and tax collection systems.

Under Somoza García the Nicaraguan state made major advances in currency and trade regulation, national and municipal government organization, social security and labor legislation, and the promotion of economic development. Under the joint rule of the brothers Somoza Debayle in the 1950s and 1960s, the Central Bank and certain other administrative agencies developed further institutionally, eventually outstripping other parts of the Nicaraguan bureaucracy. The development of these relatively modern and capable institutions enhanced the Somozas' control over Nicaraguan society and their personal enrichment within it. As I will note later, however, not even those institutions vital to the dictatorship escaped severe problems of corruption and manipulation.

The personality of each Somoza may have had a significant impact on the nature of each regime.[8] By virtually all accounts, all three shared the personality traits of gregariousness, considerable personal charm, intelligence, craftiness, and ruthlessness. Luis and his father each ruled with a mix of repression and co-optation, leavened with a willingness to employ reform when it might strengthen the regime or buy off or neutralize some enemy. However, the personality of Anastasio the younger introduced several problematic features. Having been reared in the presence of tortures and having participated in them as a youth may well have contributed to a particularly violent and repressive streak that many people observed in him. Pedro Joaquín Chamorro, later editor of the opposition newspaper *La Prensa*, has graphically described his own torture in 1956. Falsely accused of participating in the 1956 assassination of Somoza García, Chamorro was held for several months and repeatedly tortured by security officials, at times including Anastasio Somoza Debayle himself. Chamorro also reported that certain prisoners during that era were held in cages next to wild animals in a Somoza family zoo in the garden of the presidential residence.[9]

Anastasio Somoza Debayle also developed a serious and worsening problem with alcohol that increasingly manifested itself in the early 1970s. His older brother Luis apparently feared the possible results of these tendencies, for until his death in 1967 Luis opposed his younger sibling's assumption of the presidency. Many aspects of the quick decay of the third Somoza's regime may fairly be laid at the door of these circumstances—increasing corruption of both the leader and his appointees, the breakdown of formerly regime-sustaining alliances with critical segments of the national bourgeoisie, and the increasing violence and repressiveness of the National Guard.

Regime

Each Somoza's regime manifested to some degree most of the fundamental characteristics outlined by Chehabi and Linz in their introductory chapters. Each practiced constitutional hypocrisy; the constitution was frequently altered by a compliant legislature dominated by PLN loyalists to suit the wishes of the dictator who controlled legislative seats and the payoffs they engendered. Both Anastasios nominally left the post of commander of the National Guard in order to be eligible for the presidency yet retained effective continual control of the institution via a deputy. Thus the appearance of constitutionality was usually maintained even though the constitution and national institutions were largely at the whim of the Somoza in power at the moment. The Somozas' sham constitutionalism, holding of elections (always fraudulently manipulated), and extolling of democracy were helpful in keeping the external support of the United States. This fig leaf of constitutionalism helped to sustain flows of foreign economic and military assistance and to retain the tolerance or outright friendship of several U.S. administrations.

The degree of personalism in the Nicaraguan state was extreme. The Somozas practiced nepotism extensively, for both corrupt and tactical purposes. With regard to the tactical uses of nepotism, the Somozas married well— Anastasio the elder, from a second-tier Liberal family of declining economic fortunes, gained status by marrying into the Debayle clan, an influential Liberal family. This practice continued in the next generation. Somoza relatives also occupied key positions of power. For instance, General José Somoza, illegitimate brother of Luis and Anastasio Jr., served as commander of the Guard's major infantry force, the Third Battalion, during the 1970s. Anastasio Somoza Portocarrero, son of Anastasio Somoza Debayle, commanded the Basic Infantry Training School (EEBI). Somoza Portocarrero was widely viewed in Nicaragua as heir apparent to the regime when his father's government fell in 1979.

The Nicaraguan *state* under the Somozas manifested something of a split personality. On the one hand, after the decay wreaked by almost twenty years of U.S. occupation and civil wars, the country was significantly modernized and made more competent for promoting economic growth.[10] On the other hand, for much of the life of the dynasty, the state was widely characterized by bureaucratic corruption and a lack of legal-rational bureaucratic norms. In addition to pursuing developmental goals, Somoza García expanded the government and its functions so as to increase the resources for the patronage with which he purchased loyalty. His collaborators received lucrative government concessions and contracts, public jobs, access to bribes, and tax exemptions.

Many "ghost" public employees—some on several agency payrolls, never appeared at their jobs except to pick up their paychecks. The dictator himself received honoraria, salaries, fees, and administrative "rights" from dozens of public agencies and concessions such as lumbering and mining. Somoza Debayle did ostensibly expand the state to ameliorate growing social strains in the 1960s and 1970s. Among agencies created for such purposes, often doing little but siphoning off their resources, including considerable U.S. economic aid, were the Agrarian Institute, the National Agricultural Technology Institute, the Institute for Peasant Welfare, the Family Center for Rural Education, the Nicaraguan Housing Bank, and the National Housing Institute. But Somoza and the increasingly corrupt cohorts he put in charge of these agencies looted them at an accelerating rate. As I have written elsewhere, "Bigger government meant more resources to steal or with which to buy friends. Corruption of all kinds abounded, diverting public resources to private ends. For example, more and more Somoza relatives held key public offices. . . . [T]he traditional forms of corruption, the main cement of the regime, continued—bribery, conflict of interest, embezzlement, theft, and fraud."[11] Competency played a much less important role in obtaining positions and advancement than personal or partisan connections to the ruler. Not all public employees in Nicaragua were corrupt or in personal thrall to the dictator, of course, but so many were that the prevailing ethos of the public sector was exploitative, venal, and often abusive of the clientele.

As head of the national reconstruction committee established after the 1972 Managua earthquake, Anastasio the younger profiteered heavily and shamelessly from foreign relief funds and from public reconstruction efforts. He invested heavily in myriad enterprises that could profit from the reconstruction process, the shape and details of which he personally controlled. He purchased extensive tracts of land and resold them to the state for development, urban relocation, and reconstruction projects. He invested in real estate, the sale of demolition and construction equipment and supplies, and the concrete and paving businesses. Much of this was new investment that intruded into economic sectors once reserved for bourgeois allies of the regime. Somoza Debayle's personal wealth reportedly multiplied rapidly because of such rapacity.[12]

The least corrupt and most competent area of the public sector under each of the Somozas involved the promotion of economic development, which directly benefited the national bourgeoisie and the by then immensely wealthy Somoza family. Carlos Vilas notes, "The expansion, diversification, and modernization of the economy that began in the 1950s was greatly assisted by the state, especially through the construction of a road and electricity infrastructure and through financing provided by the Banco Nacional [National Bank]. . . . [T]he state provided cheap loans and technical assistance for the promotion of such activities as tobacco, beef, shrimp, bananas, irrigated rice—in many of which the Somoza family had a share."[13] The Central Bank, the National Bank, the National Foreign and Internal Commerce Institute, the National Development Institute, certain planning agencies, and utilities and road building programs contributed significantly to promoting and managing Nicaragua's rapid economic growth, infrastructure development, and industrialization. Despite favoritism in some programs, under the Somozas bureaucratic competence prevailed in economic development promotion.

Deprofessionalization of the Armed Forces

Within the National Guard, the core of their political power, the Somozas used a mix of legal and illegal, positive and negative, humane and cruel ends to keep the institution consistently functioning as an instrument of their personal will. The Guard became efficient yet corrupt, modernized yet paternalistic, and it was simultaneously isolated from the populace and insinuated into the most intimate crannies of Nicaraguan society.[14] The Guard exercised an enormous array of functions, operating the postal service, national radio and telegraph networks, the national health service, and the railways as well as customs and immigration. It conducted all police, espionage, and military business. The military branch of the Guard was expanded, its functions and responsibilities were increased, and training and equipment were frequently upgraded in order to build institutional capacity, morale, and esprit. (The United States played a key role in the modernizing of Guard equipment and personnel by supplying money, equipment, advisers, and training in Nicaragua and at U.S. bases in both the United States and Panama.) National Guard pay and benefits were regularly increased to keep both officers and enlisted men content and generally loyal to each other, the institution, and the Somozas.

On the negative side, the Somozas encouraged a servile loyalty within the Guard that undermined the very professionalism otherwise being promoted. The Somozas were highly paternalistic with Guard officers and troops, dispensing personal favors to win loyalty. Many Somoza family members held Guard posts, and other internal spies abounded. Punishment of malcontents or of plotters against the regime was often draconian. Assignments and retirements were manipulated to disrupt suspected potential conspirators. Corruption at both grand and petty scales, abuse of power, and even criminal behavior were tolerated in order to buy loyalty. Such practices in themselves alienated the civilian population, of course, but the Guard was deliberately isolated from the general population. Its officers and troops lived on bases or in housing segregated from civilians, enjoying special commissaries and other material privileges as well as virtual exemption from prosecution for crimes. The repressive behavior of the National Guard and its flagrant corruption eventually caused most citizens to fear and detest the organization.

Under the tutelage of Anastasio Somoza Debayle, by the 1970s the Guard had become even more corrupt and less disciplined, despite further improvements in size, training, and equipment. So eroded was the institution's discipline that when the Managua earthquake struck in 1972, the National Guard effectively disbanded as soldiers attended to their personal lives and families and officers looted and profiteered from international relief aid. However, when confronted with its ultimate test, the 1979 final Sandinista offensive, the National Guard, despite its brutality and ruthlessness, fought hard and acquitted itself better militarily than most outsiders expected.[15]

Absence of the Rule of Law

Under each of the Somozas the rule of law was badly flawed or distorted, often practiced only symbolically and superficially at best, and sometimes not at all. Consistent with the constitutional hypocrisy of the regime, the courts and law were invoked to provide a mask of legalism for government corruption and criminality. Police and courts were corrupt, abused their authority for their own enrichment, and accepted, solicited, and coerced bribes. Even the police reportedly were deeply involved in criminal activity of many kinds. Judges and prosecutors at all levels were beholden to the Somozas for their appointments and manipulated judicial proceedings to fulfill the expressed desires of the regime, including the intimidation and harassment of opponents. Friends of the regime were virtually exempt from criminal prosecution. Special secret tribunals were used to prosecute political enemies and suspected military plotters. When ordinary judicial proceedings were insufficient to the task, the National Guard employed torture, imprisonment in inhumane conditions, and murder. Human rights violations were frequent and often severe. States of constitutional exception were declared on several occasions, suspending normal constitutional protections (badly honored, to be sure) in order to free the security forces for their repression of opposition. All these problems with the rule of law, present from the beginning of the dynasty, intensified sharply under the rule of Anastasio Somoza Debayle in 1967 and marked his regime as the most fully sultanistic of the three.[16]

Unlike many other sultanistic rulers, the Somozas did tolerate a "semiop-position," that is, "those groups that are not dominant or represented in the governing group but that are willing to participate in power without fundamentally challenging the system."[17] The large, regionally based population of Conservative Party identifiers, elites, and bourgeoisie in Nicaragua existed throughout the three Somozas' regimes. At least during certain periods, key Conservative elements played the role of semiopposition by tolerating the Somozas in power, in part because under the rule of Somoza García and his elder son Luis their enterprises and economic security were respected. At other times Conservatives were co-opted into collaborating with the regime with positions, patronage, and sharing of spoils. *La Prensa*, an opposition newspaper owned by the Conservative Chamorro family, was frequently intimidated and harassed, but it was never closed down and for four decades served as a symbol of resistance to the dynasty.

At times when a real Conservative opposition, alone or in coalition (as in 1948 or 1967, for instance), threatened an effective electoral challenge to the regime, it suffered the much greater repression characteristic of other sultanistic regimes discussed in chapters 1 and 2. The opposition's leaders would be repressed and supplanted by the Somozas with a fully collaborationist Conservative slate, which Nicaraguans always referred to derisively as *zancudos* (mosquitoes). Other opposition parties also existed but were harassed and repressed, especially when they allied with the Conservatives to challenge the government in an election. The reformist Independent Liberals broke away from the PLN the late 1940s. A Social Christian movement arose in the 1960s and split into two parties. There was also the pro-Moscow Nicaraguan Socialist (Communist) Party, which, with its unions, collaborated with the regime of Anastasio Somoza García against the 1948 pro-democracy struggle before being driven underground. This collaboration between the regime and the communists and unions occurred when Somoza García's rule was challenged by pro-democracy forces in the mid-1940s. Somoza García "extended a hand to organized labor and the political left . . . in order to reconstruct a new political coalition favorable to the regime."[18] Later, from among these parties and other opposition sectors there sprang more than twenty rebel groups in the early 1960s, but only the Sandinistas survived the National Guard's counterinsurgency measures.

Exile movements against the dynasty were commonplace, centered especially in other Central American capitals. Dissidents within Nicaragua often traveled to neighboring countries to meet and plan, especially to Costa Rica, where many Nicaraguans had worked and had family. The two nations had a history of border conflicts and interference in each others' internal affairs.[19]

Costa Rica's democratic traditions apparently made many people and officials there sympathetic to anti-Somoza plots. Costa Rican president José Figueres Ferrer supported a Nicaraguan exile effort to overthrow the Somoza brothers in 1959. In 1978–79 San José, the Costa Rican capital, became a center of anti-Somoza organizing and recruiting among exile Nicaraguans and sympathetic Costa Ricans. Several Sandinista National Liberation Front (Frente Sandinista de Liberación Nacional—FSLN) training camps and bases existed inside Costa Rica's northern border with the tolerance of Costa Rican President Rodrigo Carazo Odio and other authorities. The opposition coalition's shadow government, the National Reconstruction Junta and its cabinet, resided very publicly in San José during the final three months of the war that eventually toppled the last Somoza.

Social Base

At the time of Anastasio Somoza García's rise to power in 1936, Liberalism was widely recognized as having broader support among Nicaraguans than Conservatism. Each partisan grouping was a collection of clans with backing that cut across class lines and was led by prominent families. Somoza García's rechristened Liberal Nationalist Party at the outset enjoyed a significant natural base among Liberal identifiers. The loyalty of many upper- and middle-class Liberals was reinforced and encouraged over the decades with the jobs, patronage, and access to corrupt gains made possible by government appointments and service. However, in time the Somozas' corruption and repression, especially in its most noxious forms as practiced by the National Guard, alienated many Nicaraguans. By the 1970s the depredations of the last Somoza regime had disgusted and angered enough people that many former allies of Anastasio Somoza Debayle had turned against him, his government, and the National Guard and joined the opposition.

Economic elites were long tolerant of the Somozas because of the dynasty's success in promoting growth. Many, including Conservatives, had benefited from enterprises or sectors of production effectively reserved for them. Certain businesses or areas of the economy appear to have been tacitly conceded to important bourgeois families, sometimes with explicit agreements of the Somozas not to compete with them in exchange for shares in their firms. As Walter writes, Somoza "seems to have been very respectful of the more important Conservative capitalists and their business ventures."[20] But from the outset each of the Somozas in power had also extracted tribute from other capitalists. One common technique was to demand, with no investment by a Somoza, a substantial share of the stock in a new enterprise. The Somozas also received substantial bribes masquerading as consulting and advisory fees from both domestic and foreign firms. They set up in business and invested with members of their own clan, whose privileged access to state capital and contracts led Wheelock Román to call it the "loaded dice group."[21] The Somozas were therefore never hostile to capital or business in general, even that of other bourgeoisie or party groups, and helped create and nurture a development process that generally enriched the upper class.

By the mid-1970s, however, the political crises of the last regime and its economic mismanagement became seriously threatening to the interests of the collaborating bourgeoisie. Moreover, Anastasio Somoza Debayle's excessive greed and his encroachment on the economic turf traditionally reserved for other bourgeois sectors in the wake of the 1972 earthquake represented a great threat to many fortunes. Somoza Debayle moved into or aggressively expanded his investments in several businesses such as construction, building materials, and equipment. In so doing he intruded on a large share of the profits of the investors who had, by tacit accord, long dominated those industries before the earthquake. Influential economic groups became increasingly mobilized politically in reformist causes, and by late 1978 virtually all of the bourgeoisie had deserted the regime.[22]

Foreign aid on occasion constituted a substitute for domestic allies during moments of political difficulty for the Somozas. United States military assistance programs strengthened the National Guard during World War II and during the 1960s and early 1970s, and the enhanced strength of his principal instrument of coercion helped Somoza García weather the pro-democracy movement of the late 1940s. The multiple guerrilla insurgencies of the early 1960s were effectively contained by a National Guard strengthened by U.S. financial assistance, training, and advice. For example, in 1962 under the Alliance for Progress, U.S. economic aid to the regime more than doubled, while military aid rose sevenfold.[23]

One of the most remarkable demonstrations of the importance of foreign assistance in a moment of crisis for the regime occurred immediately after the Managua earthquake in December 1972, when the National Guard temporarily collapsed. Troops and officers left their posts to assist their families and attend to their property. For a couple of days Somoza could not pull together even a company of soldiers. Troops from the United States and other CONDECA forces were brought into Managua to reestablish and maintain public order. CONDECA, the Central American Defense Council, was a cooperative joint command of U.S. and Central American forces (excluding Costa Rica) organized to operate under the orders of the Panama-based U.S. Southern Command in case of a regional emergency. Another example of the value of U.S. assistance was provided by Ambassador Turner Shelton, appointed to Managua by President Nixon in the late 1960s. During a period of political and economic crisis for Anastasio Somoza Debayle, Shelton repeatedly shored up the dictator. In addition to arranging for the CONDECA troop deployment to Nicaragua after the quake, Shelton effectively suppressed negative reports and criticism of the regime by his own embassy staff, arranged for Somoza to visit President Nixon in Washington during a 1971 political crisis, and helped the regime negotiate a settlement of that crisis with the Conservative Party.

Anastasio Somoza Debayle assiduously cultivated other U.S. friends and supporters—in Congress, the executive branch, the military, and the business community—with gifts, hunting and vacation trips to Nicaragua, other entertainment, and joint business ventures. To supplement this "Somoza lobby" in Congress and the U.S. administration, during the 1970s the regime also employed public relations and advertising firms to shore up Nicaragua's faltering image in the press.[24] Many who experienced Anastasio Jr.'s considerable personal charm or received his favors and blandishments were persuaded. One former U.S. military attaché in Managua once said to me, referring to the brutal and degenerate dictator with a nostalgic sigh: "Ah, that Tacho! He was a great party guy!"

Breakdown of the Last Somoza Regime

The collapse of the regime of Anastasio Somoza Debayle was the result of a national revolt[25] against his authoritarian and corrupt rule. The revolt was driven by sociopolitical and economic forces that were widespread in the Central American isthmus, and similar rebellions were occurring virtually simultaneously in El Salvador and Guatemala.[26]

Socioeconomic Roots of Class Conflict in the Third Somoza Regime

From 1960 to 1970 Nicaragua's gross domestic product rose 95 percent, and GDP per capita increased 58 percent. For the decade of 1961–70, the average annual growth of per capita GDP was 4.0 percent, then it slowed a bit to 3.1 percent per year for 1971–74. From 1975 through 1978, however, per capita GDP growth fell to −1.8 percent, and it plunged at least ten more points in the first half of 1979.[27] As the Central American Common Market (CACM) boom began to cool in the 1970s, relative and absolute income, employment, and relative wealth eroded among working-class groups in Nicaragua.

After a decade of industrialization and rapid general production growth, the 1973 OPEC oil embargo and subsequent rapid escalation of oil prices drove up consumer prices for the rest of the decade. In Nicaragua, for example, the average annual change in the consumer price index (CPI) for 1963–72 was only 4.0 percent, but it jumped to 15.3 percent for 1973–79.[28] Real wages began to slide in 1967 with rising inflation, then declined sharply in 1973 after the Managua earthquake. Real wages then recovered briefly but plunged again after 1975. By 1978 real wages among working-class Nicaraguans stood at only 64 percent of their 1967 level.[29] As prices rose and real wages fell, employment failed to keep up with the growth of the workforce in Nicaragua during the CACM boom.[30] Despite a dramatic increase in the level of industrialization driven by CACM-related investment policies, from 1970 through 1978, the year the insurrection began, reported unemployment rose fourfold—from 3.7 percent to 14.5 percent.[31]

The rapid economic transformations in Nicaragua under Anastasio Somoza Debayle were rapidly eroding the living standards of working-class Nicaraguans. One may reasonably assume that they noticed these dramatic changes in their pocketbooks and market baskets and that they became more and more aggrieved about them throughout the 1970s.

There are several indicators of growing inequality of wealth and real income during the governments of the brothers, especially that of Anastasio Jr. Concentration of landownership in Nicaragua increased during the 1950s through the 1970s, especially in the fertile and populous Pacific zone. High cotton prices and the expansion of beef production for export permitted speculating large landholders to squeeze subsistence cultivators off the land and into an already oversupplied wage labor market.[32] Agricultural development tended to concentrate landownership and also income.[33] By 1977 the 1.4 percent of farms larger than 350 hectares contained 41.2 percent of the cultivated land, but roughly sixty thousand campesinos had no land at all. Small farms (less than 4 hectares) made up 36.8 percent of Nicaragua's farms but occupied only 1.7 percent of cultivated land. Moreover, the wealthiest fifth of the Nicaraguan populace earned 59.9 percent of the national income, and the poorer half earned only 15 percent of the income.[34] In the 1950s and 1960s Nicaragua's government implemented policies that preferentially benefited agroindustries belonging to the Somozas and their cohorts. Benefits included "not only financial, trade, and credit policies . . . but also the use of the public budget and institutions to supply them with labor, machinery, electricity, administrators, transport, etc."[35]

As I already noted, during the 1960s and 1970s Nicaragua's three major capitalist factions began to intertwine their once separate investments. But after the Managua earthquake the aggressive expansionism of the Somoza faction began to undermine the other investor groups' relative positions and profits. The killer earthquake that took ten thousand Managuans' lives in late 1972 also hit working-class people extremely hard. It destroyed thousands of jobs and brought them additional reconstruction tax levies and longer workweeks with no increase in pay. The quake destroyed housing and left tens of thousands living in ruins, squatter settlements, or relocated to new projects and developments on which Somoza and his cohorts profiteered. Growing political and labor unrest caused many Nicaraguan capitalists to doubt the regime's capacity to promote orderly growth. Anastasio Somoza Debayle's growing backing among the upper classes began to break down during the mid-1970s and thus arrested the development of a unified bourgeoisie.

Popular Mobilization in Nicaragua

The erosion of working-class income and wealth, the Managua earthquake, and dissatisfaction among competing elites contributed to popular mobilization, reformist demands upon the regime of Anastasio Somoza Debayle, and protests of public policies in the 1970s.

As the ranks of the aggrieved increased owing to socioeconomic conditions, the number of organizations in Nicaragua multiplied, as did their activities.[36] The decline of working-class wages in the late 1960s and early 1970s revitalized the nation's long-suppressed industrial labor movement, which stepped up organization and used work stoppages and strikes to seek wage gains in 1973–75. The decline of middle-class living standards also led to considerable unionization and to strikes among such white-collar employees as health workers and teachers. Catholic social workers, missionaries, and priests had begun organizing unions among Pacific zone peasant wage laborers. Clergy also organized small groups of the urban and rural poor into Christian base communities (*comunidades eclesiales de base*—CEBs) for catechism and community self-help in the late 1960s.[37] The peasant union movement gained great momentum after 1975.

Peasant unions increasingly pressed for wage gains, and CEBs called for better urban services and housing. CEBs and Protestant self-help groups among the urban poor multiplied rapidly after the Managua quake. Economic decline first stimulated the formation of Nicaraguan private sector pressure organizations, which in turn increasingly demanded political and economic reform, especially after 1974. For example, the Unión Democrática de Liberación, an association headed by business leaders, appeared in 1974. Such private sector groups as the Nicaraguan Development Foundation (INDE) promoted working-class cooperatives. New opposition political parties (Social Christian, Popular Social Christian) also became increasingly active in Nicaragua in the 1960s and 1970s, and new anti-Somoza factions of the old Conservative and Liberal Parties appeared during the 1970s. Student opposition to the regime also swelled during the 1970s. The FSLN, the only rebel group to survive among some twenty that had appeared between 1959 and 1962, greatly expanded its links to university student groups and support from them during the 1970s.

Government Response to Popular Mobilization and Its Effects upon the Opposition

Anastasio Somoza Debayle declared a state of siege in December 1974 after an embarrassing incident of hostage taking by FSLN, and thus began a three-year reign of terror that took several thousand lives in rural Nicaragua and eventually spread to urban areas. Following the January 1978 assassination of *La Prensa* editor Pedro Joaquín Chamorro, bourgeois elements began to desert and even to oppose the regime. Key business interests such as the Consejo Superior de la Iniciativa Privada (COSIP) joined with unions and moderate forces to support general strikes, and to form the Frente Amplio Opositor (FAO), which sought to negotiate an end to the Somoza regime before the FSLN could overthrow it. The National Guard brutally crushed spontaneous and FSLN-led popular revolts in several cities in late 1978. The FSLN, split for several years over tactics, realized that popular outrage at the Guard's atrocities had doomed the regime and rendered such factional differences sterile. The three FSLN wings quickly reunified in early 1979. The Sandinistas then built a network of prominent citizens (the Grupo de los Doce) to publicly oppose Somoza, forged two broad-front antiregime coalitions (the Movimiento Pueblo Unido and the Frente Patriótico Nacional—MPU and FPN) that included virtually all the opposition forces in Nicaragua and rapidly increased FSLN military strength. In early 1979 a provisional government was formed in Costa Rica, formalizing the opposition's revolutionary claim to sovereignty.[38]

Resource Mobilization and the Outcome of the Contest over Sovereignty

Chehabi and Linz's observation that sultanistic regimes are likely to generate elite and middle-class opposition from landlords, businessmen, clerics, and professionals resentful of economic monopolization, suppression of ideas and the press, dependence on foreign powers, and general corruption certainly held true for the regime of Anastasio Somoza Debayle. The degeneracy, repression, and policy errors of the dictatorship alienated virtually every sector of Nicaraguan society by the late 1970s, including many social forces that had once supported the regime. The government of Anastasio the younger became increasingly debilitated by popular hostility, loss of its powerful allies, and ultimately by the breakdown of the capacity and loyalty of its own functionaries.

As the Carter administration became increasingly critical of Somoza's human rights abuses, it pressured him to perform better and threatened to curtail U.S. military and economic assistance. Although the flow of U.S. aid already in the pipeline was never completely stopped, new military aid was curtailed in 1977 and new economic assistance was ended in 1979. The United States also intervened with other nations to prevent the delivery of arms to Nicaragua. The United States, though reluctant to see the FSLN-led rebels come to power, announced its desire for the end of the Somoza regime and in 1978 supported an effort of the Broad Opposition Front (FAO) coalition to reach a negotiated settlement to the conflict that would exclude the FSLN from a significant role in the new government. This negotiation failed largely because Somoza Debayle refused to negotiate in good faith with the FAO. Other nations also criticized the Somoza regime and began to assist the FSLN-led rebel coalition. These problems—the curtailment of vital funding and military supplies, growing international isolation, and especially the symbolically critical withdrawal of U.S. support and tolerance—badly discouraged Somoza and weakened the loyalty and resolve of supporters in late 1978 and 1979.[39]

Officials of the government and the National Guard began sending their families out of Nicaragua in 1978, and more began fleeing themselves in early 1979. The single event that finally shattered what remained of the regime was the National Guard's 20 June 1979 murder of ABC television correspondent Bill Stewart in front of his own camera crew. Its revelation to the world the following day and the outraged reaction it caused sowed panic among the Somocistas. A stampede to exile ensued, accompanied by a frenzied looting of public resources. On 6 July Somoza Debayle placed his resignation in the hands of the United States, which was attempting to negotiate an end to the war.[40] On 17 July Somoza abandoned Managua for Miami, and two days later the interim government surrendered power to the rebel junta.

The Nicaraguan National Guard did not break down in the face of either the rising organized armed opposition from the FSLN or the burgeoning spontaneous popular resistance it encountered. Increasingly beleaguered by the growth of the rebellion and by combat on several fronts, the Guard nevertheless fought on through June and half of July 1979 despite deteriorating morale and discipline, rising casualties and desertions, the hatred of the populace, and some reduction in its supply of munitions. Last-minute efforts to keep revenue flowing to the Guard and government and to call up reserve forces were largely unsuccessful.

In June the National Guard ceded the northern part of the country to the FSLN and made its stand in Managua and on the southern front against the invading force led by Edén Pastora. Late that month the Guard rallied and drove the FSLN from Managua, temporarily reversed the rebel advance in Rivas, and held León for two weeks against a strong FSLN push. By mid-July, however, the Sandinista forces had pushed the Guard back to Managua. It was only on the resignation and departure of the man with whom their fates had become so identified, Anastasio Somoza Debayle, that the National Guard collapsed. As high officers left the country by air, many troops and lower-ranking officers fled to Honduras. Roughly half the National Guard's peak force of fourteen thousand was captured by FSLN forces.[41] Some have argued that the much-hated Guard personnel fought so tenaciously (and viciously) against the FSLN and the Nicaraguan people out of fear of the revenge the enraged populace might exact from them if they lost.

The FSLN-led coalition of rebels in late 1979 rapidly accumulated organizational capacity, popular and organizational endorsement, military capacity and supplies, and vital external support. The U.S.-backed FAO negotiation effort to remove Somoza Debayle failed in early 1979. The FSLN then quickly gathered in new allies from among those who had given up on the failed FAO. The success of the Grupo de los Doce (a group of a dozen noted professionals and entrepreneurs of various party backgrounds who began to work with the FSLN and were proposed as new cabinet members in 1977, but who had to flee Nicaragua and work against Somoza from exile), the rapid growth of the MPU and FPN coalitions led by the Sandinistas, the rapid recruitment of thousands of new volunteers into the FSLN, the spontaneous assumption of arms against the regime by the people, and the formation of a coalition government in San José all constituted key parts of the rapidly growing resource base of the FSLN just before and during the final offensive. The rebel coalition also was able to count on external support from Costa Rica, Venezuela, Panama, and Cuba that provided arms, secure bases for training and staging of the final offensive, and hospitality and recognition for the shadow government. The rapidly improving resource base and organizational position of the FSLN-led coalition in mid-1979 corresponded with the declining fortunes of the sultanistic dictatorship. The rebels rode this constellation of growing advantages to victory on 19 July 1979.

Legacies of Sultanism

Chehabi and Linz argue that weakness of opposition under sultanism contributes to the emergence of a revolutionary movement under the old regime or the development of revolution after its fall. Under the Somozas the civic opposition was repressed, co-opted, and divided. The most sincere and consistent civic opposition elements (the Social Christians and the Independent Liberals) were small; collaboration with the Somozas upon the Conservatives had divided and corrupted the party. Nicaragua's turbulent history, marked by long periods of dominant regimes opposed by weak and divided oppositions and an opportunistic and mutually distrustful culture among political elites, left the FSLN's allies in the victorious anti-Somoza coalition weak, disorganized, and in disarray.

In sharp contrast, the FSLN had been honed and its organizational skill successfully tested time and again by eighteen years of struggling to survive under fierce repression. The Sandinistas' military victory had also earned them the enthusiastic backing of most Nicaraguans (at least for the short run) and placed them in the enviable position of dominating the new revolutionary security forces. Moreover their ideology, a mix of Marxism-Leninism, populism, and nationalism, gave the leaders of the revolutionary coalition a blueprint for action that other elements of the coalition lacked. It was relatively easy for the FSLN to outorganize and outmaneuver its allies in the coalition and to emerge in a position of complete dominance of the revolution within six months. Although the FSLN deliberately eschewed a cult of personality around any individual leader, many Sandinista leaders were charismatic and this, plus the achievements of the entire movement, may well have given to the party something akin to a collective charisma that enhanced its position within the revolutionary alliance.

Other legacies of sultanism may be noted in the Nicaraguan polity since 1979. First, although the Sandinistas made an effort to avoid a cult of personality and sought to instill an ethos of asceticism, self-abnegation, and honesty among public employees, there emerged vestiges of the corruption and greed that characterized the Somoza dynasty. The Sandinistas were generally successful in avoiding the elevation of any member of the National Directorate to a position of significant superiority until the election of 1984 placed Daniel Ortega in the presidency. Even as he accumulated power and visibility in the office, President Ortega did not appear to be raised to anywhere near the level of official and informal adulation that has characterized Cuba's Fidel Castro, for example. Most of the FSLN National Directorate's top commanders, however, acquired beautiful and spacious homes in extensive compounds, were attended by large numbers of military personnel, staff, and servants, and developed luxurious habits of personal consumption. These homes were justified as needed for security, and the *comandantes'* levels of consumption appeared to be rather normal for upper-class Nicaraguans and short of the luxury known to the Somozas. Nevertheless, this standard of living was far from austere, so the *comandantes* were frequently satirized by the opposition and others as not very different from the previous regime and as hypocritical in light of the revolution's ideology and repudiation of old regime corruption.

After the first few years corruption developed into a significant problem for the revolutionary regime. There were rumors of corruption among top Sandinista officials, and evidence emerged of corrupt practices among some high- and middle-ranking government officials. As the economy deteriorated some rank-and-file government and public sector enterprise employees began to steal and profiteer to supplement their meager incomes. There were prosecutions and convictions for such behavior, so corruption and criminality were not regularly condoned (much less encouraged) as they had been under the Somozas.

Another great legacy of sultanism, external interference by the United States, was extreme and eventually contributed heavily to the electoral defeat of the FSLN.[42] The Carter administration worked hard to shape the policies of the fledgling revolution in 1979 and 1980. Most notable, of course, was the determined effort by the Reagan and Bush administrations to topple the FSLN. The United States deployed an extraordinary array of measures against the revolutionary government: organizing, directing, and financing the contras; a trade embargo; a diplomatic campaign to discredit Nicaragua and isolate the country internationally; a propaganda campaign to spread fear and alienate citizens from the revolutionary government; overt and covert espionage and sabotage; efforts to disrupt and discredit the 1984 election; and vigorous financial and moral support for the successful Nicaraguan Opposition Union (UNO) opposition coalition in the 1990 election. Given the extensive record of U.S. involvement and interference in Nicaraguan affairs since the 1850s, it seems reasonable to conclude that despite the end of the Sandinista revolution with the 1990 election U.S. interference in Nicaraguan affairs will occur for the foreseeable future whenever a U.S. administration sees something amiss in Nicaragua.

Conclusions

To varying degrees the rule of all three Somozas manifested sultanistic tendencies. Constitutional hypocrisy, personalism, corruption of the state, absence of the rule of law, manipulation and repression of opposition, and periodic reliance on an external sponsor when domestic challenges arose characterized them all. Nicaragua also deviates partially from patterns of sultanism observed elsewhere, especially in the presence of a semiopposition and the coexistence of military professionalism and competence within the National Guard despite the deprofessionalizing pressures of manipulation and corruption. Under the rule of Anastasio Somoza Debayle from 1967 to 1979 the characteristics of sultanism became most pronounced.

In many respects the rebellion of Nicaraguans against Anastasio Somoza Debayle was motivated by economic forces and by a regime response to popular mobilization quite similar to the reaction to rebellions in Guatemala and El Salvador, even though neither of those regimes was sultanistic.[43] Thus the rebellion against the Somoza dynasty should probably be viewed not as the product of sultanism, but as the result of more general socioeconomic and political processes just as likely to occur in other types of authoritarian regimes.

The victory of the Sandinista-led rebel coalition in 1979 was the product both of successful organization and resource mobilization by the insurgents and of Somoza Debayle's failure to accomplish the same ends. That the Salvadoran and Guatemalan regimes survived their national revolts has much to do with their relatively far greater success at resource mobilization. El Salvador's regime persevered in the face of intense opposition through the massive efforts and expenditures by the United States to increase its capabilities and contain its enemies. The regime negotiated a political settlement of the civil war in 1992 and has moved toward stabilization by making concessions to its erstwhile opposition. Guatemala's military-dominated system also survived the challenge to its sovereignty because of its much greater internal strength and resources and a skillful use of carefully managed reforms. In 1996 Guatemala too negotiated an end to its civil war with the insurgent Left, and an elected civilian government remains in power.[44]

In contrast to these cases, it seems certain that the political rot of Somocismo accounted for much of its eventual weakness in the face of a strong challenge. It is also manifest that some of Nicaraguans' vehement antipathy toward the old regime was born in the viciousness and degeneracy of the Somozas, the government they spawned, and their principal tool, the National Guard. Thus, although sultanism was by no means the sole cause of the Nicaraguan national revolt, its corrosive effects contributed directly to the collapse of the regime.

7

. . . .

The Duvalier Regime in Haiti

David Nicholls

From the early days of independence Haitian leaders and intellectuals have pictured their country as a modern nation, following the legal-rational model of nineteenth-century European constitutional states. Although the first head of state, Jean-Jacques Dessalines (1804–6), owed his position to having led a successful military campaign against the French armies of Leclerc and Rocham-beau, his claim to continued legitimacy as governor-general and then emperor depended on his governing in the context of a constitution, formulated in 1805. After his assassination the following year, the succeeding regimes of Alexandre Pétion and Henry Christophe were both keen to stress the legal basis of their authority. Pétion's regime in the south and west appealed to constitutional ideas of Enlightenment republicanism, while the apologists of Christophe's northern state (which became a kingdom in 1811) looked to the more conservative British model of constitutional monarchy. The baron de Vastey, a mulatto spokesman of Christophe's kingdom, claimed that the legitimacy of the northern govern-ment stemmed from the consent of the people, and that liberty and the rule of law are more likely to flourish in constitutional and limited monarchies than under republican forms of government. Republics, he claimed, have produced a multitude of despotic rulers, and "there has never existed a more frightful tyranny than that of Robespierre."[1]

Throughout the nineteenth century and up to the present day, Haitian regimes have been concerned to maintain constitutional forms of government and have claimed that their legitimacy stems from election or ratification ac-cording to legal-rational criteria.[2] Even the imperial regimes of Dessalines and

Faustin Soulouque and the kingdom of Christophe claimed legal legitimacy based on a constitution. The institution of president for life, adopted by the northern state in 1807 and by Pétion's republic in 1816 and copied by Bolívar and later by François Duvalier, was enshrined in constitutional form.

Accepting for the moment the Weberian classification, it would certainly be necessary to say that successive Haitian heads of state have also made claims to authority on the grounds of tradition and charisma. For the first century of independence the head of state was invariably a military officer, who had normally come to prominence as a result of his military position. Heads of state, however, needed to be "elected" in some form or other in order to claim more than de facto power.

Many Haitian presidents also attempted to reinforce their legitimacy with pretensions to paternal authority. They were frequently known as Papa. Pétion, for example, was called Papa Bon Kè (Papa Good Heart); Alexis Nord at the beginning of the present century was known as Papa Nord; and François Duvalier encouraged people to call him Papa Doc. Such paternalism would probably be included in the Weberian category of the traditional form of legitimacy, though it could also be part of a more general attempt to establish a charismatic claim to obedience. In Haiti the term *papa* also refers to some of the voodoo spirits and to leading *houngans* (voodoo priests). Despite exploiting these connections with Haitian traditional religion, Duvalier also frequently pointed to the work of the Turkish modernizing leader, Kemal Atatürk, claiming to be following this model in Haiti.

The legacies of slavery and the colonial system have been important in influencing the understanding of political authority in Haitian culture. This dual legacy has tended to reinforce an authoritarian style of politics based on the military model. Throughout the country's history most Haitians have seen the state as an alien set of institutions, hostile to the ordinary citizen. The vast majority have had no expectation that the state would be a channel of welfare or benefits for them. It exists to tax, inhibit, imprison, and ultimately execute. Mats Lundahl calls it the "predatory state." Papa Doc and his son certainly refined the techniques of oppression and financial corruption, but they should be seen as following in a long succession of predatory leaders.[3] What welfare systems exist are established on a local and extended family level through friendly societies, secret societies, voodoo temples, church groups, informal banks, and above all remittances from Haitians living and working abroad.[4] Haitians generally have little conception of a common good embracing the whole population, and state institutions are regarded with disdain. In contrast, however, particularly in the countryside, there is a strong sense of local community, and social control is largely maintained without the assistance of state agencies. The popular proverb *Apré bondié se leta* (After God comes the state), is to be understood with reference to a God who is believed to be remote and potentially threatening.

The influence of the voodoo religion has been pervasive in the history of Haiti. It consists in the worship of God (Bondié or Granmèt), and of the spirits (*lwas*). It is an amalgam of African cults, containing elements of Christianity, and has assumed somewhat different forms in several Caribbean islands and some South American countries. In Haiti it is the religion of the majority of the people, most of whom would also regard themselves as Catholics. Its predominant social effect, like that of most religions, has been conservative, tending to reinforce the authority of current rulers. For the Haitian masses, however, it has constituted a link with their African past and a means of reasserting their ethnic identity. As such its effects have sometimes been radical, and it has played an important role in resisting foreign colonial and quasi-colonial adventures.[5] Many of the *lwas* are portrayed in military uniform, and the master of ceremonies in a voodoo celebration is known as *laplace,* from the colonial *commandant de la place.* If these institutions reflect the militarism of colonial and postcolonial regimes, the name God or Lord, Granmèt (great master or lord), is clearly derived from the master-slave relationship on the plantation. Heads of state, like the Roman Catholic hierarchy, have varied in their approach to voodoo—from hostility and persecution to attempts to wean devotees away from the cult toward more "respectable" forms of religion. Some astute politicians, however, have sought to use the voodoo religion as a means of recruiting popular support for their movements.[6]

The Genesis of the Haitian Regimes

From 1804 until the United States invasion of 1915, Haitian heads of state frequently came into office as a result of their personal power as military officers. This would be true in the case of Dessalines (1804–6), Christophe (1806–20), Pétion (1806–18), Fabre Nicolas Geffrard (1859–67), Silvain Salnave (1867–69), most heads of state from Alexis Nord (1902–8) to the U.S. invasion, and more recently Paul Magloire (1950–56). Some, like Jean-Pierre Boyer (1818–43) or Jean-Claude Duvalier (1971–86), were handed power by an immediate predecessor. Others, such as Faustin Soulouque (1847–59) and Tiréas Simon Sam (1896–1902), were compromise candidates in the context of conflicting and powerful generals, each too weak to defeat his rival; often these were black leaders who, like Philippe Guerrier (1844–45) and Soulouque himself, were put forward as puppet presidents by mulatto politicians (in both these cases the Ardouin brothers figured prominently). This was known as *la politique de doublure* (politics of the understudy). Philippe Sudre Dartiguenave (1915–22) and Louis Borno (1922–30) were put into office by the U.S. marines. Others again, including Louis Etienne Lysius Félicité Salomon (1879–88), Sténio Vincent (1930–41), and François Duvalier (1957–71), came to power as skillful politicians able to assemble an alliance of interests and of military influence sufficient to defeat their rivals. All these heads of state found it necessary to legitimate their position by some form of election and frequently by promulgating a new constitution.

Of the rulers mentioned above, those who most clearly exhibit the characteristics of sultanism are Dessalines, Christophe, Soulouque, Salomon, Magloire, and the two Duvaliers. Three came to power as a result of military preeminence, two by political skill, one by inheritance, and one by *doublure* (which soon backfired on his mulatto sponsors). It is therefore difficult to generalize about the immediate genesis of these regimes. Many presidents would have liked to rule sultanistically, but because much of the country was controlled by rival generals or by *cacos* (rural guerrilla) groups, they were unable to exercise effective autocratic power. From the time of independence, achieved after a long and bloody struggle, many peasants retained their arms and were prepared to resist perceived threats to their way of life or attempts to remove them from land on which their families had squatted for generations.[7] The effective rule of governments was thus often limited to the capital and the larger provincial towns, and sultanistic developments were thereby checked. Most Haitian regimes, indeed, may be said to have manifested a partially realized sultanism, the long-term genesis of which might properly be traced back to the authoritarian character of the French colonial regime.

Colonialism is an authoritarian form of rule in which locally resident officials have enormous discretionary powers (particularly before the development of the telegraph). In colonial Saint Domingue the governor was invariably a military officer, responsible not to local residents, but to the metropolitan government in Paris. This government indeed exercised ex post facto powers of disciplining the governor, but while he was in office he had wide-ranging powers. Governor Edward Eyre of Jamaica would be another example, or Warren Hastings in India.[8]

The colonial economy, depending as it frequently did on a plantation system that exported one or a few primary products to the metropolitan country, led postcolonial countries to see in customs duties the easiest method of tax revenue; it is a system by which the ordinary small producer can be taxed almost without his realizing it. An effective system of income tax has never been developed in Haiti.

A further characteristic of sultanist regimes is centralized administration and an adequate communication system. Before the first U.S. occupation of Haiti (1915–34), the central government was often weak and communications were bad; most people lived on properties they effectively owned. Poor road transport meant that much overseas trade was conducted from provincial ports, like Jérémie, Les Cayes, Cap Haïtien, and Jacmel. Consequently there was a thriving economic and cultural life in the provincial towns. All this decentralization helped thwart the sultanist tendency of most regimes.

With the occupation, however, the peasants were disarmed, communications were improved, administration was centralized, and the slow disintegration of the colonial system that had occurred over the previous century was put into reverse. As Michel-Rolph Trouillot has recently observed, a new type of army was created by the U.S. occupation, the Garde d'Haïti, whose concerns were solely internal.[9] At independence the Haitian army had been founded to defend the country against European invasion and was later employed in preemptive attacks against the Dominican Republic. Furthermore, the army, like the medieval church in Europe, was one of the few channels through which a poor, nonelite person could rise to power. By the late nineteenth century it had become a fairly ramshackle affair, with real control in the hands of regional commanders. The new Garde was, in contrast, a highly centralized force whose purpose was to strengthen the hand of the government in suppressing discontent among the people. The U.S. authorities thus put in place an infrastructure upon which an autocratic regime could be established. The pattern is not dissimilar to that found in Cuba, Nicaragua, the Dominican Republic, and most recently, Panama. Attempts to restructure the Haitian economy, however, replacing the small landowning peasantry with a plantation system producing crops for export, were unsuccessful. This failure was due largely to the determination of rural Haitians and the complicated property laws. The withdrawal of the marines in 1934 meant that a principal bulwark against presidential autocracy was removed.

The Rise of Papa Doc

François Duvalier was born in 1907 and was brought up near Port-au-Prince by Duval Duvalier, a journalist, teacher, and justice of the peace. He attended the Lycée Pétion in the capital and studied at the medical school of the university. Duvalier benefited from the emphasis the American occupation placed on technical and practical education, and he later worked with the American medical mission, studying for a year at the University of Michigan. Duvalier was influenced by the ethnological movement led by J. C. Dorsainvil and Jean Price Mars, who were among the first intellectuals to develop the idea of *négritude*.[10] He identified with the *noiriste* tendency in Haitian politics[11] and emphasized the African contributions to Haitian culture. He was therefore an outspoken critic of the francophile mulatto elite and was part of the group that founded the journal *Les Griots* in the 1930s. Though favorably disposed to president Sténio Vincent (1930–41), Duvalier was critical of his intransigent and corrupt successor, Elie Lescot (1941–46). He welcomed Lescot's removal and the election of the black (and mildly *noiriste*) president Dumarsais Estimé (1946–50), in whose government he served as a minister. With Estimé's overthrow in 1950 by the same military triumvirate that disposed of Lescot, and with the succession of Paul Magloire, Duvalier joined the clandestine opposition to the new dictator. He considered Magloire, though himself black, a defender of the old mulatto elite, reversing the small gains made by the black middle classes under Estimé.

Like many Haitian presidents, Duvalier came from a small but significant black *classe intermédiaire*. He was elected in 1957 as a defender of black interests and an opponent of the elite. His knowledge of Haitian popular culture convinced him of the vital importance of the voodoo religion, and he carefully cultivated a number of key *houngans* (voodoo priests). This, together with his hostility to the francophile elite, brought Duvalier into conflict with the Roman Catholic hierarchy, who had generally supported Magloire. Nevertheless, before the election he was careful not to emphasize these religious and cultural factors openly. He put forward a rather bland program of national unity and economic "equilibrium." By the time of the presidential election the number of viable candidates had been whittled down to three. Duvalier had support from the army leadership, and whereas his principal opponent, Louis Déjoie, a mulatto businessman, was backed by the U.S. embassy, Duvalier was regarded as an acceptable candidate and was indeed favored by some in the embassy. Although not free from corruption and irregularities, the election probably reflected opinion in the country, and Duvalier was elected with a large majority.

François Duvalier dealt ruthlessly with all signs of opposition, and he anticipated such resistance by depriving of political power any groups that might form the basis of challenge to his regime. He enjoyed support from an important black middle class in the cities and of middle-level peasants in the countryside. Through these he extended his control over the whole population. The Volontaires de la Sécurité Nationale (VSN), generally known as the Tonton

Macoutes (after a figure in Haitian folklore), used terror to deal with potential opponents but also served as a means of recruiting some popular support for the regime throughout the country.

When he died in 1971, Duvalier had eliminated potential opponents and was able to hand over power to his teenage son, Jean-Claude, who became "president for life," a title his father had adopted in 1964. The transition from father to son was accomplished smoothly because opposition to the regime in the country was dispersed and disorganized. The army was firmly under civilian control and Macoute leaders owed personal allegiance to the Duvaliers, knowing this was where their interests lay. A key role in the transition was played by Simone Ovide Duvalier, Papa Doc's wife, who in the early years of Jean-Claude Duvalier's presidency ensured loyalty to the regime by her personal contacts with senior army officers and Macoute leaders. She nipped in the bud attempts by her daughters and their husbands to take power. The marriage of Jean-Claude ("Baby Doc") to Michèle Bennett in 1980 brought an end to his mother's power and symbolized the change that had taken place between the regime of father and son. A further reason for the smooth transition was the belief of the U.S. government that any destabilizing of the Haitian situation might lead to a Cuban-style regime bent on radical policies. Steps were taken to prevent an exile invasion; two U.S. warships were stationed off the coast, and the airspace was secured. In the absence of any credible opposition within the country, those discontented with the regime of Papa Doc hoped for a gradual change under his son. The constitutional and legal aspects of the transition were orchestrated by Hervé Boyer, a close confidant of François Duvalier.

Characteristics of the Duvalier Regime

François Duvalier's principal concern after his election to office on 22 September 1957 was to avoid the fate of former president Dumarsais Estimé, who had been overthrown by the army at the end of his constitutional single term of four years, on the grounds that he was planning a change in the constitution so that he could run for a further term. Duvalier therefore dealt effective blows to the army and to other potential centers of opposition in the country. After skillfully changing the army leadership more than once and suppressing principal opposition groups, he turned his attention to the church and to schoolteachers (many of whom were priests or from religious communities). He also reduced the political power of the U.S. embassy, the press, the business community, the university, and freelance intellectuals and finally the trade unions.

Insofar as the government of Papa Doc was guided by ideology, it was in terms of an ethnic nationalism, which emphasized the African elements in Haitian culture, resenting the cultural domination by a small francophile, Catholic, literate elite. This system was perpetuated by the control of the education system by a church that was itself run largely by expatriate clergy. When Duvalier took office in 1957 ten of the eleven bishops were white foreigners, and the religious orders that operated the best schools in the country were led by Europeans. After a six-year battle in which bishops were repatriated, nuns imprisoned, and Jesuits expelled, and Duvalier himself was excommunicated, a new concordat was reached with the Vatican in 1966, and a fresh hierarchy was appointed. By the time he died in 1971 ten of the eleven bishops were black or mulatto Haitians. Duvalier's moves conveniently coincided with the Vatican's own policy of appointing indigenous hierarchies in Third World countries. As a result of the new concordat, Duvalier was able to claim cynically that his regime could now count on "the support of the highest moral authority in the world" and that it was a vindication of his struggle, since the 1930s, for a Haitian episcopate.[12] The role of the church in education was somewhat reduced, school syllabi were changed, and Haitian history could be taught only by Haitian nationals. Little, however, was done to promote the Creole (*kréyol*) language, though under Jean-Claude Duvalier some hesitant steps were taken in this direction. Haitian Creole became an official language of the country only in the 1987 constitution.

In addition to some positive characteristics that will be considered in due course, sultanism as an ideal type entails the absence of a mass movement supporting the ruler and of a significant ideology influencing his actions. In these two respects it is clearly distinct from a totalitarian regime. Insofar as a regime is totalitarian—or rather manifests totalitarian tendencies in a high degree—to that extent it avoids being categorized as sultanistic. Elsewhere I have argued that it is a mistake to think of Duvalierism as a form of totalitarian government; it is equally misleading to call the regime fascist, though opponents found the temptation to do so hard to resist.[13] In an orgy of conceptual confusion, one Marxist writer referred to Papa Doc's Haiti as an example of "*créole* fascism," corresponding to a "feudal or semi-feudal society," exhibiting a "medieval" form of government![14] Fascism was a form of totalitarianism; if we can show that Haiti under the Duvaliers was not totalitarian, to describe it as fascist is inappropriate.

A principal characteristic of totalitarianism is that the regime has a concern for the totality of the life of the people. Not only is the government concerned with social order and the economy, but it also oversees the religion, culture, and leisure of the population. No sphere is left untouched by the overall plan for transforming (or on other occasions for conserving) social order. There is little evidence that Papa Doc, and even less his son, made serious efforts to impose some total vision on the population. Apart from a few symbolic issues, there is little indication of any desire to mold the whole life of the country, to impose an overall or total ideology. The rhetoric of black power was largely window dressing. Although the black middle classes benefited to some marginal degree from government posts and patronage, nothing was done to disturb the social and economic dominance of the mulatto elite in the three decades of Duvalierist rule.

In his recent works, however, Trouillot portrays Duvalierism as constituting a move from authoritarian to totalitarian politics.[15] Indeed, the second part of the English-language edition of his book is titled "The Totalitarian Solution." Although he presents a generally accurate and sophisticated interpretation of the Haitian past, I believe he errs in this matter.

In the first place, he ignores the most important characteristic of a totalitarian regime: the desire to impose a dynamic and total way of life on the nation, a concern with every aspect of the people's daily existence. At one point Trouillot gives his case away. "Duvalierism," he states, "had no program other than power for power's sake."[16] A regime whose sole program is to gain and retain power cannot properly be called totalitarian. Trouillot even refers to the "totalitarian inclinations" of the autocratic Paul Magloire, which suggests a very curious concept of totalitarianism. It would be hard to think of any Latin American ruler who conformed less to the totalitarian model than did the playboy Magloire. The politics of Magloire and of the Duvaliers are much closer to sultanism than to totalitarianism. How different from the dynamic and fanatical desire to remold the Italian nation, or to purify the German *Volk* of non-Aryan blood, or to collectivize the peasants into a total communist state!

Although much of what Trouillot says about the Duvalier regime is correct—its ruthless extension of terror into the massacre of women and children, its successful undermining of every institution in the country likely to constitute a center of resistance to the ruler, its recruiting of the masses through the civil militia (VSN)—these are not distinguishing features of a totalitarian regime. They are to be found in nontotalitarian forms of despotism, particularly in its populist form.

One aspect of Duvalierism Trouillot refers to would indeed suggest a totalitarian tendency if it were an accurate representation of the situation. "By the mid-1960s, only two options remained: one was either a Duvalierist or an anti-Duvalierist."[17] Leslie Manigat made a similar point some years ago: "Such is the encroachment of politics on all aspects of life that if a man does not go into politics, politics itself comes to him."[18] Although this may have been so for a small class of intellectuals, aspiring politicians, rich businessmen, and other elite figures, most of the population for most of the time could maintain a detached attitude, neither for nor against the regime. Certainly the country-wide organization of the VSN and unscrupulous behavior by local Macoute leaders meant that no one was assured of being left alone. Even in the days of nineteenth-century caciques (guerrilla leaders), however, like Mérisier Jeannis and the *cacos* leaders, many peasants involuntarily became involved in the political struggles of the day.

Under the Duvaliers there was very little pressure on most of the population to become explicitly involved in politics; an outward conformity was sufficient. Businessmen were generally left to get on with making money, though they were sometimes encouraged to share it, by threats from Macoutes or by tempo-rary imprisonment in the palace. There was no concern for ideological purity even among Duvalierists themselves. Opportunists were welcomed. The Du-valiers recruited Marxists (Lucien Daumec), former fascists (Gérard de Cata-logne), and technocratic socialists (the Blanchet brothers) as well as *noiristes* (Clovis Désinor). This is in stark contrast to Nazi Germany, where ortho-doxy and sincere devotion to the party were demanded; the legal theorist Carl Schmitt, for example, who leaned over backward to conform to the Hitler regime, was expelled from office in the party in 1936 as an opportunist who did not conscientiously believe the pure teachings of the party. The fearful indif-ference that Duvalierist terror inspired—the desire to know nothing and be seen to know nothing about politics—is a classical characteristic of traditional despotism. Carl Wittfogel refers to the incident in *The Arabian Nights* where a body is moved from outside one door to another, since no one wants to be found with it in the morning.[19]

Supernatural powers and qualities were frequently ascribed to Papa Doc. Many of his words and actions had symbolic meaning in the voodoo religion. Thousands of posters appeared as the Péligre dam was about to be opened proclaiming that "Duvalier alone is able to harness the energy of Péligre and give it to his people." Others showed Jesus with his hand on Duvalier proclaim-ing, "I have chosen him." Versions of the Lord's Prayer and other Christian devotions were published substituting the name of Duvalier. A form of con-fession begins, "We confess that we did not vote for you in 1957." But all this is nothing unusual in sultanistic or totalitarian states. Bishop Paul Robert of Gonaïves welcomed presidential candidate Paul Magloire into the city in 1950 with the words (spoken to Jesus by the disciples of John the Baptist) "Art thou he that should come or do we look for another?"[20]

Although it is certainly true that totalitarian governments attack autonomous or semiautonomous centers of power as Papa Doc did, so too do traditional despotic regimes. Discussing the ways to preserve a tyranny, Aristotle wrote: "One of them is the forbidding of common meals, clubs, education and anything of a like character. . . . A second measure is to prohibit societies for cultural purposes, and any gathering of a similar character; in a word, the adoption of every means for making every subject as much of a stranger as is possible to every other."[21]

A further characteristic of sultanism is arbitrary personal power. Undoubtedly the presidency in Haiti has throughout history been the only office that counts. Influential politicians have indeed existed from time to time, like Anténor Firmin in the late nineteenth century or Sténio Vincent before his election, but their eyes are always set on the presidency. The rule of the Duvaliers, however, marks a new stage in the personalization of power. Practically all the institutional restraints on presidential power were demolished one by one. Individual ministers or other national figures became powerful during the thirty years of Duvalierism but were soon cut down to size; they were sent into exile, imprisoned, killed, given ambassadorial posts, or just left out in the cold. This happened to Clément Barbot, Jean Magloire, Clémard Joseph Charles, the Blanchet brothers, Hervé Boyer, Max Dominique, and many other army officers, Roger Lafontant, Luckner Cambronne, and a host of Macoute chiefs. Sometimes after a cooling-off period they were brought back into favor. Often the ruler himself hardly needed to act, because at the least sign of a particular minister's achieving preeminence, the rest would unite against him and secure his downfall. This happened to Hervé Boyer at the time of the transition from father to son in 1971. It looked at one point as though Papa Doc was about to make him prime minister, but other ministers resisted this move.

Government revenue under the Duvaliers was raised principally by taxes on imports and on coffee exports. Income tax was inefficiently and corruptly organized and largely avoided by the rich. According to the World Bank 1 percent of the population received 44 percent of the national income but paid only 3.5 percent of the income tax in 1983.[22] When faced by a financial crisis François Duvalier would imprison a rich businessman on some bogus charge and hold him in the presidential palace until he signed a check for government bonds, costing perhaps $2 million. Other businesses were forced to make payments by threats from leading Macoutes.

Although there was a professional civil service, it was continually undermined by personal appointments made by the president himself, or by a particular minister, who would often put members of his own family into important positions in his ministry. Powerful Macoute leaders would ensure that their wives were given sinecures in some ministry or other.[23] Such family patronage is a further characteristic of sultanism.

Malversation has been common in Haiti since the days of Dessalines, who coined the celebrated phrase, "Pluck the chicken, but don't let it squawk." It has always been taken for granted that a president has the right to take reasonable steps to secure a moderately comfortable retirement, which as likely as not would have to be spent in exile. François Duvalier undoubtedly stole large sums of government money, but he was much more interested in power than in money and was in any case determined to die in office. A number of ministers and others made illicit gains during his regime, mostly by diverting foreign aid and by means of a number of financial institutions that were publicly unaccountable, including the infamous Régie du Tabac, which had power to tax almost fifty different products. Corruption was sometimes overlooked, but on other occasions its perpetrators were made to pay dearly for their greed. Clémard Joseph Charles, for example, was imprisoned for many years for his corrupt practices.

Under Jean-Claude Duvalier conventional limits on corruption were overstepped, by the president himself and by his wife Michèle and her family. Their corruption and extravagant lifestyle caused scandal even in Haiti itself and undoubtedly contributed to the downfall of Duvalierism. With the help of such operators as Frantz Merceron, the presidential family was able to send millions of dollars out of the country into private bank accounts. During the last years of Baby Doc, Merceron is said to have managed an account worth over $70 million.[24] Expensive contracts for unneeded factories led to huge "backhanders"; profits made by state enterprises were skimmed off. Michèle's brother was arrested in Puerto Rico for drug trafficking, and other members of her family were closely involved with Colombian drug barons. Foreign aid remained a principal source of corruption throughout the regime of Baby Doc. For example, an International Monetary Fund grant was made to Haiti in December 1980. Within a month $20 million had disappeared into private accounts.[25]

The armed forces under the Duvaliers were organized in such a way that the president had close control over appointments and over the general administration of the forces. The presidential guard was organized separately from the regular army, with its head reporting directly to the president. The police force was also a branch of the army, but Duvalier made sure that the police chief was again directly responsible to him. Rural administration was governed by the *chef de section*, who was invariably a military officer. With the aid of the Tonton

Macoutes Papa Doc had ensured civilian control of the armed forces, and Baby Doc was able to maintain supremacy over the military until the end.[26]

The army rarely numbered more than seven thousand men, including the police. Haiti has been known since the early nineteenth century as a peaceful and nonviolent country with respect to social life. There is a strong system of social control informally administered. Politics, to be sure, has always been characterized by violence. Under the Duvaliers incipient revolts were quashed by the army or the Macoutes. The principal challenges to the government have in the past come from the army, but Papa Doc effectively put an end to the army as an independent variable in political life. This civilian control over the army was maintained by his son. After the popular antigovernment demonstrations of December 1985, it took weeks before the army leaders made any moves to take over the country, which they eventually did, largely at the behest of Duvalier and the U.S. embassy, on 7 February 1986.

The separately organized VSN and other Macoute organizations, which owed personal loyalty to the president, were able to watch the activities of the army throughout the country and report directly to him. In the early days of François Duvalier's regime, the civilian militia was controlled by Clément Barbot. The president, however, became wary of Barbot's ambition, his contacts with the U.S. embassy, and his personal influence among the Macoutes. Barbot was indeed plotting to assassinate Duvalier, probably with the encouragement of elements in the U.S. embassy. He was eventually killed along with his brother in a gun battle with forces loyal to the president. The number of Macoutes varied from time to time, between twenty thousand and thirty thousand. They retained an important role during the long presidency of Baby Doc, though in the post-1980 period divisions between various factions became noticeable. By 1986 few Macoutes showed enthusiasm for defending the regime.

The Decline and Fall of Baby Doc

Baby Doc left the country in February 1986 as a result of widespread popular demonstrations and growing opposition from much of the population. By losing the backing of important sectors of the black middle class, his regime had become vulnerable to overthrow, either from external (U.S.) intervention or from internal disaffection and protest.[27] With the demonstrations in November and December 1985, beginning in Gonaïves and spreading to Petit Goâve, Cap Haïtien, and other towns, the extent of discontent became obvious. The church gave tacit support to the protests by holding high-profile requiems for those killed and by spreading news of the demonstrations through Radio Soleil.

Duvalier had lost the support of many Macoute leaders, who were not inclined to stick out their necks to protect him. The army was divided but was clearly unwilling to risk unpopularity by a total and violent suppression of the demonstrations. Early protesters indeed carried placards reading *Vive l'armée*. On the other hand neither the Macoutes nor the army felt prepared to initiate action that would directly cause the overthrow of the regime. So far from being a conspirator, all the evidence points to a somewhat unwilling General Henri Namphy's being persuaded by Baby Doc and the U.S. embassy to take power and ensure a smooth transition. Washington promised massive military and financial aid, which strengthened the army and set the scene for the massacre of scores of voters in the abortive elections of 29 November 1987. Certainly Namphy appears to have acquired a taste for political power, but his unwillingness to initiate revolutionary action against the Duvaliers was due to thirty years of unremitting pressure to keep the military under civilian control. François Duvalier, as we have noted, succeeded in bringing the army firmly under his command. By its actions in 1985–86 the U.S. government reversed this process and gave back to the army a pivotal role in the politics of Haiti.

The contribution of exiles to the overthrow of Duvalierism was insignificant. They had mostly lost touch with events in the country, with key people in local communities, and with the general political ethos. They tended to denounce as collaborators Haitians who had stayed at home, while these in turn attacked exiles for abandoning the country for an easier life abroad. There was some truth in both accusations, but it was manifest that Duvalierism fell as a result of opposition from those who remained in the country. When exiles began to return there was considerable tension between the two groups and much resentment on both sides. Leslie Manigat, who became president as a result of a bogus election in January 1988, exemplifies these weaknesses of the returned exile. He was put into office by the military and taken out by the military; he had little popular support and few real friends in key positions. His miscalculations and mishandling of the situation illustrate the effects of almost twenty-five years of exile.[28]

The Roman Catholic Church played a key role in the decline and fall of the Duvalier regime. François Duvalier had dealt a series of blows to the power of the church in the early 1960s. The church was humiliated and eventually negotiated a new concordat with Duvalier, largely on his own terms. A subservient hierarchy was instituted, and the church was deprived of its key political role. Gradually, under Baby Doc, some bishops and other church people began to make cautious criticisms of certain of the more notorious practices of government ministers, such as the export of blood by Hemo-Caribbean, owned by Luckner Cambronne, minister of the interior.[29] The pope's visit of 1983 strengthened the bishops' hands, and they began to denounce contraventions of human rights. More important, at the local level small development projects, literacy campaigns, and peasant cooperatives blossomed in many parts of the country. These were often sponsored by church groups and by small non-government aid agencies. The church also formed a network of "base communities," known as *ti legliz*, where church people would meet to consider their situation in the light of the gospel. They were often led by laypeople or by radical clergy and were regarded with some suspicion by the hierarchy, which felt that they were beyond its control. Many of these groups provided the leadership for the protest movements of 1985–86.

In general Protestant churches in Haiti have been less explicitly involved in politics, but individual members of the Eglise Episcopale (Anglican) and Methodist Church have from time to time played an important role. Many black middle-class supporters of François Duvalier, particularly in the capital, were members of the Eglise Episcopale, and its bishop, C. A. Voegeli, gave strong support to Duvalier in the campaign of 1957. An Anglican priest was godfather to one of Papa Doc's children, and the bishop traveled with an "official" number plate on his car. The Bennetts are Anglicans, and Jean-Claude's wife, Michèle, would regularly send flowers from the palace to the Anglican cathedral. By contrast, Methodist minister Alain Rocourt played a leading role in the work of the Provisional Electoral Council, which organized the abortive election of November 1987, and was widely seen as an opponent of Duvalierism. Rocourt comes from the region of Jérémie, where a significant sector of the mulatto elite has been Methodist for many generations.[30]

Other Protestant churches, including Baptist and African Methodist Episcopal, have been well established in Haiti for decades. Some retain strong links with the United States and are generally conservative. Pastor Wallace Turnball has been for some time typical of this tendency. He has done evangelistic work and sponsored rural projects, run on paternalistic lines; he discourages active involvement in politics among his congregation. Other Protestant groups, however, have become more Haitianized and have provided the context within which a political leader like Sylvio Claude could emerge. Pastor Nerée, the Baptist, has also been outspoken in his criticisms of the regime.

In recent years there has been an influx of fundamentalist groups from the United States, which are aggressive in their evangelism and radically pro-American in their political stance. They have sometimes allied themselves with the richer peasants against organizations of smaller peasants linked to the Roman Catholic Church, such as Tet Ansanm (all together, or heads together). The violent clashes in the northwest, around the town of Jean Rabel, in July 1987, when hundreds of poorer peasants were massacred by the army, had a religious aspect to them.[31]

Thus several factors contributed to the decline and fall of the Duvalier dynasty. Most important was the growing structural weakness of Baby Doc's regime owing to its gradual loss of support from that key sector in Haitian politics, the black *classe intermédiaire*. The regime became more and more dependent on the goodwill of the elite, who are notoriously volatile in their political preferences. The government was thus vulnerable to opposition movements.

In the late 1970s President Jimmy Carter's policy of linking foreign aid to an increasing liberalization of the country and respect for human rights led to a widespread discontent openly manifested in newspapers that were readily available on the streets. Much more important (in a country with perhaps 80 percent illiteracy) was the radio. Such commentators as "Compère Plume" (Evans Paul) and Jean Dominique made devastating attacks on the government in their popular Creole programs. Attempts to suppress opposition, with the advent of Ronald Reagan, were only partially successful, owing to the brave resistance of such men as Sylvio Claude and the open criticism of repressive measures by church leaders. Combined with this resistance was the growing confidence of peasant groups in rural areas and provincial towns.

When Baby Doc began to sense that he was losing support from the key black middle classes, he attempted to appeal to the people at large, over the heads of these men. Programs on Radio Nationale encouraged people to phone in, or otherwise communicate, local cases of injustice or incompetence. The president tried to pose as the defender of the ordinary peasant against the local bureaucracies. This move backfired because it further alienated key local figures, who were still able, through their control of patronage and of the Macoute organizations, to mobilize some popular support for a regime. The most the attempt could have achieved is some dispersed goodwill toward the president. Community councils also were set up to give the appearance of local democracy. Most of these were controlled by Duvalierists and had little effect. Some, however, grew teeth and became centers on which significant demands for change were focused.

Economic decline and the compulsory slaughter of black pigs (supposedly necessary because of swine fever), which was decreed by the Organization of American States, affected the daily life of millions throughout the country. These pigs were a principal means of savings for poor families, so that when some emergency occurred, such as illness or death, they could be sold to raise cash. Disgust among most sections of the population with the extravagant style of life adopted by the presidential entourage, and blows to national pride with the scandals of the boat people and the "sale" of sugar workers to the Dominican Republic, added fuel to the flames. Even the business community, which had prospered during the mid-seventies and early eighties, came to see Jean-Claude's government as at best a *pis-aller* (lesser of two evils) and at worst an albatross round the country's neck.

Forward-looking army officers began to recognize that Duvalierism was not eternal; therefore they were not going to defend it at any cost. With all these movements, and in the light of widespread protests and demonstrations, the United States also decided that Duvalier must go, and at this point it played a key role in negotiating the flight of Baby Doc. To ascribe the end of the regime either to an army coup or to United States intervention is seriously to misconceive the situation. The role of army and embassy was to determine the manner and the moment.

The Interregnum

The fall of Baby Doc was followed by five years of military-controlled governments. The early period was dominated by General Henri Namphy, an apparently inoffensive mulatto officer who had been a favorite of Pap Doc, who called him *mon ti grimmaud, grimmaud* being a word for a light-skinned Haitian. Namphy, however, soon acquired a liking for power. He and his fellow generals strengthened the armed forces, incorporating many former Macoutes. In 1987 a new constitution, drawn up by a specially appointed commission, received popular endorsement in a referendum (to many people's surprise). Elections were scheduled for 29 November 1987. Most Duvalierist candidates were disallowed, and violent opposition from this sector, resulting in widespread death and destruction, led to the elections' being called off.

The military junta organized new elections in January 1988, which were widely boycotted by the people and by the leading candidates in the November elections. Leslie Manigat was pronounced victor and acted as president for some months, until he quarreled with General Namphy and was escorted out of the country. Pressure from inside and outside Haiti forced Namphy to resign; he was replaced by Prosper Avril and later by Hérard Abraham. A provisional civilian government under Ertha Pascal-Trouillot supervised the election of December 1990.

The sultanistic pretensions of the junta were limited by their tenuous control of the country and, indeed, of the army itself. In the post-Duvalier years corruption and violence were privatized, and even Generals Namphy and Avril found it impossible to control their subordinate officers. The weakness of the army was clearly exhibited on those occasions when the elites of the country united to oppose some particular action of theirs, for example, when they attempted to take control of the electoral commission. Popular protest forced the junta to back down. Pressure at home and from abroad eventually succeeded in compelling them to appoint a civilian administration, under Trouillot, to oversee elections.

Aristide

Father Jean-Bertrand Aristide took office in February 1991, after a stunning victory in the elections of the previous December, in which he received over two-thirds of the votes cast (though one should remember that probably fewer than half those eligible bothered to register and vote). His nearest rival, Marc Bazin, obtained a mere 15 percent. An attempted coup in January 1991, led by Roger Lafontant, a leading Duvalierist, was foiled. The complicity of the archbishop of Port-au-Prince, François Wolff Ligondé, led to popular attacks on church property, and the papal nuncio was reportedly chased into the street in his underwear. Apart from these incidents Aristide (popularly known as "Titid") moved peacefully into the presidential palace in February 1991 with enthusiastic backing from the masses and with varying degrees of acquiescence from political elites (with the obvious exception of the largely discredited Duvalierists). The masses clearly expected miracles. Political elites were willing in general to give him a chance. What went wrong? How, riding on such a wave of goodwill, did he come tumbling down so soon?

Aristide, born in 1953 at Port-Salut in the southwest of the country, came from a modest background.[32] His father died soon after he was born, and he was brought up by his grandfather, a small landowner and justice of the peace. He was educated at a school in the capital run by the Salesians. He entered the Salesian seminary at Cap Haïtien in 1966, where he learned several foreign languages. He finished seminary at age twenty-one and after a year in the Dominican Republic as a novice he returned to Haiti and studied philosophy and psychology at the state university. He studied for a time in Israel and was ordained a priest in 1982. After further education abroad he returned to Haiti in 1985, where he worked with the Salesians, teaching and working in the parish of St. Jean Bosco in a poor district of the capital. His sermons, explicitly condemning the military regime in the strongest language, drew huge crowds. His church was eventually burned down, and many of his congregation were killed or injured by Duvalierist thugs. His superiors attempted to send him abroad, but his supporters resisted this move. He was eventually expelled from the Salesian order.[33] He retired to run an orphanage for street children, but he maintained a militant opposition to the regime. It was only at the last moment that he emerged as a candidate for the presidency.

The Legislature and the Black Middle Class

It must be clearly recognized that Aristide never enjoyed full support in the legislature. Although one principal political grouping—the National Front for Change and Democracy (FNCD)—backed him in the election and achieved a significant representation in the two chambers, Aristide never really saw eye to eye with the parliamentarians. The much-celebrated constitution of 1987, however, gives the legislature substantial powers to restrict the president in important ways. Haiti has indeed been described, with some exaggeration, as having "a constitutionally powerless president."[34] Hegel said that Napoleon gave the Spanish people a constitution that was much too good for them. In a similar way the new Haitian constitution ignores the political culture of the country. Throughout their history Haitians have assumed the existence of a powerful executive; the president was everything, taking credit for what went well and suffering the consequences of political disasters. Yet under the new constitution his powers are severely limited.

In choosing his cabinet, Aristide largely ignored the claims of elected politicians, even those who had supported him. He chose people he thought he could trust, including mulattoes from the bourgeoisie. The cabinet contained former priests or seminarians, like Ernst Verdieu (Social Affairs) and Renaud Bernardin (Planning), or people who had previously been involved with nongovernmental aid agencies, like Marie-Michèle Rey (Finance). It was called a government of pals, with no serious attempt to represent powerful interests. Aristide thus made little effort to secure effective support from the legislature. He encouraged the growth of a popular, nonparliamentary movement, called Lavalas from the slogan he adopted for his election campaign (a word popularly used for the deluge of water and mud that sometimes descends into the capital after a storm, carrying all before it). The predominantly black politicians retaliated by refusing to endorse some of his diplomatic nominations and delaying or modifying his policy proposals. As early as May, Communist Party leader René Théodore denounced the government as "autocratic." This charge was compounded when former provisional president Ertha Pascal-Trouillot was arrested on charges of corruption and complicity in the January 1991 coup; she was soon released, however, partly owing to pressure from Venezuela and the United States.

Aristide's relations with the legislature reached their nadir in August 1991 with the attempt by mostly left-wing deputies to remove the prime minister, René Préval. A mob composed of a thousand Aristide supporters manhandled one of the opposition legislators and threatened to burn others alive. They also set fire to the CATH (trade union) headquarters, ransacking the offices of the FNCD (the radical party that had supported Aristide in the elections) and of the KID (Democratic Unity Confederation). The leader of both CATH and KID, mayor of Port-au-Prince Evans Paul, denounced "banditry, threats, and violence" by government supporters. Many deputies were afraid to sleep in their own homes.

Aristide, far from discouraging this violence, actually commended the mob who intimidated judges in the trial of Roger Lafontant (organizer of the Duvalierists' attempted coup). These events reinforced the hostility toward the president from important sectors. With the president demonstrating such scant respect for law and for constitutional procedures, some feared the shades of a neo-Duvalierism. There was an increasing personalization of power. A Haitian architect who was supervising some work in the presidential palace told me that the Department of Public Works was totally bypassed and he dealt only with Aristide's formidable personal assistant, Gladys Lauture.

Then the government began sacking thousands of civil servants, partly in response to recommendations from international agencies like the World Bank that government expenditures be cut. Certain departments were manifestly overstaffed, and numerous employees were unqualified political appointees of the Duvalier regime or of successive military juntas. Nevertheless, firings went beyond this, and many were dismissed because of personal vendettas. The black middle classes, who had been among François Duvalier's principal supporters in 1957 but had mostly become disillusioned with Baby Doc, were unnecessarily alienated from the new government by such moves.

The Business Community

For most businesspeople in Haiti Aristide was by no means the favored candidate; his denunciations of capitalism as *un péché mortel* (a deadly sin)[35] and his castigation of the rich led them to oppose him. They feared he might attempt to introduce a socialist economy and oppose the interests of big business. He was, however, viewed as someone who would at least deal firmly with the Duvalierist threat. This led some elements among the Haitian bourgeoisie to support him. Among his principal backers was Antoine Izmery, a Palestinian business-man, who financed much of Aristide's election campaign; he was not alone.

In the event, many businessmen saw Titid's landslide victory as promising at least some political stability and a much needed break with the corrupt military-dominated regimes that had succeeded Baby Doc. He thus came to power with the acquiescence of this sector and indeed made conciliatory gestures toward them, appealing to the "patriotic" members of the bourgeoisie to cooper-ate with his government. These appeals, however, sometimes contained thinly veiled threats that the uncooperative might find the poor helping themselves.

The privileged status of the small francophile, educated, cultured bour-geoisie should be emphasized. Even in the midst of frightful poverty and de-spite years of national economic decline, this small sector of the population continues to enjoy a high standard of living and many servants, who are depen-dent on them for survival. Numerous rich people have left for Miami, New York, or Montreal but retain homes and property in Haiti, returning periodi-cally to manage them or delegating this task to relatives. Although Aristide's attempt to raise the national minimum wage annoyed them, a compromise was reached. In addition, they were favorably impressed by the government's "rea-sonable" approach to commercial matters and its ability to secure promises of increased foreign aid. What, then, accounts for the determination of these elite groups to rid the country of Titid? If his policies did not threaten the business interests of this class in any significant way, what led them to collaborate in the military coup under the mulatto general Raoul Cédras?

The answer is to be found not in commerce but in social attitudes. The very presence of the black populist priest in the presidential palace had instilled new confidence in the masses both in the countryside and in the capital. The popu-list rhetoric (curiously similar at times to the language Papa Doc used in his early days) was leading the poor to question their subordinate and subservient role. Organizations of small peasants in the countryside became more out-spoken in demanding land reforms and the restoration of property stolen in the Duvalier years. Servants began challenging the orders of their wealthy masters, hinting that the large house and two cars might one day be theirs. A social structure going back to the nineteenth century and closely related to color differences was being called into question. Duvalierism had already staked out the claims of the black middle classes; the rhetoric of Titid brought the good news to the poor. It was the apprehension that they would lose their privileged position, together with a plausible fear of mob rule, that led the bourgeoisie to support a military coup. It was not what Aristide *did* that was important, but what he *was* and what he symbolized in the eyes of the masses.

The Army

Army officers, heavily subsidized with American aid, effectively ran Haiti from February 1986 to February 1991. with disastrous consequences. Drug trafficking and contraband were rife, and there were numerous human rights violations. Chronic political instability led to further economic decline.

After having connived at the violence before and during the abortive elections of November 1987 and having managed the fraudulent elections of January 1988, the army, under its new commander General Hérard Abraham, decided to protect the electoral process in December 1990; this was due partly to pressure from the United States and the presence of over a thousand foreign observers. Furthermore, the army helped suppress the attempted Duvalierist coup of January 1991. At his inauguration, Aristide replaced five senior officers, and with the "resignation" of Abraham in July, he appointed Raoul Cédras, who had played an important role in protecting the elections of the previous year. Surely here was someone he could rely on! A whole new generation of Cédras's contemporaries moved into top posts.

The army, of only about seven thousand men, feared losing power and jobs with Aristide's plan for establishing a Swiss-trained police force and a separate presidential guard. Furthermore, the president was determined to protect the rural poor from larger landlords by abolishing the rural *chefs de sections* and bringing local administration under civilian control. It was through the *chefs de sections* that dictatorial regimes, based in the capital, were able to impose their rule on the rural population. Having powers of arrest and detention, they normally sided with the local *gros nègs* against the poor.[36]

Aristide moved to restrict contraband and drug trafficking in the army, thus giving some officers cause to dislike him. It should be remembered that the rank and file of the army, though not particularly well paid, are a relatively privileged group in a very poor country. They saw in Aristide's reforms a threat to their position, despite his efforts to woo these lower ranks by inviting them to parties in the presidential palace. When the coup against Aristide took place there appears to have been no significant split in the army, though it is possible that if he had remained in the country certain army units would have rallied to him.

The Church

Aristide was a Roman Catholic priest, expelled from the Salesian order and suspended from the public performance of his priestly duties. Nevertheless he was in "good standing" and able to say mass privately if he chose to do so.

Owing to pressure from the hierarchy, he resigned his priesthood late in 1994. Since the concordat of 1860, the church hierarchy has played an important role in Haitian politics, almost invariably siding with the elite. In contrast to the Dominican Republic, where the church sees itself as identifying with national aspirations (two archbishops have served as presidents in the past), the Haitian church has always been something of an alien institution, dominated by foreign white clergy. They saw the masses as superstitious in their adherence to the African spirits of the voodoo religion and as needing guidance from an autocratic state in conjunction with an authoritarian church. Politicians claiming to speak for the black masses, like Salnave and Salomon in the nineteenth century, have opposed the hierarchy, identifying rather with freemasonry, Protestantism, or even voodoo.

A hierarchy led by the ambitious archbishop of Cap Haïtien (Msgr. François Guyot) was fearful that with the growth of *ti legliz* things were getting out of hand; its own leadership seemed threatened. The bishops closed the countrywide literacy campaign, Misyon Alfa, many of whose activists were politically radical. The outspoken and inflammatory sermons of Père Aristide, parish priest of St. Jean Bosco, had alarmed them, and they tried to silence him or have him transferred abroad. This he resisted, and relations between Aristide and the church broke down. As already noted, the archbishop of Port-au-Prince was implicated in the failed Duvalierist coup of January 1991 and fled into exile. Among the bishops only Msgr. Willy Romélus, of Jérémie, has shown any sympathy with Aristide. Elements in the church appear to have given surreptitious support to the coup that overthrew Aristide, and the Vatican was the only state in the world to recognize the brutal military regime.

The voodoo priests suffered in the post-Duvalier years from the association many of them had with the Macoutes. Aristide himself was violently critical of the Macoutes in his years at St. Jean Bosco. Since that time, however, some voodoo priests have emerged as politically radical and socially progressive. Titid himself, as president, participated in the two hundredth anniversary of the Bois Caïman voodoo ceremony of August 1791.

International Reactions

The Organization of American States and European Community members, together with the United Nations Security Council, reacted swiftly to condemn the coup of 30 September 1991, and many governments called for Aristide's reinstatement. The OAS imposed an embargo, which the European Community and the United Nations later endorsed. Few, however, were prepared for military intervention. The ousted president's return would therefore depend on strong support in Haiti itself, and it is not clear that key groups were prepared to risk the violence that might follow such a move. The army was vigorously opposed to his return but was pressured into accepting him by the threat of a U.S. invasion. As a result of an agreement brokered by former president Jimmy Carter, U.S. troops landed peacefully, and after some weeks Aristide was re-installed in the presidential palace and the military junta left the country.

Efforts by the military to claim a veil of constitutionality after the coup of 1991 were denounced as bogus by the French government, whose ambassador referred to Jean-Jacques Honorat, de facto prime minister, as an *imbécile et crétin*. The oil embargo was largely ineffective; huge profits have been made by marketing contraband supplies at inflated prices. Like most embargoes it was only partially applied and did little harm to those in power. Some assembly plants were closed, though not all, resulting in unemployment among the working classes in the capital. The embargo encouraged dealing in contraband among military officers and corrupt tradesmen. It raised the cost of transport and has therefore hit the rural population. It was a fine gesture of solidarity by these nations but little more. Owing to the poverty of Haiti it had little effect on their own economies, and it is unlikely that they would have been willing to impose such an embargo on a more wealthy Hispanic trading partner. Why did they not take similar steps after the Peruvian coup? The embargo and freezing of foreign aid hurt some businessmen, who sent a delegation to Washington to persuade OAS governments that it would harm the poor (exhibiting a some-what uncharacteristic and unconvincing concern for their less fortunate fellow citizens). A rise in the cost of basic imports affected the very poor, and the effects on public health and nutrition levels have become visible.

Among foreign influences, the attitudes and actions of the United States government have been the most important and most complex. On arriving in Haiti during the military regime of General Prosper Avril, ambassador Alvin Adams made clear the United States' support for "the democratic process." His quoting the Haitian proverb *Bourik chajé pas kampé* (A loaded ass must keep going) not only confirmed this position but left him with the nickname by which he was universally known in Haiti (*Bourik chajé*). Washington was clearly alarmed at the prospects of a president coming to power who had frequently denounced the United States government as evil and diabolic. Nevertheless (as with François Duvalier in 1957), rhetoric was modified and a working relationship developed. Adams used his considerable influence with the army to suppress the January 1991 coup, thus ensuring Aristide's succession.

He gave critical support to Aristide once in office but made himself unpopular in Haiti by his high profile and overt meddling in domestic politics.

The advent of Titid certainly gave new hope to the mass of Haitians, reflected in the dramatic decline of illegal migration to the United States (the "boat people"). This brought a favorable American reaction to his regime. The massive increase in boat people since the coup confirms the contrast with the brutal military regime that has followed. The resumption of Haitian migration on a large scale was one of the few cards Aristide held in pressing Washington to support his return.

Although Titid's handling of the U.S. connection might be seen as one of his successes, his relationship with the Dominican Republic was quite otherwise. Hundreds of thousands of Haitians live and work in the neighboring republic, most of them in the cane fields. Since 1920 Haiti has supplied significant numbers of laborers to its eastern neighbor, sometimes by contract between the two governments and more often by Haitians' illegally crossing the border in search of paid labor. The Dominican reaction is ambivalent. They rely on Haitians to do work that Dominicans refuse to perform, but they resent the presence of this large black migrant population, especially in times of economic hardship. In 1937 dictator Trujillo massacred tens of thousands of Haitians as part of his policy of "de-Africanizing" the border. President Joaquín Balaguer shared the racist philosophy of his former master and manifests a deep-seated prejudice against Haitians, as clearly evinced in his book, *La isla al revés*.[37]

The material conditions Haitian migrants live in are very bad, but no worse than those they left in Haiti. One must also remember that most of them chose to go to the Dominican Republic, and some even bribed their way there. More important is the lack of human rights and the disrespect they endure. Also, many cases have been documented of coercion approaching slavery.[38] Aristide outspokenly denounced the Dominican Republic in the international forum. This gave Balaguer an excuse to expel thousands of undocumented Haitians, leading to a major confrontation between the two states. The Dominican Republic thus became a safe haven where Duvalierists and other opponents of Aristide could plot his downfall.

Père Aristide and Papa Doc

Despite Aristide's considerable success in obtaining promises of increased foreign aid—from Washington, from the European Union, and from some Latin American countries—this was not enough to counteract the mistakes he had made by alienating so many key groups in Haiti at the same time. I have drawn a comparison with François Duvalier. Both were small, black, nonelite figures with extraordinary charisma. They were both brought up by men from the key *classe intermédiaire;* Aristide's grandfather, like Duval Duvalier, was a justice of the peace. Both wished to challenge the privileges of the predominantly mulatto elite—the unjust structures of wealth in a country of startling contrasts. One was a country doctor, the other an urban priest; both wrote poems, but their charisma worked differently. Duvalier was a calculating and ruthless manipulator of complex situations who could skillfully play one group off against another until all his potential opponents were eliminated. He also retained considerable popular support, particularly in the rural areas where 80 percent of the population lives. François Duvalier's use of terror became notorious throughout the world through Graham Greene's *The Comedians.* Eventually he spent so much energy trying to stay in office and stay alive that he achieved little of lasting value. He made only a marginal shift in the structure of wealth, by providing a certain amount of state patronage for a small sector of the black middle class and some Arab and nonelite mulatto families like the Mevs and the Bennetts. Even his replacing foreign bishops by Haitian nationals seems merely to have exchanged white faces for black, under the same conservative miters. "My government has not been what I had hoped for," he confessed to a close collaborator just before his death in 1971.[39]

Aristide, on the other hand, is a brilliant orator with an extraordinary appeal to the poor and outcast. He puts many of their deepest feelings into words, while playing on these feelings to forward interests he believes to be theirs. Not many will doubt his sincerity in wishing to improve the lot of the poor. He bravely resisted the iniquities of the military junta in the post-1986 years, but he is manifestly inexperienced in political affairs and easily manipulated by those around him. If he had remained a prophetic thorn in the flesh of the politicians rather than becoming one of them, he might have performed an invaluable function in Haiti. It is a great temptation to believe that if only a good man could sit in the presidential palace all could be changed for the better. Aristide's seven months there did, however, see a rise in tax revenue, promises of foreign aid, an increase in the minimum wage, and attempts to bring the police force and rural administration under civilian control.

The really important development in Haiti over the past thirty years has been the growth of thousands of peasant groups throughout the country. Some are backed by local clergy, some even sponsored by forward-looking voodoo priests, and many are supported by nongovernmental aid agencies. These groups thrived under Baby Doc, survived under the military interregnum, received government aid under Titid, but suffered grievously after his overthrow. Since his return in late 1994 they have reemerged as an important factor in Haitian politics.

After the Coup

The desire to avoid what is seen as the only alternative frequently drives people to support, or acquiesce in, regimes they would otherwise abhor and oppose. So long as a government can restrict the perceived options to ones that powerful groups find totally unacceptable, it is able to survive. For years Cheddi Jagan, the radical leader of the opposition, was a principal weapon in the armory of President Forbes Burnham in Guyana. The possibility of Jagan's coming to power was for some years all that stood between Burnham and defeat. As a result Jagan became—despite himself—a principal bulwark against change in Guyana. Both Jagan himself and the international situation changed dramatically, however, and Jagan was elected president in 1993. Likewise Aristide was for some time a trump card in the hands of the junta. Elite groups were persuaded to acquiesce in a brutal, corrupt, and monumentally inefficient military regime, which in other circumstances they would have opposed, largely because they saw Aristide's return to power as the sole alternative. Only when it became clear that effective constraints on his freedom of action would be in place did these groups accept his return.

I have tried to account for the overthrow of Aristide and have pointed out some of his mistakes. In doing so I have no wish to justify the coup and even less desire to excuse the outrages of the military regime under General Raoul Cédras, which has been ruthless, violent, corrupt, and oppressive. Its feeble attempts to appear constitutional by involving the two houses of the legislature have proved a fiasco, convincing no one (except the pope!). The coup leaders inaugurated an interim president—Appeal Court head Joseph Nerette, something of a political nonentity—and a new prime minister, the whimsical Jean-Jacques Honorat, former Duvalierist intellectual turned human rights activist. An outspoken opponent of Aristide since before his election, he was not widely trusted and had problems constructing his cabinet. In June 1992 the military dropped both men, leaving the office of president vacant. Their new puppet prime minister, Marc Bazin, could not claim legal legitimacy, for according to the constitution a prime minister must be chosen by the president; and the only person who could make any claim to this office was Aristide.

As part of a compromise brokered by the U.S. State Department in July 1993 (known as the Governor's Island Accord, accepted by Aristide and Cédras),

Aristide appointed a new prime minister, Robert Malval, on the understanding that he would prepare for the president's return within four months. Such a move would clearly be resisted by the military, which was also implicated in the assassination of the justice minister. Malval, finding himself in an impossible position, resigned in December 1993, later denouncing Aristide as "egoistic, disloyal, and incompetent." A new provisional president was installed by the junta in May 1994, but he was recognized by no country (apart, presumably, from the Vatican).

On 15 October 1994 Aristide returned to Haiti, but with wings clipped and claws pared. Not only was he restricted by a constitution that gives major powers to the prime minister and to a legislative assembly he did not control (these legal limits had existed in his earlier period in power), but the country was effectively controlled by U.S. troops. The possibility was removed that Lavalas mobs would put pressure on the legislature by demonstrations and threats of violence, as they did in 1991. Aristide, in conjunction with the prime minister he had chosen, appointed a cabinet in which most key positions (apart from minister of defense) were in the hands of mulattoes from the bourgeois elite; this was designed primarily to reassure the business community and the United States that radical policies would be abjured. The Haitian constitution barred Aristide from succeeding himself, and so in February 1996 René Préval was elected to the presidency by an overwhelming vote. Aristide's Lavalas Party also won the election to both houses of parliament. But both victories were obtained while the most important opposition parties boycotted the elections. The Haitian government is faced with a dilemma: it has to satisfy its social base among the poor, but it also has to live up to U.S. expectations as to orderly government.

Conclusion

Most Haitian regimes, including those of the Duvaliers, can be seen to have manifested sultanistic tendencies. They have been authoritarian and autocratic; their despotic propensities have normally been inhibited by certain institutional factors, including (up to the first U.S. occupation) an inability to control the whole country. With the centralization imposed by the occupation, later governments were able to rule more effectively. François Duvalier certainly went further than any other government in eroding the institutional restraints on presidential power, and only gradually have countervailing power centers reemerged.

Exiles frequently lose touch with realities at home, experiencing a decline in popular support. On other occasions, as with Khomeini, Perón, or Lenin, exile enhances a person's reputation and prepares the way for a messianic return. At this time is not clear where Titid stands. He may be able to call on mass support to ensure that his candidates gain control of the legislature and then to set about claiming a further term of office, which seems to have some plausibility since three years of his five-year term were spent in exile.

The greatest danger Haiti faces today is the attempt to impose "democracy" on the country in terms of a strong and highly centralized regime. The constitution of 1987 made a valiant attempt to embody a degree of devolution, but it is likely that a popularly elected president, backed by the army, would soon ensure that such local decision making was ineffective. The hope for the country is to be found not merely in elections, but in the general strengthening of local and regional groups and institutions as bulwarks to sultanistic tendencies and as effective means by which ordinary Haitians will be able to participate in decisions that affect their daily lives.

8

. . . .

The Pahlavi Regime in Iran

Homa Katouzian

Empirically, the Pahlavi state presented a unique experience. Yet its basic features were firmly rooted in thousands of years of Iranian history. In normal periods Iran's social and economic system has been one of arbitrary rule based on the absence of property *rights;* therefore in abnormal periods (the collapse of arbitrary regimes caused by domestic or external forces) it has been visited for relatively long stretches by chaos, confusion, plunder, and the absence of proper central authority before the next arbitrary regime has eventually been established. That is also why until the beginning of the twentieth century the term *enqelab,* now used as the equivalent of "revolution," meant sociopolitical chaos and calamity.

The system of arbitrary rule was based on the state monopoly of property rights and the concentrated, though not necessarily centralized, economic, bureaucratic, and military power it gave rise to. There could be no rights of private property, only *privileges* that were granted to individuals by the state and that could therefore be withdrawn at a clap of the hands. There always existed social classes, in terms of differences of wealth, position, and occupation; there were always landlords, merchants, artisans, peasants, and so on. But unlike the situation in Europe, in Iran the composition of the various social classes constantly changed, since the state could and would arbitrarily withdraw a privilege from a person, family, clan, or community and grant it to others. Consequently there could be no established aristocracy, and an unusual degree of both upward and downward mobility obtained in society.

The absence of law and politics in the Western sense was the institutional counterpart to this sociological base. Where there are no rights there is no law. Where the law constitutes little more than the arbitrary decisions, whims, or desires of the lawgiver, the concept of law itself becomes redundant, despite the existence of a body of public rules and regulations at any moment in time. Only independent rights, not dependent privileges, can form the basis for real economic and social power by individuals and social classes. Therefore the absence of rights means the absence of law, and the absence of law must mean the absence of politics. Note that it is not merely just laws and rational politics (usually associated with the rise of modern European society in the past few centuries) that are absent, but law and politics themselves, just or unjust, traditional or rational.

European society, whether ancient, medieval, or modern, has always been founded on some kind of written or unwritten law and contract, between the state and society, or on deeply entrenched custom. To be sure, this differed between, say, Greek city-states and modern European democracies in terms of the scope and limit of the power of the state, the extent of its social base and political legitimacy, and the way its administration of justice affected various social groups and classes. Yet the state's power has been subject to varying but definite limits, and these limits have been determined by the rights of the social classes. Given this continuity, law and politics have always existed in Europe, which means that European revolutions were fought not for law itself but against the existing legal and constitutional arrangements, with the aim of extending (or restoring) the scope of social rights as well as their application.

In Iran, by contrast, the power of the state was limited not by any tacit or explicit law, contract, or custom but by the extent of that power itself. Absence of law did not mean absence of rules of conduct: on the contrary, it meant that the state could arbitrarily make or break "laws" at will and to the limits of its physical power. *Estebdad* literally means arbitrary rule, and where decisions are routinely arbitrary there can be no meaningful state of law. This explains why Iran's constitutional revolution of 1905–6 aimed for freedom from arbitrary rule, that is, for law itself.[1] Expressed in terms of Isaiah Berlin's notion of negative and positive liberty,[2] the constitutionalists wanted freedom from arbitrary rule and the right to secure and predictable living, guaranteed by an independent and inviolable legal framework.[3]

Premodern Iranian society was thus prelegal as well as preconstitutional and prepolitical. And that is how the state (*dowlat*) stood not only above but also opposite the people (*mellat*). Toward the end of the nineteenth century, when Iran came into close contact with Europe and Western ideas, the terms *polteek* and *polteeki* were adopted for "politics" and "political" in reference only to

European politics. *Siyasat* and *siyasi*, which later replaced the foreign borrowings, had originally meant "punishment," or the art of effective government for arbitrary rulers.[4] The historical absence of a true state of law, with the insecurity and unpredictability it entails, has been both a product and a cause of the absence of feudalism (in the European sense) in Iranian society. Furthermore, these conditions provided the strongest barriers against the accumulation of financial and (later) physical capital in industry and agriculture alike, for history and experience taught that earthly possessions could easily be lost, not infrequently along with the lives of their owners.

The resulting social psychology and pattern of public behavior is thus easy to discern. *Dowlat* is, as a matter of principle, regarded as an actual and potential enemy by both individuals and social classes, including its own servants. The systemic arbitrariness (*estebdad*) and the consequent individual examples of injustice (*zolm*) create an acute sense of fear and insecurity, mistrust, disbelief, frustration, resentment, and alienation. There may be loyalty and attachment to one's own family and community, the popular (nonstate) culture, or even the whole of the country. But once a regime comes to be identified as yet another avatar of the age-old system of arbitrary governance, it lasts not by consent, sectional or class loyalty, or overriding considerations for the defense of the realm, but merely by the dialectics of force and fear. The moment the state's seemingly inexorable force begins to weaken, for whatever reason, it loses its grip on the population. The fear that the state then generates in the community turns into explosive energy, giving rise to a new force.

This is not a matter for purely psychological analysis. Since the state monopolizes all rights, it must also monopolize all obligations. In contrast, the society, having no rights, feels no obligation toward the state. It follows that at times of acute domestic or external crisis the people either side with the state's enemies or refuse to pull its chestnuts out of the fire. In fact, when it is widely believed that the state is about to fall, public reaction either helps bring about a collapse that might otherwise have been averted or shortens the death agony.[5]

The social psychology of Iranian upheavals and revolutions—the suddenly emerging sense of a strong public bond among individuals and classes, the oneness of purpose, the idealism, heroism, and self-sacrifice—is not different from the social psychology of other revolutions.[6] Where Iran is different is in the unity of all social classes in the struggle to topple a regime identified with arbitrary rule; the implicit belief that once the regime collapses the entire arbitrary state will have been destroyed; the role of an individual leader as savior; the "good" counterpart to the "bad" person in power; and the consequent lack of a program for dismantling the arbitrary state itself.[7] As a result, the arbitrary state tends to survive under the new regime.

The summary above is not meant to recount Iran's long history, nor am I suggesting there has been no change in Iranian history since the fall of Adam. Rather, it is intended as an abstract and simple theory to help make sense of the *longue durée*. Compared with Europe, Iran has gone through too many changes rather than too few, at least partly because of the basic social features described above. The one change that is yet to occur, however, is the final and complete destruction of the arbitrary state and the arbitrary society.

The Pahlavi State: Dictatorship, Interregnum, and Sultanism

Like all the regimes preceding it, that of the Pahlavis was an arbitrary one, although it took time for both Reza Shah and Mohammad Reza Shah to establish their absolute and arbitrary rule in the later stages of their reign. Strictly speaking, the period of Reza Shah's sultanism falls between 1933 and 1941, and that of his son between 1963 and 1977.

As I already mentioned, the constitutional revolution of 1905–11 had been fought, first and foremost, to establish a legal framework (*qanun*) and, later, parliamentary government in the country under a constitutional monarchy of the Qajar dynasty.[8]

The constitutional revolution was led by merchants, landlords, religious leaders, and modern intellectuals. It was bound to diffuse political power and strengthen private property, both in land and in merchant capital. The abolition of land assignment (the age-old system whereby the state assigned land to whomever it willed, making landlords assignees rather than owners) by the first Majlis (parliament) provided a constitutional sanction for the existing ownership of land, turning the landlord's privilege into a contractual right of ownership. It also served the merchants' interest to the extent that it reduced the political and economic power of the state, reaffirmed the property rights of those bigger merchants who had acquired land by purchase, encouraged other merchants who wished to do the same, and strengthened the ownership of capital.

It is therefore not surprising that Reza Shah's rise to power between 1921 and 1926, when he became first minister of defense, then prime minister, and finally shah, was generally resisted by a combined landlord and merchant opposition but helped by army officers, bureaucrats, and intellectuals who were either actual or potential clients of the state. After his coronation in 1926, when he established the new Pahlavi dynasty, Reza Shah's rule was still authoritarian rather than downright sultanistic, since he depended on the advice of a small band of important politicians with roots in the Qajar era, and, to a lesser extent, on parliament.

By 1933, however, the Majlis had been reduced to no more than a powerless instrument of the state, and almost all of the Shah's early advisers (not to mention critics and opponents) had been dismissed, banished, jailed, murdered, or driven into complete subservience. In that year Abdolhosein Teimurtash, the extremely powerful minister of the court, was arrested and subsequently murdered in jail, to be followed shortly by Ja'farqoli Khan Sardar As'ad Bakhtiari, the Shah's close friend and minister of war. The fall of Teimurtash was both symbolic and symptomatic. It was symbolic because he had hitherto been regarded as the second most powerful man in the country and had wielded considerable independent power and authority. It was symptomatic because it revealed the growing shift from authoritarian dictatorship to arbitrary sultanism, when the men who had provided the backbone of the new regime became its victims.[9]

It is anybody's guess how Reza Shah's regime would have evolved had the Allies not invaded Iran in 1941. Officially the country was neutral, but the official as well as unofficial popularity of Germany's cause was evident, and Iran's strategic location south of the Soviet Union and north of the Persian Gulf (together with its implications for Britain's oil supply routes) were too sensitive not to attract attention.

Reza Shah abdicated in favor of his son, Mohammad Reza, but the Allies did not formally take over the administration of the country. According to a treaty signed in Tehran, Allied troops would remain in Iran and use the country's facilities until the end of the war, but they would otherwise respect Iran's independence and integrity. Had Reza Shah had a social base in the country, he could have concluded the treaty himself and remained on the throne, as he was ready to do. His quick fall from power was thus due not only to the invasion but also to his having alienated most Iranians. There was not a single social class that identified with his rule. Furthermore, most civil servants and politicians were highly critical, and even the army, Reza Shah's most cherished accomplishment, was dispirited. The minute he declared his abdication, even before he had left the country, the Majlis deputies, who had been handpicked by the government rather than elected by the people, began to accuse him of dictatorship, arbitrariness, corruption, and plunder of private property.[10]

The years 1941–53 can best be described as an interregnum. Landlords and conservative politicians, in an informal alliance with the religious establishment,[11] made up the most powerful and influential social group in the country. The new shah largely depended on the landlord-ulema alliance, although he was also keen to enhance his personal power through the army as well as foreign support. The Tudeh Party, initially a coalition of Marxist, socialist, and democratic elements, demanded democratic and distributive reforms, but it increasingly tended toward Marxism-Leninism and the Soviet Union. There were elements in the army, notably General Ali Razmara, who were aiming to create a modern military dictatorship, possibly to the exclusion of the Shah himself.

This period was marked by relative openness and power struggles, although it cannot accurately be described as a democratic era: between 1941 and 1951 no fewer than seventeen cabinets came and went without any notable achievements to their credit, and political conflict was carried out in a destructive rather than constructive fashion.[12] Mohammad Mosaddeq's government (1951–53) made an attempt at establishing parliamentary democracy, but this was in the wake of the nationalization of Iranian oil, and the government was faced with serious economic constraints as well as hostility from the Shah, parts of the army, landlords, the religious establishment, Britain, and in the end America. The combination of these forces led to Mosaddeq's overthrow by the famous coup d'état of 1953.[13]

In the subsequent decade the Shah headed an authoritarian regime that was supported by landlords, the religious establishment, and the army. Iran's economic and political dependence on the United States grew. Between 1953 and 1960, taking advantage of regular (though not yet vast) amounts of oil revenues in addition to American grants and technical assistance, the Shah managed to increase his personal power at the expense of his allies and advisers. But the economic crisis of 1960–62 forced him to give way to demands of reformist (although loyal) forces from within the regime, which aimed at checking the Shah's personal power and wished to implement a land reform policy in the interest of social and economic development.

Ali Amini's government (April 1961–July 1962) was a product of this power struggle. It faced the more radical and popularly based Second National Front, led by Mosaddeq's former colleagues and supporters. Amini enjoyed the goodwill of the Kennedy administration, but the Shah had only grudgingly accepted him, he was distrusted by landlords and religious leaders because of his land reform policy, and most of the Mosaddeqists opposed him.[14] Not surprisingly, he did not last long and resigned after a disagreement with the Shah over the size of the military budget.

The Shah then managed to consolidate his own power by taking over the land reform policy (though in a diluted form) and adding a few other measures in a concocted referendum that he described as the White Revolution (January 1963). Having lost the confidence of landlords, traditional politicians, and the religious establishment, and lacking a social base among the urban lower and middle classes, he had to face the combined revolt of all these classes, whose leadership had by then fallen into the hands of the landlords and religious leaders. He won the battle against the riots of June 1963, which brought Ayatollah Ruhollah Khomeini to national prominence, and from that moment on he became the absolute and undisputed leader of the land.

The years 1963–77 are the period of the Shah's sultanistic rule. Two principal factors made this fundamental change possible. First, the land reform had eliminated the landlords as an independent social class and transferred their sociopolitical power directly to the state. At the same time, the confrontation with the religious opposition and its defeat helped remove its autonomous influence in social and political affairs and reduced its economic power base by bringing major religious endowments under state administration. Second, the increasing flow of oil revenues paid directly to the state provided the Shah with great sources of domestic finance and foreign exchange from outside the domestic economic system. As is well known by now, much of the oil revenue is not a return on the use of domestic inputs but a kind of economic rent paid for the use of scarce resources or, alternatively, a kind of financial capital realized as the result of liquidating physical assets. Either way, this revenue is directly received and disbursed by the state, enabling it to finance development projects, expand its military-bureaucratic network, and expand its clientele among technocrats and intellectuals.[15] Thus the Shah, who effectively was the state, became increasingly independent from the economy and the society, while the latter became increasingly dependent on him and his decisions. It is important to emphasize that the change from authoritarianism to sultanism was the result both of the Shah's abandonment of his former alliance with the landlords and the religious establishment and of his growing independence from the domestic economy (and foreign aid) owing to rising oil receipts.

The year 1977 saw the inauguration of President Jimmy Carter. His pronouncements in defense of human rights in Eastern Europe and among America's Third World allies played a critical psychological role both in encouraging vocal opposition to the Shah's rule and in shaking the Shah's confidence in the hitherto uncritical support he had enjoyed from his Western (especially American) allies. The swift and complete collapse of his rule was characteristic of a regime that lacks a social base and cannot depend on the unswerving loyalty and support even of its own civil and military apparatus at times of acute crisis.

The fundamental reason for the rise of sultanism under the Pahlavis remained, as it had always been, the weakness of private property and the related absence of strong autonomous classes as a social base for the formation, or persistence, of a dictatorial or democratic state. The question, nevertheless, is why the constitutional revolution, the abdication of Reza Shah, or even the (class-based) coup d'état of 1953 failed to prevent the reemergence of sultanism in modern guise. Several factors help explain this failure. The ideology of modernism and nationalism (on which more below) encouraged the formation of a highly centralized as well as concentrated state machinery. Independent political parties (as opposed to occasional mass movements) were rare, did not take root, and did not last long enough. The near absence of institutions that make up the foundation of modern civil societies meant there could be no automatic balance against the growth of the state power beyond authoritarian dictatorship. Lack of genuine political experience ensured that not even politicians, let alone the citizenry, could play the game of politics by the rules of competition and compromise, as opposed to deadly struggle. Parliament itself, whenever it operated relatively freely, was often a battleground, and this exercise of freedom without a commensurate sense of responsibility rendered effective government extremely difficult. The use of imported modern techniques and technology in building up the instruments of fear and coercion—the army, the security services, the paramilitary organizations, and so on—increasingly made it easier to control urban discontent and to subdue the autonomy of nomad groups. Foreign aid helped the process, and massive oil revenues later completed it.

The State and Ideology

By definition, and in contrast to a modern totalitarian regime, traditional arbitrary rule does not require an ideology for social and intellectual legitimation and organization. The Qajar state lacked such an ideology and was not so much actively legitimized as passively accepted by traditional religion. Traditional religions are in any case different from modern ideologies in many respects, even though there are important similarities.

The Pahlavi state, on the other hand, was not a traditional system of arbitrary rule, but one that was strongly identified with certain notions of nationalism and modernism. There were no nationalist and modernist overtones in the constitutional revolution, but the very ideas of constitutional and parliamentary government were modern, even though they were commonly explained and justified in traditional Islamic terms.[16] Besides, many modern intellectuals aspired to the development of a modern infrastructure for the country, including modern education, banking, roads, and railways. Apart from that, there was an intellectual undercurrent of nationalism in the proper European sense of the term, that is, not merely anti-imperialism and aspirations toward complete sovereignty and independence, but an aggressive belief in ancient glories and a romantic desire to turn Iran into a fully Europeanized—if not European—society. This type of aggressive and vitalistic European nationalism grew and spread rapidly among modern intellectuals and professionals during and after World War I.[17]

Therefore the founders of the Pahlavi state were not limited to Reza Khan and a handful of army officers or, as the strong popular myth has it, the British government. Nationalist and modernist sentiments grew rapidly among modern intellectuals and educated elites during World War I when Iran's neutrality was grossly violated by all sides and Russian and British interference in the country's affairs rose to its peak. And they exploded against the British-sponsored 1919 agreement, which these groups all saw as an attempt to turn Iran into a British protectorate.[18] In fact, the 1919 agreement was denounced by both the old constitutionalists and the growing nationalist and modernist elements who were far more radical in their aspirations and very impatient to realize them. But the unity of purpose between the two groups was not to last long.[19]

The extent to which the 1921 coup by Seyyed Zia and Reza Khan was welcomed by nationalists and modernist intellectuals is not yet widely acknowledged, partly because of the later realization that British officers and diplomats in Iran had a hand in organizing the coup, but mainly as a result of the dictatorial regimes that sprang from it. The rise of official nationalism that followed the coup and became the dominant ideology of the Pahlavi state was inevitably associated with the growth of dictatorship (1923–33). This surprised many of the literary and intellectual nationalists, some of whom fell out with Reza Khan even before he became Reza Shah. It did not, however, surprise the hardheaded military and civilian officials who themselves played an important role in bringing it about. They were to be puzzled, dismayed, and disillusioned only when it changed into an arbitrary system and turned against them.

When the romantic nationalist movement began to gather momentum, it was still a nationalism not of the rulers but of the ruled, a novel and dynamic wave with a firm popular base among the discontented modern intellectuals. It was motivated by anger and shame because of cultural decline, economic backwardness, and political impotence and propelled by the real and imagined achievements of ancient Persia. It was contemptuous, sometimes even ashamed, of many of the existing norms and traditions but was proud, instead, of the romanticized glories of the bygone ages. It was embarrassed by the ordinary people and their ways and self-conscious about what Europeans might think of "us" because of "them," but it blew its trumpets about Cyrus, Darius, Anushiravan, and the "Aryan race." It is highly instructive that as late as 1935 no less than Reza Shah himself told Mokhber al-Saltaneh, his former prime minister, that the reason he had ordered men to wear European hats was to ensure that the Europeans "would not laugh at us."[20] Yet hundreds of men and women perished in a pool of blood in Mashad when they held a protest meeting in defiance of the compulsory hat change.[21]

At the same time, Europe was busy producing racist theories and ideologies. Theories about the superiority of the Aryan race were already widespread when the Nazis began to make their presence felt in Germany. During the Great War the exclusive model for embryonic Iranian nationalism had been the Kaiser's Germany, the enemy of both Britain and Russia, and the hotbed of modern theories of racism in general. Later the Bolshevik revolution supplied another model that captured the imagination of a minority of modernist-nationalist intellectuals. Both radical nationalist trends cooperated in bringing down the constitutional regime and replacing it with Reza Shah's dictatorship. Not surprisingly, Nazism and Nazi Germany became the model of official nationalism later under Reza Shah, and the two countries' political and economic relations rapidly got closer until the Allies invaded Iran in 1941.[22] Under Mohammad Reza Shah, official Europeanism gave way to Americanism, both during his authoritarian phase and, especially, in his sultanistic phase after 1963. However, official Aryanist and pan-Persian propaganda was, if anything, enhanced in the 1960s and 1970s. This propaganda taught that Iranians were an Aryan people who had founded one of the greatest civilizations (if not *the* greatest), but this civilization had declined, both materially and intellectually, in consequence of the Arab conquest, Islam, the Turkic and Mongol invasions, and later, European imperialism—all external forces. The high point of official nationalism was reached when the 2,500th anniversary of the founding of the Persian empire was celebrated in Persepolis with the participation of many foreign heads of state.

Political Parties

Early in Reza Shah's regime steps were taken to organize an official political party, called the Iran-e Now (new or modern Iran) Party. At first the move enjoyed Reza Shah's backing, but he quickly realized that the organizers—his chief lieutenants Teimurtash, Nosrat al-Dowleh, and Ali Akbar Davar—had intended to turn the party into a political instrument that, though it would not pose a threat to the dictatorial regime, would act as a check on the Shah's aspirations for unlimited power. That was why the Shah ordered it disbanded even before it had been properly launched: the contrast is striking with Turkey, where Kemal Atatürk, to whom Reza Shah is often compared, founded a party that institutionalized his regime and later democratized it.[23] When Mostafa Fateh, the Anglo-Persian Oil Company's most senior Iranian employee, was asked by the party's organizing triumvirate to join, he replied: "This party is like a cure after the ill man's death. . . . In the beginning you did not take the people into account, and now you regret that and wish to use this party as a kind of protection against the Shah's ever-increasing power. But you are making a mistake once again, for neither will he allow such a party to thrive, nor will the neglected and ignored people welcome your party."[24] And after his summary dismissal, just before he was arrested, tried, and murdered in prison for obscure reasons, Teimurtash wrote in his notes: "[The Shah] is afraid lest the remnants of the New Iran Party—which was disbanded in anticipation of a day like this— might have a nucleus which would come to my help and support."[25]

Under Mohammad Reza Shah, events took a different turn. Fascism was no longer available as an acceptable external model, and the Shah's Western allies were all democracies. A few years after the 1953 coup, when all independent party activity had been suppressed, two parties were suddenly created to show that Iran was a two-party democracy along Anglo-American lines: Melliyun (intended to mean nationalists and led by then prime minister Manuchehr Eqbal) was meant to replace Mosaddeq's National Front, and Mardom (people), which was to be the more popular party in the absence of the Tudeh Party. It was window dressing largely intended for external consumption.

The Iran-e Novin Party (also meaning new or modern Iran) was launched in 1963 at the beginning of the Shah's "revolutionary" phase. It effectively replaced the Melliyun, which disappeared unceremoniously. Mardom was retained, and the Pan-Iranist Party, a small band of Iranian chauvinists that went back to the 1940s but had been inactive since the 1950s, was encouraged to resume activity. The new party was taken somewhat more seriously, since its founders were young technocrats whom many saw as the backbone of the Shah's new reformist course. After the assassination of Hasan-Ali Mansur, the Shah's prime minister between 1964 and 1965, and his replacement with the less independent Amir-Abbas Hoveida, it failed to become an independent force in Iranian politics. Most ministers, deputies, and high state officials joined, but it never attracted any public participation. Its most important function, perhaps, was to act as the administrative machinery for the selection of the Majlis deputies, who were then declared as duly elected in general elections.[26] Mardom was still the main "opposition" party, but it was a pseudo-opposition. The Pan-Iranist Party was in many ways a semi-opposition within the regime, but when in 1971 it denounced Iran's acquiescence in the independence of Bahrain, which official propaganda had called Iran's "fourteenth province" until then, it was no longer tolerated. Soon the Mardom Party followed, but not before demonstrating the nature of the regime.

In 1974 a by-election took place in the northern city of Shahsavar. The new general secretary of the party, Ameri, had persuaded the government to allow his candidate to campaign freely for the seat. Election fever gripped the city; the pseudo-opposition's candidate acted like a genuine opposition candidate and denounced the Hoveida administration. In spite of a last-minute campaign by many Iran-e Novin leaders, the Mardom candidate won a large majority—except that his victory was not acknowledged by the government, which declared its candidate elected. Ameri denounced the election fraud in public, but about the same time the Shah, on a state visit to India, pointed to the by-election as proof that Iran was democratic. Soon Ameri resigned, and he was killed when his jeep hit a cow.

In 1975 official party politics took a dramatic turn. At a suddenly called press conference, the Shah, who had once written that he would never institute a single party because that was what the communists and Hitler had done,[27] declared that to enable all Iranians to cooperate for the benefit of their country, the existing parties were disbanded and replaced with a single party, the Rastakhiz-e Melli (national resurgence) Party. Its three programmatic points were the imperial order, constitutional monarchy, and the white revolution. Membership in the new party was effectively made mandatory for all Iranians. In a famous speech, the Shah classified his subjects into three groups: the great majority, who, he said, were behind the regime; those who were passive and neutral and should therefore "expect nothing from us"; and dissidents and critics, for whom there was no room in the country and who were free to apply for passports and leave Iran.

The state was thus no longer satisfied with the passive obedience of the public but expected active commitment. Membership books were sent to all state offices, including universities, and their staff members were told to join or face punitive action. The psychological impact of this treatment on the public is not difficult to guess. Instead of creating a popular base for the regime, it alienated the people. Abolhasan Ebtehaj, Iran's first and most able technocrat, who, having been sacked by the Shah, had founded a private bank, remembers that the Shah founded a single party, and warned that whoever disagreed must leave [the country]. . . . I telephoned [Prime Minister] Hoveida, who was the party's general secretary. I said "this means that I have to join the party, because I can't leave Iran." "Yes," he said. I said "what should I do?" He said he would send me a piece of paper to sign. They sent a piece of paper which I signed, meaning that I had become a party member. That's all, just a signature. . . . After all [the Shah] had declared war, hadn't he? . . . This warning [about party membership] was formal, meaning that whoever remained [in the country] and did not become a party member should not expect any help if anything happened to him. That meant that if someone out in the street beat me up violently and hurt me, if I raised my voice I would be told "we told you so!" This is what Iran had become, an Iran which enjoyed the support of two democratic Western states. Isn't this shameful?[28]

A single party in which membership is automatic rather than a privilege cannot serve the purpose of institutionalization. Only three years after the new party's founding, the people of Iran, described in the party constitution as its membership, revolted against the state in a massive and united fashion, whose like has seldom been experienced in history.

Armed Forces and Security Networks

Both Pahlavi shahs were trained military men. At the same time, they regarded the armed forces as their ultimate instrument of internal security (against regional unrest and urban revolts), and under Mohammad Reza Shah they were also seen as a means to control the Persian Gulf region. Furthermore, the armed forces were seen as a physical expression of their pan-Iranian beliefs and propaganda. Under both father and son, as the Shah grew more powerful, the ones who were stronger and more prosperous, but also more dependent and subservient, were the army officers. High military expenditures were a feature of both regimes. The magnitude of the last Shah's military spending in the 1970s is so well known that it hardly needs detailed description. These expenditures would not have been possible without the bounty of the oil revenues. But high military spending went back to the 1950s when Abolhasan Ebtehaj, then managing director of the Plan Organization, had objected strongly to the use of relatively scarce development funds for military purposes,[29] and the 1960s, when Ali Amini had to resign from the premiership because he disagreed with the Shah over the size of the military budget.[30] However, it is worth mentioning that under both shahs the official figures for military expenditures understated the total amount spent, partly because some expenditures were included in other items, and partly because some infrastructural constructions—for example, roads, railways, and ports—were to some extent intended for military use.

The power and privileges of army officers went considerably beyond their unusually good pay and conditions. Their military uniforms, which they regularly wore in public, conferred extraordinary authority, and they could intimidate ordinary people in routine contacts. Military organizations could also encroach on private property (especially urban land) whenever it suited their purpose. Every province had a military commander in addition to the civilian governor, both appointed by the Shah and sent from Tehran. As a rule, the military commander (usually a general) had more power, and the military units under his command, together with the gendarmerie, which was a paramilitary force, had a tight grip on provincial affairs. In authoritarian periods they would play a leading role in rigging elections in favor of the official candidates,[31] but in the sultanistic periods they would no longer be needed, for the outcome of "elections" would then be a foregone conclusion.

Yet as powerful as the military personnel and organizations were in relation to the ordinary public, they were powerless on issues concerning their own professional tasks and activities. Here decision making was even more concentrated than in civilian matters, and the decision maker par excellence was the Shah, whose explicit permission had to be obtained even for such routine activities as moving a column from one barracks to another. He was personally in charge of all arms purchases, he made all the appointments and promotions of the senior and general staff, and heads of services, departments, and operations had to report directly to him. There was no normal chain of command; everything was dependent on the Shah alone. Thus the armed forces were technically weak and dependent and could not act effectively whenever the supreme commander himself was in trouble or was out of the country. Reza Shah (whose personality was incomparably stronger than his son's) could personally beat up his war minister and chief of staff for wavering in the face of serious danger, but this itself is an indication of the nature of their relationship in good times as well as in bad.[32]

General Fereidun Jam, the urbane, popular, and professional chief of staff (1969–71) and former brother-in-law of the Shah, found it almost impossible to function in circumstances where "none of the commanders had any power in his field of command which stems from responsibility; that is, they were all responsible without having power. . . . Not even the army commander had the right to use more than a company in his area. In Tehran, they had to obtain [the Shah's] prior permission even for nightly operations. . . . It is clear that such an army which in normal times would have to seek permission to breathe, will have no one to lead it in a crisis, and will disintegrate . . . exactly as it in fact did."[33]

General Jam, General Hasan Tufanian, and Admiral Amir Abbas Ramzi Ata'i are all at one in emphasizing the lack of coordination between various military establishments and the requirement that all the service chiefs both report directly to the Shah and obtain permission from him for the slightest decision. As a result, says Jam, uncoordinated reports used to be sent to the Shah, and similarly "uncoordinated, illogical, and ill-prepared orders were sent down."[34] According to Tufanian, the Shah "had created an ineffective ministry of war, and a general staff . . . which was even more ineffective, and we were all in it."[35] Ramzi Ata'i remembers twice having asked Hoveida why he did not throw his weight around, and on both occasions the prime minister had replied "with embarrassment" that he in fact was "no more than a private secretary." He added: "You see, ministers would go straight to the Shah. As the navy chief, I would take my work directly to His Majesty. Departmental undersecretaries would take their work directly to His Majesty. As a result the prime minister was bypassed, the chief of general staff was bypassed—hierarchy was not observed in Iran."[36]

Jam complains that the Shah decided, and Tufanian directly executed, the army's purchase orders, though even here there was no logic or coordination, so that "every day they would order some [military] equipment and then say, 'Do something with it.' "[37] In fact the general staff had no knowledge at all (not even through Tufanian) of what was being purchased for what purpose. On the other hand, Tufanian independently confirms Jam's point about the Shah's interference in every little detail: "After all, we used to call the Shah the supreme commander, and even the officers' leaves had to be reported to [him]— appointments, everything, everything. Therefore officers were used to a certain system, [and] when the system's head went away, I believe it was almost bound to disintegrate."[38]

Jam relates an astonishing story about Iraq's ultimatum to Iran over the use of the Shatt al-Arab waterway in 1969. As the acting chief of general staff, he merely heard a rumor that such an ultimatum had been received by the Foreign Ministry. The ministry confirmed the rumor to him, but it turned out that the prime minister had not been informed of the ultimatum, which had been received a few days before, because the foreign minister (Ardeshir Zahedi) was on bad terms with him. Jam had to raise the alarm, and between them he and the prime minister managed to take the necessary steps while the Shah was out of the country. And yet when the Shah returned to Iran the prime minister asked Jam whether he had packed his bags for both of them to go to prison because they had made those decisions on their own, without contacting the Shah in Tunisia, where he had been on a state visit.[39] The quick collapse of the Shah's regime in 1979 had many long- and short-term causes of a political as well as technical variety, one of which was precisely this dependence of every decision on one person alone in an otherwise complex and modernizing society.

Apart from questions of external security (and from the mid-1960s, external ambitions as well) the army was intended and used as a security force for subjugating ethnic and nomadic peoples and deployed against serious urban revolts. Putting such cases aside, however, internal security was entrusted to various police and security forces. Under Reza Shah, the central police force grew stronger over time, so that by 1933 even ministers and state dignitaries began to live in constant fear of negative reports about their views and activities—true or false—sent to the Shah. A well-known feature of the periods of arbitrary rule under both shahs was that censorship reached a stage where people were afraid of passing any critical comments on the state of affairs, even in private conversations. They knew that such comments could well reach the ears of the state, and there was a risk of severe retribution once this happened. Commenting on the withdrawal of parliamentary immunity and the arrest of three Majlis deputies under Reza Shah, one of his former prime ministers wrote in his memoirs: "Whoever so much as mentioned the Shah's name, they could grab and ask him what he meant, and would sometimes make whatever they wished out of it. It was a means of making [silence] money for the police as well. We had reached the stage that the Shah was demanding faith in himself."[40]

SAVAK, founded in 1957, was Mohammad Reza Shah's secret police, though there were other security and intelligence-gathering organizations in and outside the army: the Special Bureau, the army intelligence, the army counterintelligence, the Imperial Inspectorate, the Imperial Commission, and so on. They too were parallel organizations that reported directly to the Shah, and there was an intense—at times destructive—rivalry among them. General Hasan Alavi-Kia, an acting SAVAK chief, said he had once jokingly told the Shah that the competition between security organizations might have been the consequence of the Shah's own policy of "divide and rule."[41] Jam confirms that the army had little or no contact with the general staff, was in touch with the Shah, and spent some of its time and energy fighting off other security organizations.

SAVAK was a large and ruthless security organization whose power, influence, and sphere of operations grew from the mid-1960s in consequence of the interrelated growth of the Shah's arbitrary power as well as the steady, and later explosive, increases in oil revenues. SAVAK's operations and methods against political activists and urban guerrillas are well known. What is not so well known is the widespread fear it struck in the hearts of high and low alike in an attempt to obviate any word of criticism of the regime, even in private. This played an important role in spreading anger and frustration because of the fear and humiliation it led to. In this way SAVAK managed to politicize large numbers of people, apparently to stop them from interfering in politics. Incidentally, this to some extent explains the large discrepancy between the official figures and estimates by international human rights associations of the number of political prisoners under the Shah. The official figures (about 2,500) referred to those who had been convicted and sentenced in military courts, whereas the figures quoted by the human rights organizations (70,000 to 100,000) were based on the number of political detainees, many of whom would spend months in jail without trial, in punishment for minor misdemeanors that posed hardly any threat to the security of the state.

The State and Official Corruption

Official corruption is not an exclusive peculiarity of sultanistic states, traditional or modern; it is found in most authoritarian and dictatorial regimes and even in some industrial democracies. Yet its forms, its depth and breadth, and the channels and techniques by which it is practiced are—among other factors—a function of the basic features of the political system. Under Reza Shah Iran was still poor, and the state was being reconstructed along European lines. Both these factors tended to limit public corruption compared with later periods. The modernization of the state helped remove from the surface some of the corrupt official practices that were openly exercised until the constitutional revolution. Reza Shah's own attitude toward official corruption was peculiar, at least compared with that of his son. He took extreme exception to it and would not tolerate the slightest public corruption whenever it was found. But at the same time he himself amassed a great fortune by systematic encroachments on public and private property. There was a popular saying that the Shah allowed no one to steal except himself. Nevertheless, considerable public corruption did exist, to the extent that many politicians and state officials were involved in embezzlement as well as sale and purchase of official posts; this extended well down the administrative and military hierarchy.

Under Mohammad Reza Shah, different economic and political circumstances led to different levels and intensities of public corruption. In 1941–53 embezzlement and bribery became more widespread, but persisting poverty and relative political openness set a certain limit. Between 1953 and 1963 the continuous flow of rising (though still modest) oil revenues, foreign aid, and the growth of dictatorship further spread and intensified official corruption; the economic growth of the 1960s added to the rise of sultanism made matters worse; and the great oil bonanza of the 1970s plus the high tide of sultanism raised the level of corruption to unprecedented levels.

It was in the 1950s that the Pahlavi Foundation was created, ostensibly as a public charity but in fact as the Shah's main instrument for vast financial operations both inside and outside the country. Marvin Zonis found it the most powerful economic force in the country after the government itself: "Resources devoted to charity rather than commercial undertakings appear relatively slight."[42] According to Robert Graham, "Behind a smokescreen of charity, the Foundation is used in three key ways to assist the regime: as a safe and institutionalized conduit for 'pensions'; as a means of exerting economic control and influence by investing in specific sectors of the economy; and as a source for funds for royal ventures."[43]

Writing in more recent times, Bostock and Jones unambiguously declared that the "Pahlavi Foundation, nominally a charitable foundation, fostered official corruption."[44] Mohammad Baheri, a onetime minister of justice and deputy minister of the royal court, has given an outspoken account of the operations of the Pahlavi Foundation under Mohammad Ja'far Behbahanian, the court's chief accountant, the Shah's personal treasurer, and director of the foundation.[45] The most important single asset held by the foundation was all the shares of Bank Omran ("Development Bank"). Rather than giving loans for agricultural development, however, it effectively became an agency for collecting debts from the peasants who had received land from the Shah's vast estates, acquired or requisitioned by his father. Later Bank Omran became highly active in urban property development. By 1977 its assets stood at U.S. $1.05 billion, its capital had been increased to U.S. $81 million, and its declared dividend was U.S. $4.2 million, which was paid to the Pahlavi Foundation.[46]

Yet this was just the tip of the iceberg of official and dynastic corruption inside and outside Iran. No less than a Central Intelligence Agency report of the mid-1970s described the royal court as a "center of licentiousness and depravity, of corruption and influence peddling."[47] Both Ali Amini (prime minister 1961–62) and Dariush Homayun (minister of information 1977–78) mention a cast of "untouchables" who were free of any constraints in wielding economic power and influence.[48] A CIA report of 1976 declared that Princess Ashraf, the Shah's twin sister, had a "near legendary reputation for financial corruption" and noted that her son Shahram was a "wheeler-dealer with holdings in some twenty companies," some of these providing "a cover for Ashraf's quasi-legal business ventures."[49] Mohammad Baheri's detailed information on court corruption is impressive, coming as it does from a deputy minister of the court itself. The empress, the Shah's siblings, and his other relatives all imported goods (including investment goods for their business ventures) totally exempt from customs duties. They sometimes even arranged for others in the private sector to benefit from such exemptions. As a result, court officials became involved in this and other corrupt practices as well.[50] He notes: "I know a person who obtained power of attorney from Princess Ashraf for the purchase of one-tenth of the [agricultural?] lands of Khuzistan. . . . He gave a ten percent share to Princess Ashraf in this big business and took the remaining ninety percent himself . . . and then opium smuggling and . . . some people would gather round Princess Ashraf . . . whenever she saw someone is clever at making money she would bring him under her own protective umbrella."[51]

Baheri further explains that a group of wheeler-dealers had penetrated the court to obtain "business licenses, land . . . or any privilege that the government could grant. The Shah's siblings were also somehow involved in all this, for example, [Prince] Abdorreza and Princess Shams," as was, albeit to a lesser extent, the queen.[52] Commenting on the theme of official corruption, General Tufanian implies that there were strong pressures to misuse the colossal arms purchase funds; he was personally responsible for these funds and took his orders directly from the Shah. When scolded by the Shah for having publicly complained about the problem, he had replied: "This has been one hundred percent in His Majesty's own interest, because they say everywhere that the royal family is corrupt."[53]

Yet the problem of official corruption was by no means confined to a few "untouchables" or to the Shah's relatives and court officials. As early as the 1950s Abolhasan Ebtehaj was finding it increasingly difficult to combat powerful vested interests that were out to benefit from the Plan Organization's extensive development expenditures. The case of the Shiraz chemical fertilizer plant became notorious—and symbolically led to Ebtehaj's resignation and fall from grace in 1959 because it involved bribes to a minister and a high official[54] as well as use of influence by one of the Shah's mistresses.[55]

Khodadad Farmanfarmaian, a leading technocrat, governor of the Central Bank, and head of the Plan Organization, has said that some ministers used the secret ministerial budget (for which no account had to be given) for their personal purposes. Yet he explains that the main center of corruption was not within the cabinet itself but around it, in the rest of the government and the court. People connected with the royal family, the prime minister, and the heads of the armed services acted as influence peddlers, project promoters, or simply dealers. In the years following the oil price increase, corruption "reached the level of billions of dollars." Actual costs of some government projects rose to twenty or thirty times the original estimate because of corruption. "The only thing I could reasonably do was to make enough noise against the project and dissociate myself and the Plan Organization from it." The prime minister was not happy with this state of affairs, "but he faced the tremendous vested interests behind these projects." He adds that Hoveida did not like this state of affairs but played the game.[56]

The Logic and Psychology of Arbitrary Rule

The attitude and behavior of the security forces and organizations mentioned before almost completely reflected the arbitrary way the two Pahlavi shahs viewed their own position and behaved even toward some of their closest and most loyal servants. Mokhber al-Saltaneh, Reza Shah's prime minister for several years, quoted his monarch's address to Parliament, adding his own comments in parentheses: "Insofar as Iran has made any progress, it has been a product of the application of my force and power (as is obvious from the ministry of justice). And as soon as this force disappears, progress will end at whatever point it may have reached (this is the inevitable consequence of a one-man regime)."[57]

When the same prime minister began to think about resigning, he consulted the minister of war, Sardar As'ad Bakhtiari, who was very close to the Shah (and was himself murdered in jail soon afterward). The latter told him that his resignation might be "against the Shah's wishes, [in which case he] would be hurt,"[58] and promised to let him know if he learned the Shah wanted him to resign. In the end the Shah himself asked for his resignation. When Ali Akbar Davar, an exceptionally able finance minister and former justice minister, committed suicide, leaving a humble note begging the Shah to care for his family, Reza Shah "talked extensively [in the cabinet meeting] about this action, and added that he had no sympathy for such people."[59] Clearly, Davar's suicide had been construed as an act of defiance, a "resignation" without prior permission, for the Shah put a stop to preparations for a state funeral for him.[60]

Nosrat al-Dowleh, the minister of finance and eldest son of Prince Farman-farma, under whom Reza Khan had served as a soldier earlier in his career, was suddenly arrested for no obvious reason, though a highly incredible bribery charge was later laid against him. Yet the Shah's response to intervention on his behalf by Teimurtash was, "I no longer need him."[61] By law, ministers had to be tried in the Supreme Court, and it still being the period of authoritarianism rather than sultanism, some appearances had to be observed. However, both Davar and Teimurtash had to stress to the Supreme Court president, Nayyer al-Molk, that "Nosrat al-Dowleh must be convicted, or we would all be condemned. At that time, not even members of parliament enjoyed [de facto] immunity, although that was guaranteed [de jure]. Apparently, the sentence given by the court was thought [by the Shah] to be too lenient, therefore Nayyer al-Molk was forced to resign."[62] Nevertheless, a few years later Nosrat al-Dowleh was quietly arrested, taken to a provincial city, and murdered by the police.

The examples above—and one could cite many more—show that no one was immune from unceremonious dismissal, arbitrary arrest, imprisonment, banishment, and murder. The assault on private (especially landed) property escalated as the dictatorship deteriorated into sultanism. Numerous landlords who owned superior properties were forced to part with them in favor of the Shah or to sell them at nominal prices.[63] In 1921, when Reza Khan and Seyyed Zia carried out their coup, the former owned no estate at all. In 1941, when he abdicated, he owned 5,600 estates.[64] This was almost 10 percent of all private as well as state-owned estates in the country, though in terms of quality (location, water supply, produce) it was in fact much more. In the early 1940s many of their original owners successfully sued the former Shah and recovered some estates. By the 1970s, however, the Pahlavi Foundation was bringing pressure on some of the owners of such properties (notably along the Caspian Sea) to pay the Foundation their market value, even though they themselves had bought the property from the previous owners.

Under Mohammad Reza Shah, all genuine opposition had effectively been banned since 1953. But the Shah became increasingly intolerant of any advice given by loyal but independent-minded politicians and public servants. Such men were no longer murdered in jail, but they were summarily dismissed and banished from political life and sometimes even jailed, with or without trial. Such was the fate of several post-1953 prime ministers, including General Fazlollah Zahedi, the leader of the coup, Hosein Ala, who replaced Zahedi, and Ali Amini, whose travails have been mentioned before. Khodadad Farmanfarmaian, then a high official in the Plan Organization, recalls: "About three months before Dr. Amini resigned . . . I approached him with a draft bill for the budget function transfer to the Plan Organization. [Amini] said: 'I haven't got the power to do it anymore.' . . . I said, 'I don't wish to work when the country's prime minister doesn't have the power to carry out what he himself believed in, and what he himself instructed me to do.' I resigned."[65]

Ebtehaj, who had earlier resigned in frustration as the head of the Plan Organization, recalls that the Shah did not like anybody to resign; they had to be dismissed. He adds that the Shah "regarded the army as his own property, the oil revenues as belonging to him. Many a time I saw him on television saying 'I, I, my money, my oil, my revenues'—he did not at all believe that the revenues belonged to the people." Worse, according to Ebtehaj, no steps were taken to meet the moral and material needs of the people: "Only base qualities were encouraged in Iran. Everyone was spying against everyone else. Each person was jealous of the other. They all lied about each other. These were the paths of [personal] advancement. Well, what was the consequence? As soon as a match was lighted, [the whole thing] blew up."[66]

When the revolutionary movement got under way, the Shah became somewhat more susceptible to advice, and at later stages he even sought independent opinions. His constant encouragement to the American and British ambassadors to express their views about his handling of the revolutionary situation must have been—at least in part—because he believed their governments had sinister intentions toward him.[67] Even his last ambassador in London found, on a trip to Tehran, that the Shah would now listen to independent remarks. But when he saw Hoveida, by now minister of the court, he was told that the Shah would not willingly give up any power, even when "the dams have burst."[68] When a few months earlier the British ambassador had asked Hoveida why the Shah did not want to enter a dialogue with the people, Hoveida had replied: "You know His Majesty's definition of a dialogue. It is—I speak, you listen. He will not change."[69] The same impression was also gained by Ali Amini, who, after sixteen years out in the cold, had been asked by the Shah to advise him. He says that when he brought up the subject of a transfer of power, the Shah answered: "Transfer—what about me?" Amini reminded him of his promise to become a constitutional monarch but realized that "as [Mehdi] Bazargan had told me, [the Shah] was not being truthful. I mean, he was then in trouble. Bazargan said that as soon as he managed to get out of trouble he would go back to what was before."[70]

Reza Shah's personality was in many ways different from his son's. A self-made man who had risen from the lowest of the military ranks, he was highly intelligent, extremely able, and very adaptable to unfamiliar circumstances. He was open and direct in his approach and could be abrasive, arrogant, and even rude, yet he was capable of keeping his plans and grudges so close to his chest that he caught everyone by surprise each time he revealed his hand. He had an independent, self-reliant and highly self-confident personality, as well as an iron will that saved his life or position on several occasions. The worst moment of his life was when the Allies invaded Iran and he had to abdicate; but still he acted with courage, dignity, and forbearance.

Mohammad Reza Shah was also intelligent and, like his father, had a powerful memory. Deep down, however, he was a shy, if not timid, man whose seeming arrogance was a smoke screen to cover his basic lack of self-confidence. He displayed weakness in the face of adversity during the three major crises of his reign: Mosaddeq's premiership, the riots of June 1963, and the revolution of 1977–79, but he appeared to be strong in favorable circumstances. He had an ambivalent attitude toward his own father; he was proud of his father's achievements but wanted to be compared favorably with him. Mosaddeq had also made a negative impact on his psyche: he was jealous of his public popularity and was anxious to prove that he was no less (if not more) patriotic. Several observers have pointed to his physical illness as an important factor affecting his weak and indecisive behavior during the revolution. Yet given how he had behaved in earlier crises, one could argue that he would not have acted differently had he been well. In short, there were elements of narcissism in his personality that revealed themselves in both bad times and good times.

Since he was the country's sultanistic ruler, the Shah's personality affected the revolution and its outcome, although many more important factors contributed to its causes and consequences. A thorough analysis of the revolution is beyond the scope of this chapter,[71] but one can briefly ask whether the revolution itself was inevitable and whether it had to proceed and succeed over such a relatively short period.

From the observations above it must be clear that the system of petrolic sultanism could not have survived much longer, although it could well have been changed with the Shah or his successor still on the throne. The revolution was the product of the unity of all social classes in opposing the state and, hence, one man alone. That is why almost every conceivable ideology and political program was represented in it: Islamist, religious democratic, non-religious democratic, and all the main varieties of Marxist-Leninist ideas and parties. The civil service entirely sided with the revolutionaries by joining the general strike, and this played an important role both in solidifying the struggle and in quickening the pace of its development. From September 1978 on, in particular, the army was weak and wavering in its resolve, both horizontally among its commanders and vertically within its ranks.

The "liberalization" of 1977, since it entailed no attempt, or indeed intention, of thoroughly reforming the sultanistic system, could only open the floodgates to total insurrection. Soon after President Carter's election and his pointed campaigns against human rights violations around the globe, both the Shah and the people became convinced that the West (America, Britain, or both) was determined to topple his regime. The impact of this false perception on the psyche of both sides, and the intensity and speed of the revolutionary process, can hardly be exaggerated: in other circumstances the people might have hoped for some reform, and the Shah would have been more resolute in dealing with the movement.

That as part of the logic of sultanism the army (as well as the administration) had been used to depending entirely on one person's direct and uncoordinated decisions clearly made it difficult to cope with the situation, especially in the last few weeks when the Shah himself had left the country. It also meant there was no one in the regime who could credibly negotiate a pact with the opposition, so as to effect an orderly transition to a different regime.[72]

But other factors also fostered a quick revolutionary triumph. The general strike was an extremely potent weapon that could hardly have been ended by such "shows of strength" as indiscriminate bombardments of civilian targets in Qom or Tehran. Besides, the Shah's (and the regime's) psychological dependence on the West would have prevented the use of such tactics; the West would certainly have disapproved at that time, a problem the Syrian and Iraqi regimes, for example, did not face when they drowned the insurrections of Hama (1982) and Najaf (1991) in blood.

In short, the regime's absolute lack of a social base, the belief that the West was in favor of fundamental change in Iran, the Shah's psychology, and the absence of an autonomous military and civilian administration all played important roles both in bringing about the revolution and in determining its speed.

9
· · · ·

The Marcos Regime in the Philippines

Mark R. Thompson

> I shall have the occasion to bare the gory and intimate
> details, as only a trusted (erstwhile) insider could have
> gleaned, of the notorious scandal going on in the
> Philippines that would make Watergate a drop in the bucket
> and President Nixon a piker placed side by side with
> Marcos. As an insider, I must cry out with all the vehement
> protest I could muster that the martial law regime of Marcos
> was nothing but an ill-disguised plot to perpetuate himself,
> his wife and/or son in power by consolidating the political
> and economic resources of the country under his control.
>
> PRIMITIVO MIJARES,
> 20 February 1975

Highly personalistic dictatorships are vulnerable to public revelations by dis-affected insiders. Embarrassing "tell-all" accounts have been written about many kinds of governments, democratic and nondemocratic alike, but they are particularly dangerous for those regimes that govern in a fundamentally illegiti-mate manner. It is not just a leader's personal foibles or abuse of power that come under scrutiny but *the corruption of the form of rule itself*. "Sultanism" serves no higher ideological purpose or even the interests of a particular social class or state institution. Rather, power is exercised for the benefit of the ruler, his family, and his close friends. When collective good is sacrificed to personal gain, all legitimacy is lost. Efforts to make such regimes more palatable through "constitutionalism" and "social reformism" can easily be undercut by a traitor from the inner circle who reveals that the emperor has no clothes.

In the Philippines, the 1975 public defection of Primitivo Mijares, President Ferdinand E. Marcos's chief media propagandist and one of his closest advisers, was a major public relations blow to the martial law regime. Portraying himself as the Filipino John Dean, Mijares testified before a subcommittee of the U.S. House of Representatives, wrote *The Conjugal Dictatorship of Ferdinand and Imelda Marcos*, and undertook what he called a "truth safari" to Filipino-American groups around the United States.[1] Marcos obviously took Mijares' tattling very seriously. He offered him a $50,000 bribe not to appear before Congress. Although Mijares went ahead with his testimony, Marcos promised him $100,000 if he gave up writing a book further detailing his charges and left the United States.[2] Presidential adviser Guillermo de Vega, who had negotiated with Mijares for Marcos, was mysteriously murdered in Malacañang (the presidential palace) shortly after the U.S. Justice Department ordered an investigation of the bribe attempts. When Mijares' book appeared, Marcos agents plundered copies in bookstores and libraries throughout the United States.[3]

Mijares was either lured or tricked into making a fatal return journey to the Philippines. There, in a terrible act of revenge, his son was kidnapped and probably tortured to death in front of Mijares before he himself was also killed, in all likelihood by soldiers working for General Fabian Ver.[4] Tragically, Mijares seems to have ignored his own advice about Marcos: "The man will exact his vengeance in his own sweet time on the unsuspecting enemy whom he had lulled into a false sense of security."[5]

Although Marcos was greatly offended by Mijares' revelations, most scholars of Philippine politics have paid them little attention,[6] perhaps in part because of Mijares' morally dubious reputation, which made him easy to discredit and difficult to defend.[7] Mijares' style was highly polemical, and he was obviously trying to curry favor with wealthy members of the United States–based opposition. But his way of looking at the Marcos regime was also different from that of many academics. They stressed the regime's developmental ideology, its bureaucratic authoritarian character, and its corporatist organization.[8] Mijares claimed the regime's ideology was meant for public consumption, not as a policy guide, that Marcos had subverted the military to ensure its loyalty to him, while technocrats had been outmaneuvered by cronies, and that government was little more than a "protection racket" run by the first family, their relatives, and their friends.[9]

This chapter is an effort to develop Mijares' insights into an argument about the origins of the Marcos regime, its sultanistic character, and its breakdown.

Mijares will be a frequent witness in this presentation, but his claims will be carefully cross-examined against other evidence that has since become available. As Josephus showed, traitors often leave behind the best historical accounts.[10] Marcos will be heard from less often, since I hold the view that though he often told the truth about his enemies, he was, as George Will phrased it, an "inveterate liar" about his own actions.[11] Social science analysis can benefit greatly from the information an erstwhile insider can provide about a highly personalistic regime.

The Decline of Clientelist Democracy

Why did Philippine democracy break down to be replaced by personalistic dictatorship?[12] One influential theory is that the country's democracy was highly clientelist and that it was in a state of terminal decline long before martial law was declared in 1972.[13] This was said to be most clearly demonstrated by the mounting costs and growing violence of elections. It is certainly true that between the inauguration of an independent republic in 1946 and the declaration of martial law in 1972, the Philippines had a rough and tumble democratic regime that observers labeled "raw democracy."[14] Elections were characterized by rampant vote buying, localized violence, and occasional fraud. The two major parties had a common origin (the Liberals were a breakaway faction of the Nacionalistas founded under U.S. colonial rule), had the same elite social composition, and were ideologically identical. Party switching was common, with even presidential candidates changing sides. Elections were largely competitions between the two parties' clientelist networks, making them among the most expensive in the world.[15] Murders committed by rival local political leaders were common.

Elections were expensive and violent largely because the economic rewards of victory were great. Senate president Jose Avelino's response to charges of bribe taking in government ("What are we in power for? . . . Why should we pretend to be saints when in reality we are not?") summarizes the attitude the victorious party took toward the state.[16] Patronage, pork barrel, bribes, the illegal sale of government licenses, and occasional outright plundering of state financial institutions were considered prerogatives of the incumbents.

But there were certain constraints on "raw democracy" that kept elections highly competitive and placed limits on corruption. The two major parties in the Philippines regularly alternated in power. When a party won the presidency, the key political office, opportunists from the opposition often defected to reap the material rewards of power. But pork barrel and patronage were in short

TABLE 9.1

Victors of Philippine Pre–Martial Law Presidential Elections

Election Year	President Elected	Party
1946	Manuel Roxas	Liberal
1949	Elpidio Quirino	Liberal
1953	Ramon Magsaysay	Nacionalista
1957	Carlos Garcia	Nacionalista
1961	Diosdado Macapagal	Liberal
1965	Ferdinand Marcos	Nacionalista
1969	Ferdinand Marcos	Nacionalista

supply because a landlord-controlled Congress opposed all but indirect taxes and placed tight limits on foreign borrowing.[17] As an election approached, disadvantaged members of the ruling party would jump to the challengers' side in hopes of gaining a larger piece of the political pie should they win. Also, revelations of "anomalies" in government by the lively (when not libelous) media inevitably turned the growing middle-class, educated, urban segment of the electorate against the ruling party. Warning that a corrupt incumbent endangered democracy (whose breakdown, it was feared, might lead to communist revolution), oppositionists were twice able to solicit substantial covert support from the U.S. government.[18] This balance between the incumbents and the opposition explains why the presidency changed hands between the two major parties four times during the pre–martial law period, as table 9.1 shows.

In fact, a regular political cycle accompanied this alternation in power. This can best be shown by gubernatorial elections held every four years between presidential polls. The dominant party (the party of the president) won on average nearly 80 percent of the votes during its first presidential term in office. This can be explained by the patronage advantage enjoyed by the newly elected incumbents. But over time, demands for government favors outstripped supply, leading to increased dissatisfaction with the ruling party and defections to the opposition. This shows up in gubernatorial elections during a president's second term, in which the average proportion of races won slipped to 60 percent (see table 9.2).

The declining success of the ruling party at the local level foreshadowed its defeat in the next presidential election. By taking turns in power, neither party could monopolize state resources indefinitely.

Elections put distributive pressures on the two major parties. Vote buying was common in pre–martial law elections, with an estimated one-fourth of the electorate being directly bribed.[19] Pork barrel allocations and patronage jobs distributed at election time were other inducements. With government reve-

TABLE 9.2
Percentage of Dominant Party Governors Elected

First Term			Second Term		
Dominant Party	Year	%	Dominant Party	Year	%
Liberal	1947	82	Liberal	1951	50
Nacionalista	1955	81	Nacionalista	1959	65
Liberal	1963	75	—	—	—
Nacionalista	1967	80	Nacionalista	1971	66
AVERAGE		79	AVERAGE		60

SOURCE: James A. Curry, "Continuity and Change in Philippine Electoral Politics: A Re-evaluation," *Journal of Southeast Asian Studies* 7, no. 2 (1976): 230.

nues limited, even elite politicians from the ruling party often had to dig into their pockets to finance their campaigns. This constituted a major redistribution of income from rich political leaders to the poor electorate at election time. Not only did this keep powerholders from overconcentrating state resources in their own hands, it also helped undercut revolutionary sentiment during most of the pre–martial law period because of cross-class clientelist ties.[20]

Though party politics revolved around patronage, state institutions retained some autonomy from the powerholders of the regime. Most important was the military. Although provincial commanders were often under the sway of local strongmen, top military officers usually stayed neutral during presidential elections.[21] This neutrality helps explain why the Philippines, unlike several Latin American countries, had no tradition of *continuismo*. There was no precedent for overstaying in office, no established formula for legitimizing it, and no guarantee the military would accept a political innovation of this sort. Another crucial institution, the Commission on Elections (Comelec), could not prevent all vote rigging, but it nonetheless made it difficult for an incumbent president to steal a national election. Although regional courts were often corrupted by powerful elites, the Philippine Supreme Court maintained its reputation for integrity and helped referee national politics. As David Wurfel wrote, "In 1961, for instance, the court invalidated an act enlarging and reapportioning the House of Representatives just before the election even though its ruling threw the [ruling] Nacionalista party into turmoil and may have contributed to its subsequent defeat at the polls. But no serious consideration was apparently given to ignoring the court's ruling."[22]

Thus, although Philippine pre–martial law politics was far from the ideal type of democracy, electoral competition and institutional autonomy kept it in equilibrium. An important study of clientelist democracy written shortly before Marcos's presidency stressed the stability of the system.[23] This stability suggests that the structural argument about the inevitability of the collapse of the pre–martial law order has overlooked a crucial contingency: that Marcos broke the informal rules of Philippine democracy and later changed the game altogether by launching a dictatorship. Not that the democratic system did not have weaknesses, but it had survived until confronted with a president determined to stay in power indefinitely.

Marcos used what Filipinos call "guns, goons, and gold" to an unprecedented extent during his legal presidency. Throughout the pre–martial law period, rising campaign costs by ruling party candidates caused a political business cycle—government deficit spending and inflationary pressures in election years and austerity and economic slowdown in off years—but not fiscal crisis.[24] In other words, the ruling party's use of patronage for electoral purposes was not carried to such an extreme that it bankrupted the state. Marcos changed this pattern by allocating an unprecedented amount of pork barrel financing to improve his future electoral prospects. He then spent an estimated $200 million on his 1969 reelection campaign, "more than all other campaign funds spent in all the post-war presidential campaigns put together"![25] With the state's coffers already empty, this huge campaign expenditure caused a major fiscal crisis.

The number of election-related deaths had remained relatively constant until Marcos's presidency. Nonpresidential elections were particularly violent; the ruling party's efforts to secure a provincial base for the next presidential polls were compounded by the fact that local elections have historically been more intensely contested in the Philippines than national ones. But since the early 1950s, the armed forces had not intervened extensively in elections on the side of the ruling party. This changed during the 1967 polls, when military and paramilitary groups supported many pro-Marcos candidates (see table 9.3).

It is impossible to say how much of this increased bloodshed is directly attributable to growing militarization under Marcos. But it is striking that more

TABLE 9.3
Deaths and Injuries during Nonpresidential Elections, 1955–1967

Year	President	Deaths	Injuries
1955	Ramon Magsaysay	34	38
1959	Carlos Garcia	24	a
1963	Diosdado Macapagal	23	59
1967	Ferdinand Marcos	75	108

SOURCE: Philippine Constabulary reports on electoral terror and Willem Wolters, *Politics, Patronage and Class Conflict in Central Luzon* (Quezon City: New Day, 1984), 143.

aUnknown.

than twice as many killings occurred during the 1967 election as during any polls since 1955. This sharp rise in electoral violence can be seen as part of Marcos's effort to break out of the political cycle that would soon lead to opposition victory. Marcos's reelection in 1969 was also marred by terror.[26] Though the "body count" was lower than 1967, consistent with the pattern of less violent national elections, it was higher than during most previous presidential polls and led to unusually loud charges of "terrorism" from the opposition.

Mijares rightly blamed Marcos's "win at all costs" strategy for much of the political turmoil during and after the election.[27] Electoral overspending had plunged the country into economic disaster. Embittered opposition politicians backed radical student demonstrators, many of whom claimed the marred election proved revolution was necessary. The rise of an Islamic secessionist movement in the southern part of the country was also supported by opposition Liberals trying to "punish" Marcos's rule breaking. Outraged oppositionists even tried to assassinate the Philippine president.

But Marcos skillfully exploited this mounting political polarization. He intentionally exaggerated the strength of a motley band of a few dozen intellectuals and several hundred peasant guerrillas who made up the Communist Party of the Philippines (CPP). His agents had infiltrated the Keystone Kops assassination conspiracy of the opposition and later used it to extort properties from wealthy enemies. There was a string of bombings in Manila that American intelligence officials have linked to Marcos.[28] As the finale, he staged a fake ambush of defense secretary Juan Ponce Enrile to justify martial law. Marcos was always one step ahead of his enemies.

A Crisis of Sovereignty

A second theory of democratic breakdown in the Philippines relates to the country's "crisis of sovereignty." In an unusual experiment in "colonial democracy," the United States quickly held local and then national elections for a Philippine legislature after colonizing the country at the beginning of this century.[29] These democratic institutions were imposed on a feudal social structure and used by local, largely Chinese mestizo landowners to consolidate their political hegemony. With the right to vote at first limited to the wealthy, the elite Nacionalista Party won control of the national legislature established by American authorities in 1907. It continued to dominate politics throughout the colonial era using patron-client ties to mobilize peasant voters as suffrage was gradually expanded. Politics were nonideological, since the Nacionalista Party leaders, although officially favoring immediate independence, struck a modus vivendi with the colonizer in which American patronage was exchanged for acquiescence to foreign rule. Unlike the Dutch in neighboring Indonesia, the Americans built a relatively weak colonial state and quickly surrendered effective control of it to the Philippine elite.

The unorthodox process of decolonization contributed to "neocolonialism" during the early independence period. Neither a violent struggle nor widespread civil disobedience was necessary to drive out the colonizer; the United States willingly granted the Philippines commonwealth status in 1935 and independence ten years later. The World War II alliance between Filipino guerrilla fighters and returning American troops against the Japanese strengthened emotional ties between colonizer and colonized, as symbolized by the often-cited promise of Douglas MacArthur: "I shall return." (A notable exception was the anti-Japanese Huk guerrillas, who felt betrayed by U.S. support for elite repression of their movement after the war.) Even U.S. links to the Philippine elite, which largely cooperated with the Japanese, were cemented as MacArthur supported the candidacy of Manuel Roxas, who pardoned his fellow "collaborators" after winning the newly independent Republic of the Philippines' first presidential election. A "parity" agreement (giving American investors full access to the Philippine market) with the United States in return for war reparations and the establishment of American military bases in the Philippines in the late 1940s were agreed to by a grateful Filipino political leadership under little nationalist pressure.

But nationalism gradually gathered strength, first with criticism of the "parity" agreement and the U.S. bases, and then among student activists in the 1960s, with protests against American intervention in Vietnam, foreign investment, and the Philippine constitution (which had been approved by Franklin Roosevelt in 1935). During the so-called First Quarter Storm of 1970, there were dozens of large student demonstrations and riots. Under mounting nationalist sentiment, at least among elite groups, the Philippine Congress passed legislation restricting foreign investment and the Philippine Supreme Court ruled that American properties would be automatically nationalized after the expiration of the United States–Philippine trade agreement in 1974. A constitutional convention was convened with high hopes for strengthening sovereignty and achieving social reform.

It has been argued that "an anti-system-change coalition" composed of the American business community in the Philippines, the U.S. government, and most of the Filipino elite emerged to combat these populist and nationalist pressures through authoritarianism.[30] Although these groups welcomed the declaration of martial law, Marcos pursued a Machiavellian strategy of arousing nationalist passions so that he could emerge as the savior of threatened U.S. and Filipino elite interests. Several other authors have reached Mijares' conclusion that Marcos was funding some of the radical student demonstrators.[31] Marcos may also have been behind the calling of a constitutional convention, and there is no doubt that he manipulated the proceedings through outright bribery. He convinced the U.S. government that he could best protect its (largely military) interests in the Philippines even if he had to destroy democracy in the process. The U.S. had often tried to influence the course of Philippine politics, but previous efforts had been directed against incumbents deemed to have become too dictatorial. Skillfully playing the Cold War card, Marcos convinced the American government to back him in what he pictured as an anticommunist crusade.

The Development of the "Marcos Style"

The limitations of these two theories of the breakdown of Philippine democracy—clientelist collapse and the crisis of sovereignty—require a closer look at what Mijares said onetime Marcos executive secretary Rafael M. Salas Cañizares called the "Marcos style," in which "any type of dissimulation or chicanery or bribery or coercion is applicable."[32] As is typical of sultanistic rulers, Marcos's relatively humble origins rendered him an upstart among the elite and made him less constrained by its mores. Marcos was born into a family on the fringe of the Filipino oligarchy in Ilocos Norte, a province north of Manila noted for the particular brutality of its politics. His mother was a poor relation of a wealthy Chinese mestizo family; his father was the son of the former town mayor whose fortunes had later declined, and he was himself briefly a congressman, though he could sometimes barely feed his family. After Marcos's father lost a congressional election in 1935, the winning candidate was murdered. The young Marcos was convicted of the killing, but he appealed his case to the Supreme Court and was let off on a technicality. This was apparently due to the sympathy Justice Jose P. Laurel (father of Corazon C. Aquino's vice president, Salvador Laurel) felt for the young Marcos (the older Laurel had committed a similar crime as a young man).[33]

Marcos's tales of "heroism and courage" as an anti-Japanese guerrilla during the Second World War "are straight out of Walter Mitty," Mijares charged.[34] Recent research has verified these accusations.[35] What is most interesting is how Marcos was able to turn these lies to his political advantage. During the war Marcos had organized an Ilocano gang of "forgers, pickpockets, gunmen, and racketeers" engaged in extortion and the black market.[36] He transformed his "guerrilla" group into a political machine that built up a constituency by claiming war benefits from the U.S. government and got him overwhelmingly elected to Congress in 1949. The fake war medals he received as a political favor a decade and a half later were evidence of how much influence he had gained in the legislature.

As a leading opposition congressman in the 1950s (eventually he became House minority leader), Marcos was a master of anticorruption rhetoric that won him plaudits from reporters (several of whom he kept on his payroll).[37] As chairman of the committee in charge of allocating import licenses, however, Marcos was notorious for extorting payoffs and being harsh with those who opposed him. Mijares connected Marcos with the killing of Ilocos warlord Floro Crisologo, who was shot to death (while praying in a church) after he had asked for a bigger share of the profits from a tobacco smuggling scheme the two politicians ran together.[38] "Among his peers," Sterling Seagrave reports, "[Marcos] had a reputation for cutthroat tactics that frightened even the corrupt old lions in Congress."[39]

Marcos married Imelda Romualdez out of careful political calculation, Mijares claimed.[40] Although she was a poor relation, Imelda was still a Romualdez, a member of one of the most prominent families in the Philippines in the 1950s.[41] Two of her uncles and a cousin were, respectively, mayor of Manila, Supreme Court justice, and Speaker of the House of Representatives. Imelda's father had been much less successful, however, and as a product of his second, unhappy marriage she lived in a garage during much of her childhood. Although this deprivation would later nurse her compulsive hoarding behavior and her desire for revenge on those in the elite she perceived as having wronged her, at the time of her marriage to Marcos she provided him with connections to a powerful family from another region (the Visayas) and another party (the Romualdezes were Nacionalistas; at that time Marcos was a Liberal). This helped Marcos make a successful bid for a seat in the Philippine Senate, then the Senate presidency, and finally the Philippine presidency itself. That Marcos already had a common-law wife and three children at the time of his marriage did not deter him, because Imelda was more politically useful. This *Heiratspolitik* is similar to that of other sultanistic rulers who tried to build an alliance with the old elite through marriage.

Mijares claimed Marcos was planning to declare martial law from the first day of his legal presidency.[42] Marcos's diaries reveal that he was considering such an action at least as early as February 1970.[43] There is also evidence that he sent aides to Spain "to study how Franco had stayed in power so long."[44] Marcos's initial move was to serve as his own defense secretary for his first thirteen months in power while he undertook the largest reorganization of the military in its history. He retired many top officers, replacing them with loyalists from his own Ilocos region and junior officers who had supported him during his presidential campaign. Marcos bestowed patronage on the armed forces under the guise of giving them a greater role in economic development. He carefully nurtured the military's grudge against the Philippine Congress, whose favor had to be courted for confirmation of most officer-level appointments. His success in winning the support of the armed forces was clear from the results of a secret survey of top officers in 1972 showing that the overwhelming majority favored declaring martial law.[45] With military support, Marcos declared martial law in September 1972.

From Clientelism to Sultanism

In pre–martial law politics the quest for patronage, the heart of the clientelist system, was tempered by democratic constraints: free media, an outspoken opposition, tightly contested elections, and orderly succession in power. With polls canceled, the press censored, Congress abolished, and the constitution ignored, restraints were removed on Marcos's accumulation of wealth in office. Once he had declared a dictatorship, Marcos "shared an endless bounty of profits derived from government-sponsored contracts and concessions as well as private deals . . . with his wife and relatives, and with selected friends who belonged to his inner entourage and became part of the functioning Marcos dynasty."[46]

Marcos also began to fuse previously independent state institutions with his regime, which is typical of sultanism.[47] He moved quickly to gain personal control over the military hierarchy. Previously an officer had needed congressional pull to advance in rank. Now Marcos was the sole benefactor of all top brass. Right after declaring martial law, he promoted officers one grade, increased their salaries 150 percent, raised benefits, and set up a company to help them invest their new wealth.[48] In return for their loyalty, he tolerated corruption among top officers, which undermined professionalism and increased inequality within the military: "Officers controlled or extorted payments from the black market for dollars; they controlled car-theft rings, marijuana syndicates, illegal logging, gambling, prostitution, fishing, mining, gunrunning, and robbery. Smaller racketeers were principally the province of junior-ranking officers and enlisted men whose basic pay and living conditions had not significantly improved."[49] By allowing officers to "overstay" past mandatory retirement through repeated six-month extensions, he could command their obedience more easily than that of those whose tenure had not yet expired. The pervasiveness of this practice is shown by the sixteen-month average tenure of top officers under the democratic regime as opposed to over one hundred months during the dictatorship.[50]

Mijares reported, however, that "Marcos does not really love his generals. He monitors their movement every inch of the way."[51] In particular, Marcos distrusted Philippine Constabulary (PC) head Fidel Ramos (whose West Point background and reputation for personal integrity made him politically suspect, although he was a cousin of the president) and defense secretary Juan Ponce Enrile (whose presidential aspirations were transparent). In the martial law military buildup, the army and paramilitary were enlarged most rapidly as a counterweight to Ramos's PC. Marcos chose loyalist Fabian Ver over Ramos as his new chief of staff in 1981. Marcos also took operational command of the military away from Enrile in 1983.

Ver was an "integree officer" (attending an ROTC university program rather than a military school) in the Philippine Constabulary. In 1963 his relative and patron Ferdinand Marcos arranged for him to be sent to the United States for intelligence training to avoid investigation in a smuggling scandal. On his return he served as Marcos's chauffeur, head of security during the 1965 campaign, and then as chief secret policeman by running, with his three sons, the Presidential Security Command (PSC) and the National Intelligence Coordinating Agency (NICA). These security and intelligence forces were made up predominantly of Marcos's and Ver's fellow Ilocanos, whom they considered most trustworthy, and were designed to spy more on Marcos's opponents in and outside the armed forces than on the enemies of the state.[52] (In the "his and hers" style of government, Imelda Marcos also cultivated a coterie of top-ranking officers, including her former bodyguard, her former yacht captain, and her brother-in-law.)

Marcos also undermined the independence of the judiciary. Lower-level judges had always been vulnerable to political pressure. Marcos further politicized the courts with his power to dismiss any judge arbitrarily. He also restricted the jurisdiction of civilian courts, putting all crimes committed by public officials and most of those against public order under the domain of newly created military courts. Especially concerned about the loyalty of the Supreme Court, Marcos increased retirement pay for high court judges but withheld it if retirees had been critical of his regime. Mijares reported that the most effective way to cow the Supreme Court was with leaks from the presidential palace that if an adverse decision were reached, the court would be abolished and a revolutionary government established.[53] The sultanization of the high court became evident to all when Chief Justice Enrique Fernando held a parasol over Imelda Marcos's head during a public gathering. Marcos had "destroyed not only the substance of the democratic process but particularly the principle and practice of legal and public accountability, which, despite the weaknesses of the Philippine system of government over the years, had survived until this time, and . . . served as a watchdog of the commonweal."[54]

A Changing Political Economy

Exercising arbitrary power because constitutional constraints had been discarded and independent state institutions undermined, the Marcos regime began to dramatically change the character of the Philippine political economy. By removing congressional limitations on foreign loans, providing government guarantees for loans to presidential cronies, and courting foreign bankers, Marcos was able to nearly triple borrowing during the first five years of dictatorial rule, from $2.7 billion in 1972 to $8 billion in 1977. By 1980 it was $17 billion, reaching $25 billion by 1983.[55] The Philippines debt crisis, the only one in Southeast Asia in this period, can be directly attributed to Marcos's skillful attraction of foreign capital, which was then largely frittered away through corruption.[56]

Marcos expropriated wealth from foreign investors and the politically weakened landlord class through direct confiscation, bribery, and cronyism. Non-Filipinos wanting to do business in the Philippines had to make payoffs to high officials in government. Foreign businessmen already operating in the country often found that if their investments became too lucrative they were targeted for takeover by government officials or friends of the president. Corazon Aquino's brother and other wealthy pre–martial law elites were forced to sell out their corporations to Marcos's associates at less than market price.[57] This tactic resulted in a massive income redistribution from old economic and political elites to state-linked "influentials." In a survey made in 1975, half of the country's pre–martial law elite had dropped out of the most influential category. Thirty-one of the thirty-five top "influentials" had close ties to the president.[58]

Marcos (during his legal term) and his predecessor, Diosdado Macapagal, had both attacked the excessive political and economic influence of the Lopez brothers, who were the country's leading sugar *hacenderos,* media magnates, industrialists, and kingmakers, but had later been forced to back down. With his martial law powers, however, Marcos was able quickly to humble this once mighty clan. He seized their television and radio stations and extorted their industrial holdings, including the Manila Electric Company, by promising (falsely) to free the imprisoned son of family patriarch Eugenio Lopez, who had been jailed in connection with an assassination attempt. (The properties were given to Marcos' brother-in-law, Benjamin "Kokoy" Romualdez.) Mijares quoted Imelda Marcos as commenting: "We cannot give Geny Lopez his freedom as long as the Lopezes are still in possession of great wealth. They must divest themselves first of their economic power. They might use this again to fight us."[59]

Marcos's favorite modus operandi, however, appears to have been the old-fashioned bribe. Mijares claimed that every new company and many established firms had to give Marcos or his associates 10 percent to 25 percent of their equity *"gratis et amore,"* an account that other evidence confirms.[60] Westinghouse paid a $17 million "commission" to Marcos through presidential associate Herminio Disini to win the bid to build a nuclear reactor in the Philippines for $1.1 billion, edging out General Electric, which had offered to build *two* reactors for $700 million.[61] Mijares described how a typical business "deal" with Marcos was made:

"Mr. President, you know, there is a proposal which has been submitted to you and which (Secretary Melchor or so and so) has already endorsed favorably."
"Oh, huh."
What do you think, Mr. President?"
"What are the requirements of your company? Perhaps, you should send me a new memorandum because the one sent by Secretary Melchor has been filed away by Fe. . . ."
At this point, an experienced man, who knows the mentality of the President, would immediately state:
"Sir, the new company's stock structure will be divided among (the names of the persons). . . . Do you think it would be all right to include any more?"
"Bakit naman panay Intsik (o Hapon) iyang mga iyan?" (Why are they mostly Chinese [or Japanese]?)
"Mabuti seguro . . . ay . . . isama mo sina (he gives the names).
"Yes, sir. And, sir . . . (in whispers) in whose name should we register the 20 percent equity?"[62]

"Crony Capitalism"

"Cronyism" under Marcos was a kind of subcontracting of corruption that relied on state power to provide monopolies for private accumulation. Through a corporation controlled by his college fraternity brother Roberto Benedicto, Marcos took over the sugar industry from the grower landlords who had been the most powerful elite faction in the country before martial law. By presidential decree, Benedicto's National Sugar Trading Corporation was made the sole exporter of sugar and captured P11 to P15 billion (about $1.7 to $2.3 billion) from producers between 1974 and 1983 by paying less than market price.[63] The sugar landlords, the leading power brokers of the pre–martial law era with their media outlets and congressional connections, not only were weakened politically by the declaration of martial law but now faced bankruptcy or at least reduced profitability owing to this government monopoly. Through the sugar monopoly, then, the Marcos regime had gained a new source of revenue and further undercut the strength of the sugar landlords.

Cronies came to dominate almost all areas of the economy. Marcos imposed a levy on coconut producers that generated P4 billion between 1973 and 1978.[64] The money was deposited in a bank bought from Corazon Aquino's family and controlled by defense minister Juan Ponce Enrile and Eduardo Cojuangco. As Marcos's leading crony, Cojuangco later used his coconut-generated wealth to buy San Miguel, the country's largest corporation, and became a political "warlord" in the Central Luzon region. Enrile, the other major crony in the coconut industry, monopolized the lumber industry through military crackdowns on "illegal" loggers and exclusive government franchises and licenses. He also built up one of the country's largest corporate empires and was the political master of his native Cagayan province.[65]

Rodolfo Cuenca, a onetime Marcos fund-raiser, built a multi million-dollar empire through government construction contracts and the exclusive right to ship cargo from the Philippines to the United States. Herminio Disini, who set up the Westinghouse nuclear power plant deal, controlled the $1 billion Herdis group, which had gotten its start in the tobacco industry after Marcos imposed a 100 percent tariff on his competitors' imported materials, while he had to pay only 10 percent. Disini, married to Imelda Marcos's first cousin and a regular golf partner of Marcos, was also granted a 500,000-acre logging concession by the president and, like all cronies, received, a number of government-guaranteed loans. Other presidential friends met with similar success. Ricardo Silverio's Toyota affiliate won control of the domestic automobile parts industry through a decree that forced Ford and General Motors out of the market. Jose Campos dominated pharmaceuticals, Ramon Cruz Jr. the airlines, and Antonio Floirendo the banana industry. Each crony had his respective "kingdom": Benedicto was the "sugar king," Cojuangco the "coconut king," Floirendo the "banana king," Campos the "drug king," and so on. But "according to the buttons on the intercom system at Malacanang Palace, Ferdinand Marcos was simply 'The King.' "[66]

"The Conjugal Dictatorship"

Edward Banfield's principle of "amoral familism" is applicable to Philippine politics: widespread nepotism in government arises out of a sense of obligation to family members and a distrust of others.[67] Before martial law, however, Philippine presidents had to balance family ties with the scrutiny of the press and the opposition, the coalitions and patronage distribution needed to win elections, and the powers of an independent judiciary and military. Family dynasty building was also limited by the frequent alternation of the major parties in power.

But under martial law, Marcos's authority was no longer restrained, nor was his time in office limited like that of his presidential predecessors. Many of his and his wife's close relatives were economic cronies. Family members also controlled portions of the state apparatus. Imelda's favorite brother, Benjamin "Kokoy" Romualdez, controlled the Bureau of Customs, the General Auditing Commission, and the Bureau of Internal Revenue. Imelda's sister, Alita Martel, was the "franchise holder" of the Central Bank and the Department of Agriculture.[68] The president's brother, Pacifico Marcos, ran the Medicare Commission, which was plagued by corruption. Even Marcos's elderly mother had her sphere of influence, the Rice and Corn Administration.[69] In addition, several family members were elected officials in the regime: Marcos's sister was governor of their home province until his son, Ferdinand Jr., took over the post. A Marcos daughter, Imee, was an assemblywoman to the legislature, as was Imelda Marcos. The Marcos family had become the core of the regime-state.

The first lady was unquestionably the second most powerful person in government. Marcos appointed her to important government positions—governor of Metro Manila in 1975 and head of the newly created Ministry of Human Settlements in 1977—which, along with her considerable informal powers, led Mijares to label the dictatorship "conjugal."[70] She was the country's ambassador at large, traveling to the United States, the Soviet Union, China, Libya, and elsewhere, combining diplomatic missions with international shopping. The state of the Marcoses' marriage was a great political importance. A fragile compromise of her tolerating his many affairs as long as he exercised discretion was shattered when Marcos's relationship with American starlet Dovie Beams became a public scandal in 1970.[71] At this point Imelda began demanding economic concessions from Marcos for herself and her family as expiation. In a highly comical account, Mijares reported that her brothers and sisters organized their own corps of spies to catch Marcos in flagrante delicto, while counteragents moved to shield the president from their prying eyes.[72] Another insider account, from former information minister Francisco Tatad, claims that Imelda's later appointments to government posts were acts of appeasement after Imelda's intelligence network had discovered further Marcos transgressions.[73] The presidential palace began to polarize into two hostile camps, with

Imelda receiving visitors in a separate waiting room and making her own government decisions.

It is doubtful that Marcos would have given in to his wife so easily, however, had he not seen certain benefits for his regime. For all their conflict, he could trust her. She could not break with him politically (and in the Philippines there is no divorce). When his health worsened, she was a safe regent. Her personal excesses made a convenient lightning rod for the general corruption of the regime. Her projects were part of his deliberate strategy of "bread and circuses" to distract people's attention. Her Ministry of Human Settlements, a "government within a government," was the largest patronage machine in the country. With the revival of elections, her clientelist network proved very useful.

Although Imelda was an integral part of the Marcos dynasty, she did represent an extreme tendency in the regime that may have *accelerated* the process of sultanization. Her personal extravagance is too well known to rehash here. She was much more materially greedy than Marcos, who had simple tastes.[74] The high cost and low utility of her many projects, such as the Miss Universe pageant and the Ali-Frazier fight, symbolized the waste of the regime. She was an enemy of its few technocrats, leading the 1983 attack against prime minister and finance minister Cesar Virata, whom she called "Dr. No" because he opposed her more inane schemes. Mijares claimed she was obsessed with succeeding her husband, which subsequent accounts have confirmed.[75] Seeing Enrile as a rival, she hounded him from the beginning of martial law onward, contributing to his break with the regime.[76] There is considerable evidence that she and General Ver had Benigno S. Aquino Jr. assassinated to get another potential competitor out of the way while Marcos was undergoing a kidney operation that it looked as if he might not survive.[77] Imelda had an impulsive, vengeful side, whereas Marcos was more calculating, though equally ruthless.[78] Running the government day to day as de facto president for much of 1984–85 while Marcos recovered, she was in part responsible for the extreme corruption and political drift during the final years of the regime.

A Personality Cult and Populist Gestures

The increasingly personalistic character of the regime became evident in the efforts the ruling duo made to glorify themselves. During the early years of martial law, the Marcoses were discussing whether to declare themselves emperor and empress, Mijares reported.[79] Pictures of the Marcoses in a very imperial pose were distributed throughout the Philippines (and hung in every government office). Imelda Marcos also had her husband and herself painted as the Malay version of Adam and Eve, Malakas (Strong) and Maganda (Beautiful), in the presidential palace. The culmination of this self-exaltation was reserved for Ferdinand Marcos alone, however. He had a massive bust of himself built north of Manila, overlooking the Marcos Golf and Country Club, near the Marcos Highway that, like Ozymandias, seems to say: "Look on my works, ye Mighty, and despair!"[80]

Despite the obvious indications of personalism in the regime, many foreign scholars and some Filipino intellectuals were blinded by Marcos's claim that he was using martial law to carry out extensive reform. Even before martial law, Marcos had articulated an ideology of "revolution from the center" as an alternative to a corrupt oligarchical democracy and violent communist rebellion.[81] With authoritarian powers, Marcos declared that a "new society" would be built by restoring order, carrying out social reform, bringing about economic development, and cleaning up government. Results seemed impressive. Crime was down, half a million guns were confiscated, demonstrations were banned, and (in a precedent-setting move) a notorious drug dealer was executed. The urban elite, fearing anarchy, applauded this law and order campaign. Land reform was declared "the cornerstone" of his program, which raised the hopes of the peasantry. Although they could no longer strike, workers were organized into a single union that held tripartite negotiations with a newly merged business federation and government representatives. Incentives for foreign investment were decreed and nationalist Supreme Court decisions overturned. So-called economic technocrats believed they could finally implement their program of export industrialization that had been blocked by a protectionist Congress. Economic growth was impressive in the early years, reaching 9.6 percent in 1973 and averaging 6.3 percent for the next four years.

Mijares reported that Marcos's "ideology" was the concoction of two socialists the president had brought into the cabinet to give it a radical veneer. In practice, the regime had no real guiding philosophy: "The highly-touted new reforms of the dictatorial regime are meant only to affect certain 'grand issues' and nothing was really supposed to change when it comes to the members of the ruling clique's comfort and convenience, and economic and political interests."[82] There is much evidence to support Mijares' position, particularly after the first few years of martial law. By then crime was at a record high, guns were being redistributed to paramilitary groups and warlords loyal to Marcos, and drug dealers were again bribing their way out of jail.[83] Land reform had come to a standstill, having largely served to undermine his wealthy landlord opponents and not to lessen inequality in the countryside.[84] The leadership of the Trade Union Congress of the Philippines (TUCP) was compromised by government favors and failed to protest a 30 percent decline in real blue-collar wages between 1972 and 1978, while the business federation was run by a notorious Marcos crony.[85] Businessmen in the private sector found their interests subordinated to the cronies who enjoyed special privileges from the state. The technocrats were marginalized in the regime. Foreign investment slowed as bribery and forced buyouts affected the business climate after the first two years of martial law. (At the same time, however, international borrowing increased because of government loan guarantees.) Economic growth fell to the lowest in Southeast Asia after the early martial law commodity boom ended and politically painful market liberalization measures were repeatedly postponed by the regime. The head of the anticorruption crusade, executive secretary Alejandro Melchor, was himself purged in 1975 after having stepped on too many important toes, particularly the first lady's.

Marcos and the United States

Before Marcos came to power, it was the *opposition* that was often able to win U.S. backing to save democracy from an incumbent whose corruption might make the country vulnerable to revolution. But the Nixon administration, entangled in the Vietnam War and skeptical about the efficacy of democracy in the Third World, accepted Marcos's argument that "emergency rule" was necessary to defeat a communist threat and achieve political stability.[86] Receiving assurances that it could keep its large military bases in the Philippines, the U.S. government did not condemn martial law and increased assistance to his regime.

By winning American support, however, Marcos became very dependent on it, as have many other sultanistic dictators. In a country psychologically oriented toward the United States, perhaps more so than any other land in the world, close relations with the Americans had been essential to all Philippine presidents, and Marcos was no exception. But as an authoritarian strongman he was particularly reliant on U.S. military aid to support his enlarged armed forces. Without an ideology or a broad base of support, he was vulnerable if the Americans turned against him. This explains why Marcos was so afraid of U.S. efforts to destabilize his regime. (When he fell, it was the United States he blamed most.)[87] But this dependence on the Americans did not mean he was incapable of manipulating them. Until the Aquino assassination, Marcos had the upper hand in his relationship with the U.S. government. Publicly, Filipino radicals labeled Marcos a *tuta* (little dog) of the United States:

Privately, of course, the Left's leadership was well aware that Marcos was actually the *least* docile of the country's presidents. . . . Ferdinand was vastly more astute than his opposite numbers in Washington. He had Carter's vain mini-Kissinger, Assistant Secretary of State for East Asian and Pacific Affairs Richard Holbrooke, in his pocket and charged half a billion dollars for a new five-year bases agreement. . . . Reagan, an old friend from the 1960s, bundled his fatuous Vice-President off to Manila [after the 1981 Philippine presidential election] to inform Marcos that "we love your adherence to democratic principle and the democratic process".[88]

Marcos's Constitutional Hypocrisy

Marcos was anxious to show, particularly to the U.S. government, that he had "not grabbed power."[89] Legitimizing his dictatorship abroad was a more difficult task than that faced by other authoritarian rulers because of the Philippines' reputation abroad as the Asian "showcase of democracy."[90] Over the years Marcos would argue that he had established a "constitutional authoritarian" regime to "save democracy" from a state of rebellion. The judiciary, though shorn of any real power, was allowed to continue to function so that the constitutionality of the "new society" could be certified.

But Marcos faced a major obstacle in keeping up appearances as a good democrat: his second, and constitutionally final, term expired in December 1973. Through threats and bribes he got the reconvened constitutional convention to approve a document that allowed him to serve indefinitely both as president under the old constitution and as prime minister under the new. Then, because of mounting opposition, he canceled the scheduled plebiscite on the new constitution, instead having local "citizens' assemblies" decide on it by a show of hands. Mijares claimed he was part of a committee that manufactured the "results" of the voting in the presidential palace.[91] An intimidated Supreme Court ruled that although the constitution had been unconstitutionally ratified, there was no "legal" obstacle to its implementation. American government officials realized the new constitution had been fraudulently approved, but they had an interest in giving the impression that the Philippine president enjoyed democratic legitimacy so their pro-Marcos stance would not be questioned.

Needing to prove the popularity of martial law, particularly to foreign financiers whose loans were crucial to the regime, Marcos held five plebiscites between mid-1973 and late 1977. He announced one of them in front of a gathering of Chase Manhattan Bank officials in 1975 and promised he would return the country to parliamentary rule if it was defeated. Needless to say, it was not (all plebiscites during martial law were approved by between 83 percent and 95 percent).[92] Another referendum was timed to please delegates at an International Monetary Fund–World Bank meeting held in Manila in 1976. Finding that the claim to be democratic without a legislature had become a bit strained, Marcos announced the revival of elections in front of the World Law Conference held in Manila in 1977, which had (with unintended irony) "human rights" as its theme.

But massive cheating marred the 1978 legislative elections, and after a second fraudulent election in 1980 (for local offices), the opposition had had enough. Their boycott of the 1981 presidential polls left Marcos desperate for an opponent. He encouraged (and probably paid) an obscure provincial politician who worked for his government to run against him. The candidate, General Alejo Santos, managed to carry the vote only in his (small) hometown; 50 percent of registered voters in Manila may have boycotted the election.[93] But this did not keep Marcos from claiming democratic legitimacy, nor did it deter U.S. vice president George Bush from affirming it on a state visit to the Philippines.

Opposition to Sultanism and Democratization in the Philippines

This is not the place to discuss in detail the nature of the opposition to Marcos and democratization.[94] The point here is that the transition to democracy in the Philippines followed a fundamentally different logic than did most Latin American and Eastern European democratizations because of the sultanistic character of the Marcos regime. More institutionalized nondemocratic regimes— whether communist and noncommunist, civilian or military—are likely to arrange for an orderly transition rather than risk being overthrown. This is due to common goals within the regime that authoritarian rulers believe will be served by democratization: winning free elections, maintaining the high status of a state body (for example, the "military as institution"), retaining key bureaucratic positions, limiting investigations of human rights violations during the authoritarian period, and gaining firm economic footing once out of power. Personal rule does not involve such collective interests. In particular, sultanistic rulers are so reviled that they have no legitimate interests they can protect once they relinquish power (when they are usually forced into exile, if not executed). This makes them "stand pat" dictators. Marcos had to be brought down, because he would never have stepped down. Augusto Pinochet, by contrast, could surrender authority to a democratic regime while remaining head of the military and retaining support among a substantial minority of the population.

Opposition to Marcos therefore often more closely resembled the revolutionary path of Cuba or Nicaragua or the coup pattern of Haiti. The unyielding character of the Marcos regime gave an advantage to armed opponents, as did its massive corruption and arbitrary exercise of power. The Philippine communists grew from a tiny army of student romantics to a major challenge to the regime in the late authoritarian period. The loss of electoral patronage contributed to rising social tensions in the countryside. Corruption and land grabbing by regional political elites allied with Marcos, as well as human rights abuses by the military, further fueled discontent.[95] The communists capitalized on this explosive situation, and their recruiting proved particularly successful in coconut- and sugar-growing regions where crony monopolies had kept commodity prices and wages low. With elite military battalions concentrated in Manila to protect Marcos, the communists' rural-based insurgency grew from only several hundred troops before martial law to eight thousand soldiers by 1980, reaching twenty thousand by 1983.[96]

Discontented military leaders, Enrile and later Ramos, mobilized officers disgusted by the patrimonializing of the armed forces to plot against the regime. The military rebel opposition began in the late 1970s or early 1980s as a core group of officers close to defense minister Enrile, who had been on the losing end of a power struggle with General Ver and the first lady. Although the group was a vehicle for Enrile's political ambitions, it was able to win the sympathy of many junior and some senior officers because of several symptoms of sultanism: delayed promotions owing to extendee generals, excessive personal enrichment by top officers, and a growing communist insurgency. But it was only after 1983, when Marcos became very ill, Aquino was assassinated, and U.S. policy changed, that the military rebel opposition gained momentum. Behind a carefully planned public protest at the Philippine military academy in 1985, Enrile's "core group" of the Reform the Armed Forces Movement (RAM) was making contacts with General Ramos (who commanded the loyalty of a less conspiratorial but larger faction of the military). It also established links to the U.S. government and civilian opposition groups to gain support for a military coup.

Anti-Marcos pre–martial law politicians invoked the country's long democratic tradition, but this helped them little with balloting canceled under martial law. Aside from exile activity in the United States, the traditional opposition was largely ineffective until Marcos restored "elections" in 1978.[97] Although these polls were rigged, the opposition, led by Benigno S. Aquino Jr., was able to mobilize considerable support, as an hours-long "noise barrage" in Manila indicated. But blatant manipulation of subsequent local polls and in the run-up to the 1981 presidential election led to a boycott by opposition politicians in alliance with the communists.

Widespread corruption and favoritism had turned most independent businessmen into covert oppositionists by the late 1970s, but only a few were willing to act on their displeasure, as was shown by their limited support for a small, unsuccessful terrorist bombing campaign led by a handful of businessmen, opposition politicians, and social democratic activists. A turning point came in 1981 when the flight of a Chinese businessman close to the president caused a financial panic that forced Marcos to bail out many of his cronies. Leading businessman Jaime Ongpin (later finance minister under Aquino) began attacking Marcos publicly, while others organized the Makati Business Club, which also took an antiregime stance. The economic crisis that followed the Aquino assassination made the Makati business district a major opposition center.

Church opposition emerged in response to the regime's violations of human rights. Although by the standards of other authoritarian regimes Marcos's was not extraordinarily repressive, the frequent use of torture, the employment of private armed groups ("lost commands" and "secret marshals"), and the use of selective political murder ("salvaging") to carry out vengeance and heighten fear led to intense hatred of its military apparatus.[98] Failing in its efforts to constrain the military ("Church-Military Liaison Committee"), the church sponsored a human rights group and progressive bishops began openly criticizing the regime. After the Aquino assassination, the moderate bishops led by Cardinal Jaime Sin lent moral support to antigovernment demonstrations.

Marcos's failing health and the decline of the economy beginning in the late 1970s severely weakened the regime. Aquino was killed on government orders in the midst of a personalized power struggle, rather than being put into jail or under house arrest as more institutionalized military regimes did with returning exile opposition leaders in Korea and Uruguay. The communists seemed likely to benefit most from the massive protests that followed the Aquino assassination. But the U.S. government, concerned about political succession and worried about the growing revolutionary movement, changed its policy and began pressuring Marcos to hold fairer elections. With the backing of the Catholic Church and businessmen, the traditional opposition made a respectable showing in the 1984 legislative polls, which the communists boycotted. The continued hard-line tactics of the radical left ruined any possibility of reviving a united front, and Marcos called a snap presidential election to head off growing American criticism. The pre–martial law opposition politicians chose a seemingly nonpartisan candidate, Corazon Aquino, who could make moral appeals to the electorate and would attract campaign volunteers to compensate for Marcos's patronage advantage. Church and business backing was crucial in setting up an electoral watchdog group, which raised the cost of cheating. The Aquino camp kept in close contact with Enrile's RAM, which it knew was plotting a coup against the regime. After the fraudulent election, RAM's plan for a putsch was discovered, leading Cardinal Sin to call for civilian bodyguards to protect the rebels. This prompted "people power," which brought Aquino to power and the Marcoses to Hawaii. The traditional opposition had defeated a dynastic dictatorship.

The Philippines was the first country to democratize directly after sultanism. (The Dominican Republic democratized, but only after several authoritarian periods and a brief civil war following Trujillo's assassination. Nicaragua's democratic transition came after a decade of nondemocratic Sandinista rule.) But the legacies of Marcos's regime contributed to a very troubled transition to democracy.[99] Marcos left a ruined economy drained of billions in stolen wealth, a communist insurgency, and a politicized military. Unlike the situation in Latin America, coup attempts against the Aquino government were less an effort to preserve military prerogatives under civilian rule than a continuation of a military rebel plot to capture state power. Highly competitive elections helped stabilize the system as the old rules of the game gradually gained acceptance. Violence and vote buying returned, while social reforms failed. "Raw democracy" was slowly restored after the end of a "conjugal dictatorship."

NOTES

. . . .

Acknowledgments

1. Juan J. Linz and Alfred Stepan, *Problems of Democratic Transition and Consolidation: Southern Europe, South America, and Post-Communist Europe* (Baltimore: Johns Hopkins University Press, 1996).

2. See Michael Bratton and Nicolas van de Walle, *Democratic Experiments in Africa: Regime Transitions in Comparative Perspective* (New York: Cambridge University Press, 1997).

1 • A Theory of Sultanism 1

We thank Don Babai, Jorge Domínguez, Jonathan Hartlyn, Raimund Krämer, the late David Nicholls, Said Saffari, Brian Smith, Richard Snyder, Mark Thompson, and Richard Turits for their extensive comments on earlier drafts of the first two chapters.

1. The initial formulation of a sultanistic regime is in Juan Linz, "Totalitarian and Authoritarian Regimes," in *Handbook of Political Science*, vol. 3, ed. Nelson Polsby and Fred Greenstein (Reading, Mass.: Addison-Wesley, 1975). For an updated classification of nondemocratic regimes see Juan J. Linz and Alfred Stepan, *Problems of Democratic Transition and Consolidation: Southern Europe, South America, and Post-Communist Europe* (Baltimore: Johns Hopkins University Press, 1996), chaps. 3 and 4.

2. Although even there Poland was already a posttotalitarian polity, a type of governance that would later spread to most of the Soviet bloc in the years before the collapse of communism. For an analysis see Linz and Stepan, *Problems of Democratic Transition and Consolidation*, 42–51.

3. Originally formulated by Guillermo O'Donnell in *Modernization and Bureaucratic Authoritarianism: Studies in South American Politics* (Berkeley: Institute of International Studies, University of California, 1972). See also David Collier, "Overview of the Bureaucratic-Authoritarian Model," in *The New Authoritarianism in Latin America*, ed. David Collier (Princeton: Princeton University Press, 1979).

4. For a recent attempt to classify them see Leonardo Morlino, "Authoritarianism," in *Contemporary Political Systems: Classifications and Typologies*, ed. Anton Bebler and Jim Seroka (Boulder, Colo.: Lynne Rienner, 1990).

5. Max Weber, *Economy and Society: An Outline of Interpretive Sociology*, ed. Guenther Roth and Claus Wittich (Berkeley: University of California Press, 1978), 231 and 232; emphasis in the original.

6. See Guenther Roth, "Personal Rulership, Patrimonialism, and Empire-Building in the New States," *World Politics* 20 (January 1968). A little earlier Aristide Zolberg had analyzed the emerging patrimonialism in Africa in his *Creating Political Order: The*

Party-States of West Africa (Chicago: University of Chicago Press, 1966). A case study on pre-Mobutu Zaire was provided by Jean-Claude Willame, *Patrimonialism and Political Change in the Congo* (Stanford: Stanford University Press, 1972).

7. For a good summary of the differences between patrimonialism and neopatrimonialism see Jean-François Médard, "The Underdeveloped State in Tropical Africa: Political Clientelism or Neo-patrimonialism?" in *Private Patronage and Public Power,* ed. Christopher Clapham (New York: St. Martin's Press, 1982).

8. One rare exception is Norbert Elias, who wrote in 1969 (without elaborating) that the rule of Louis XIV in France could perhaps be classified as a traditional domination on the way from patrimonialism to sultanism. See his *Die höfische Gesellschaft* (Frankfurt: Suhrkamp, 1992), 40.

9. Juan Linz, "An Authoritarian Regime: The Case of Spain," in *Mass Politics: Studies in Political Sociology,* ed. Erik Allardt and Stein Rokkan (New York: Free Press, 1970); idem, "From Falange to Movimiento-Organización: The Spanish Single Party and the Franco Regime, 1936–1968," in *Authoritarian Politics in Modern Society: The Dynamics of Established One-Party Systems,* ed. Samuel P. Huntington and Clement H. Moore (New York: Basic Books, 1970); and idem, "Opposition to and under an Authoritarian Regime: The Case of Spain," in *Regimes and Oppositions,* ed. Robert Dahl (New Haven: Yale University Press, 1974).

10. Galíndez's degree was conferred posthumously by Columbia University and the work was later published. See Jesús de Galíndez, *The Era of Trujillo: Dominican Dictator,* ed. Russell H. Fitzgibbon (Tucson: University of Arizona Press, 1973). See 11–18 for an account of this tragedy.

11. Linz, "Totalitarian and Authoritarian Regimes," 259–63.

12. Crawford Young and Thomas Turner, *The Rise and Decline of the Zairian State* (Madison: University of Wisconsin Press, 1985), 182.

13. Terry Lynn Karl, "Petroleum and Political Pacts: The Transition to Democracy in Venezuela," in *Transition from Authoritarian Rule: Latin America,* ed. Guillermo O'Donnell, Philippe Schmitter, and Laurence Whitehead (Baltimore: Johns Hopkins University Press, 1986), 199, 206; H. E. Chehabi, *Iranian Politics and Religious Modernism: The Liberation Movement of Iran under the Shah and Khomeini* (Ithaca: Cornell University Press, 1990); John Thayer Sidel, "Beyond Patron-Client Relations: Warlordism and Local Politics in the Philippines," *Kasarinlan* 4, no. 3 (1989); Mark R. Thompson, *The Anti-Marcos Struggle: Personalistic Rule and Democratic Transition in the Philippines* (New Haven: Yale University Press, 1995); Samuel P. Huntington, *The Third Wave: Democratization in the Late Twentieth Century* (Norman: University of Oklahoma Press, 1991), 111.

14. Vilfredo Pareto, *The Rise and Fall of Elites: An Application of Theoretical Sociology* (New Brunswick, N.J.: Transaction, 1991), 27. Pareto writes that this method was recommended by the French physiologist Claude Bernard.

15. Richard Sandbrook with Judith Barker, *The Politics of Africa's Economic Stagnation* (Cambridge: Cambridge University Press, 1985), 89.

16. Weber, *Economy and Society,* 232.

17. Ibid., 1020.

18. For this see Bryan S. Turner, *Weber and Islam: A Critical Study* (London: Routledge & Kegan Paul, 1974); Wolfgang Schluchter, "Einleitung. Zwischen Welteroberung und Weltanpassung. Überlegungen zu Max Webers Sicht des frühen Islams," in *Max*

Webers Sicht des Islams: Interpretation und Kritik, ed. Wolfgang Schluchter (Frankfurt: Suhrkamp, 1987), especially 84–99; and Olivier Carré, "A propos de Weber et l'Islam," *Archives de Sciences Sociales des Religions* 61 (1986). Carré (143) argues that Weber's notion of "sultanism" is prefigured in Ibn Khaldun's typology of forms of rule.

19. See Haim Gerber, *State, Society, and Law in Islam: Ottoman Law in Comparative Perspective* (Albany: State University of New York Press, 1994), which systematically confronts Weber's ideal types with evidence from Ottoman history. Gerber concludes that "the Ottoman political system was much more bureaucratic—that is, based on objective rules rather than being rapacious, despotic, and whimsical—than is usually thought" (127). For an interesting interpretation of how the Ottoman ruler acquired the negative image of an arbitrary despot in the West see Lucette Valensi, *The Birth of the Despot: Venice and the Sublime Porte,* trans. Arthur Denner (Ithaca: Cornell University Press, 1993). The conclusions of such detailed studies of the Ottoman Empire cannot, of course, be extended to the case of Iran, whose premodern legacy is touched on by Homa Katouzian's chapter in this book.

20. Weber, *Economy and Society,* 493.

21. See Max Weber, *The Religion of China: Confucianism and Taoism* (New York: Free Press, 1964), 44, 138–39, 195.

22. Halil Inalcik, "Comments on 'Sultanism': Max Weber's Typification of the Ottoman Polity," *Princeton Papers in Near Eastern Studies* 1 (1992): 49–72.

23. When the sultanate was abolished in Turkey in 1922, the caliphate was maintained for another year. Moreover, in fourteenth-century Spain, even Christians referred to their king as "Sultan Don Pedro." Guy Hermet, *Histoire des nations et du nationalisme en Europe* (Paris: Seuil, 1996), 45.

24. Inalcik, "Comments," 53.

25. The absence of traditional legitimation is important and shows the incorrectness of Jeane Kirkpatrick's characterization of Somoza and the Shah as "traditional autocrats." See her *Dictatorships and Double Standards: Rationalism and Reason in Politics* (New York: Simon & Schuster, 1982), 24–25.

26. These same regimes are also the object of a brief comparative analysis by Didier Bigo. See his *Pouvoir et obéissance en Centrafrique* (Paris: Karthala, 1988), 319–28.

27. Alain Rouquié, *The Military and the State in Latin America,* trans. Paul E. Sigmund (Berkeley: University of California Press, 1987), 182.

28. Marcial Antonio Riquelme, "Toward a Weberian Characterization of the Stroessner Regime in Paraguay (1954–1989)," *European Review of Latin American and Caribbean Studies,* no. 57 (1994).

29. Linz and Stepan, *Problems of Democratic Transition and Consolidation,* 336–65.

30. Sandbrook with Barker, *Politics of Africa's Economic Stagnation,* 89; Robert H. Jackson and Carl G. Rosberg, "The Political Economy of Personal Rule," in *Political Development and the New Realism in Sub-Saharan Africa,* ed. David E. Apter and Carl G. Rosberg (Charlottesville: University Press of Virginia, 1994).

31. Naomi Chazan, Robert Mortimer, John Ravenhill, and Donald Rothchild, *Politics and Society in Contemporary Africa* (London: Macmillan, 1988), 129–46.

32. See Michael Bratton and Nicolas van de Walle, "Neopatrimonial Regimes and Political Transitions in Africa," *World Politics* 46 (July 1994).

33. The first three had the added distinction of being, to various degrees, mentally

deranged. See Samuel Decalo, *Psychoses of Power: African Personal Dictatorships* (Boulder, Colo.: Westview, 1989).

34. Given how out of proportion repression was, we wonder whether in these two cases it might be useful to turn to older terms like "tyranny" or "despotism" rather than "sultanism" to characterize their rule. The main distinction between these two regimes and that of the Khmer Rouge in Cambodia was that the latter destroyed society and killed off citizens in the name of a well-defined ideology. For an attempt to classify modern-day tyrannies see Daniel Chirot, *Modern Tyrants: The Power and Prevalence of Evil in Our Age* (New York: Free Press, 1994).

35. For Romania see Linz and Stepan, *Problems of Democratic Transition and Consolidation,* chap. 18, which discusses the mixture of totalitarianism and sultanism under Ceaușescu and compares his regime both with other communist regimes and with other sultanistic regimes.

On Grenada see Tony Thorndike, "Grenada: Maxi-crisis for Mini-state," *World Today* 30 (October 1974). The corruption of democracy in Antigua and Barbuda is well captured in the novelist Jamaica Kincaid's essay about her country, *A Small Place* (New York: Penguin, 1988).

36. This is in some ways analogous to what Weber did with Ferdinand Tönnies's famous concepts of *Gemeinschaft* and *Gesellschaft* when he introduced the notions of *Vergemeinschaftung* and *Vergesellschaftung*. See *Economy and Society,* 40–41.

37. Robert Fishman, "Rethinking State and Regime: Southern Europe's Transition to Democracy," *World Politics* 42 (April 1990).

38. A good example is provided by Chile, where the professionalism of the armed forces under democracy was rooted enough to survive the fall of Allende and was used by Augusto Pinochet to consolidate his authoritarian rule: one analyst has termed this reformulation "tarnished professionalism" (*profesionalismo desvirtuado*). See Genaro Arriagada Herrera, "The Legal and Institutional Framework of the Armed Forces in Chile," in *Military Rule in Chile: Dictatorship and Oppositions,* ed. J. Samuel Valenzuela and Arturo Valenzuela (Baltimore: Johns Hopkins University Press, 1986), 123.

39. This fusion can also appear in totalitarian systems, such as in the vanguard role of the parties in all communist regimes, the *Kaderpolitik* in the German Democratic Republic, or the "unity of party and state" under Nazism, but under sultanism this fusion is not based on ideological imperatives, as in totalitarian systems. The difference between sultanism and totalitarianism will be discussed below.

40. The features of a modern bureaucracy are taken from Max Weber's chapter on democracy in *Economy and Society,* 2:956–58.

41. Willame, *Patrimonialism and Political Change in the Congo,* 131, 138.

42. Paul D. Hutchcroft, "Oligarchs and Cronies in the Philippine State: The Politics of Patrimonial Plunder," *World Politics* 43 (April 1991): 429, 430.

43. Raul V. Fabella, "Trade and Industry Reforms in the Philippines: Process and Performance," in *Philippine Macroeconomic Perspective: Developments and Policies,* ed. Manuel F. Montes and Hideyoshi Sakai (Tokyo: Institute of Developing Economics, 1989), 197, as quoted in Hutchcroft, "Oligarchs and Cronies in the Philippine State," 434.

44. Anne Greene, *The Catholic Church in Haiti: Political and Social Change* (East Lansing: Michigan State University Press, 1993), 35.

45. Greene, *Catholic Church in Haiti,* 35.

46. For a good description of security forces in Zaire see Jean-Claude Willame, *L'automne d'un despotisme: Pouvoir, argent et obéissance dans le Zaïre des années quatre-vingt* (Paris: Editions Karthala, 1992), 45–53.

47. Bigo, *Pouvoir et obeïssance en Centrafrique*, 111. See also 110 for the text of an ordinance that allowed Bokassa to override all promotion criteria in the armed forces.

48. This is documented in the memoirs of the Shah's last chief of staff. See Arteshbod Abbas Qarabaghi, *E'terafat-e zheneral: Khaterat-e arteshbod Qarahbaghi* (The general's confessions: The memoirs of General Qarabaghi)(Tehran: Nashr-e Ney, 1986), 91–101. For an account of how arms purchases by officers responsible for ordnance in the Nicaraguan National Guard led to dissatisfaction see J. A. Robleto Siles, *Yo deserté de la guardia nacional de Nicaragua* (Ciudad Universitaria Rodrigo Facio, Costa Rica: Editorial Universitaria Centroamericana, 1979), 189–91.

49. Samuel P. Huntington, "Social and Institutional Dynamics of One-Party Systems," in Huntington and Moore, *Authoritarian Politics in Modern Society,* 41.

50. For an early warning against confusing the claim to charisma with charismatic authority itself, see Roth, "Personal Rulership, Patrimonialism, and Empire-Building in the New States," 200. One leader who still seemed to enjoy a degree of genuine charisma was Antigua's V. C. Bird, who belonged to the first generation of Caribbean trade union leaders who led their islands to independence.

51. Willame, *L'automne d'un despotisme*, 20.

52. Vladimir Tismaneanu, "Personal Power and Political Crisis in Romania," *Government and Opposition* 24 (spring 1989): 195.

53. Ferdinand Marcos, *An Ideology for Filipinos* (Manila: Cid Reyes, 1983).

54. Mobutu Sese Seko, *Les grands textes du Mobutisme* (Kinshasa: Forcad/Institut Makanda Kabobi, 1984).

55. Robert L. Youngblood, *Marcos against the Church: Economic Development and Political Repression in the Philippines* (Ithaca: Cornell University Press, 1990), 35–40.

56. As used in Eric Hobsbawm and Terence Ranger, eds., *The Invention of Tradition* (Cambridge: Cambridge University Press, 1994).

57. The last point is particularly interesting, since until then Romanian nationalists had insisted on the Latin heritage of their country to demarcate it from its Slavic neighbors. For this purpose Romînia became România, and the English Rumania became Romania.

58. This purge led to the decimation of the population of the island of Annobón by a cholera epidemic in the 1970s, after he refused to allow medical help to reach the people. Decalo, *Psychoses of Power*, 33.

59. Linz, "Totalitarian and Authoritarian Regimes," 196.

60. See the contributions of Homa Katouzian and David Nicholls in this volume.

61. Tismaneanu, "Personal Power and Political Crisis in Romania," 195.

62. This dimension is reflected in the similar titles of books and articles on these regimes. Examples are Charles W. Anderson, "Nicaragua: the Somoza Dynasty," in *Political Systems of Latin America,* ed. Martin Needler (New York: Van Nostrand Reinhold, 1970), and Richard Millett, *Guardians of the Dynasty* (Maryknoll, N.Y.: Orbis Books, 1977) on Nicaragua; An Observer [David Nicholls], "Dynastic Republicanism in Haiti," *Political Quarterly* 44 (January–March 1973); Sterling Seagrave, *The Marcos Dynasty* (New York: Harper & Row, 1988); Vladimir Tismaneanu, "Byzantine Rites, Stalin-

ist Follies: The Twilight of Dynastic Socialism in Romania," *Orbis* 30 (1986), and idem, *Romania: A Case of "Dynastic" Communism* (New York: Freedom House, 1989); and Tai Sung An, *North Korea in Transition: From Dictatorship to Dynasty* (Westport, Conn.: Greenwood Press, 1983).

63. Greene, *Catholic Church in Haiti*, 35–39.

64. Lela Garner Noble, "Politics in the Marcos Era," in *Crisis in the Philippines: The Marcos Era and Beyond*, ed. John Bresnan (Princeton: Princeton University Press, 1986), 94, 97.

65. Mary Ellen Fischer, "Idol or Leader? The Origin and Future of the Ceauşescu Cult," in *Romania in the 1980's*, ed. Daniel Nelson (Boulder, Colo.: Westview, 1981), 131.

66. "Du bist zu groß für ein so kleines Volk," *Der Spiegel*, 1 December 1986, 190. In addition a number of Ceauşescu's brothers held top posts in the security apparatus. For a list of the dynasty's members see Tismaneanu, "Personal Power and Political Crisis in Romania," 192–93.

67. Decalo, *Psychoses of Power*, 62. For a glimpse of politics in Equatorial Guinea in 1996 see "Trouble in Oily Waters," *Economist*, 24 February 1996, 50.

68. For details see Robert Coram, *Caribbean Time Bomb: The United States' Complicity in the Corruption of Antigua* (New York: William Morrow, 1993); *Keesing's Contemporary Archives* 40 (March 1994): 39905–6.

69. Omar Bongo of Gabon also played with the idea of founding a kingdom. Both he and Mobutu apparently abandoned their plans after the negative publicity generated by Bokassa's extravaganza. On this episode see Bigo, *Pouvoir et obéissance en Centrafrique*, 143–62.

70. Of course the borderline is fluid: Indira Gandhi did promote the political careers of her two sons. See Subrata K. Mitra, "India: Dynastic Rule or the Democratization of Power," *Third World Quarterly* 10 (1988), and Jad Adams and Phillip Whitehead, *The Dynasty: The Nehru-Ghandi Story* (London: Penguin, 1997).

71. Miriam Ferguson was elected governor of Texas in 1924 after her husband James E. Ferguson's impeachment in 1917, and Lurleen Wallace was elected governor of Alabama in 1966 when her husband George C. Wallace was barred by his state's constitution from succeeding himself. See Stephan Lesher, *George Wallace: American Populist* (Reading, Mass.: Addison-Wesley, 1994), 352–86, esp. 359.

72. Rouquié, *Military and the State in Latin America*, 157. Rouquié adds, somewhat implausibly, that he was also "inspector of public latrines for the Rockefeller Foundation."

73. German E. Ornes, *Trujillo: Little Caesar of the Caribbean* (New York: Thomas Nelson, 1958), 29–33.

74. Rouquié, *Military and the State in Latin America*, 174.

75. Decalo, *Psychoses of Power*, 5.

76. On contemporary traditional systems see Linz, "Totalitarian and Authoritarian Regimes," 253–59. Ethiopia under Emperor Haile Selassie presented an interesting case of a traditional patrimonial monarchy that had a constitution, but one that was "honest" and conferred all powers on the emperor. See Jackson and Rosberg, *Personal Rule in Black Africa*, 120–26.

77. See, as a sample, Rafael Leónidas Trujillo, *The Evolution of Democracy in Santo Domingo* (Ciudad Trujillo: Editora del Caribe, 1955); Ferdinand E. Marcos, *The Demo-*

cratic Revolution in the Philippines (Englewood Cliffs, N.J.: Prentice-Hall, 1979), and idem, *The New Republic: A Third World Approach to Democracy* (Manila, 1982); or Nicolae Ceauşescu, *La démocratie socialiste en Roumanie* (Bucharest: Meridane, 1980).

78. See Guy Hermet, Richard Rose, and Alain Rouquié, *Elections without Choice* (New York: John Wiley, 1976).

79. For details see John Booth, *The Ending and the Beginning: The Nicaraguan Revolution* (Boulder, Colo.: Westview, 1985), 98–100.

80. Tismaneanu, "Personal Power and Political Crisis in Romania," 187.

81. For an early conceptualization of "pseudo-opposition" see Linz, "Opposition to and under an Authoritarian Regime, 191n.

82. For a somewhat apologetic account of these see Jerzy J. Wiatr, "The Hegemonic Party System in Poland," in Allardt and Rokkan,*Mass Politics: Studies in Political Sociology.*

83. On elections under the monarchy see A.-H. Banisadr, A. Ghazanfarpour, S. Ghazanfarpour, and P. Vieille, "Les elections et leurs fonctions en Iran," *Revue Française de Science Politique* 27 (February 1977).

84. "Du bist zu groß," 178.

85. Alexis de Tocqueville, *The Old Régime and the French Revolution*, trans. Stuart Gilbert (New York: Anchor Books, 1955), 45.

86. See Ervand Abrahamian, *Iran: Between Two Revolutions* (Princeton: Princeton University Press, 1982), 118–35.

87. Omari H. Kokole and Ali A. Mazrui, "Uganda: The Dual Polity and the Plural Society," in *Democracy in Developing Countries: Africa*, ed. Larry Diamond, Juan J. Linz, and Seymour Martin Lipset (Boulder, Colo.: Lynne Rienner, 1988), 271.

88. See Amir Asadollah Alam, *The Shah and I: The Confidential Diary of Iran's Royal Court* (New York: St. Martin's Press, 1992). On the pro-Pahlavi lobby in America see James A. Bill, *The Eagle and the Lion: The Tragedy of American-Iranian Relations* (New Haven: Yale University Press, 1988), 170–76, 319–22, 355–67, 374–78.

89. Hutchcroft, "Oligarchs and Cronies in the Philippine State," 429. For details see Raymond Bonner, *Waltzing with a Dictator* (New York: Vintage Books, 1988).

90. For details see Rouquié, *Military and the State in Latin America*, 165.

91. Weber, *Economy and Society*, 238–40, 1095, 239, 1097.

92. See Stanislas Andreski, "Kleptocracy as a System of Government in Africa," in *Bureaucratic Corruption in Sub-Saharan Africa*, ed. Monday U. Ekpo (Washington, D.C.: University Press of America, 1979).

93. Decalo, *Psychoses of Power*, 8. Bokassa also nationalized enterprises to divert their profit into his own pockets, established personal monopolies on the distribution of such products as cement and steel, and owned farms that supplied the capital with food. For details see Bigo, *Pouvoir et obeïssance en Centrafrique*, 114–22.

94. See, for instance, Carlos Alberto Floria and César García Belsunce, *Historia de los argentinos*, vol. 1 (Buenos Aires: Larousse, 1992), 432–39, for a discussion of the relation between provincial caudillos and Buenos Aires.

95. On caudillismo see François Chevalier, " 'Caudillos' et 'caciques' en Amérique: Contribution à l'étude des liens personnels," in *Mélanges offerts à Marcel Bataillon, Bulletin hispanique* 64 bis (Bordeaux: Féret & Fils, 1962); Eric R. Wolf and Edward C. Hansen, "Caudillo Politics: A Structural Analysis," *Comparative Studies in Society and History* 9 (1967); K. H. Silvert, "Caudillismo," in *International Encyclopedia of the Social*

Sciences, vol. 2 ([New York]: Macmillan, 1968); and Linz, "Totalitarian and Authoritarian Regimes," 263–64.

96. See, for instance, his 1952 speech in Joaquín Balaguer, *La palabra encadenada* (Santo Domingo: Editora Taller, 1985), 63–66.

97. This is superbly documented in Raidza Torres, "Indian Self-Rule: A Historical and Political Perspective of the Interactions between the Nicaraguan State and the Miskito Indians on the Question of Autonomy" (senior thesis, Departments of Government and History, Harvard University, 1988).

98. Such privatization occasionally also occurs under nonsultanistic regimes, such as Argentina's military dictatorship.

99. For a discussion of human rights violations under sultanism and authoritarianism see Juan J. Linz, "Types of Political Regimes and Respect for Human Rights: Historical and Cross-national Perspectives," in *Human Rights in Perspective: A Global Assessment,* ed. Asbjørn Eide and Bernt Hagtvet (Oxford: Blackwell, 1992), 193–208.

100. Let us not forget that two years after he led the attack on the Moncada Barracks in 1953 Fidel Castro was let out of prison before the completion of his sentence and allowed to go into Mexican exile.

101. For details see Decalo, *Psychoses of Power,* chap. 2, and Jackson and Rosberg, *Personal Rule in Black Africa,* 245–51.

102. See Yossi Shain, *The Frontiers of Loyalty: Political Exiles in the Age of the Nation-State* (Middletown, Conn.: Wesleyan University Press, 1989).

2 • *A Theory of Sultanism 2*

1. This corresponds to the "funnel strategy" proposed by James Mahoney and Richard Snyder "Integrative Strategies for the Study of Regime Change," in *The Challenges to Democratic Theory,* ed. Sten Vgelvik Larsen, Social Science Monographs (New York: Columbia University Press, forthcoming).

2. Max Weber, *Economy and Society: An Outline of Interpretive Sociology,* ed. Guenther Roth and Claus Wittich (Berkeley: University of California Press, 1978), 1090.

3. Terry Lynn Karl, "Petroleum and Political Pacts: The Transition to Democracy in Venezuela," in *Transition from Authoritarian Rule: Latin America,* ed. Guillermo O'Donnell, Philippe Schmitter, and Laurence Whitehead (Baltimore: Johns Hopkins University Press, 1986), 199, 206.

4. Homa Katouzian, *The Political Economy of Modern Iran: Despotism and Pseudo-modernism, 1926–1979* (New York: New York University Press, 1981), 213–73.

5. Robert H. Jackson and Carl G. Rosberg, "The Political Economy of Personal Rule," in *Political Development and the New Realism in Sub-Saharan Africa,* ed. David E. Apter and Carl G. Rosberg (Charlottesville: University Press of Virginia, 1994), 305.

6. On the borrowing binge see Bernardo Villegas, "The Economic Crisis," in *Crisis in the Philippines: The Marcos Era and Beyond,* ed. John Bresnan (Princeton: Princeton University Press, 1986), 168–71.

7. Elizabeth Abbott, *Haiti: The Duvaliers and Their Legacy* (New York: McGraw-Hill, 1988), 175–77.

8. James Ferguson, *Papa Doc, Baby Doc: Haiti and the Duvaliers* (New York: Basil Blackwell, 1987), 70.

9. John Booth, *The Ending and the Beginning: The Nicaraguan Revolution* (Boulder, Colo.: Westview, 1985), 89.

10. Jackson and Rosberg, "Political Economy of Personal Rule," 305.

11. Samuel Decalo, *Psychoses of Power: African Personal Dictatorships* (Boulder, Colo.: Westview, 1989), 59.

12. Robert Coram, *Caribbean Time Bomb: The United States' Complicity in the Corruption of Antigua* (New York: William Morrow, 1993), 131.

13. For a definition of "crisis of sovereignty" see H. E. Chehabi, *Iranian Politics and Religious Modernism: The Liberation Movement of Iran under the Shah and Khomeini* (Ithaca: Cornell University Press, 1990), 7–9.

14. See Paul W. Drake, "From Good Men to Good Neighbors," in *Exporting Democracy: The United States and Latin America, Themes and Issues,* ed. Abraham F. Lowenthal (Baltimore: Johns Hopkins University Press, 1991).

15. Charles Cheney Hyde, *International Law, Chiefly as Interpreted and Applied by the United States* (Boston: Little, Brown, 1922), 25–36.

16. For a study expounding the thesis that an ongoing crisis of sovereignty has warped the political development of the country, see Jan Knippers Black, *The Dominican Republic: Politics and Development in an Unsovereign State* (Boston: Allen & Unwin, 1986).

17. Neill Maccaulay, *The Sandino Affair* (Durham: Duke University Press, 1985).

18. Maurice Halperin, *The Rise and Decline of Fidel Castro* (Berkeley: University of California Press, 1974), 4–5.

19. Jorge I. Domínguez, *Cuba: Order and Revolution* (Cambridge: Belknap Press of Harvard University Press, 1978), 13.

20. See Louis A. Pérez Jr., *Cuba under the Platt Amendment, 1902–1934* (Pittsburgh: University of Pittsburgh Press, 1986). For the effect of this interference on domestic politics in Cuba see Domínguez, *Cuba,* chap. 2.

21. See Andrew S. Zimbalist and John Weeks, *Panama at the Crossroads: Economic Development and Political Change in the Twentieth Century* (Berkeley: University of California Press, 1991).

22. John Weeks and Phil Gunson, *Panama: Made in the USA* (London: Latin America Bureau, 1991).

23. Hyde, *International Law,* 36.

24. David Steinberg, "Tradition and Response," in Bresnan, *Crisis in the Philippines,* 50.

25. V. I. Lenin, "On the Slogan for a United States of Europe," in *Collected Works,* vol. 21 (New York: International Publishers, 1967), 339–43.

26. On Iran see Firuz Kazemzadeh, *Russia and Britain in Persia, 1864–1914: A Study in Imperialism* (New Haven: Yale University Press, 1968), and Mark Gasiorowski, *U.S. Foreign Policy and the Shah: Building a Client State in Iran* (Ithaca: Cornell University Press, 1991).

27. Henry L. Roberts, *Rumania: Political Problems of an Agrarian State* (New Haven: Yale University Press, 1951), 18.

28. René Lemarchand, "The C.I.A. in Africa: How Central? How Intelligent?" *Journal of Modern African Studies* 14 (1976): 410–11.

29. Coram, *Caribbean Time Bomb,* 35–36.

30. U.S. aircraft land at any hour and with no prior notice, they pay no landing fees, and the crews do not go through customs or immigration. Ibid., 125–26.

31. For Antigua's strategic importance to the United States see Coram, *Caribbean Time Bomb,* chaps. 12 and 13.

32. And in the case of pre–World War II Iran, Russia and Britain.

33. One might speculate that the reason Puerto Rico, the third former Spanish colony in the Antilles, escaped sultanism is precisely that it never received its independence, although the personal integrity of Luis Muñoz Marín, founder of the Commonwealth, is also an important factor. See Laurence Whitehead, "The Imposition of Democracy," in Lowenthal, *Exporting Democracy,* 220–26.

34. Decalo, *Psychoses of Power,* 9–10, 50, 95–96.

35. See Henry Kissinger, *White House Years* (Boston: Little, Brown, 1979), 1261.

36. This point is made for Nicaragua in Morris H. Morley, *Washington, Somoza, and the Sandinistas: State and Regime in U.S. Policy toward Nicaragua* (New York: Cambridge University Press, 1994).

37. The breakdown of most clientelist democracies does not lead to sultanism, however: Brazil in the 1950s and early 1960s and Peru from the 1940s to the 1960s are cases in point.

38. On parties in Nicaragua see Virgilio Godoy Reyes, "Nicaragua 1944–84: Political Parties and Electoral Processes," in *Political Parties and Democracy in Central America,* ed. Louis W. Goodman, William M. LeoGrande, and Johanna Mendelson Forman (Boulder, Colo.: Westview, 1992), 175–81.

39. Juan M. del Aguila, *Cuba: Dilemmas of a Revolution* (Boulder, Colo.: Westview, 1984), 29–30.

40. For an influential early work on patron-client relations in the Philippines see Carl H. Lande, *Leaders, Factions, and Parties: The Structure of Philippine Politics,* Monograph Series 6 (New Haven: Yale University Southeast Asia Studies, 1966).

41. Lela Garner Noble, "Politics in the Marcos Era," in *Crisis in the Philippines: The Marcos Era and Beyond,* ed. John Bresnan (Princeton: Princeton University Press, 1986), 79–80. See also Mark Thompson's chapter in this volume.

42. Max Weber, *The Religion of China: Confucianism and Taoism* (New York: Free Press, 1964), 44, 195.

43. It must be pointed out, however, that this term coincided with World War II, a period when the struggle against the fascist powers begot greater political openness in the Allied camp.

44. Richard Sandbrook with Judith Barker, *The Politics of Africa's Economic Stagnation* (Cambridge: Cambridge University Press, 1985), 83–85.

45. Jackson and Rosberg, "Political Economy of Personal Rule," 300.

46. Accordingly it is in Senegal, where municipal self-government of the four historic communes dates back to the eighteenth century, that impersonal state institutions are most developed and a somewhat more democratic form of government prevails. See G. Wesley Johnson Jr., *The Emergence of Black Politics in Senegal: The Struggle for Power in the Four Communes: 1900–1920* (Stanford: Stanford University Press, 1971).

47. For an analysis of the regime's working see Samir al-Khalil, *Republic of Fear: The Politics of Modern Iraq* (London: Hutchinson, 1989).

48. See "The House That Saddam Built," *Economist,* 29 September 1990, 43–44, and

Isam al-Khafaji, "State Terror and the Degradation of Politics," in *Iraq since the Gulf War: Prospects for Democracy,* ed. Fran Hazelton, (London: Zed, 1994).

49. See Dankwart Rustow, "Succession in the Twentieth Century," *Journal of International Affairs* 18 (1964).

50. Timothy Colton, *The Dilemma of Reform in the Soviet Union* (New York: Council on Foreign Relations, 1986), 27.

51. Clement H. Moore, *Tunisia since Independence: Dynamics of a One Party State* (Berkeley: University of California Press, 1965).

52. Lisa Anderson, *The State and Social Transformation in Tunisia and Libya, 1830–1980* (Princeton: Princeton University Press, 1986), 241.

53. *Le Monde,* 24 June 1986, 6.

54. By analogy with an "authoritarian situation," as defined by Juan Linz, "The Future of an Authoritarian Situation or the Institutionalization of an Authoritarian Regime: The Case of Brazil," in *Authoritarian Brazil: Origins, Policies, and Future,* ed. Alfred Stepan (New Haven: Yale University Press, 1973), 233–35.

55. See Joel Podolny, "The Role of the King in the Spanish Transition to Democracy," in *Politics, Society, and Democracy: The Case of Spain,* ed. Richard Gunther (Boulder, Colo.: Westview, 1992), and Charles Powell, *Juan Carlos: Spain's Self-Made Monarch* (London: St. Antony's/Macmillan, 1995).

56. See Mark Gasiorowski, "The Failure of Reform in Tunisia," *Journal of Democracy* 3, no. 4 (1992), and Eva Bellin, "Civil Society in Formation: Tunisia," in *Civil Society in the Middle East,* ed. Augustus Richard Norton (Leiden: E. J. Brill, 1995), esp. 126–41.

57. Some of these traits can of course also be found in other nondemocratic leaders, such as Stalin. Under him the workings of the Kremlin's inner circle may have approximated sultanism, but structurally the Communist Party contained elements that prevented the transformation of his despotic rule into a sultanistic regime.

58. Since we are not competent in psychological approaches, and even less in psychoanalytical approaches, we do not comparatively analyze the personality of this type of ruler, but we think this would be a fruitful area for further research.

59. See also Juan J. Linz and Alfred Stepan, *Problems of Democratic Transition and Consolidation: Southern Europe, South America, and Post-Communist Europe* (Baltimore: Johns Hopkins University Press, 1996), chap. 4, for a synoptic view of the implications of various nondemocratic regime types for transitions to democracy.

60. Michael Bratton and Nicholas van de Walle, "Neopatrimonial Regimes and Political Transitions in Africa," *World Politics* 46 (July 1994): 374–75.

61. On Turkey see Kemal H. Karpat, *Turkey's Politics: The Transformation to a Multiparty System* (Princeton: Princeton University Press, 1959); on Senegal see Christian Coulon, "Senegal: The Development and Fragility of Semidemocracy," in *Democracy in Developing Countries: Africa,* ed. Larry Diamond, Juan J. Linz, and Seymour Martin Lipset (Boulder, Colo.: Lynne Rienner, 1988); on Eastern Europe see Juan J. Linz and Alfred Stepan, *Problems of Democratic Transition and Consolidation: Southern Europe, South America, and Post-Communist Europe* (Baltimore: Johns Hopkins University Press, 1996); on Cape Verde and São Tomé e Principe see Michel Cahen, "Vent des îles: La victoire de l'opposition aux îles du Cap-Vert et à São Tomé e Principe," *Politique Africaine* 43 (October 1991). On Taiwan see Tun-jen Cheng and Stephan Haggard, eds., *Political Change in Taiwan* (Boulder, Colo.: Lynne Rienner, 1992), and Chi-hsiang Chang

et al., *Taiwan's Electoral Politics and Democratic Transition: Riding the Third Wave* (Armonk, N.Y.: M. E. Sharpe, 1996).

62. A case in point is Turkey, where the military has intervened three times since Kemal Atatürk's death and handed back power each time. See Ergun Özbudun, "Paradoxes of Turkish Democratic Development: The Struggle between the Military-Bureaucratic 'Founders' of Democracy and New Democratic Forces," in *Politics, Society, and Democracy: Comparative Studies,* ed. H. E. Chehabi and Alfred Stepan (Boulder, Colo.: Westview, 1995).

63. Samuel P. Huntington, *The Third Wave: Democratization in the Late Twentieth Century* (Norman: University of Oklahoma Press, 1991), 175–80.

64. See Robert E. Martínez, *Business and Democracy in Spain* (Westport, Conn.: Praeger, 1993), and Leigh A. Payne, *Brazilian Industrialists and Democratic Change* (Baltimore: Johns Hopkins University Press, 1994).

65. In the 1988 plebiscite in Chile, for instance, it was the armed forces that persuaded Pinochet not to tamper with the results of the vote against him and to respect it. The legalistic thinking still dominant among the military impeded his using it in the interest of remaining in power.

66. Somoza was assassinated in 1980; the Shah was hounded around the globe and narrowly escaped being handed over to the revolutionary authorities in Iran by Manuel Noriega, then Panamanian intelligence chief (see William Shawcross, *The Shah's Last Ride: The Fate of an Ally* [New York: Simon & Schuster, 1988], 334–38); Ceauşescu was executed within Romania after an ignominious show trial.

67. Sidney Verba, "Some Dilemmas in Comparative Research," *World Politics* 20 (October 1967): 114–15.

68. Anne Greene, *The Catholic Church in Haiti: Political and Social Change* (East Lansing: Michigan State University Press, 1993), 44, and Anthony P. Maingot, "Problems of a Transition to Democracy in an Authoritarian Soft State," *Journal of Interamerican Studies and World Affairs* 28 (winter 1986–87): 80–83.

69. But let it also be said that the somewhat less than adequate response of the authorities revitalized civil society in Mexico.

70. As if to confirm the revolutionaries' charge that they were foreign puppets, the leaders interpret the weakness of external support in the last days of their regime as a foreign plot against them: the theme of betrayal looms large in their reminiscences. See Fulgencio Batista, *Cuba Betrayed* (New York: Vantage, 1962); Anastasio Somoza, as told to Jack Fox, *Nicaragua Betrayed* (Boston: Western Islands, 1980); Mohammad Reza Pahlavi, *Answer to History* (New York: Stein & Day, 1980), especially chap.11.

71. Jeff Goodwin and Theda Skocpol, "Explaining Revolutions in the Contemporary Third World," *Politics and Society* 17 (December 1989).

72. On the fall of Eric Gairy see George C. Abbott, "Grenada: Maverick or Pace-Maker in the West Indies?" *World Today* 36, no. 4 (1980).

73. Weber, *Economy and Society,* 1111–12; see also Robert C. Tucker, "The Theory of Charismatic Leadership," *Daedalus* 97 (summer 1968).

74. Weber, *Economy and Society,* 494.

75. In January 1960 the new archbishop of Santo Domingo, Zanini, dramatically switched the course of the Catholic Church, leading to a repression that delegitimized Trujillo in the eyes of the peasantry and contributed to his downfall.

76. The archbishop of Havana and primate of Cuba was neutral, whereas the archbishop of Santiago, traditionally Cuba's second most important bishop, opposed Batista.

77. On the radicalization of Nicaraguan Catholics (and Protestants), see Michael Dodson and Laura Nuzzi O'Shaughnessy, *Nicaragua's Other Revolution: Religious Faith and Political Struggle* (Chapel Hill: University of North Carolina Press, 1990), 116–39.

78. See Greene, *Catholic Church in Haiti*, chap. 5, and Martin-Luc Bonnardot and Gilles Danroc, eds., *La chute de la maison Duvalier* (Paris: Editions Karthala, 1989), 71–96.

79. Robert L. Youngblood, *Marcos against the Church: Economic Development and Political Repression in the Philippines* (Ithaca: Cornell University Press, 1990), 76–93.

80. For an article discussing the parallels between Shariati's thought and liberation theology in Nicaragua see Bahman Baktiari, "Religion and Revolution in Iran and Nicaragua," in *Central America and the Middle East: The Internationalization of the Crisis,* ed. Damián J. Fernández (Miami: Florida International University Press, 1990).

81. For the role of the Catholic Church in democratic transitions see Samuel Huntington, *Third Wave,* 72–85.

82. On Nicaragua see Dodson and O'Shaughnessy, *Nicaragua's Other Revolution,* 134–39. On the Philippines see Raymond Bonner, *Waltzing with a Dictator* (New York: Vintage Books, 1988), 305–7.

83. Victor Turner, *The Ritual Process: Structure and Anti-structure* (Ithaca: Cornell University Press, 1977), especially chap. 3.

84. The event, which was also significant in terms of Afro-Cuban religious symbolism, was captured on film. See WGBH.TV Educational Foundation, "Castro's Challenge," first broadcast over the U.S. Public Broadcasting System in 1985, Jorge I. Domínguez series editor.

85. *New York Times,* 31 March 1986, 1 and 6. On Cardinal Sin's role in Marcos's overthrow see Henry Wooster, "Faith at the Ramparts: The Philippine Catholic Church and the 1986 Revolution," in *Religion, the Missing Dimension of Statecraft,* ed. Douglas Johnston and Cynthia Sampson (New York: Oxford University Press, 1994).

86. This is not to repeat the old idea that in the Islamic world there is no separation between secular and religious structures of authority (or that such a separation is a Western import), which has been convincingly refuted: see Hamid Dabashi, "Symbiosis of Religious and Political Authorities in Islam," in *Church-State Relations: Tensions and Transitions,* ed. Thomas Robbins and Roland Robertson (New Brunswick, N.J.: Transaction Books, 1987). However, this separation has no grounding in dogma, unlike the situation in the Christian world.

87. On this tension within the clerical hierarchy in Iran see H. E. Chehabi, "Religion and Politics in Iran: How Theocratic Is the Islamic Republic?" *Daedalus* 120 (summer 1991).

88. For a discussion of provisional governments see Yossi Shain and Juan J. Linz, *Between States: Interim Governments in Democratic Transitions* (Cambridge: Cambridge University Press, 1995).

89. See Joseph S. Tulchin and Knut Walter, "Nicaragua: The Limits of Intervention," in Lowenthal, *Exporting Democracy.*

90. It is too early to tell whether the election of S. Mohammad Khatami to the Iranian presidency in May 1997 will presage a democratization of Iranian political life.

The election does prove that the Islamic Republic is not sultanistic, however, since most Iranian officials supported the losing candidate.

91. See Jack A. Goldstone, "Revolutions and Superpowers," in *Superpowers and Revolutions,* ed. Jonathan R. Adelman (New York: Praeger, 1986).

92. James Clad, "Still in the Family," *Far Eastern Economic Review,* 26 March 1987, 70.

93. See, for instance, Henry F. Carey, "Irregularities or Rigging: Romania's 1992 Parliamentary Elections," *East European Quarterly* 29 (spring 1995). For an analysis see Linz and Stepan, *Problems of Democratic Transition and Consolidation,* chap. 18. One might even go back further and ask whether the corruption and institutional decay of the Ceauşescu years were not to some extent a legacy of the sultanistic rule of King Carol (r. 1930–40), under whom "administrative and political corruption, always healthy plants in Rumania, blossomed in full splendor" and "public ethics hit a new low." Roberts, *Rumania,* 208. Mattei Dogan calls Romania's interwar period "mimic democracy." See his "Romania 1919–1938," in *Competitive Elections in Developing Countries,* ed. Myron Weiner and Ergun Özbudun (Durham, N.C.: Duke University Press, 1987).

94. Weber, *Economy and Society,* 1112.

95. Raimund Krämer, "Der alte Mann und die Insel," *Berliner Debatte* 2 (1993).

96. See Asghar Schirazi, *The Constitution of Iran: Politics and the State in the Islamic Republic* (London: I. B. Tauris, 1997).

97. For a suggestive account of how postrevolutionary Nicaragua's politics were affected by the sultanist heritage see Arturo Cruz Jr., "The Absurdity of Nicaragua," *New Republic,* 16 November 1987, 26–36.

98. It is interesting that whereas Castro and Khomeini were both allowed to go into exile after their first challenge to Batista and the Shah (the Moncada Barracks incident in 1953 and the uprising of 1963), they dealt far more harshly with Batista's and the Shah's supporters when they came to power in 1959 and 1979.

99. Mass emigration of mostly middle-class Cubans and Iranians has further diminished the prospects of democratization.

100. Although in Zaire some of the de facto autonomous provinces seem to have been more competently governed than they were under Mobutu. See Howard W. French, "A Neglected Region Loosens Ties to Zaire," *New York Times,* 18 September 1996.

101. John Thayer Sidel, "Beyond Patron-Client Relations: Warlordism and Local Politics in the Philippines," *Kasarinlan* 4, no. 3 (1989): 26–28.

102. Guillermo Donnell, "The State and Democratization," *World Development* 21 (1993): 1358.

103. On the importance of local politics see Joel S. Migdal, "The State in Society: An Approach to Struggles of Domination," in *State Power and Social Force: Domination and Transformation in the Third World,* ed. Joel S. Migdal, Atul Kohli, and Vivienne Shue (Cambridge: Cambridge University Press, 1994).

104. See *Wall Street Journal* (Europe), 29–30 November 1996.

3 • *Paths out of Sultanistic Regimes*

Portions of the analyses of Haiti, Zaire, and the Philippines are adapted from my article "Explaining Transitions from Neopatrimonial Dictatorships," *Comparative Politics* 24, no. 4 (1992): 379–99. The integrative explanatory framework introduced in this chapter also draws in part on structural variables employed in the earlier work. I thank H. E. Chehabi, David Collier, Ruth Berins Collier, John Foran, Jeff Goodwin, Juan Linz, and James Mahoney for their helpful comments and suggestions. This material is based on work supported by a National Science Foundation Graduate Fellowship.

1. See Robert H. Dix, "Why Revolutions Succeed and Fail," *Polity* 16 (1983): 423–46; Jack A. Goldstone, "Revolutions and Superpowers," in *Superpowers and Revolutions*, ed. Jonathan R. Adelman (New York: Praeger, 1986), 38–48; Manus I. Midlarsky and Kenneth Roberts, "Class, State, and Revolution in Central America: Nicaragua and El Salvador Compared," *Journal of Conflict Resolution* 29, no. 2 (1985): 163–93; Farideh Farhi, "State Disintegration and Urban-Based Revolutionary Crisis: A Comparative Analysis of Iran and Nicaragua," *Comparative Political Studies* 21, no. 2 (1988): 231–56; Farideh Farhi, *States and Urban-Based Revolutions: Iran and Nicaragua* (Urbana: University of Illinois Press, 1990); Jeff Goodwin and Theda Skocpol, "Explaining Revolutions in the Contemporary Third World," *Politics and Society* 17, no. 4 (1989): 489–509; Timothy P. Wickham-Crowley, "Understanding Failed Revolution in El Salvador: A Comparative Analysis of Regime Types and Social Structures," *Politics and Society* 17, no. 4 (1989), 511–37; and John Foran, "A Theory of Third World Social Revolutions: Iran, Nicaragua and El Salvador Compared," *Critical Sociology* 19, no. 2 (1993): 3–27. On the *outcomes* of revolutions against sultanistic rulers see John Foran and Jeff Goodwin, "Revolutionary Outcomes in Iran and Nicaragua: Coalition Fragmentation, War, and the Limits of Social Transformation," *Theory and Society* 22 (1993): 209–47.

2. See Samuel P. Huntington, *The Third Wave: Democratization in the Late Twentieth Century* (Norman: University of Oklahoma Press, 1991), esp. chap. 3; Giuseppe Di Palma, *To Craft Democracies: An Essay on Democratic Transitions* (Berkeley: University of California Press, 1990), esp. chap. 8; and Guillermo O'Donnell and Philippe C. Schmitter, *Transitions from Authoritarian Rule: Tentative Conclusions about Uncertain Democracies* (Baltimore: Johns Hopkins University Press, 1986), 32–33. The concept of "waves" of democratization is from Huntington.

3. I refer here to structural explanations of revolution by scholars such as Theda Skocpol, Jeffrey Paige, and Charles Tilly that constitute what Goldstone calls the "third generation" of theories of revolution and also to subsequent research, mainly from the 1980s, that "deepened" this generation. See Jack A. Goldstone, "Theories of Revolution: The Third Generation," *World Politics* 32, no. 3 (1980): 425–53. On the deepening of this generation during the 1980s, see the essay by John Foran, "Theories of Revolution Revisited: Toward a Fourth Generation?" *Sociological Theory* 11, no. 1 (1993): 1–20.

4. The most widely cited work on transitions from authoritarianism exemplifying such a voluntarist approach is Guillermo O'Donnell, Philippe Schmitter, and Lawrence Whitehead, eds., *Transitions from Authoritarian Rule: prospects for Democracy*, 4 vols. (Baltimore: Johns Hopkins University Press, 1986). See especially O'Donnell and Schmitter's theoretical volume, *Tentative Conclusions about Uncertain Democracies* (Baltimore: Johns Hopkins University Press, 1986). See also James M. Malloy and Mitchell A. Seligson, eds., *Authoritarians and Democrats: Regime Transitions in Latin America* (Pittsburgh: University of Pittsburgh Press, 1987); Enrique Baloyra, ed., *Comparing New Democracies: Transitions and Consolidation in Mediterranean Europe and the Southern Cone* (Boulder, Colo.: Westview, 1987). Note that the voluntarism of many of these works was a reaction against earlier deterministic explanations of regime change that focused on "precondi-

tions" for democracy. For a critique of the preconditions approach see Terry Lynn Karl, "Dilemmas of Democratization in Latin America," *Comparative Politics* 23, no. 1 (1990): 1–21; esp. 2–5.

5. Foran notes that a focus on the role of human agency is a key feature of the emerging "fourth generation" of theories of revolution. See Foran, "Theories of Revolution Revisited," 6–8. For efforts to "bring agency back in" see, in addition to Foran, William H. Sewell Jr., "Ideologies and Social Revolutions: Reflections on the French Case," *Journal of Modern History* 57, no. 1 (1985), 57–85; Michael S. Kimmel, *Revolution: A Sociological Interpretation* (Philadelphia: Temple University Press, 1990); James Mahoney, "Social Structure and Political Culture in the Explanation of Third World Social Revolutions: Iran and Cuba Compared," unpublished MS, Department of Political Science, University of California, Berkeley, 1992; and Eric Selbin, *Modern Latin American Revolutions* (Boulder, Colo.: Westview, 1993).

6. Karl and Schmitter use the rubric "from contingent choice to structured contingency" to describe this integrative agenda. See Terry Lynn Karl and Philippe C. Schmitter, "Modes of Transition in Latin America, Southern and Eastern Europe," *International Social Science Journal* 128 (May 1991): 270–71. For a discussion of alternative strategies for integrating agency and structure in the analysis of regime change and the difficult conceptual challenges confronting the would-be integrator, see James Mahoney and Richard Snyder, "Integrative Strategies for the Study of Regime Change," in *The Challenges of Theories on Democracy,* ed. Sten Ugelvik Larsen, Social Science Monographs (New York: Columbia University Press, forthcoming).

Critiques of the extreme voluntarism of the transitions literature that emphasize the need to combine agency and structure in the explanation of regime change include Daniel H. Levine, "Paradigm Lost: Dependence to Democracy," *World Politics* 40, no. 3 (1988): 377–94; Nancy Bermeo, "Rethinking Regime Change," *Comparative Politics* 22, no. 3 (1990): 359–77; Karl, "Dilemmas of Democratization in Latin America"; Karen L. Remmer, "New Wine or Old Bottlenecks? The Study of Latin American Democracy," *Comparative Politics* 23, no. 4 (1991): 479–95; Herbert Kitschelt, "Political Regime Change: Structure and Process-Driven Explanations?" *American Political Science Review* 86, no. 4 (1992): 1028–34; and Gerardo L. Munck, "Democratic Transitions in Comparative Perspective," *Comparative Politics* 26 (April 1994): 355–75.

7. Impressionistic evidence suggests that the study of contemporary revolutions has been undertaken predominantly by sociologists, while the study of regime transitions has been undertaken predominantly by political scientists.

8. Other analyses that self-consciously seek to combine elements of these two literatures are Robert M. Fishman, "Rethinking State and Regime: Southern Europe's Transition to Democracy," *World Politics* 42, no. 3 (1990): 422–40, and Matthew Soberg Shugart, "Guerillas and Elections: An Institutionalist Perspective on the Costs of Conflict and Competition," *International Studies Quarterly* 36 (1992): 121–52.

9. Although Romania had elements of a staged revolution.

10. Some of the cases I analyze here, such as Zaire under Mobutu (before 1991) and Haiti under François Duvalier, are not strictly sultanistic because the ruler's circle of clients extended beyond a narrow clique of cronies. In an earlier analysis I used the term "neopatrimonial" to refer to the set of regimes discussed here. See Richard Snyder, "Explaining Transitions from Neopatrimonial Dictatorships," *Comparative Politics* 24,

no. 4 (1992): 379–99. On the concept of neopatrimonialism see S. N. Eisenstadt, *Revolution and the Transformation of Societies: A Comparative Study of Civilizations* (New York: Free Press, 1978), 277–89. For an application of the concept to the African context, see Michael Bratton and Nicholas van de Walle, "Neopatrimonial Regimes and Political Transitions in Africa," *World Politics* 46 (July 1994): 374–75. On patrimonial rule more generally, see Guenther Roth, "Personal Rulership, Patrimonialism, and Empire-Building in the New States," *World Politics* 20 (1968): 194–206, and Christopher Clapham, *Third World Politics: An Introduction* (Madison: University of Wisconsin Press, 1986).

11. This approach to the definition of actors draws on Guillermo O'Donnell, "Transitions to Democracy: Some Navigation Instruments," in *Democracy in the Americas*, ed. Robert A. Pastor (New York: Holmes & Meier, 1989), 62–75; and O'Donnell and Schmitter, *Tentative Conclusions*, 4–5, 15–17. I have also benefited from the discussions of theoretical issues involved in the definitions of actors in Adam Przeworski, "Some Problems in the Study of the Transition to Democracy," in *Transitions from Authoriarian Rule: Comparative Perspectives*, ed. Guillermo O'Donnell, Philippe C. Schmitter, and Laurence Whitehead, (Baltimore: Johns Hopkins University Press, 1986), 47–63, and in David Collier and Deborah L. Norden, "Strategic Choice Models of Political Change in Latin America," *Comparative Politics* 24, no. 2 (1992): 229–43. According to Przeworski (53–54), defining actors in terms of strategic postures is risky because "strategic postures may remain the same but the particular groups or individuals that hold them may change," hence, there is a temptation to look to institututional and structural roles to explain why these shifts occurred. I would note the additional risk of creating an ontological dualism that isolates agents from structures, stripping actors from their social moorings and treating them in an "undersocialized" fashion. On undersocialized conceptions of human agency see Mahoney and Snyder, "Integrative Stragegies for the Study of Regime Change."

12. This effort to specify the "margins of maneuverability" for actor discretion allowed by structural factors resembles in some respects Alfred Stepan's analysis of the collapse of democracy in Brazil in 1964. See Alfred Stepan, "Political Leadership and Regime Breakdown: Brazil," in *The Breakdown of Democratic Regimes: Latin America*, ed. Juan J. Linz and Alfred Stepan (Baltimore: Johns Hopkins University Press, 1978), 110–37. However, in contrast to Stepan's analysis, which relies on a single case study, this analysis compares multiple cases to gauge the latitude for actor discretion during transitions. The implications of this difference are discussed in the chapter's conclusion. For an analysis of Stepan's "funnel" strategy for integrating agency and structure in the explanation of regime change, see Mahoney and Snyder, "Integrative Strategies for the Study of Regime Change."

A more fully integrative approach than the one employed here would not be limited to "mapping" structural contexts but would also emphasize how these structures were created, reproduced, and eventually transformed by human agents.

13. These labels and the discussion that follows are adapted from O'Donnell, "Transitions to Democracy," 64–68, and O'Donnell and Schmitter, *Tentative Conclusions*, 15–17. O'Donnell and Schmitter emphasize that these four groups are themselves usually composed of several factions. This analytic scheme also corresponds to Huntington's fourfold typology of "standpatters," "reformers," "moderates," and "extremists" in *Third Wave*, 122.

14. Soft-liners are not necessarily reformists or democrats; they can be as ruthless as dictators.

15. As O'Donnell points out, regime hard-liners and the maximalist opposition are "in effect allies in promoting a polarization that threatens to eliminate the soft-liners from important positions in the regime" and to undercut the position of moderates. O'Donnell, "Transitions to Democracy," 65.

16. On the fusion of public and private characteristic of sultanistic regimes, see Chehabi and Linz, chapter 1 of this volume.

17. The presence of hard-liners, however, can be assumed more safely than the presence of the other three groups, because the very definition of these regimes entails a ruling clique committed to retaining power.

18. Differentiating cases of "missed" structural opportunities (that is, *failures* to act) from cases where such opportunities did not exist poses formidable empirical and epistemological challenges. In both cases the "outcome" is usually the same: that predicted by structural factors. Close empirical scrutiny of cases to uncover evidence of intent (or its absence) may be the only remedy. The data requirements for demonstrating intent or its absence are often quite daunting for cases of regime change.

19. Of course repression is also an important, if not unique, feature of sultanistic regimes. See Juan J. Linz, "Totalitarian and Authoritarian Regimes," in *Handbook of Political Science*, vol. 3, *Macropolitical Theory*, ed. Nelson W. Polsby and Fred I. Greenstein (Reading, Mass.: Addison-Wesley, 1975), 175–357. See esp. 259–60.

20. On the radial nature of patrimonial authority structures see Karen L. Remmer, "Neopatrimonialism: The Politics of Military Rule in Chile, 1973–1987," *Comparative Politics* 21, no. 2 (1989): 149–70, esp. 165.

21. On the military in sultanistic regimes see Alain Rouquié, *The Military and the State in Latin America* (Berkeley: University of California Press, 1987), chap. 6. On indicators for measuring military autonomy see Alfred Stepan, *Rethinking Military Politics: Brazil and the Southern Cone* (Princeton: Princeton University Press, 1988), and David Pion-Berlin, "Military Autonomy and Emerging Democracies in South America," *Comparative Politics* 25, no. 1 (1992): 83–102.

22. Joel S. Migdal aptly calls this imperative confronting personalistic rulers the "politics of survival." See his *Strong Societies and Weak States: State-Society Relations and State Capabilities in the Third World* (Princeton: Princeton University Press, 1988), chap. 6.

23. And hence can help avoid the reification of this structure. Reification refers to the loss of "the awareness that, however objectivated, the social world was made by men [and women]—and, therefore, can be remade by them." Quoted from Peter L. Berger and Thomas Luckmann, *The Social Construction of Reality: A Treatise in the Sociology of Knowledge* (New York: Doubleday, 1966), 89.

24. Toward the end of his rule, Ceaușescu in Romania also moved in this direction, relying increasingly on the paramilitary Securitate as his support base and isolating the regular armed forces.

25. See Elizabeth Abbott, *Haiti: The Duvaliers and Their Legacy* (New York: McGraw-Hill, 1988), 306–7.

26. On the important role of caretaker governments in transitions from nondemocratic regimes, see Yossi Shain and Juan J. Linz, "The Role of Interim Governments," *Journal of Democracy* 3, no. 1 (1992): 73–89.

27. Of course the existence of this political space does not automatically lead to the growth of moderate and maximalist opposition groups, since actors may neither be able nor choose to use this space to organize.

28. Dix, "Why Revolutions Succeed and Fail," 436–38, 443–46; Goldstone, "Revolutions and Superpowers," 43–44; and Midlarsky and Roberts, "Class, State, and Revolution in Central America," 185–90.

29. Midlarsky and Roberts, "Class, State, and Revolution," 187.

30. Dix, "Why Revolutions Succeed and Fail," 432–38.

31. Goodwin and Skocpol, "Explaining Revolutions," 498–501.

32. The term "political cultures of opposition" is from Foran, "Theories of Revolution Revisited," 13.

33. O'Donnell and Schmitter, *Tentative Conclusions about Uncertain Democracies,* 18. For a reconsideration of this position by Schmitter in light of the collapse of communist regimes in Eastern Europe, see Philippe C. Schmitter, "The International Context of Contemporary Democratization," *Stanford Journal of International Affairs* 2, no. 1 (1993): 1–34.

34. Since the set of sultanistic regimes includes some of the most overtly "dependent" superpower client regimes, it is especially fertile ground for exploring the limits of superpower influence in the international system. See Robert A. Pastor, "Preempting Revolutions: The Boundaries of U.S. Influence," *International Security* 15, no. 4 (1991): 54–86. Juxtaposing cases of sultanistic regimes characterized by extreme dependence on the United States alongside cases characterized by the *absence* of such dependence could be especially fruitful for testing the boundaries of superpower influence.

35. This does not mean that international conditions should be ignored in the analysis of other types of regimes.

36. Farhi, "State Disintegration," 241–45; Goldstone, "Revolutions and Superpowers," 44–47.

37. Direct intervention by a foreign power is well illustrated by the United States' invasion of Panama in 1989 to remove General Manuel Noriega. On the Panamanian case see Steve C. Ropp, "Explaining the Long-Term Maintenance of a Military Regime: Panama before the U.S. Invasion," *World Politcs* 44, no. 2 (1992): 210–34.

38. Furthermore, the divergent regime outcomes in Romania (rule by civilian soft-liners) and Haiti (rule by military soft-liners) indicate that the relative strengths of oppositions cannot by themselves predict outcomes of transitions from sultanism.

39. See, for example, Samuel P. Huntington, *Political Order in Changing Societies* (New Haven: Yale University Press, 1968), 3. As Karen Remmer points out, "Particularly telling is the contrast Huntington draws between the instability of the Stroessner regime and the stability of Chilean democracy (Huntington, p. 80), which collapsed only five years after the publication of his book." See Remmer, "Neopatrimonialism," 170.

40. David Nicholls, *Haiti in Caribbean Context: Ethnicity, Economy, and Revolt* (New York: St. Martin's Press, 1985), 219.

41. The flight abroad of large segments of the Haitian middle class and professional class further drained the potential support base of moderate opposition groups. By 1980 approximately one million Haitians, or 14 percent of the country's potential population, had left the country. See James Ferguson, *Papa Doc, Baby Doc: Haiti and the Duvaliers* (New York: Basil Blackwell, 1987), 67.

42. Abbott, *Haiti*, 86–88.

43. Ibid., 85–87. For a historical analysis of the Haitian military, including the Duvalier period, see Michel S. Laguerre, *The Military and Society in Haiti* (Knoxville: University of Tennessee Press, 1993).

44. Abbott, *Haiti*, 160–61, 301.

45. Quoted in Nicholls, *Haiti in Caribbean Context*, 229.

46. Georges Fauriol, "The Duvaliers and Haiti," *Orbis* 32 (1987): 587–607; see esp. 595–97.

47. Nicholls, *Haaiti in Caribbean Context*, 223.

48. Thomas Turner, "Decline or Recovery in Zaire?" *Current History* 87 (1988): 213–16, 230; quotation at 215.

49. Michael G. Schatzberg, *The Dialectics of Oppression in Zaire* (Bloomington: University of Indiana Press, 1988), 4.

50. Crawford Young and Thomas Turner, *The Rise and Decline of the Zairian State* (Madison: University of Wisconsin Press, 1985), 28.

51. Ibid., 161–62.

52. Turner, "Decline or Recovery in Zaire?" 216. Turner mentions the dissolution in 1987 of the domestically based opposition party, the Union for Democracy and Social Progress (UDPS). Most of the UDPS leaders were absorbed into Mobutu's MPR, Zaire's only legal party at the time. As is discussed below, a revitalized UDPS appears to have emerged after 1991.

53. Quoted in Young and Turner, *Rise and Decline of the Zairian State*, 262.

54. Ibid., 264.

55. Schatzberg, *Dialectics of Oppression*, 66.

56. Young and Turner, *Rise and Decline of the Zairian State*, 265–67.

57. Ibid., 393–95; Kenneth B. Noble, "Pretoria Said to Advise Zairian Army," *New York Times*, 17 August 1991, 2.

58. Young and Turner, *Rise and Decline of the Zairian State*, 255–58.

59. Zaire has extensive mineral resources, including rich deposits of copper, tin, cobalt, iron ore, and diamonds. And Zaire's border with Angola made it strategically important to the United States during the 1970s and 1980s, when superpower proxies fought one another in the Angolan civil war.

60. Young and Turner, *Rise and Decline of the Zairian State*, 395.

61. Quoted in Turner, "Decline or Recovery in Zaire?" 213.

62. Kenneth B. Noble, "Hope for Change Fades in Zaire as Feuds Flare," *New York Times*, 14 August 1991, A5. On runaway inflation and Zaire's enormous debt see Kenneth B. Noble, "In Zaire, Fear and Despair Grow as Economy Slides into Chaos," *New York Times*, 4 November 1991, A4.

63. Kenneth B. Noble, "Zaire's Dictator Agrees to Share Power with Foe," *New York Times*, 30 September 1991, A1, A6.

64. See "Mobutu Ousts Foe and Renews Chaos," *New York Times*, 21 October 1991, A5; "Riots Continuing over Ouster of Mobutu Foe," *New York Times*, 25 October 1991, A6.

65. René Lemarchand, "Africa's Troubled Transitions," *Journal of Democracy* 3 no. 4 (1992): 98–109, at 105.

66. See "Witnesses Say Police Killed Three People in Zaire Riot," *New York Times*, 4 September 1991, A5; "Troops in Zaire Capital Go on a Looting Spree," *New York Times*, 28

September 1991, 3; Kenneth B. Noble, "Anti-Mobutu Protests Set off Violence," *New York Times*, 11 October 1991, A3; "Soldiers Open Fire in Zaire, Killing 13," *New York Times*, 17 Februrary 1992, A3.

67. See Kenneth B. Noble, "Zaire's Chief Vows to Stay in Power and Warns West Not to Meddle," *New York Times*, 28 October 1991, A6; "U.S. Blames Mobutu for Violence in Zaire and Tells Him to Resign," *New York Times*, 22 July 1993, A4.

68. A similar configuration of actors in Panama at the end of the 1980s led to a stalemate between Noriega and civilian moderates. This stalemate was eventually broken by the U.S. invasion in 1989.

69. See the works cited in note 1.

70. Goodwin and Skocpol, "Explaining Revolutions," however, are careful not to link sultanism and revolution in a mechanical fashion. They emphasize that not all sultanistic regimes are toppled by revolutionaries.

71. Midlarsky and Roberts, "Class, State, and Revolution," 187.

72. The brevity of this discussion, as well as its lumping together the Iranian, Nicaraguan, and Cuban regimes, obviously obscures important differences among these cases. For example, the Cuban military's capacity for autonomous action seems to have been somewhat greater than that of the Nicaraguan and Iranian armed forces. And the strength of the moderate opposition in Nicaragua seems to have been significantly greater than in the other two countries, leading to an "unconsolidated" revolutionary regime plagued by endemic conflict between moderates and maximalists after Somoza's ouster.

73. Although, in contrast to the rulers in the three revolutionary cases, Mobutu has not been highly dependent on a single foreign power.

74. Foran, "Theories of Revolution Revisited," 13. In a more structuralist vein, one could argue that the weakness of maximalists in Zaire is due more to a *lack* of "political cultures of opposition" than to actors' failures to utilize them.

75. On the role of "cultural idioms" in revolutionary change see Theda Skocpol, "Cultural Idioms and Politial Ideologies in the Revolutionary Reconstruction of State Power: A Rejoinder to Sewell," *Journal of Modern History* 57, no. 1 (1985): 86–96.

76. On African Marxist-Leninist regimes, see Marina Ottoway and David Ottoway, *Afro-Communism* (New York: Holmes & Meier, 1981).

77. See Selbin, *Modern Latin American Revolutions;* Foran, "Theory of Third World Social Revolutions"; and Mansoor Moaddel, "Ideology as Episodic Discourse: The Case of the Iranian Revolution," *American Sociological Review* 57, no. 3 (1992): 353–79.

78. For a critique of recent comparative studies of revolution that conceptualize state and societal actors in radically different terms, ignoring the moral discourses and ideologies that motivate and shape the behavior of incumbent state elites, see Jeff Goodwin, "Toward a New Sociology of Revolutions," *Theory and Society* 23 (1994): 731–66.

79. For an analysis of the Paraguayan case see Snyder, "Explaining Transitions from Neopatrimonial Dictatorships," 390–92.

80. A father-to-son transfer of power also occurred in Nicaragua in 1956. As in Haiti, this transition led to a lengthy continuation of sultanism followed eventually by regime breakdown. In both cases the collapse of sultanism resulted in part from the son's inability to maintain the system of patronage and elite co-optation constructed by the father.

81. Nicholls, *Haiti in Caribbean Context,* 226–28.

82. Ferguson, *Papa Doc, Baby Doc,* 54–55.

83. Nicholls, *Haiti in Caribbean Context,* 228.

84. Abbott, *Haiti,* 288–90.

85. Ibid., 290.

86. Ferguson, *Papa Doc, Baby Doc,* 91–92, 110–11.

87. On the role of the Haitian Catholic Church in Duvalier's ouster see Abbott, *Haiti,* 261–92, and Ferguson, *Papa Doc, Baby Doc,* 76–111.

88. My account of the U.S. role in the transition is based on Abbott, *Haiti,* 302–5, 328–30, and Ferguson, *Papa Doc, Baby Doc,* 112.

89. According to Ferguson (*Papa Doc, Baby Doc,* 129), after Duvalier's departure the United States quickly sent the $26 million in suspended aid to the military's National Council of Government (CNG), headed by General Namphy, and added $10 million in emergency relief assistance, including $400,000 in antiriot equipment for the police and army.

90. The discussion in this paragraph and the following one draws on Pamela Constable, "Haiti's Shattered Hopes," *Journal of Democracy* 3, no. 1 (1992): 41–51.

91. On the coup that removed Aristide see "Haitian Soldiers Seize President; Twenty-six Reported Killed in Uprising," *New York Times,* 1 October 1991, A1; Howard W. French, "Army Strikes Back," *New York Times,* 2 October 1991, A6. According to Constable ("Haiti's Shattered Hopes," 46), reports circulated that wealthy Haitians had encouraged the military to revolt against Aristide by offering cash payments and weapons shipments from abroad.

92. As should Haiti's "crisis of sovereignty," which culminated in U.S. invasion and occupation of the country from 1915 to 1934 and again in the summer of 1994.

93. The cases of Nicaragua and Paraguay can be regarded as *indirect* transfers of power to nonrevolutionary civilian rule after intervening periods of institutionalized authoritarian regimes. In Paraguay the armed forces, which ousted Stroessner, ceded control to civilian moderates after several months in power. In Nicaragua the revolutionary Sandinista leadership held relatively open and fair elections in 1984, which it won, and relinquished power after losing subsequent elections in 1990.

94. On the Dominican Republic, see Jonathan Hartlyn's contribution to this volume.

95. The case of Panama in 1989, where power was also transferred directly to civilians, does not fit the pattern described here because the regime transition was orchestrated by a U.S. invasion.

96. For an excellent analysis of the Philippine transition see Mark R. Thompson, *The Anti-Marcos Struggle: Personalistic Rule and Democratic Transition in the Philippines* (New Haven: Yale University Press, 1995).

97. Claude A. Buss, *Cory Aquino and the People of the Philippines* (Palo Alto, Calif.: Stanford Alumni Association, 1987), 92. On the U.S. role in RAM's formation see Raymond Bonner, *Waltzing with a Dictator: The Marcoses and the Making of American Policy* (New York: Vintage Books, 1988), 372.

98. Bonner, *Waltzing with a Dictator,* 438–46.

99. By contrast, in the revolutionary cases of Nicaragua, Iran, and Cuba the moderate oppositions were weak and divided.

100. The NDF was the political front of the New People's Army (NPA). On the NDF role in the transition see William Chapman, *Inside the Philippine Revolution* (New York: W. W. Norton, 1987), 215–18.

101. Bonner, *Waltzing with a Dictator,* 441–43.

102. Quoted in ibid., 445.

103. The relative strength of the Philippine moderate opposition is undoubtedly due in part to the size of the Philippine middle class and business community, which were much larger than their counterparts in the other cases of sultanism examined here.

104. Marcos relied more heavily on the regular armed forces to maintain internal control than did the Duvaliers, for example, who delegated this function to the Tonton Macoutes. On the role of the Philippine armed forces under Marcos see Felipe Miranda, "The Military," in *The Philippines after Marcos,* ed. R. J. May and Francisco Nemenzo (Kent, Eng.: Croom Helm, 1985), 45–69.

105. The loyalty of the armed forces to Aquino fluctuated after she became president. There were several coup attempts against her government by right-wing military factions. See Don Chapman, "Can Democracy Survive in the Philippines?" *Editorial Research Reports,* 10 August 1990, 446–59; John McBeth, "Who Are YOU? A New Military Reform Group Grows out of RAM," *Far Eastern Economic Review,* 7 June 1990, 24–26.

106. The post-Ceauşescu regime's opponents have characterized it as "neocommunist" and described the transition as a "revolution betrayed." See John Sislin, "Revolution Betrayed? Romania and the National Salvation Front," *Studies in Comparative Communism* 24, no. 4 (1991): 395–411.

107. Ronald H. Linden, "Socialist Patrimonialism and the Global Economy: The Case of Romania," *International Organization* 40, no. 2 (1986): 346–80.

108. My characterization of the Ceauşescu regime draws on Mary Ellen Fischer, *Nicolae Ceausescu: A Study in Political Leadership* (Boulder, Colo: Lynne Rienner, 1989); Vladimir Tismaneanu, "Personal Power and Political Crisis in Romania," *Government and Opposition* 24, no. 2 (1989): 177–98; William E. Crowther, "'Ceausescuism' and Civil-Military Relations in Romania," *Armed Forces and Society* 15, no. 2 (1989): 207–25; Daniel N. Nelson, *Romanian Politics in the Ceausescu Era* (New York: Gordon & Breach, 1988), esp. chap. 9 on ruler-military relations; and Walter Bacon, "Romanian Secret Police," in *Terror and Communist Politics: The Role of the Secret Police in Communist States,* ed. Jonathan R. Adelman (Boulder: Westview, 1984), 135–54. Ceauşescu's formula for stability bears striking resemblances to that of Stroessner in Paraguay, who counterbalanced the Colorado Party against the military. On Stroessner's regime see Snyder, "Explaining Transitions from Neopatrimonial Dictatorships," 390–92.

109. The RCP's disenchantment with Ceauşescu is revealed by an open letter addressed to him in March 1989 that was signed by six former top RCP leaders, including two former general secretaries. This letter denounced Ceauşescu for, among other things, human rights abuses by the Securitate, economic mismanagement, and his "systematization" rural resettlement program. For the text of the letter and an analysis see Vladimir Tismaneanu, "The Rebellion of the Old Guard," *East European Reporter* 3, no. 4 (1989): 22–25. On military discontent with Ceauşescu see Crowther, "'Ceausescuism' and Civil-Military Relations in Romania."

110. The leadership of the FSN included an assortment of former Communist Party officials who had fallen out of favor with Ceauşescu, military officers, and political

dissidents. Ion Iliescu, the FSN's leader, had served as secretary of the Romanian Communist Party Central Committee until 1971 and continued to be a Politburo member for several years afterward. See Mark Almond, "Romania since the Revolution," *Government and Opposition* 25, no. 4 (1990): 484–96. For a comparative analysis of the Romanian transition see Jeff Goodwin, "Old Regimes and Revolutions in the Second and Third Worlds," *Social Science History* 18, no. 4 (1994): 574–604.

111. Although the Securitate, like the Tonton Macoutes, seems to have partially survived the transition. See Sislin, "Revolution Betrayed?" 408.

112. In terms of international factors, however, there are important differences between the Haitian and Romanian cases. First, Ceauşescu, unlike Jean-Claude Duvalier, was not highly dependent on a single superpower patron. Second, the effects of regional "demonstration effects" (which Huntington, *Third Wave,* refers to as "snowballing") were clearly more relevant in the Romanian case.

113. Path-dependent and "critical juncture" frameworks for political-historical analysis may be especially promising as strategies for embedding sultanistic regimes within long-term trajectories of change. Recent exemplary applications of such frameworks include Ruth Berins Collier and David Collier, *Shaping the Political Arena: Critical Junctures, the Labor Movement and Regime Dynamics in Latin America* (Princeton: Princeton University Press, 1991), and Dietrich Rueschemeyer, Evelyne Huber Stephens, and John D. Stephens, *Capitalist Development and Democracy* (Chicago: University of Chicago Press, 1992). See Mahoney and Snyder, "Integrative Strategies for the Study of Regime Change," for a discussion of the strengths and limitations of path-dependent analyses.

114. The literature on whether authoritarian interludes "freeze" or transform politics seems especially relevant here. For an overview of this literature and the issues involved in analyzing politics after regime change see Frances Hagopian, "After Regime Change: Authoritarian Legacies, Political Representation and the Democratic Future of South America," *World Politics* 45, no. 3 (1993): 464–500.

115. See Fishman, "Rethinking State and Regime," who stresses the importance of the conceptual distinction between regime and state for explaining varied paths of transition in southern Europe.

116. Stepan, "Political Leadership and Regime Breakdown."

117. On the critical role of counterfactuals in Stepan's analysis and in social science explanation in general, see James D. Fearon, "Counterfactuals and Hypothesis Testing in Political Science," *World Politics* 43 (January 1991): 169–95.

118. One could argue, however, that structural factors other than the ones I have focused on are sufficient to explain the outcomes in these cases; hence there is no need to bring in "voluntarist" factors, only additional structural ones. This would be a rival to the explanatory claim made here that contingent choices and human agency "mattered."

119. See Gerardo L. Munck, "Between Theory and History and Beyond Traditional Area Studies: A New Comparative Perspective on Latin America," *Comparative Politics* 25, no.4 (1993): 475–98, and Karl, "Dilemmas of Democratization," both of whom cite Collier and Collier's *Shaping the Political Arena* as an example of a path-dependent analysis that combines agency and structure in explaining regime change. The rest of this paragraph draws on Mahoney and Snyder, "Integrative Strategies for the Study of Regime Change."

120. I am referring here to the nonintegrative, purely structural path-dependent analyses of regimes exemplified by Barrington Moore Jr., *Social Origins of Dictatorship and Democracy: Lord and Peasant in the Making of the Modern World* (Boston: Beacon, 1966), and Gregory M. Luebbert, *Liberalism, Fascism, or Social Democracy: Social Classes and the Political Origins of Regimes in Interwar Europe* (New York: Oxford University Press, 1991).

4 • The Trujillo Regime in the Dominican Republic

I gratefully acknowledge critical comments by Bernardo Vega, Evelyne Huber, Lars Schoultz, and the volume editors, H. E. Chehabi and Juan Linz.

1. Howard J. Wiarda, *Dictatorship and Development: The Methods of Control in Trujillo's Dominican Republic* (Gainesville: University of Florida Press, 1968), 179.

2. On the centrality of the Trujillo regime in inspiring Linz's initial formulation of the concept of sultanism, and for a further discussion of the traits that characterize these types of regimes, see chapter 1 of this volume.

3. Linz has defined "semiopposition" as "those groups that are not dominant or represented in the governing group but that are willing to participate in power without fundamentally challenging the system" (see also the editors' introduction to this volume, chaps. 1 and 2).

4. Bernardo Vega, *En la década perdida* (Santo Domingo: Fundación Cultural Dominicana, 1990), 157–58; Isis Duarte et al., *Cultura política y democracia en la República Dominicana: Informe final de la Encuesta Cultura Política y Democracia (DEMOS 94)* (Santo Domingo: Pontificia Universidad Católica Madre y Maestra, 1996), 205.

5. See H. Hoetink, "The Dominican Republic, c. 1870–1930," in *The Cambridge History of Latin America*, vol. 5, *Ca. 1970 to 1930*, ed. Leslie Bethell (Cambridge: Cambridge University Press, 1986), 287–98; see also Frank Moya Pons, *Manual de Historia Dominicana,*7th ed. (Santo Domingo: Universidad Católica Madre y Maestra, 1983), 281–426 passim.

6. Heureaux used large numbers of spies to control the country's population; co-opted or bribed many of his opponents, sending others into exile or murdering them; arranged for enemies overseas to be murdered; and massively enriched himself and his coterie through massive corruption. See Howard J. Wiarda, *Dictatorship, Development and Disintegration*, vol. 1 (Ann Arbor: Xerox University Microfilms, 1975), 221. For a fascinating fictional dialogue between Heureaux and Trujillo, see Bernardo Vega, *Domini canes: Los perros del señor* (Santo Domingo: Fundación Cultural Dominicana, 1988).

7. Hoetink, "Dominican Republic," 296. As Wiarda notes, before 1899 presidents were usually of a racially mixed background; after that date until Trujillo assumed power, all presidents but one were white and of an aristocratic background. Wiarda, *Dictatorship, Development and Disintegration*, 363.

8. Moya Pons, *Manual*, 468–70.

9. See Bruce Calder, *The Impact of Intervention: The Dominican Republic during the U.S. Occupation of 1916–1924* (Austin: University of Texas Press, 1984), xix; also Hans Schmidt, *The United States Occupation of Haiti, 1915–1934* (New Brunswick: Rutgers University Press, 1971), esp. 13–16.

10. Stephen M. Fuller and Graham A. Cosmas, *Marines in the Dominican Republic, 1916–1924* (Washington, D.C.: History and Museums Division, Headquarters, U.S. Marine Corps, 1974), 45–52; Calder, *Impact of Intervention*, 54–60; Moya Pons, *Manual*, 477–78.

11. Abraham F. Lowenthal, "The Dominican Republic: The Politics of Chaos," in *Reform and Revolution: Readings in Latin American Politics*, ed. Robert Kaufman and Arpad von Lazar (Needham Heights, Mass.: Allyn & Bacon, 1969), 53.

12. See Robert Crassweller, *Trujillo: The Life and Times of a Caribbean Dictator* (New York: Macmillan, 1966), 39–51. As Crassweller notes later, "The one thing that pleased him [Trujillo] as much as his humiliation of the high-born was their homage and admiration" (104).

13. Crassweller, *Trujillo*, 69–70; electoral figures from Jesús de Galíndez, *The Era of Trujillo: Dominican Dictator*, ed. Russell H. Fitzgibbon (Tucson: University of Arizona Press, 1973), 19. As mentioned in Crassweller and cited in Galíndez, the U.S. minister in the country at the time asserted that Trujillo's vote total exceeded the number of voters in the country at the time. In fact, those conducting subsequent elections under Trujillo would never admit to the abstention rate reported for these elections.

14. Crassweller, *Trujillo*, 62, argues Trujillo's support for the complex Santiago plot to overthrow Vásquez was based on his calculation of the U.S. response. For a detailed analysis and useful compilation of documents regarding Trujillo and the U.S. military, see Bernardo Vega, *Trujillo y las fuerzas armadas norteamericanas* (Santo Domingo: Fundación Cultural Dominicana, 1992). His book provides considerable evidence supporting the notion that for much of the Trujillo era there was a "dual track" policy by the United States, with the military largely favorable to the regime and the civilians seeking to keep their distance. There was a more unanimous, favorable outlook from about 1955 to mid-1958 and a unanimously antagonistic outlook beginning in 1960; see 463–67. See also Jonathan Hartlyn, "The Dominican Republic: The Legacy of Intermittent Engagement," in *Exporting Democracy: The United States and Latin America*, ed. Abraham F. Lowenthal (Baltimore: Johns Hopkins University Press, 1991).

15. In contrast, President Roosevelt agreed to see Trujillo, but only in a private meeting, and Trujillo's meeting with Secretary of State Cordell Hull was also quite formal. Bernardo Vega, *Nazismo, fascismo y falangismo en la República Dominicana* (Santo Domingo: Fundación Cultural Dominicana, 1985), 159–60; Crassweller, *Trujillo*, 172–75; *Who Was Who in America*, vol. 2 (Chicago: A. N. Marquis, 1950), 78.

16. See Vega, *Trujillo y las fuerzas armadas norteamericanas*, 464; and Bernardo Vega, *Los Estados Unidos y Trujillo*, vol. 2 (Santo Domingo: Fundación Cultural Dominicana, 1986), 860. The corrupt and venal qualities developed by these types of regimes as their sultanistic tendencies increase over time often make them unable to respond adequately to natural disasters, with a profound negative impact on their stability; for example, on Somoza Debayle and the 1972 earthquake in Nicaragua, see John Booth, *The End and the Beginning: The Nicaraguan Revolution*, 2d ed., rev. (Boulder, Colo.: Westview, 1985), esp. 277, 286. In contrast, in 1930 Trujillo dealt effectively with the cyclone, even as he used it to his political advantage, centralizing power and resources.

17. See Frank Moya Pons, "The Dominican Republic since 1930," in *The Cambridge History of Latin America*. vol. 7, ed. Leslie Bethell (Cambridge: Cambridge University Press, 1990), 511–12. Note that Trujillo's ability to become the richest man in the country

after only four years reflected the relative poverty of the country's oligarchy as much as the effectiveness of his efforts.

18. Moya Pons, "Dominican Republic since 1930," 514; see also David Nicholls, "Lebanese of the Antilles: Haiti, Dominican Republic, Jamaica and Trinidad," in *The Lebanese of the World: A Century of Emigration,* ed. Albert Hourani and Nadim Shehadi (London: Centre for Lebanese Studies and Tauris, 1992).

19. Quotation from Crassweller, *Trujillo,* 257; Martin Murphy, *Dominican Sugar Plantation: Production and Foreign Labor Integration* (New York: Praeger, 1991), 24–26. In 1956 Trujillo purchased the vast holdings of the United States–owned West Indies Sugar Company in his own name for $35.8 million, including an initial $10 million down payment, employing state resources. The public debt of the two major state banks increased dramatically, stimulating further deterioration of the country's economic situation. See Bernardo Vega, *Trujillo y el control financiero norteamericano* (Santo Domingo: Fundación Cultural Dominicana, 1990), 602.

20. For a discussion of "elections" under Trujillo, see Galíndez, *Era of Trujillo,* 94–101.

21. The kidnapping and assassination of the Spanish (Basque) exile Jesús de Galíndez, who had completed a doctoral dissertation at Columbia University harshly analyzing Trujillo, became an international cause célèbre, even as Galíndez's manuscript, one copy of which evaded Trujillo's agents, became a best-seller throughout Latin America. With the murder of the U.S. pilot who had transported Galíndez to the Dominican Republic in December 1956, in 1957 the case became a source of growing tension between the United States and the Trujillo regime.

22. See Bernardo Vega, ed., *Control y represión en la dictadura Trujillista* (Santo Domingo: Fundación Cultural Dominicana, 1986).

23. The U.S. naval attaché ended a 1940 report on the Dominican military on this note; see Vega, *Trujillo y las fuerzas aéreas norteamericanas,* 243.

24. The record year for military expenditures was 1959, as the regime found itself increasingly besieged. In that year, even as the overall government budget contracted (from $164.9 million in 1958 to $155.7 million), 26.4 percent of the total budget was earmarked for the armed forces and an additional 9.6 percent for the police and justice ($56.0 million total). In the subsequent two years, as the government budget continued to contract (to $143.7 million in 1960 and $137.2 million in 1961), the amounts devoted to the armed forces and police did so as well (to $44.1 million in 1960 and $40.6 million in 1961). Oficina Nacional de Planificación, Secretaría Técnica de la Presidencia, *Plataforma para el desarrollo económico y social de la República Dominicana (1968–1985)* (Santo Domingo, 1968), 445, 459. 480.

25. Crassweller, *Trujillo,* 130; Vega, *Trujillo y las fuerzas armadas norteamericanas,* 227, 240, 307, 353, 372, and Bernardo Vega, personal communication, September 1994.

26. Bernardo Vega, *Trujillo y Haití,* vol. 1, *1930–1937* (Santo Domingo: Fundación Cultural Dominicana, 1988), esp. 390–95; Bernardo Vega, *Trujillo y Haití,* vol. 2, *1937–1938* (Santo Domingo: Fundación Cultural Dominicana, 1995), esp. 345; Murphy, *Dominican Sugar Plantation,* 129–34. Based on his research for his second volume on Haiti, Vega lowered his original estimate of the number of deaths from 12,000 to about 5,300 (personal communication, September 1994).

27. After the massacre, important intellectuals at the service of Trujillo, such as Manuel Arturo Peña Batlle and Joaquín Balaguer, articulated anti-Haitian arguments.

For example, in an essay written in 1944 and translated into English, which never mentions the 1937 massacre, Joaquín Balaguer provides an extensive defense of Trujillo as the organizer of Dominican nationality and statehood because of his critical efforts in the areas of population, territory, and sovereignty. The first two are related essentially to the issue of Haiti, and the book includes an appendix titled "Invasions and Acts of Vandalism Perpetrated by Haiti against the Dominican Republic." The book explains why the Dominican authorities wanted to stem Haitian immigration, including such reasons as "the loss of its national character," "the disappearance of its customs and the undermining of its morality," "the danger of totally losing the purity of its original appearance," and the authorities' hopes that they could attract "a powerful migratory stream formed of Caucasian elements"; see Joaquín Balaguer, *Dominican Reality: Biographical Sketch of a Country and a Regime,* trans. Mary Gillard (Mexico City: n.p., 1949, 145. Balaguer continued to articulate anti-Haitian themes into the 1990s.

28. For valuable analyses of the mythical, ideological, and cultural elements of the Trujillo regime, see Andrés L. Mateo, *Mito y cultura en la era de Trujillo* (Santo Domingo: Librería La Trinitaria, 1993); Moya Pons, "Dominican Republic since 1930," 517; Rosario Espinal, *Autoritarismo y democracia en la política dominicana* (San José, Costa Rica: CAPEL, 1987), 51–77; José Luis Saez, "Catolicismo e Hispanidad en la oratoria de Trujillo," *Estudios Sociales* 21 (July 1988): 89–104; and Murphy, *Dominican Sugar Plantation,* 129–44. Trujillo's obsession with race even led him to use face whiteners to lighten his skin (he had Haitian Afro-Caribbean ancestry through his maternal grandmother); see Crassweller, *Trujillo,* 84–85.

29. Indeed, President Vásquez usually sought United States approval in advance for all expenditures for capital improvements; Crassweller, *Trujillo,* 182.

30. The Dominican Republic was the last country in which the United States retained a customs receivership, and even after the treaty was signed, all funds collected by Dominican customs were deposited in the Dominican branch of a U.S. bank representing foreign bondholders, to distribute the funds between them and the Dominican government. In a careful review of Trujillo's actions, Bernardo Vega deflates much of the nationalist aura that still pervades common views of Trujillo's financial actions. He argues these actions during the 1930s probably prevented the debt from being paid off before 1947 (and perhaps even at discounted rates and with additional commercial concessions), and that Trujillo left the country saddled with extensive debt that was not even greater primarily because the United States refused several loan requests from his regime. Both the 1940 convention and the 1947 cancellation of the country's debt imitated steps taken by Haiti, in the first case some six years earlier, in the second some five days before. Although the monetary system established in 1947 was solid, Trujillo was able to manipulate it for his personal benefit. See Vega, *Trujillo y el control financiero norteamericano,* esp. ii–iii and 451, and Frank Moya Pons, "Dominican Republic since 1930," 516–17.

31. On the late emergence of economic elite opposition, see Wiarda, *Dictatorship, Development and Disintegration,* 370–74. Estimates of Trujillo's economic holdings are from Moya Pons, "Dominican Republic since 1930," 515.

32. See Wiarda, 1975 *Dictatorship, Development and Disintegration,* 439–59; Frank Moya Pons, *El pasado dominicano* (Santo Domingo: Fundación J. A. Caro Alvarez, 1986),

65–68. Moya Pons estimates that Trujillo's material beneficence toward the church was worth about $26 million.

33. One of the only strikes during the Trujillo period broke out in the sugar lands of La Romana and San Pedro de Macorís in January 1946. The leader of that strike, Mauricio Báez, was killed four years later, apparently on Trujillo's orders, while in exile in Cuba. In spite of Trujillo's initial opposition, Dominican sugar mills continued to exploit Haitian labor to cut cane, bringing Haitians across the border for the harvest and then returning them. This contrasts sharply with the case of Cuba, where beginning in 1933 the cheap foreign labor was gradually deported and Cubans, increasingly organized and better paid, began to cut cane: one thing that made this possible was that much larger quantities of Cuban sugar entered the U.S. market under a preferential price. See Bernardo Vega, *En la década perdida*, 115–26.

34. See Hartlyn, "Dominican Republic," and Vega, *Trujillo y las fuerzas armadas norteamericanas*, 463–67.

35. For a three-part framework and a more extensive analysis of the failed transitions of 1961–62 and 1966 in the country and the successful one of 1978, see chapters 3 and 4 of Jonathan Hartlyn, *The Struggle for Democratic Politics in the Dominican Republic* (Chapel Hill: University of North Carolina Press, forthcoming 1998). Those chapters analyze the transitions in terms of three interrelated clusters of factors: the nature of the preexisting authoritarian regime and its relations to key actors, the international geopolitical and economic context, and the transition process itself. The continuing neopatrimonial nature of the country's post-1978 democratic regime is analyzed in the book's subsequent chapters.

36. See the chapter in this volume by Richard Snyder as well as the editors' introductory chapters. On sultanism, provisional governments, and democratic transitions, see also the discussion in Juan Linz and Alfred Stepan, *Problems of Democratic Transitions and Consolidation: Southern Europe, South America, and Post-Communist Europe* (Baltimore: Johns Hopkins University Press, 1996), chaps. 3 and 4; and Yossi Shain and Juan J. Linz, *Between States: Interim Governments and Democratic Transitions* (Cambridge: Cambridge University Press, 1995), esp. 28–30.

37. The conditions highlighted above as helpful for a democratic transition from neopatrimonialism all held in 1978 much more than in 1961, especially a strong moderate opposition with a basis in independent societal economic actors as well as opposition political parties and a weak revolutionary opposition. However, that the military was somewhat autonomous worked contrary to what was expected: in this case it was Balaguer himself who eventually negotiated a transition with the moderate opposition forces, leaving key military officers to their fate.

38. From 1958 to 1960, military and police forces grew from eighteen thousand to thirty-one thousand. See Vega, *Trujillo y las fuerzas armadas norteamericanas*, 225, 428–53, and Bernardo Vega, *Eisenhower y Trujillo* (Santo Domingo: Fundación Cultural Dominicana, 1991), 221–24. One of the paramilitary groups, a "foreign legion," had a few foreign mercenaries. Other advisers of Trujillo, such as Balaguer, tried to encourage him to seek reconciliation rather than confrontation with the church and the United States.

39. Jerome Slater, *Intervention and Negotiation: The United States and the Dominican Republic* (New York: Harper & Row, 1970), 7.

40. Jerome Slater, *The OAS and United States Foreign Policy* (Columbus: Ohio State University Press, 1967), 193–94. The measure barely passed, as Argentina, Brazil, Guatemala, Haiti, Paraguay, and Uruguay abstained.

41. For Trujillo's assassination, see Piero Gleijeses, *The Dominican Crisis: The 1965 Constitutionalist Revolt and American Intervention,* trans. Lawrence Lipson (Baltimore: Johns Hopkins University Press, 1978). Gleijeses asserts that at least twelve of the fourteen conspirators "were motivated by fear for their own security and privileges . . . and by desire for a revenge that at last seemed possible" as well as by hopes of power and riches; social reform and political democracy were of little interest to them (303). The United States, which at first had strongly encouraged the conspirators, became nervous after the Bay of Pigs debacle. It feared that a power vacuum in the country if Trujillo were to be killed could be taken advantage of by Dominican radicals with ties to Fidel Castro. On the U.S. Navy operations, see Abraham F. Lowenthal, *The Dominican Intervention* (Cambridge: Harvard University Press, 1972), 11, 26.

42. After his resignation, he went on a three-day drinking orgy, personally killed the six remaining imprisoned assassins of his father (two were never captured), who had been brutally tortured, and then left on the family yacht, with his father's body and reportedly $90 million. Gleijeses, *Dominican Crisis,* 44–46.

43. Lowenthal, *Dominican Intervention,* 11; Gleijeses, *Dominican Crisis,* 46–47; Slater, *OAS and United States Policy,* 198–200.

44. See also Rosario Espinal, "An Interpretation of the Democratic Transition in the Dominican Republic," in *The Central American Impasse,* ed. Giuseppe Di Palma and Laurence Whitehead (New York: St. Martin's Press, 1986).

45. For a brief analysis of neopatrimonial democracy, see Jonathan Hartlyn, "Crisis-Ridden Elections (Again) in the Dominican Republic: Neopatrimonialism, Presidentialism, and Weak Electoral Oversight," *Journal of Interamerican Studies and World Affairs* 36 (winter 1994), 91–144. That article also analyzes the Dominican Republic's crisis-ridden elections since 1978, especially that of 1994, in which fraud provided Balaguer the critical margin of victory, permitting his second reelection since he returned to power in 1986 but also provoking a postelectoral crisis that shortened his term to two years and led to a number of constitutional reforms. Balaguer stepped down from the presidency in August 1996. See also Hartlyn, *Struggle for Democratic Politics,* esp. chaps. 1, 7, 8, and 9, for a more extensive discussion of neopatrimonialism and of Balaguer's 1986–96 period in office.

5 • *The Batista Regime in Cuba*

1. Edmund A. Chester, *A Sergeant Named Batista* (New York: Henry Holt, 1954), 262, 263. In 1954 Chester wrote, "I have known Fulgencio Batista as a friend for twenty years" (261).

2. In this chapter I follow the approach and definitions sketched by Chehabi and Linz in their introductory chapters. To save space, I will forgo citing the same general sources they do.

3. Chester, *Sergeant Named Batista,* 1–24, 100, and Hugh Thomas, *Cuba: The Pursuit of Freedom* (New York: Harper & Row, 1971), 845.

4. For his political thought from 1933 to 1944, see Fulgencio Batista, *Revolución social o política reformista* (Havana: Prensa Indoamericana, 1944).

5. Much of the information for the next several paragraphs is documented in Jorge I. Domínguez, *Cuba: Order and Revolution* (Cambridge: Harvard University Press, 1978), 95–109.

6. In September 1944 the Communist Party's Second National Assembly approved a letter from the party to Batista stating that "we wish to reiterate that you can count on our affection and with our respect and esteem for your principles as a democratic and progressive ruler." See "Una carta del Partido Socialista Popular a Batista," *Fundamentos* 4, no. 38 (October 1944): 376.

7. Louis A. Pérez Jr., *Army Politics in Cuba, 1898–1958* (Pittsburgh: University of Pittsburgh Press, 1976), 116–27.

8. Fulgencio Batista, *Respuesta* (Mexico City: Manuel León Sánchez, 1960), 443–56.

9. Thomas, *Cuba*, 776–77.

10. Batista, *Respuesta*, 25.

11. Batista, *Respuesta*, 19–20.

12. Pérez, *Army Politics*, 146–47.

13. Text of letters reproduced in José Suárez Núñez, *El gran culpable* (Caracas, 1963); see 157, 169, 174.

14. Alfred E. Stepan, ed., *Authoritarian Brazil* (New Haven: Yale University Press, 1973), chap. 2.

15. Suárez Núñez, *El gran culpable*, 10–11.

16. Fulgencio Batista, *Piedras y leyes* (Mexico City: Ediciones Botas, 1961), 417, 430.

17. Batista, *Piedras y leyes*, 153.

18. República de Cuba, *La Jurisprudencia al día* (1954), 1586–87.

19. Batista, *Piedras y leyes*, 153–60.

20. U.S. Bureau of Foreign Commerce, *Investment in Cuba* (Washington, D.C.: U.S. Government Printing Office, 1956), 120–21.

21. Ibid., 123.

22. Efrén Córdova Cordovés, "Problemas actuales de la intervención del estado en la economía laboral cubana," *Anuario de la Facultad de Ciencias Sociales y Derecho Público* (1955–56), 276–77.

23. Domínguez, *Cuba: Order and Revolution*, 74.

24. Private correspondence, 12 August 1973, cited as written, except for protection of author's confidentiality.

25. Suárez Núñez, *El gran culpable*, 20–24.

26. Earl E. T. Smith, *The Fourth Floor* (New York: Random House, 1962), 155; for Batista's appreciation of Ambassador Smith, see *Piedras y leyes*, 52, 416.

27. Computed from Rolando Bonachea and Nelson P. Valdés, eds., *Revolutionary Struggle, 1947–1958: The Selected Works of Fidel Castro* (Cambridge: MIT Press, 1972).

28. Ted Robert Gurr, *Why Men Rebel* (Princeton: Princeton University Press, 1970), 239–40.

29. Fulgencio Batista, *Paradojas* (Mexico City: Ediciones Botas, 1963), 23–27.

30. Batista, *Paradojas*, 118–21.

31. U.S. Department of State, *Foreign Relations of the United States, 1955–1957*, vol. 6, *American Republics,* (Washington, D.C.: U.S. Government Printing Office, 1987), 840–41; quoted as printed; omissions in original.

32. See the excellent Ph.D. dissertation by Alfred L. Padula Jr., "The Fall of the Bourgeoisie: Cuba, 1959–1961" (University of New Mexico, 1974).

33. This section owes much to Ramón Barquín, *Las luchas guerrilleras en Cuba,* 2 vols. (Madrid: Playor, 1975).

34. For the mutual recriminations that eventually became public, see especially Batista, *Respuesta,* and the Tabernilla Dolz letters in Suárez Núñez, *El gran culpable.*

6 • *The Somoza Regime in Nicaragua*

1. This material is drawn mainly from John A. Booth, *The End and the Beginning: The Nicaraguan Revolution* (Boulder, Colo.: Westview, 1985), 46–49, as well as Donald C. Hodges, *Intellectual Foundations of the Nicaraguan Revolution* (Austin: University of Texas Press, 1986); Richard L. Millett, *Guardians of the Dynasty: A History of the U.S.– Created Guardia Nacional de Nicaragua and the Somoza Family* (Maryknoll, N.Y.: Orbis, 1977); and Knut Walter, *The Regime of Anastasio Somoza: 1936–1956* (Chapel Hill: University of North Carolina Press, 1993).

2. Walter, *Regime of Anastasio Somoza,* chaps. 3–5.

3. Ibid., chap. 4; see also Jeffrey L. Gould, *To Lead as Equals: Rural Protest and Political Consciousness in Chinandega, Nicaragua, 1912–1979* (Chapel Hill: University of North Carolina Press, 1990), chap. 1.

4. Jaime Wheelock Román, *Imperialismo y dictadura* (Mexico City: Siglo Veintiuno Editores, 1979), and Rose Spalding, *Capitalists and Revolution: Opposition and Accommodation in Nicaragua, 1979–1992* (Chapel Hill: University of North Carolina Press, 1994).

5. The Banco de América group consisted originally mainly of the Conservative oligarchy, while the Banco Nicaragüense group had origins among wealthy Liberal clans involved in cotton production.

6. Most of the material on the regime is drawn from Thomas W. Walker, *Nicaragua: Land of Sandino* (Boulder, Colo.: Westview, 1981); Booth, *End and the Beginning;* Bernard Diederich, *Somoza and the Legacy of U.S. Involvement in Central America* (London: Junction Books, 1982); Jesús Miguel Blandón, *Entre Sandino y Fonseca Amador* (N.p., [ca. 1979]); Clemente Guido, *Noches de tortura,* 3d ed. (Managua: Ediciones Nicarao, 1980); and Pedro Joaquín Chamorro, *Los Somoza: Una estirpe sangrienta* (Buenos Aires: El Cid Editor, 1979).

7. Booth, *End and the Beginning,* 77–87, and Wheelock Román, *Imperialismo y dictadura.*

8. See especially Diederich, *Somoza and the Legacy of U.S. Involvement,* and Chamorro, *Los Somoza.*

9. Chamorro, *Los Somoza;* Guido, *Noches de tortura;* and Pedro Hurtado Cárdenas, *Las torturas como sistema* (Managua: Editorial Asel, 1946).

10. Walter, *Regime of Anastasio Somoza,* chaps. 3–5, and Wheelock Román, *Imperialismo y dictadura.*

11. Booth, *End and the Beginning,* 88.

12. Wheelock Román, *Imperialismo y dictadura,* 174, and Eduardo Crawley, *Dictators Never Die: A Portrait of Nicaragua and the Somoza Dynasty* (New York: St. Martin's Press, 1979), 149–50.

13. Carlos Vilas, *The Sandinista Revolution: National Liberation and Social Transformation in Central America*, trans. Judy Butler (New York: Monthly Review Press, 1986), 84.

14. Booth, *End and the Beginning*, 55.

15. Ibid., 91–93. On the history of the Guardia Nacional, see Millett, *Guardians of the Dynasty*, passim.

16. See especially Chamorro, *Los Somoza*, and Diederich, *Somoza and the Legacy of U.S. Involvement.*

17. Juan J. Linz, "Oppositions in and under an Authoritarian Regime: The Case of Spain," in *Regimes and Oppositions*, ed. Robert Dahl (New Haven: Yale University Press, 1973), 184–99.

18. Walter, *Regime of Anastasio Somoza*, xix; see also Gould, *To Lead as Equals*, 46–49.

19. See Booth, *End and the Beginning*, 130, and William J. Carroll and Mitchell A. Seligson, "The Costa Rican Connection in the Downfall of Somoza," paper presented to the Conference on Central America in the 1980s: Options for U.S. Policy, El Paso, Texas, 16–17 November 1979.

20. Walter, *Regime of Anastasio Somoza*, 198.

21. Wheelock Román, *Imperialismo y dictadura.*

22. Spalding, *Capitalists and Revolution*, and Booth, *End and the Beginning*, 101–3.

23. G. Pope Atkins, *Latin America in the International System* (New York: Free Press, 1977), 166–69, 183.

24. See Booth, *End and the Beginning*, 76–77, and Julio López C. et al., *La caída del somocismo y la lucha sandinista en Nicaragua* (San José, Costa Rica: Editorial Universitaria Centroamericana, 1979), 245–47.

25. I use the term "national revolts" as does John Walton, *Reluctant Rebels* (New York: Columbia University Press, 1984), 1–33.

26. For a comparative analysis of these cases, see John A. Booth and Thomas W. Walker, *Understanding Central America* (Boulder, Colo.: Westview, 1993).

27. Ibid., tables 1 and 2.

28. Ibid., table 3.

29. Ibid., table 4.

30. Daniel Camacho et al., *El fracaso social de la integración centroamericana* (San José, Costa Rica: Editorial Universitaria Centroamericana, 1979).

31. Booth and Walker, *Understanding Central America*, table 6.

32. Charles D. Brockett, *Land, Power, and Poverty: Agrarian Transformation and Political Conflict in Central America* (Boston: Unwin Hyman, 1988), 72–74; Donaldo Castillo Rivas, "Modelos de acumulación, agricultura, y agroindustria en Centroamérica," in *Centroamérica: Más allá de la crisis*. ed. Donaldo Castillo Rivas (Mexico City : Ediciones SIAP, 1983), 202–5; Consejo Superior Universitaria Centroamericana, *Estructura agraria, dinámica de población, y desarrollo capitalista en Centroamérica* (San José, Costa Rica: Editorial Universitaria Centroamericana, 1978), 204–54; Robert G. Williams, *Export Agriculture and the Crisis in Central America* (Chapel Hill: University of North Carolina Press, 1986), 52–73, 129–134.

33. Centro de Investigaciones y Estudios de la Reforma Agraria, *Informe de Nicaragua a la FAO* (Managua: Ministerio de Desarrollo Agropecuario y Reforma Agraria, 1983), 41.

264 • *Notes to Pages 145–152*

34. Ibid., 40–41.

35. Castillo Rivas, "Modelos de acumulación," 203.

36. Material on Nicaragua is from George Black, *Triumph of the People: The Sandinista Revolution in Nicaragua* (London: Zed, 1981), 70–72; Ricardo E. Chavarría, "The Nicaraguan Insurrection," in *Nicaragua in Revolution*, ed. Thomas W. Walker (New York: Praeger, 1982), 28–29; Thomas W. Walker, "Introduction: Revolution in General, Nicaragua to 1984," in Walker, *Nicaragua in Revolution*, 20; López C. et al., *La caída del somocismo*, 98–112; Centro de Información, Documentación y Análisis del Movimiento Obrero Latinamericano, "El movimiento obrero," in *Los Sandinistas*, ed. Gabriel García Márquez et al. (Bogota: Editorial Oveja Negra, 1979), 171–76; Booth, *End and the Beginning*, chaps. 6–7; Rafael Menjívar, "El movimiento campesino en Nicaragua," in *Movimientos populares en Centroamérica*, ed. Daniel Camacho and Rafael Menjívar (San José, Costa Rica: Editorial Universitaria Centroamericana, Facultad Latinoamericana de Ciencias Sociales, Universidad de Naciones Unidas, Instituto de Investigaciones Sociales de la Universidad Autónoma de Mexico, 1985), 409–36; Michael Dodson and Laura Nuzzi O'Shaughnessy, *Nicaragua's Other Revolution: Religious Faith and Political Struggle* (Chapel Hill: University of North Carolina Press, 1990), 116–39; and Michael Dodson and Tommie Sue Montgomery, "The Churches in the Nicaraguan Revolution," in Walker, *Nicaragua in Revolution*, 163–74.

37. Dodson and O'Shaughnessy, *Nicaragua's Other Revolution*, passim.

38. This section is drawn primarily from Booth, *End and the Beginning*, 127–82; see also Vilas, *Sandinista Revolution*, 49–126, and Black, *Triumph of the People*, 75–184.

39. Somoza himself ultimately blamed his "betrayal" by the United States for the fall of his regime and laid the responsibility for the withdrawal of U.S. support on "communists" in the State Department. See Anastasio Somoza Debayle and Jack Cox, *Nicaragua Betrayed* (Boston: Western Islands,1980).

40. The United States' aim was to reach a settlement with the rebel coalition that might exclude the FSLN from meaningful power and preserve the National Guard and PLN as counterweights to the Sandinistas. This effort failed because the FSLN had become dominant within the rebel coalition. See Booth, *End and the Beginning*, 174–82.

41. Booth, *End and the Beginning*, 174–81.

42. See, for instance, Thomas W. Walker, ed., *Reagan versus the Sandinistas: The Undeclared War on Nicaragua* (Boulder, Colo.: Westview, 1987); Latin American Studies Association, *The Electoral Process in Nicaragua: Domestic and International Influences* (Austin, Tex.: LASA, 1984); idem, *Electoral Democracy under International Pressure* (Pittsburgh: LASA, 1990); and William Robinson, *The Faustian Bargain: U.S. Involvement in the Nicaraguan Elections and American Foreign Policy in the Post–Cold War Era* (Boulder, Colo.: Westview, 1992).

43. Both Guatemala and El Salvador had been ruled for decades by institutionalized, modernizing, corporatist militaries rather than by personalistic dictators. Both regimes were highly repressive toward popular mobilization and demonstrated similar spending patterns to the regime of Anastasio Somoza Debayle; see Booth and Walker, *Understanding Central America*, chaps. 7 and 9.

44. Mitchell A. Seligson and John A. Booth, eds., *Elections and Democracy in Central America, Revisited* (Chapel Hill: University of North Carolina Press, 1995).

7 • *The Duvalier Regime in Haiti*

1. P. V. Vastey, *Essai sur les causes de la révolution et des guerres civiles d'Hayti* (Sans Souci, 1819), 148. See David Nicholls, "Pompée Valentin Vastey: Royalist and Revolutionary," *Revista de Historia de América,* no. 109 (January–June 1990): 129ff.

2. See Louis Joseph Janvier, *Les constitutions d'Haïti* (Paris: Marpon and Flamarion, 1886), and more recently, Claude Moïse, *Constitutions et luttes de pouvoir en Haïti* (Montreal: CIDIHCA, 1988).

3. See David Nicholls, *Haiti in Caribbean Context* (London: Macmillan, 1985), 220ff.; also see Mats Lundahl, *Politics or Markets: Essays on Haitian Underdevelopment* (London: Routledge, 1992), chaps. 11–14.

4. Paul Moral, *Le paysan haïtien* (Paris: Maisonneuve et Larose, 1961); Uli Locher, *Rural-Urban Migration and the Alleged Demise of the Extended Family: The Haitian Case in Comparative Perspective* (Montreal: Centre for Developing Areas Studies, 1977); Lundahl, *Politics or Markets,* chap. 18.

5. The role of voodoo in the Haitian revolution of 1789–1803 is a contentious issue among historians, but it certainly played some part in maintaining solidarity and providing inspiration, as it did in the resistance to the U.S. occupation, led by Charlemagne Péralte and Benoît Batraville (1917–19).

6. There is a considerable literature on Haitian voodoo; among the best works are Alfred Métraux, *Le vaudou haïtien* (Paris: Gallimard, 1958); Laënnec Hurbon, *Dieu dans le vaudou haïtien* (Paris: Payot, 1972); and Harold Courlander and Rémy Bastien, *Religion and Politics in Haiti* (Washington, D.C.: Institute for Cross-Cultural Research, 1966).

7. See David Nicholls, "Rural Protest and Peasant Revolt in Haiti, 1804–1869," in *Peasants, Plantations and Rural Communities in the Caribbean,* ed. Malcolm Cross and Arnaud Marks (Guildford: University of Surrey, 1979), reprinted in Nicholls, *Haiti in Caribbean Context,* chap. 9.

8. Curiously it was this combination of almost unlimited discretion with ex post facto control that Weber ascribed to the kind of democracy of which he approved. "In a democracy," he wrote, "the people choose a leader in whom they trust. Then the chosen leader says, 'Now shut up and obey me.' People and party are then no longer free to interfere in his business. . . . Later the people can sit in judgement. If the leader has made mistakes—to the gallows with him." H. H. Gerth and C. W. Mills eds., *From Max Weber* (London: Routledge, 1948), 42. Certain similarities are to be found in the "decisionism" of Carl Schmitt. See David Nicholls, *Deity and Domination* (London: Routledge, 1989), 99ff.

9. Michel-Rolph Trouillot, *Haiti, State against Nation: The Origins and Legacy of Duvalierism* (New York: Monthly Review Press, 1990), 104ff.

10. See Lilyan Kesteloot, *Les écrivains noirs de langue française: Naissance d'une littérature* (Brussels: Université Libre, 1965); Naomi M. Garret, *The Renaissance of Haitian Poetry* (Paris: Présence Africaine, 1963); J. Michael Dash, *Literature and Ideology in Haiti, 1915–1961* (London: Macmillan, 1981); David Nicholls, *From Dessalines to Duvalier: Race, Colour and National Independence in Haiti* (Cambridge: Cambridge University Press, 1979), chap. 5.

11. It is possible to distinguish two tendencies in Haiti that are closely related to ideas

about color; these are manifested particularly in conflicting interpretations of the Haitian past. On the one hand there is a mulatto legend, which regards Rigaud, Pétion, Boyer, and Geffrard as progressive leaders battling against ignorant and barbarous black leaders; on the other hand, *noiristes* see the heroes as Toussaint, Dessalines, Christophe, Soulouque, Salnave (a lone mulatto), and Salomon, providing the strong but enlightened leadership the country needs. See David Nicholls, "A Work of Combat: Mulatto Historians and the Haitian Past, 1847–67," *Journal of Interamerican Studies* 16, no. 1 (1974); idem, "The Wisdom of Salomon: Myth or Reality?" *Journal of Interamerican Studies* 20, no. 4 (1978); see also Nicholls, *From Dessalines to Duvalier.*

12. *New York Times,* 28 November 1966. See François Duvalier, *Mémoires d'un leader du tiers monde* (Paris: Hachette, 1969), 280.

13. David Nicholls, "Embryo-Politics in Haiti," *Government and Opposition* 6, no. 1 (1971): 75–85. See also Nicholls, *From Dessalines to Duvalier,* 213ff.

14. Gérard Pierre-Charles, *Radiografía de una dictadura* (Mexico City: Editorial Nuestro Tiempo, 1969), 103.

15. Michel-Rolph Trouillot, *Les racines historiques de l'état duvaliérien* (Port-au-Prince: Deschamps, 1986); the English language edition, cited in note 9, is more than a translation of the French text, as the author explains in his preface; *Haiti,* 9ff.

16. Trouillot, *Haiti,* 158–59. This is an extreme statement, which the author implicitly modifies when he speaks of Duvalier's program of "equilibrium" between black and mulatto; in the early days there is some evidence that François Duvalier really did intend to improve the lot of the poor and lower-middle-class blacks. In the event, he did nothing concrete for them.

17. Trouillot, *Haiti,* 178.

18. Leslie François Manigat, *Haiti of the Sixties: Object of International Concern* (Washington D.C., 1964), 24.

19. Karl Wittfogel, *Oriental Despotism* (New Haven: Yale University Press, 1957), 156.

20. See Nicholls, *From Dessalines to Duvalier,* 232ff.

21. Aristotle, *Politics* (London: Oxford University Press, 1948), 5:11.

22. See James Ferguson, *Papa Doc, Baby Doc: Haiti and the Duvaliers* (Oxford: Blackwell, 1987), 70, and Lundahl, *Politics or Markets,* 280ff.

23. This kind of family patronage was, however, by no means begun by Duvalier. I remember staying, on my first visit to Haiti, in a small hotel where the receptionist (Gérard Lescot) was the man who, as foreign minister, signed the United Nations charter on behalf of Haiti; he was the son of president Elie Lescot.

24. See Elizabeth Abbott, *Haiti: The Duvaliers and Their Legacy* (London: Hale, 1991), 251ff.

25. See Ferguson, *Papa Doc, Baby Doc,* 70.

26. There is a useful account of how the army actually ran under the Duvaliers and since in Michel S. LaGuerre, *The Military and Society in Haiti* (London: Macmillan, 1993); see also Kern Delince, *Armée et politique en Haïti* (Paris: Harmattan, 1979).

27. William Paley, "Power Shift Imperils Haiti's Frail Stability," *Guardian,* 13 January 1982; David Nicholls, "Haiti: The Rise and Fall of Duvalierism," *Third World Quarterly* 8, no. 4 (1986): 1239–52; idem, "Past and Present in Haitian Politics," in *Haiti: Today and Tomorrow,* ed. Charles R. Foster and Albert Valdman (Lanham, Md.: University Press of America, 1984), 253–64.

28. The predicament of Haiti's exiles follows a common pattern. See Yossi Shain, *The Frontiers of Loyalty: Political Exiles in the Age of the Nation-State* (Middletown, Conn.: Wesleyan University Press, 1989).

29. See Abbott, *Haiti,* 172–73.

30. See Leslie Griffiths, *History of Methodism in Haiti* (Port-au-Prince: Author, 1991); also Roger Gaillard, *Etzer Villaire: Témoin de nos malheurs* (Port-au-Prince: Author, 1972).

31. See Patrick Bellegarde-Smith, *Haiti: The Breached Citadel* (Boulder, Colo.: Westview, 1990), 142ff.

32. See his own account in Jean-Bertrand Aristide, *An Autobiography* (Maryknoll, N.Y.: Orbis, 1993).

33. The story from Aristide's standpoint is told in his book *La vérité! En vérité* (Port-au-Prince: Author, 1989).

34. Matthew Soberg Shugart and John M. Carey, *Presidents and Assemblies* (Cambridge: Cambridge University Press, 1992), 214n; see also 72–73.

35. Imaginatively translated by one British journalist as "a fishy motel"!

36. See Jean Comhaire, "The Haitian Chef de Section," *American Anthropologist* 57 (1955): 620ff; Pnina Lahav, "The Chef de Section: Structure and Functions of Haiti's Basic Administrative Institution," in *Working Papers in Haitian Society and Culture,* ed. Sidney Mintz (New Haven: Antilles Research Program, Yale University, 1975). On the recent situation see *Paper Laws, Steel Bayonets: The Breakdown of the Rule of Law in Haiti* (New York: Lawyers' Committee for Human Rights, 1990).

37. Joaquín Balaguer, *La isla al revés: Haití y el destino dominicano* (Santo Domingo: Librería Dominicana, 1984).

38. There is an extensive literature on migrant workers; see Maurice Lemoine, *Bitter Sugar* (London: Zed, 1985); Roger Plant, *Sugar and Modern Slavery* (London: Zed, 1987); Ramón Antonio Veras, *Inmigración, Haitianos, Esclavitud* (Santo Domingo: Taller, 1983).

39. Personal communication from Hervé Boyer.

8 • *The Pahlavi Regime in Iran*

1. A great many references could be cited to show that the central demand of the revolution was law itself, which was clearly associated, and often identified, with liberty. *Qanun,* "Law," was the name of a newspaper published in London in the late nineteenth century by Malkam Khan (Nazem al-Dowleh) to attack arbitrary government in Iran. In the same period Mostashar al-Dowleh published a book titled *Yek kalameh* (One word, i.e., Law) that was considered so dangerous that the author was arrested and jailed.

2. See Isaiah Berlin, *Two Concepts of Liberty: An Inaugural Lecture Delivered before the University of Oxford on 31 October 1958* (Oxford: Clarendon Press, 1958). For a more extensive discussion of Berlin's two concepts of liberty compared with Iranian notions during the constitutional revolution, see Homa Katouzian, *The Political Economy of Modern Iran* (New York: New York University Press, 1981), chap. 4.

3. For recent accounts of the constitutional revolution in English see Vanessa Martin, *Islam and Modernism: The Iranian Revolution of 1906* (Syracuse: Syracuse University Press, 1989), and Mangol Bayat, *Iran's First Revolution: Shi'ism and the Constitutional Revolution of 1905–1909* (New York: Oxford University Press, 1991).

4. For example, the title of Nezam al-Molk Tusi's book *Siyasatnameh*, with the alternative title *Siyar al-Moluk* (Conduct of rulers).

5. I have developed a theory of the historical sociology of Iran as well as its application to social change, past and present, in a series of books and articles. See Homa Katouzian, "Arbitrary Rule: A Comparative Theory of State, Politics and Society in Iran," *British Journal of Middle Eastern Studies* 24, no. 1 (1997): 49–73; "The Aridisolatic Society: A Model of Long-Term Social and Economic Development in Iran," *International Journal of Middle East Studies* 15 (1983): 259–81; *Political Economy of Modern Iran;* "The Execution of Amir Hasanak the Vazir: Some Lessons for the Historical Sociology of Iran," in *Pembroke Papers,* ed. Charles Melville, vol. 1 (Cambridge: University of Cambridge, Centre for Middle Eastern Studies, 1990), 73–88; *Musaddiq and the Struggle for Power in Iran* (London: Tauris, 1990); "Demokrasi, diktatori, va mas'uliat-e mellat" (Democracy, dictatorship, and the responsibility of the people), *Ettela'at-e Siasi-Eqtesadi* (Political and economic ettela'at) 7, nos. 7–8 (April–May 1993); and *Estebdad, Demokrasi va Nehzat-e Melli* (Democracy, arbitrary rule, and the popular movement of Iran) (Washington, D.C.: Mehregan, 1993).

6. For an interesting analysis see Sigmund Freud, *Group Psychology and the Analysis of the Ego* (New York: Norton, 1959).

7. The constitutional revolution departed from this model, since it consciously aimed at replacing the ancien régime with a constitutional state. The first few legislatures of the new constitutional monarchy did write legal codes for many areas of public life.

8. For an account that focuses on this aspect of the revolution, see Katouzian, *Political Economy of Modern Iran,* chap. 4.

9. See below for details. Good sources for this period are Mehdiqoli Hedayat [Mokhber al-Saltaneh], *Khaterat va khatarat* (Memoirs and hazards) (Tehran: Zavvar, 1982); Mohsen Sadr, *Khaterat-e Sadr al-Ashraf* (Memoirs of Sadr al-Ashraf) (Tehran: Vahid, 1985); Hosein Makki, *Tarikh-e bist-saleh-ye Iran* (A history of Iran, 1921–1941), vol. 5 (Tehran: Nashr-e Nasher, 1983); and Ebrahim Khajehnuri, *Bazigaran-e asr-e tala'i* (Actors of the golden era) (Tehran, 1961).

10. See, for example, Ali Dashti's powerful speech in *Bazigaran,* 286–93, and Katouzian, *Musaddiq and the Struggle for Power in Iran,* 45. See also Ervand Abrahamian, *Iran: Between Two Revolutions* (Princeton: Princeton University Press, 1982), 169–86.

11. Majid Yazdi, "Patterns of Clerical Political Behavior in Postwar Iran, 1941–53," *Middle Eastern Studies* 26 (July 1990): 281–307.

12. For a history of this period see Fakhreddin Azimi, *Iran: The Crisis of Democracy, 1941–1953* (New York: St. Martin's Press, 1989).

13. Mark Gasiorowski, "The 1953 *Coup d'Etat* in Iran," *International Journal of Middle East Studies* 19 (1987): 261–86.

14. The reasons for most Mosaddeqists' opposition to Amini are complex. See Katouzian, *Musaddiq and the Struggle for Power in Iran,* chap. 16.

15. See Homa Katouzian, "Oil and Economic Development in the Middle East," in *The Modern Economic and Social History of the Middle East in Its World Context,* ed. Georges Sabagh (Cambridge: Cambridge University Press, 1989); idem, "The Political Economy of Oil-Exporting Countries," *Peuples Méditerranéens,* no. 8 (1979); and idem, "Oil *versus* Agriculture," *Journal of Peasant Studies* 5 (April 1978): 347–69.

16. See Mohammad Tavakoli-Targhi, "Refashioning Iran: Language and Culture during the Constitutional Revolution," *Iranian Studies* 23 (1990): 77–101.

17. See Nazem al-Eslam Kermani, *Tarikh-e bidari-ye Iranyian* (History of Iranians' awakening), ed. Saidi Sirjani (Tehran: Agah-Novin, 1983); Ahmad Kasravi, *Tarikh-e mashruteh-ye Iran* (History of the constitutional revolution of Iran) (Tehran: Amir Kabir, 1977); and Homa Katouzian, *Sadeq Hedayat: The Life and Legend of an Iranian Writer* (London: Tauris, 1991), especially chaps. 1 and 5.

18. See Homa Katouzian, "The Campaign against the 1919 Agreement," forthcoming. See further, Abdollah Mostowfi, *Sharh-e zendegani-ye man* (My life), vol. 3 (Tehran: Elmi, 1946), 2–173, and Yahya Dowlatabadi, *Hayat-e Yahya* (Life of Yahya), vol. 4 (Tehran: Rudaki: 1982), chaps. 14 and 15.

19. Homa Katouzian, "Nationalist Trends in Iran, 1921–26," *International Journal of Middle East Studies* 10 (1979): 533–51.

20. Hedayat, *Khaterat*, 407.

21. See H. E. Chehabi, "Staging the Emperor's New Clothes: Dress Codes and Nation-Building under Reza Shah," *Iranian Studies* 26 (1993).: 209–33.

22. See Yair P. Hirschfeld, *Deutschland und Iran im Spiegel der Mächte: Internationale Beziehungen unter Reza Schah, 1921–1941* (Düsseldorf: Droste, 1980).

23. For an insightful discussion see Jean-François Bayart, "Republican Trajectories in Iran and Turkey: A Tocquevillian Reading," in *Democracy without Democrats: The Renewal of Politics in the Muslim World*, ed. Ghassan Salamé (London: Tauris, 1994).

24. Mostafa Fateh, *Panjah sal naft-e Iran* (Fifty years of Iranian oil) (Tehran: Payam, 1979), 299.

25. Quoted in Makki, *Tarikh*, 5:240.

26. On the organization and activities of the Iran-e Novin Party see Manuchehr Kalali (its first general secretary) in an interview recorded by Habib Ladjevardi, 8 August 1983, Nice, France, Iranian Oral History Collection, Harvard University (henceforth IOHCHU).

27. Mohammad Reza Shah Pahlevi, *Mission for My Country* (London: Hutchinson, 1960), 173.

28. Abolhasan Ebtehaj, in an interview recorded by Habib Ladjevardi, 2 December 1981, Cannes, France, IOHCHU.

29. See IOHCHU interview with Ebtehaj; and Francis Bostock and Geoffrey Jones, *Planning and Power in Iran: Ebtehaj and Economic Development under the Shah* (London: Frank Cass, 1989), chaps. 5 and 6.

30. Ali Amini, in an interview recorded by Habib Ladjevardi, 2 December 1981, Paris, France, IOHCHU.

31. For military involvement in election rigging under Reza Shah, see Hosein Makki, ed., *Doktor Mosaddeq va notqha-ye tarikhi-ye u* (Dr. Mosaddeq and his historic speeches) (Tehran: Javidan, 1979), 238ff.; for Mohammad Reza Shah see, for example, Naser Sowlat Qashqa'i, *Salha-ye bohran* (Years of crisis), ed. Nasrollah Haddadi (Tehran: Rasa, 1987), 217–29.

32. See Abbasqoli Golsha'iyan's diaries in Cyrus Ghani, ed., *Yaddasht-ha-ye Doktor Qasem Ghani*, vol. 11 (London: Cyrus Ghani, 1982), 522–604.

33. General Fereidun Jam [Djam] in an interview recorded by Habib Ladjevardi, 14 November 1981 and 10 March 1983, London, IOHCHU.

34. Ibid.

35. In an interview recorded by Zia Sedghi, 18 July 1985, Washington, D.C., IOHCHU.

36. Admiral Amir Abbas Ramzi Ata'i, in an interview recorded by Shahla Haeri, 11 July 1985, Sherman Oaks, Calif., IOHCHU.

37. IOHCHU interview with Jam.

38. Tufanian, in an interview recorded by Zia Sedghi, May–July 1985, Washington, D.C., IOHCHU.

39. IOHCHU interview with Jam.

40. Hedayat, *Khaterat,* 397.

41. In an interview recorded by Habib Ladjevardi, 1 March 1983, Paris, France, IOHCHU.

42. Marvin Zonis, *The Political Elite of Iran* (Princeton: Princeton University Press, 1971), 49.

43. Robert Graham, *Iran: The Illusion of Power* (London: Croom Helm, 1978), 155.

44. Bostock and Jones, *Planning and Power in Iran,* 169.

45. In an interview recorded by Habib Ladjevardi, 10 August 1982, Cannes, France, IOHCHU.

46. Graham, *Iran,* 159.

47. See William Shawcross, *The Shah's Last Ride* (London: Pan Books, 1989), 71.

48. IOHCHU interview with Amini, and Dariush Homayun, in an interview recorded by John Mojdehi, 21 November 1982, Washington, D.C., IOHCHU.

49. Shawcross, *Shah's Last Ride,* 159, 161.

50. IOHCHU interview with Baheri.

51. Ibid.

52. Ibid.

53. IOHCHU interview with Tufanian.

54. IOHCHU interview with Ebtehaj.

55. Bostock and Jones, *Planning and Power in Iran,* 155.

56. In an interview recorded by Habib Ladjevardi, December 1982–January 1983, Cambridge, Mass., IOHCHU.

57. Hedayat, *Khaterat,* 404.

58. Ibid., 401.

59. Makki, *Tarikh,* 6:320.

60. Hedayat, *Khaterat,* 407.

61. Quoted in Makki, *Tarikh,* 5:240.

62. Hedayat, *Khaterat,* 386.

63. For an extensive description of this process see Makki, *Tarikh,* 6:1–140.

64. See Mohammad Musaddiq, *Musaddiq's Memoirs,* ed. Homa Katouzian (London: Jebhe, 1987), 2;364–65.

65. IOHCHU interview with Farmanfarmaian.

66. IOHCHU with Ebtehaj.

67. He repeatedly expressed this view in interviews and at last in his book. See Mohammad Reza Pahlavi, *Answer to History* (New York: Stein and Day, 1980).

68. Parviz Raji, *Khaterat-e akharin safir-e shah dar Landan* (Memoirs of the Shah's last ambassador in London) (London: Ithaca Press, 1983), 221.

69. Anthony Parsons, *The Pride and the Fall: Iran, 1974–1979* (London: Jonathan Cape, 1984), 62.

70. IOHCHU interview with Amini.

71. See Mohsen Milani, *The Making of Iran's Islamic Revolution: From Monarchy to Islamic Republic* (Boulder, Colo.: Westview, 1994); Katouzian, *Political Economy of Modern Iran,* chaps. 17 and 18; H. E. Chehabi, *Iranian Politics and Religious Modernism: The Liberation Movement of Iran under the Shah and Khomeini* (Ithaca: Cornell University Press, 1990), chaps. 6 and 7; Abrahamian, *Iran: Between Two Revolutions;* and Nikki R. Keddie, *Roots of Revolution* (New Haven: Yale University Press, 1981).

72. There was an attempt to negotiate at the last minute. See H. E. Chehabi, "The Provisional Government and the Transition from Monarchy to Islamic Republic in Iran," in *Between States: Interim Governments in Democratic Transitions,* ed. Yossi Shain and Juan J. Linz (Cambridge: Cambridge University Press, 1995).

9 • *The Marcos Regime in the Philippines*

1. Mijares' wife, Judge Priscilla Mijares, generously shared her valuable insights in an interview in Manila on 2 August 1989. Alex Esclamado, publisher of the San Francisco–based *Philippine News,* provided a detailed description of Mijares' exile activities in an interview in South San Francisco on 9 and 10 September 1989. Accounts of Mijares' defection, exile, and death can be found in Steve Psinakis, *Two "Terrorists" Meet* (San Francisco: Alchemy Books, 1981), and Sterling Seagrave, *The Marcos Dynasty* (New York: Harper & Row, 1988).

2. Jack Anderson and Les Whitten, "Marcos Bribe Offer Cited by Witness," *Washington Post,* 2 July 1975, and Anderson, "New Bribe Offer in Philippine Case," *San Francisco Chronicle,* 14 July 1975, cited in Psinakis, *Two "Terrorists" Meet,* 180–81, 187.

3. Seagrave, *Marcos Dynasty,* 273–74.

4. Mijares' son's death was reported in *New York Times,* "Son of Strong Critic of Marcos Reported Slain in the Philippines," 19 June 1977, cited in Psinakis, *Two "Terrorists" Meet,* 189. A number of interviews have led me to the conclusion that Mijares and his son were killed together by General Fabian Ver's men. Seagrave, *Marcos Dynasty,* 274, holds the same opinion.

5. In Primitivo Mijares, *The Conjugal Dictatorship of Ferdinand and Imelda Marcos I* (1976; 2d ed., San Francisco: Union Square, 1986), 318.

6. Exceptions are Carl Lande, who provides a brief review of Mijares' *Conjugal Dictatorship* in "Authoritarian Rule in the Philippines: Some Critical Views," *Pacific Affairs* 55, no. 1 (1982): 89–90, and Belinda A. Aquino, *Politics of Plunder: The Philippines under Marcos* (Manila: University of the Philippines, College of Public Administration, 1987), 99 n. 5.

7. Seagrave's description of Mijares in *Marcos Dynyasty,* 268, is apt: "Mijares was a character out of the novels of Graham Greene or Eric Ambler, a highly intelligent man of ambiguous morals whose whole life was spent on the lam."

8. Alexander R. Magno, "Developmentalism and the 'New Society': The Repressive Ideology of Underdevelopment," *Third World Studies Papers,* ser. 35 (August 1983). Gary Hawes, *The Philippine State and the Marcos Regime: The Politics of Export* (Ithaca: Cornell University Press, 1987), classifies the regime as bureaucratic-authoritarian, although he also notes some of its personalistic qualities; see also Robert Stauffer, "Philippine Corporatism: A Note on the 'New Society,'" *Asian Survey* 17 (April 1977): 393–407.

9. Mijares, *Conjugal Dictatorship,* 188, 483–84, 207–9, 400.

10. Josephus, *The Jewish War,* trans. G. A. Williamson (Middlesex: Penguin Books, 1959).

11. Will is quoted in Raymond Bonner, *Waltzing with a Dictator: The Marcoses and the Making of American Policy* (New York: Times Books, 1987), 418. Marcos's own books are largely ghostwritten propaganda. Somewhat more enlightening are the interviews he gave, particularly toward the end of his regime or after his fall. See "A Talk with Marcos," *Newsweek,* 30 December 1985, 24–26; "Marcos Talks Back," *Newsweek,* 14 April 1986, 26–27; Seth Mydans, "The Marcoses' Moonlight Sonata," *Philippines Free Press,* 30 May 1987, 17, 28, 29, 47, 48 (reprinted from *New York Times*); and "Imelda and Ferdinand Marcos," *Playboy,* July 1987, 51–61. The two-thousand-page Marcos diaries, unfortunately not published by the Philippine government, which holds them in its archives, are of interest largely when describing his opponents' faults. William C. Rempel, *Delusions of a Dictator: The Mind of Marcos as Revealed in His Secret Diaries* (Boston: Little, Brown, 1993) gained access to these documents and has written an account of pre–martial law politics based on them. But one must be careful with such sources. Marcos was preoccupied with polishing his own image for future historians. As an example see Marcos, "A Defense of My Tenure," *Orbis* 33, no. 1 (winter 1989): 91–97.

12. For a more detailed account of pre–martial law politics in the Philippines see Mark R. Thompson, *The Anti-Marcos Struggle: Personalistic Rule and Democratic Transition in the Philippines* (New Haven: Yale University Press, 1995), chaps. 1–2.

13. Thomas C. Nowak and Kay A. Snyder, "Clientelist Politics in the Philippines," *American Political Science Review.* 68, no. 3 (1974), 1147–70.

14. Quoted in Stanley Karnow, *In Our Image: America's Empire in the Philippines* (New York: Random House, 1989), 360.

15. David Wurfel, *Filipino Politics: Development and Decay* (Ithaca: Cornell University Press, 1988), 98.

16. Quoted in Karnow, *In Our Image,* 21. In a pun on the country's Catholic faith and political corruption, Manila Mayor Arsenio Lacson once described government philosophy in the Philippines as "Let us prey."

17. Amando Doronila, "The Transformation of Patron-Client Relations and Its Political Consequences in Postwar Philippines," *Journal of Southeast Asian Studies* 16, no. 1 (1985): 111.

18. The United States helped the Nacionalista opposition, led by Ramon Magsaysay, defeat President Elpidio Quirino in 1953 and assisted Liberal Diosdado Macapagal in his successful 1961 campaign against incumbent Carlos Garcia, a Nacionalista. See Stephen Rosskamm Shalom, *The United States and the Philippines: A Study of Neocolonialism* (Quezon City: New Day, 1986), chaps. 3 and 4. Also, Joseph B. Smith, *Portrait of a Cold Warrior* (Quezon City: Plaridel Books, 1976), chaps.16–18.

19. Wurfel, *Filipino Politics,* 99.

20. Carl Lande, *Leaders, Factions, and Parties: The Structure of Philippine Politics* (New Haven: Southeast Asian Studies, Yale University, 1965), 47–48.

21. The exceptions are 1949, when incumbent president Elpidio Quirino employed the military against the opposition, and 1969, when Marcos did the same. See Donald L. Berlin, "Prelude to Martial Law: An Examination of Pre-1972 Philippine Civil-Military Relations" (Ph.D. diss., University of South Carolina, 1982).

22. Wurfel, *Filipino Politics,* 94.

23. Lande, *Leaders, Factions, and Parties*, 120–24.

24. Harvey A. Averch, John E. Koehler, and Frank Denton, *The Matrix of Policy in the Philippines* (Princeton: Princeton University Press, 1971), 95–114.

25. The figure is from Aurora Carbonell-Catilo et al., *Manipulated Elections* (Manila: N.p., 1985), 41, and the quotation is from Napoleon G. Rama, "The Election Campaign in Review," *Philippines Free Press*, 15 November 1969, 4, cited in Resil B. Mojares, *The Man Who Would Be President: Sergio Osmeña and Philippine Politics* (Cebu: Maria Cacao, 1986), 142.

26. The Philippine Constabulary reported forty-seven killed and fifty-eight injured. On campaign terror see *Report of the Commission on Elections to the President of the Philippines and the Congress on the Manner the Election Held on November 11, 1969* (Manila: Bureau of Printing, 1971).

27. *Conjugal Dictatorship*, 133–34.

28. Bonner, *Waltzing with a Dictator*, 242, quotes unnamed officials who said the bombings were the work of "the Monkees," a paramilitary group working for Marcos.

29. Ruby R. Paredes, ed., *Philippine Colonial Democracy* (Quezon City: Ateneo de Manila University Press, 1989).

30. Robert B. Stauffer, "The Political Economy of Refeudalization," in *Marcos and Martial Law in the Philippines*, ed. David A. Rosenberg (Ithaca: Cornell University Press, 1979), 187–98.

31. Bonner, *Waltzing with a Dictator*, 104–6, cites Philippine and American intelligence officials who said Marcos "organized demonstrations," including several in front of the U.S. embassy. Alex B. Brillantes, *Dictatorship and Martial Law: Philippine Authoritarianism in 1972* (Quezon City: Great Books, 1987), 49, interviewed two high-ranking Marcos aides who claimed the president funded student protests. Former Marcos spokesman Adrian Cristóbal told Sandra Burton that both Marcos and the opposition financed youth protest rallies; see Burton, *Impossible Dream: The Marcoses, the Aquinos, and the Unfinished Revolution* (New York: Warner Books, 1989), 76.

32. Mijares, *Conjugal Dictatorship*, 59.

33. Nick Joaquin, *Doy Laurel in Profile* (Makati: Lahi, 1985).

34. Mijares, *Conjugal Dictatorship*, 251–52.

35. Historian Alfred McCoy and *Washington Post* reporter John Sharkey did the most thorough research in 1985–86. Before that, Filipino political exile Bonifacio Gillego wrote the best exposé on the medals since Mijares' book in a 1982 article that was published in the opposition newspaper *We Forum*, which so piqued Marcos that he shut it down.

36. Seagrave, *Marcos Dynasty*, 84.

37. Lewis E. Gleeck Jr., *President Marcos and the Philippine Political Culture* (Manila: Loyal Printing, 1987), 41–43, 50.

38. Mijares, *Conjugal Dictatorship*, 151.

39. Seagrave, *Marcos Dynasty*, 162.

40. Mijares, *Conjugal Dictatorship*, 241.

41. The best accounts of Imelda Marcos's childhood and family are Carmen N. Pedrosa, *Imelda Marcos* (London: Weidenfeld and Nicolson, 1987), and Katherine Ellison, *Imelda: Steel Butterfly of the Philippines* (New York: McGraw-Hill, 1988).

42. Mijares, *Conjugal Dictatorship*, 140.

43. Cited in Theodore Friend, "What Marcos Doesn't Say," *Orbis* 33, no. 1 (1989): 103.

44. Raul Manglapus interviewed two Spanish businessmen who had lived in the Philippines; Madrid, 6 June 1985, cited in Manglapus's unpublished manuscript on democratic transition in the Philippines. Mijares, *Conjugal Dictatorship,* 140–41, reported that Marcos sent staffers to "study 'crisis governments'" to help "justify the imposition of martial law." He also claimed that Marcos "is prepared to rule for the duration of his natural life on earth in the manner that Spain's Franco did" (444),

45. Cited in Reuben R. Canoy, *The Counterfeit Revolution: The Philippines from Martial Law to the Aquino Assassination* (Manila: Philippine Editions, 1984), 23. Canoy was another former Marcos government insider who wrote a "tell-all" book.

46. Robert Shaplen, *A Turning Wheel* (New York: Random House, 1979), 220–21.

47. Robert Fishman, "Rethinking State and Regime: Southern Europe's Transition to Democracy," *World Politics* 42, no. 3 (1990): 428.

48. Mijares, *Conjugal Dictatorship,* 60, citing General Order 11, dated 30 September 1972, on pay increases. Richard J. Kessler, *Rebellion and Repression in the Philippines* (New Haven: Yale University Press, 1989), 24 on the other plums given the armed forces.

49. Kessler, *Rebellion and Repression,* 125.

50. Berlin, *Prelude to Martial Law,* 163.

51. Mijares, *Conjugal Dictatorship,* 455.

52. Carl Lande, "The Political Crisis," in *Crisis in the Philippines: The Marcos Era and Beyond,* ed. John Bresnan (Princeton: Princeton University Press, 1986), 136. Felipe Miranda, "The Military," in *The Philippines after Marcos,* ed. R. J. May and Francisco Nemezo (London: Croom Helm, 1985), 108–9, points out that in the military as a whole, Ilocanos were not "over-represented" in comparison with the pre–martial law regime. Only in the intelligence services were Ilocanos preferred.

53. Mijares, *Conjugal Dictatorship,* 418.

54. Robert Shaplen, "A Reporter at Large—from Marcos to Aquino—I," *New Yorker,* 25 August 1986, 64.

55. International Monetary Fund, "Philippines—Recent Economic Developments," 13 June 1984, 72, 136.

56. An early statement of this point is Mark R. Thompson and Gregory Slayton, "An Essay on Credit Arrangements between the IMF and the Republic of the Philippines: 1970–1983," *Philippine Review of Economics and Business* 22, nos. 1–2 (1985): 59–81. A more recent and comprehensive work is Stephan Haggard, "The Political Economy of the Philippine Debt Crisis," in *Economic Crisis and Policy Choice: The Politics of Adjustment in the Third World,* ed. Joan M. Nelson (Princeton: Princeton University Press, 1990).

57. Fox Butterfield, "Once Powerful Families in the Philippines Lose Heavily under Government Pressure," *New York Times,* 18 January 1978.

58. Perla Makil, *Mobility by Decree: The Rise and Fall of Philippine Influentials since Martial Law* (Quezon City: Institute for Philippine Culture, Ateneo de Manila University, 1975), quoted in Wurfel, *Filipino Politics,* 236–37.

59. Mijares, *Conjugal Dictatorship,* 191.

60. Mijares, *Conjugal Dictatorship,* 206. Rigoberto Tiglao, "The Consolidation of the Dictatorship," in *Dictatorship and Revolution: Roots of People's Power,* ed. Aurora Javate-de Dios et al. (Metro Manila: Conspetus, 1988), 41.

61. Aquino, *Politics of Plunder,* 46, and Walden Bello, David Kinseley, and Elaine Elinson, *Development Debacle: The World Bank in the Philippines* (San Francisoco: Institute for Food and Development Policy, 1982), 187.

62. Mijares, *Conjugal Dictatorship,* 196.

63. Dante Canlas et al., *An Analysis of the Philippine Economic Crisis—a Workshop Report* (Quezon City: University of the Philippines, School of Economics, June 1984), 86.

64. Tiglao, "Consolidation of the Dictatorship," 47.

65. Rigoberto Tiglao, "Enrile's Conglomerate," *Far Eastern Economic Review,* 19 October 1989, 44–45.

66. John Crewdson et al., "Marcos Graft Staggering: Investigators Trace Billions in Holdings," *Chicago Tribune,* 23 March 1986, 20, cited in Aquino, *Politics of Plunder,* 47–48.

67. Edward C. Banfield, *The Moral Basis of a Backward Society* (Glencoe: Free Press, 1958).

68. Mijares, *Conjugal Dictatorship,* 206–7.

69. "Some Are Smarter Than Others," in Javate-de Dios et al., *Dictatorship and Revolution,* 404–5.

70. The first lady's role in the Marcos regime was often compared to Eva Peron's in Argentina, and Imelda knew it: she had the musical *Evita* banned in the Philippines.

71. Apparently encouraged by the opposition Liberal Party, Beams held a news conference in Manila during which she played tape recordings of her bedroom trysts with the Philippine president.

72. Mijares, *Conjugal Dictatorship,* 215.

73. Tatad was interviewed by Ellison, *Imelda,* 111–12.

74. Mijares reported in *Conjugal Dictatorship* that Marcos "eats his simple Ilocano food and with his own hands. He does not drink, does not smoke, he dresses simply—all of which might perhaps be due to his Ilocano upbringing" (195).

75. Mijares' account in *Conjugal Dictatorship,* 221–23, is confirmed by Seagrave, *Marcos Dynasty,* 260–63; Ellison, *Imelda,* 214–15, 223–24; and Bonner, *Waltzing with a Dictator,* 349–50.

76. For a fascinating account of Enrile's tense relationship with Imelda see Cecilio T. Arillo (a close associate who was linked with him in the December 1989 coup attempt), *Breakaway: The Inside Story of the Four-Day Revolution in the Philippines* (Manila: CTA, 1986), 127–35.

77. The majority opinion of the so-called Agrava Commission reprinted in *Reports of the Fact-Finding Board on the Assassination of Senator Benigno S. Aquino Jr.* (Manila, Mr. and Ms. Publishing, 1984) blamed General Ver for the assassination. Bonner, *Waltzing with a Dictator,* and Burton, *Impossible Dream,* based on extensive interviews, have implicated Imelda Marcos as well.

78. The Beatles discovered this aspect of Imelda's character when they came to Manila to give a concert in 1966. Upset that the rock group had ignored the first lady's invitation to come to the presidential palace, members of her retinue chased and punched them as they were trying to board their plane.

79. Mijares, *Conjugal Dictatorship,* 192.

80. Friend, "What Marcos Doesn't Say."

81. Ferdinand E. Marcos, *Today's Revolution: Democracy* (Manila: Author, 1971).

82. Mijares, *Conjugal Dictatorship,* 188.

83. On crime see Fred Poole and Max Vanzi, *Revolution in the Philippines: The United States in a Hall of Cracked Mirrors* (New York: McGraw-Hill, 1984), 97, who cited Philippine government figures for 1981 showing that rates of all major crimes were higher than before martial law. On guns see Ellison, *Imelda*, 238–39; on drug dealers see Seagrave, *Marcos Dynasty*, 328.

84. See James Putzel, *A Captive Land: The Politics of Agrarian Reform in the Philippines* (London: Catholic Institute for International Relations, 1992), and Jeffrey M. Riedinger, *Agrarian Reform in the Philippines: Democratic Transitions and Redistributive Reform* (Stanford: Stanford University Press, 1995).

85. See Mark R. Thompson, "The Labor Movement Opposition to the Marcos Regime," in *Proceedings of the Thirteenth International Symposium on Asian Studies* (Hong Kong: Asian Research Service, 1992), 417–28.

86. Bonner, *Waltzing with a Dictator,* chap. 6, "American Acquiescence."

87. "Marcos Seizes the Offensive," *Time,* 28 April 1986, 42.

88. Benedict Anderson, "Cacique Democracy and the Philippines: Origins and Dreams," *New Left Review,* no. 169 (May–June 1988): 23 n. 76.

89. Rolando del Carmen, "Constitutionality and Judicial Politics," in Rosenberg, *Marcos and Martial Law in the Philippines,* 87.

90. Marcos found an avid defender of his legitimacy in Beth Day, an American journalist who later married Philippine foreign minister Carlos Romulo. The title of her book *Shattered Showcase of Democracy* (New York: M. Evans, 1974) takes a common perception of martial law in the Philippines and attempts to rebut it.

91. Mijares, *Conjugal Dictatorship,* 420.

92. Carbonell-Catilo et al., *Manipulated Elections,* 59.

93. Ibid., 253.

94. See Thompson, *Anti-Marcos Struggle.*

95. Gary Hawes, "Theories of Peasant Revolution: A Critique and Contribution from the Philippines," *World Politics* 42, no. 2 (1990): 277.

96. David A. Rosenberg, "Communism in the Philippines," *Problems of Communism* 32 (September–October 1984): 38.

97. On the exile opposition see Josie Shain and Mark Thompson, "The Role of Political Exiles in Democratic Transition: The Case of the Philippines," *Journal of Developing Societies* 6 (1990): 71–86.

98. Lawyers' Committee for Human Rights, *"Salvaging" Democracy: Human Rights in the Philippines* (New York: Lawyers' Committee for Human Rights, 1985). Between 1977 and 1984 there were 1,608 reported "disappearances." Also considering the early martial law period and Marcos's last full year in office, 1985, a reasonable estimate of the total number of such "extrajudicial killings" under Marcos's dictatorship would be 2,500. This is a much lower figure in terms of total population than, for example, under military rule in Argentina from 1976 to 1983. See Juan J. Linz, "Types of Political Regimes and Respect for Human Rights: Historical and Cross-National Perspectives," in *Human Rights in Perspective,* ed. Asbjørn Eide and Bernt Hagtvet (Oxford: Blackwell, 1992), 302–3 n. 19.

99. See Mark R. Thompson, "Democracy after Sultanism: The Troubled Transition in the Philippines," in *Politics, Society, and Democracy: Comparative Studies,* ed. H. E. Chehabi and Alfred Stepan (Boulder, Colo.: Westview, 1995), 329–44.

INDEX

. . . .

Abraham, Hérard, 169, 174

Africa, sultanism in, 5, 8–9, 33, 35, 37

aid, foreign, 27–28. *See also* Equatorial Guinea; Haiti; Nicaragua; Philippines; Zaire

Ala, Hosein, 202

Alabama, 16

Alam, Amir Asadollah, 21

Alavi-Kia, Hasan, 197

Albert, Lake, 15

Alemán, Arnoldo, 20

Amin, Idi, 9, 14, 20; family background and personality, 16–17, 37; overthrow of, 41; service in British army, 32

Amini, Ali, 187, 199, 202, 203

Andropov, Yuri, 36

Annobón, 235n. 58

Antigua and Barbuda, 9, 16; corruption in, 16; relations with U.S., 28, 31, 240n. 30

Antigua Labour Party, 16

Aquino, Benigno, 43, 222, 227, 228

Aquino, Corazon, 42, 59, 75, 76, 214, 228, 253n. 105

Arévalo, Juan José, 101

Argentina, 33, 36, 47

Arías, Arnulfo, 30

Arismendi Trujillo, José, 107

Aristide, Jean-Bertrand, 42, 43; election of, 74, 170; family background and personality, 170–71; ouster of, 175; presidency, 171–77; relations with armed forces, 74, 174; relations with business community, 172–74; restoration to the presidency, 179–180

Aristotle, 163

armed forces, 11, 12, 13, 38, 53–57, 68, 70–71. *See also* Batista; Cuba; Dominican Republic; Haiti; Iran; Marcos; Mobutu Sese Seko; Mohammad Reza Pahlavi; Philippines; Reza Pahlavi; Trujillo Molina; Zaire

Artigas, José Gervasio, 23

Atatürk, Kemal, 154, 192, 242n. 62

Auténtico Party (Cuba), 116, 120

authoritarian regimes, 3, 24–25, 35–37, 48; elections in, 38

Avelino, Jose, 208

Avril, Prosper, 169–70, 176

Baath Party (Iraq), 35

Baby Doc. *See* Duvalier, Jean-Claude

Baheri, Mohammad, 199

Bahrain, 193

Balaguer, Joaquín, 105, 108, 112; elections to presidency, 20, 45, 104; ideologue of Trujillo, 23–24, 257–58n. 27; presidency (1966–78), 87, 104, 106–7, 108–11; return to power (1986), 111, 260n. 45

Bandar Anzali, 15

Banyamulenge, 67

Barbot, Clément, 163, 165

Barquín, Ramón, 129

Barrios de Chamorro, Violeta, 44, 46

Batista, Fulgencio, 19; and armed forces, 115, 121–22, 129; corruption, 122–25; dictatorship (1952–58), 8, 9, 24, 25, 46, 56; election to presidency (1940), 115; family background and personality 16–17, 114, 122; lottery scheme, 22, 123; overthrow of, 40, 59, 130–31; relations with Communists, 116; viewed by U.S. officials, 113, 127–28

Bazargan, Mehdi, 203

Bazin, Marc, 170, 179

Beatles, the, 275n. 78

Belarus, 47

Ben Ali, Zine El Abidine, 36–37

Benedicto, Roberto, 219

Bennet family (Haiti), 17, 71, 164, 167, 178

Berlin, Isaiah, 183

Betancourt, Rómulo, 101, 104, 105

Bird, Lester, 16

Bird, V. C., Sr., 9

Bird, Vere, Jr., 16

Bird family, 9, 16

Bokassa, Jean-Bédel, 9, 12, 237n. 93; coronation of, 14, 41; family background and personality, 16–17, 37
Bolívar, Simón, 154
Bongo, Omar, 236n. 69
Borno, Louis, 156
Bosch, Juan, 103, 107, 108, 112
Bourguiba, Habib, 36
Boyer, Hervé, 159, 163
Boyer, Jean-Pierre, 155
Brazil, 33, 36, 47, 118, 122, 240n. 37
Breckinridge, James C., 92
Brezhnev, Leonid, 36
Bulgaria, 8, 31, 38
bureaucratic authoritarian regimes, 3, 38
Burnham, Forbes, 179
Bush, George, 151

Cabaret, 15
CACM (Central American Common Market), 144–45
Cádiz, duke of, 36
Cambodia. *See* Khmer Rouge
Cambronne, Luckner, 163, 167
Cap Haïtien, 157, 165, 170
Cape Verde Islands, 38
Carazo Odio, Rodrigo, 142
Cardenal, Ernesto, 43
Carol (king of Romania), 244n. 93
Carter, Jimmy, 30, 168, 176, 188
Castro, Fidel, 96, 105, 127; charisma, 42, 43, 150; dictatorship, 24, 46; exile, 244n. 98; leader of anti-Batista insurgency, 44, 121, 129
Castro, Raúl, 46, 129
Catherine (empress of Central African Empire), 22
caudillos, 23, 89, 90
Ceaușescu, Nicolae: dictatorship, 9, 19, 23, 37, 56; family background, 16; overthrow of, 8, 77–78; personality cult, 14–15; relations with the West, 33, 59
Ceaușescu, Nicu, 15, 37
Ceaușescu family, 15, 236n. 66
Cédras, Raoul, 173, 174, 179
Central African Republic/Empire, 9, 17; corruption in, 22, 237n. 93; diamonds, 22
Central American Common Market, 133
Chamorro, Pedro Joaquín, 43, 136, 141, 147
Chamorro, Violeta. *See* Barrios de Chamorro, Violeta

charismatic authority, 13, 41–42, 44, 45, 154
Charles, Clémard Joseph, 163, 164
Chile, 38, 234n. 38; plebiscite in, 242n. 65
China, 31, 66, 221; sultanism in, 6, 34
Christian base communities, in Nicaragua, 42, 146. *See also ti legliz*
CIA, 31, 104, 199
civil society, 20, 39, 47, 53, 55, 69, 102. *See also* Cuba; Haiti; Mexico; Zaire
Claude, Sylvio, 167
clientelism, 33–34. *See also* Cuba; Nicaragua; Philippines
Cojuangco, Eduardo, 220
colonialism, 30, 35, 154, 156
Colorado Party (Paraguay), 8, 10, 71, 253n. 108
Comintern, 116
Communism, 9, 15, 20, 23, 70, 99
CONDECA (Central American Defense Council), 143, 144
Congo-Kinshasa. *See* Zaire
Conservative Party (Nicaragua), 18, 33, 133, 135, 141, 147, 150 constitutional hypocrisy in, 17–19. *See also* Cuba; Dominican Republic; Haiti; Nicaragua; Philippines
corruption, 16, 21–23, 27–28, 35. *See also* Antigua; Batista, Central African Republic/Empire; Haiti; Iran; Mobutu Sese Seku; Mohammad Reza Pahlavi; Nicaragua; Philippines; Reza Pahlavi; Somoza Debayle; sultanism; Trujillo Molina; Zaire
Costa Rica, 141–42, 143, 147, 149
Creole language, 160
Crisologo, Floro, 215
"cronies," 11, 65, 218–20
Cuba, 8, 45–46, 149; armed forces in, 115, 118, 119, 121–22, 129; civil society in, 117, 126; clientelism, 115–17; Communists in, 115–16, 118, 261n. 6; constitutional hypocrisy in, 125–27; crisis of sovereignty in, 29, 119; economic development in, 119, 124–25, 129; economic elites in, 117, 120–21, 125, 128–29; elections in, 18, 116, 126; exiles, 46; organized labor, 118, 120, 123, 124, 128; relations with U.S., 31, 45, 46, 119; Roman Catholic church in, 42, 123, 126, 129, 243n. 76. *See also* Batista; Cuban revolution
Cuban revolution, 41, 44, 45, 56–57, 67–69, 128–31; impact on Dominican Republic, 87, 104, 105, 106
Cuenca, Rodolfo, 220

Cuervo Rubio, Gustavo, 116
customs administration, 31, 89, 99, 258n. 30

Davar, Ali Akbar, 191, 201
Déjoie, Louis, 158
d'Escoto, Miguel, 43
Dessalines, Jean-Jacques (emperor of Haiti),
    153, 155, 156, 164
Domingo y Morales del Castillo, Andrés, 126
Dominican Party, 93, 94, 100–101, 105
Dominican Republic, 4–5, 8, 15; armed forces
    in, 88–92, 103, 109, 110, 257n. 24; business
    groups, 103, 107, 109, 110; Communist
    Party in, 101, 105; constitutional hypocrisy
    in, 17, 18, 87; crisis of sovereignty in, 28–
    29, 86, 87; customs administration, 89, 99,
    258n. 30; economic development in, 88, 92,
    98, 104, 106, 109, 110; elections in, 18, 20,
    45, 91, 94, 95, 109; exiles, 95, 101, 102, 106;
    massacre of Haitians, 94, 98, 177, 257nn. 26
    & 27; relations with Haiti, 28, 88, 94, 98,
    169, 177; relations with U.S., 29, 44, 46, 88,
    91, 99, 256n. 14; relations with Venezuela,
    104, 106, 107; Roman Catholic church in,
    42, 86, 90, 99, 100, 103, 105, 107, 175, 242n.
    75, 259nn. 32 & 37; transition to democ-
    racy, 87, 106, 108, 112, 259n. 35; U.S. inva-
    sion (1965), 29, 46, 108, 112; U.S. occupa-
    tion, 87, 89, 90, 91
Dominique, Max, 163
Duvalier, François: death of, 32, 159; election
    of, 9, 158; family background and person-
    ality, 37, 157–58; and Haiti's racial cleavage,
    10, 14, 15, 19, 20, 62–63, 160–61, 178, 266n.
    16; regime, 56, 62–63, 154, 156, 159–65, 166;
    use of voodoo, 162
Duvalier, Jean-Claude, 37; marriage, 17, 71,
    159; overthrow of, 55, 72–74, 165–69, 252n.
    89; regime, 8, 9, 10, 12, 13, 28, 32, 34, 40, 71–
    72, 155, 159
Duvalier family, 15, 62, 159
dynasticism, 15–16; in Jamaica, 16; in South
    Asia, 16; in U.S. states, 16, 236n. 71

Eastern Europe, 8, 20, 38, 40, 45, 115, 188
Ebtehaj, Abolhasan, 193, 200, 202–3
Edward, Lake, 15
Eisenhower, Dwight D., 104, 106
elections, 18, 38–40. *See also* Cuba; Do-
    minican Republic; Haiti; Iran; Nicara-
    gua; Philippines

El Salvador, 144, 152
emigration of middle classes, 25, 46, 244n.
    99, 249n. 41
Enrile, Juan Ponce, 217, 220, 222, 227
Equatorial Guinea, 9, 15–16, 47, 235n. 58;
    exiles, 25; foreign aid, 28. *See also* Macías
    Nguema
Estimé, Dumarsais, 158, 159
Estrella Ureña, Rafael, 91
Ethiopia, 236n. 76
ethnic nationalism and racism: in Domini-
    can Republic, 14, 86, 98, 177; in Germany,
    161; in Haiti, 160; in Iran, 14–15, 189–91,
    194; in Romania, 14, 235n. 57
exiles, 25. *See also* Cuba; Dominican
    Republic; emigration of middle classes;
    Equatorial Guinea; Haiti; Iran; Nicaragua;
    Uganda
Eyre, Edward, 156

FAO (Broad Opposition Front [Nicaragua]),
    147–49
Farah (empress of Iran), 200
Farmanfarmaian, Khodadad, 200, 202
fascism/fascists, 30, 33, 160, 192, 240n. 43
Fateh, Mostafa, 192
Fernando, Enrique, 217
Fernando Póo, 15
Figueres Ferrer, José, 142
Firmin, Aténor, 163
Franco, Francisco, 3, 4, 5, 36, 215
FNCD (National Front for Change and
    Democracy [Haiti]), 171, 172
FSLN (Sandinista National Liberation
    Front), 142, 147

Gairy, Eric, 9, 19, 37
Galíndez, Jesús de, 4, 5, 95, 232n. 10, 257n. 21
Garcia, Carlos, 209, 211, 272n. 18
Garde d'Haïti, 32, 157
Geffrard, Fabre Nicolas, 155
Germany, East, 40, 234n. 39
Germany, Nazi, 4, 161, 162, 186, 191, 234n. 39
Gómez, Juan Vicente, 5, 27, 31
Gonaïves, 165
Gorbachev, Mikhail, 36
Grau San Martín, Ramón, 101, 114, 115, 116,
    118, 126
Great Depression, 135
Grenada, 9. *See also* Gairy, Eric
Guantánamo Bay military base, 29

Guatemala, 144, 152
Guerrier, Philippe, 155
Guyana, 179
Guyot, François (bishop of Cap Haïtien), 175
Guzmán, S. Antonio, 108

Haile Selassie (emperor of Ethiopia), 236n. 76
Haiti, 14, 15; armed forces in, 32, 53, 54, 55, 63, 72, 73, 157, 159, 164–70, 181; black middle class in, 62–63, 158, 161, 165, 168, 171–73, 178; civil society in, 74; Communist Party in, 171; constitutional hypocrisy in, 155–56; corruption in, 28; crisis of sovereignty in, 30, 252n. 92; economic development in, 163–64, 168; economic elites in, 162, 163, 172–73; elections in, 73, 74, 166, 169; exiles, 32, 159, 166; foreign aid, 28, 63, 72, 252n. 89; military dictatorship, 71–74, 169–70, 179–80; natural disasters in, 40; peasants, 162, 168; plebiscite, 169; pope's visit (1983), 43, 73, 167; Protestant churches in, 167; pseudo-opposition in, 86, 94; relations with Dominican Republic, 28, 88, 94, 98, 169, 177, 257nn. 26 & 27; relations with U.S., 30, 44, 63, 72, 155, 159, 165, 172, 179; Roman Catholic church in, 42, 43, 63, 73, 154–55, 158, 159, 160, 162, 166–68, 174–75; technocrats in, 11; U.S. embargo, 176; U.S. occupation, 157, 180
Hama, 205
Hastings, Warren, 156
Henri Christophe (king of Haiti), 153, 154, 155, 156
Heureux, Ulises, 88–89, 92, 93, 111, 255n. 6
Hispaniola, 31. *See also* Dominican Republic; Haiti
Hitler, Adolf, 24, 193
Homayun, Dariush, 199
Honorat, Jean-Jacques, 176, 179
houngans (voodoo priests), 154, 158
Hoveida, Amir-Abbas, 192, 193, 194, 196, 203
Hull, Cordell, 99
Huntington, Samuel P., 5
Hussein, Saddam, 35
Hutus, 67

ideology, 14, 23–25
Iliescu, Ion, 20, 254n. 110
Ilocos Norte province (Philippines), 15, 20, 214–16

IMF (International Monetary Fund), 11, 164, 226
Imperial Commission (Iran), 197
Imperial Inspectorate (Iran), 197
Inalcik, Halil, 6
Iraq, 35, 196, 205
Iran, 6–7; Allied occupation of, 30, 186, 191; armed forces in, 13, 194–98; coup d'etat (1953), 30, 189; constitutional revolution (1906), 34, 185, 189, 268n. 7; corruption in, 46; crisis of sovereignty in, 30; earthquakes, 39; elections in, 18, 193, 243–44n. 90; exiles, 46; Majlis (parliament), 186, 192; monarchy, 6–7, 15, 34, 191, 193; oil, 22, 27, 186–88, 191; political parties in, 189, 191–93; property rights in, 182–83, 189; relations with Great Britain, 30, 186, 190, 203; relations with U.S., 187–88, 203; rule of law, 182–85; state, 183–84; technocrats in, 11, 193–94, 200–203. *See also* Islamic revolution; White Revolution
Iran-e Novin Party, 18, 192
Iran-e Now Party, 191–92
Islamic revolution (Iran), 5, 39, 40, 41, 45, 49, 50, 56, 57–59, 67–69, 196, 203–4

Jacmel, 157
Jagan, Cheddi, 179
Jam, Fereidun, 195–97
Jean Rabel, 168
Jérémie, 157, 167
John Paul II (pope), 43, 73, 167, 179
Juan Carlos I (king of Spain), 36

Kabila, Laurent, 67
Kennedy, John, 105
Khatami, Mohammad, 243n. 90
Khmer Rouge, 25, 234n. 34
Khomeini, Ayatollah Ruhollah, 42, 180, 188, 244n. 98
Khuzistan, 200
Kim Il-sung, 9, 23, 37
Kim Jong-il, 9, 37
Kissinger, Henry, 32
Korea, North, 9, 66
Korea, South, 38

Lacayo, Antonio, 46
Lafontant, Roger, 163, 170, 172
Laurel, Jose P., 214
Laurel, Salvador, 214

Lauture, Gladys, 172
Lavalas Party, 171, 180
Laxalt, Paul, 76
Lenin, Vladimir, 30, 180
Les Cayes, 157
Lescot, Elie, 158
Liberal Nationalist Party (Nicaragua), 132, 133, 141, 142
Liberal Party (Cuba), 116, 120
Liberal Party (Nicaragua), 18, 33, 132, 133, 135, 147
Liberal Party (Philippines), 34, 208, 210, 212
liberalization, 38–41; in Tunisia, 36
liberation theology, 74, 243n. 80
Liberia, 47
Lopez, Eugenio, 218–219
Lukashenko, Alexander, 47

Macapagal, Diosdado, 209, 211, 218, 272n. 18
Machado, Gerardo, 114, 116
Macías Nguema, Francisco, 25, 32; dictatorship, 9, 235n. 58; family background and personality, 16–17, 37; personality cult, 14
Magloire, Jean, 163
Magloire, Paul, 155, 156, 158, 161, 162
Magsaysay, Ramon, 209, 211, 272n. 18
Makati Business Club, 228
Malacañang, 207
Malval, Robert, 180
Managua earthquake, 28, 40, 42, 138, 143, 145–46. *See also* natural disasters
Manigat, Leslie, 161, 166, 169
Mansur, Hasan-Ali, 192
Mao Zedong, 24
Marcos, Ferdinand, 8, 14, 115; and armed forces, 12, 53, 54; election of, 9, 18, 34, 209, 212; foreign policy of, 21; overthrow of, 57, 75–77; family background and personality, 214–15; personality cult, 222–23; sultanistic regime, 216–26; war record of, 214–15
Marcos, Imelda, 15, 215, 217–19, 221–22, 275n. 78
Marcos, Ferdinand, Jr., 15
Marcos family, 15, 216, 221
Mardom Party (Iran), 18, 192–93
Márquez Sterling, Carlos, 126
Masferrer, Rolando, 120
Mashad, 191
Medellín conference, 42
Melliyun Party, 192
Menocal, Mario G., 115

Mexico, 40, 47; civil society, 242n. 69
Mijares, Primitivo, 207–98
Mobutu Sese Seko: dictatorship, 5, 9, 10, 59, 63–67; and armed forces, 54, 55, 65; corruption, 28; opposition to, 66–67, 69–70; ouster of, 67, 69–70; personality cult, 13–14, 16; seizure of power, 31
Mohammad Reza Pahlavi (shah of Iran): and armed forces, 13, 194–98, 202–3; corruption, 15, 46, 198–201; exile, 242n. 66; foreign policy of, 21; personality, 37, 195, 203–4; personality cult, 13, 14; sultanistic regime, 17, 18, 188, 192–98, 202–3. *See also* White Revolution
monarchy: in Africa, 16, 236n. 69; in Arabian peninsula, 27; in Balkans, 3; in France, 232n. 8; in Haiti, 153–54; in Iran, 6–7, 15, 34, 191, 193; in Spain, 36
Moncada military barracks, 127, 238n. 100, 244n. 98
"mongoose men" (Grenada), 12
monopolies, 22, 94, 220, 227
Mosaddeq, Mohammad, 187, 204
Mouvement Populaire de la Révolution (MPR [Zaire]), 13, 64
Mouvement pour l'Evolution Sociale en Afrique Noire (MESAN [Central African Republic]), 13
Mujal, Eusebio, 120
Muñoz Marín, Luis, 240n. 33
Mzali, Mohammed, 36

Najaf, 205
Namphy, Henri, 59, 72, 73, 166, 169–70
National Democratic Front (Philippines), 75–77
National Front (Iran), 187, 192
National Guard (Nicaragua), 13, 44, 133; and repression, 136, 142; role, 139; and U.S. assistance, 32, 143; and war against FSLN-led insurgency, 148–49
National Salvation Front (Romania), 78, 254n. 110
Nationalist Party (Philippines), 34, 208, 210, 212
natural disasters, 39–40, 93, 256n. 16. *See also* Managua earthquake
Nayyer al-molk, 202
neopatrimonialism, 6, 9–10, 246n. 10
neosultanism, 6, 7, 8, 111
Nerette, Joseph, 179

New Society Movement (Philippines), 13

Nguza Karl-I-Bond, 12

Nicaragua: banks, 134, 262n. 5; civil wars, 134, 135, 137; clientelism, 133; Communists in, 141; constitutional hypocrisy in, 137; corruption in, 28, 40; crisis of sovereignty in, 29, 135; economic development in, 136, 138–39, 144–46; economic elites in, 134, 138, 142–43, 146; elections in, 18, 20, 137, 252n. 93; exiles, 142, 147; foreign aid, 28; Indians of Atlantic Coast, 24; organized labor, 133, 141, 146; organized peasants, 146; relations with Costa Rica, 141–42, 149; relations with U.S., 29, 44, 46, 135, 151; revolution in, 41, 44, 56–57, 67–69, 148–51; Roman Catholic church in, 42, 43, 146. *See also* FSLN; National Guard

Nixon, Richard, 144

Niyazov, Separmurad, 47

noirisme (Haiti), 9, 14, 15, 158

Nord, Alexis, 154, 155

Noriega, Manuel, 8, 17, 30, 32, 34, 41; and Shah of Iran, 242n. 66

Nosrat al-Dowleh, 191, 201–2

OAS, 105, 106, 107, 175–76

Obando y Bravo, Miguel (archbishop of Managua), 43

oil, 22, 27, 31, 110, 186, 187

Ongpin, Jaime, 228

Ortega, Daniel, 20, 46, 150

Orumieh, 15

Ottoman Empire, 6, 31, 233n. 19

Pahlavi family, 199–200

Pahlavi, Mohammad Reza Shah. *See* Mohammad Reza Shah Pahlavi

Pahlavi, Reza Shah. *See* Reza Shah Pahlavi

Pahlavi Foundation, 199, 202

Panama, 8, 19, 139, 149; relations with U.S., 29–30, 41, 44, 46

Panama Canal, 29–30, 31, 32, 135

Panama Canal Zone, 30, 104

Pan-Iranist Party, 192–93

Papa Doc. *See* Duvalier, François

Paraguay, 8, 10, 71; army in, 13, 252n. 93, 253n. 108. *See also* Colorado Party; Stroessner

parties, political, 13, 18, 24, 33–34,

Parti Socialiste Destourien (Tunisia), 36

Pascal-Trouillot, Ertha, 169, 171

Pastora, Edén, 42, 149

patrimonialism, 4, 5, 21–22, 26–27

Paul, Evans, 172

Péligre, Lake, 40

Péligre dam, 162

"people power" (Philippines), 75

Pérez Jiménez, Marcos, 5, 27, 75

Perón, Juan Domingo, 33, 180

Persian Gulf, 186, 194

personality cult, 13–14. *See also* Ceauşescu; Macías Nguema; Marcos, Ferdinand; Mobutu Sese Seku; Mohammad Reza Pahlavi; Trujillo Molina

Peru, 47, 122, 240n. 37

Pétion, Alexandre, 153, 154, 155

Petit Goâve, 165

Peynado, Jacinto, 94

Philippine Constabulary, 217

Philippines, 5, 8, 15; armed forces in, 12, 53, 54, 75–77, 216–17; breakdown of democracy in, 208–14; clientelism, 208–12; Communist Party in, 212, 227, 228; constitutional hypocrisy in, 225; corruption in, 27–28, 216, 218–19, 227; crisis of sovereignty in, 212–14; economic development in, 223–24; elections in, 18, 19, 34, 208–12, 226, 227–28; foreign aid, 218; martial law in, 8, 19, 208, 215–16; Muslim secessionists, 212; "people power," 75; plebiscite, 225–26; pope's visit (1981), 43; relations with U.S., 30, 44, 75, 76, 209, 213, 224–25, 227; Roman Catholic church in, 42, 43, 75, 228–29; supreme court, 210, 213, 217, 225; technocrats in, 11; transition to democracy in, 44, 49–50, 75–77, 227–29. *See also* Reform the Armed Forces Now Movement

Pico Duarte, 94

Pinochet, Augusto, 115, 226, 234n. 38, 242n. 65

Pittini, Ricardo (archbishop of Santo Domingo), 100

Platt Amendment, 29, 119

plebiscites, 18–19. *See also* Chile; Haiti; Philippines; Romania

posttotalitarian regimes, 15, 160–61, 231n. 2

PRD (Partido Revolucionario Dominicano), 106, 107, 108, 110

Préval, René, 172, 180

Prío, Carlos, 116, 118, 120

pseudo-opposition, 18, 40. *See also* Dominican Republic

Puerto Cabezas, 15

Puerto Rico, 240n. 33

Qajar dynasty, 185, 186, 189
Qom, 205
Quantico military base, 92
Quirino, Elpidio, 209

racial cleavages, 19, 20, 34, 117, 266n. 11
Radical Union Party (Cuba), 120
Ramos, Fidel, 217, 227
Ramzi Ata'i, Amir Abbas, 195–96
Rastakhiz Party (Iran), 13, 193, 194
Razmara, Ali, 187
Reagan, Ronald, 76, 151, 168
Reform the Armed Forces Now Movement
    (RAM), 54, 75–77, 227, 229
Reid Cabral, Donald, 108
revolution, 41–45, 49, 50, 56, 57, 67–70, 245n.
    3. *See also* Cuban revolution; Islamic revo-
    lution; Nicaragua, revolution in
Reza Pahlavi (shah of Iran): and armed
    forces, 197; corruption, 186, 198, 202; dress
    codes, 191; family background and per-
    sonality, 16–17, 37, 195, 203; and Iranian
    nationalism, 14–15; rise to power, 19, 185,
    190, 202; state builder, 10, 34; sultanistic
    regime, 186, 192, 201
Rivero Agüero, Andrés, 126
Robert, Paul (bishop of Gonaïves), 162
Rodríguez, Andrés, 8
Roman Catholic church, 42–43, 160. *See also*
    Christian base communities; Cuba; Do-
    minican Republic; Haiti; John Paul II; lib-
    eration theology; Medellín conference;
    Nicaragua; Philippines; *ti legliz*; Vatican II
Romania, 15, 18, 19, 20, 31, 32, 33, 35, 244n. 93;
    breakdown of sultanism in, 77–78;
    plebiscite in, 19
Romanian Communist Party, 19, 20, 54, 77,
    253n. 109
Romélus, Willy (bishop of Jérémie), 175
Romualdez, Benjamin "Kokoy", 219, 221
Romualdez family, 215
Roosevelt, Franklin, 90, 213, 256n. 15
Roosevelt, Theodore, 89
Roxas, Manuel, 209, 213
Rwanda, 67

Sacasa, Juan Bautista, 132
Salesian order, 170, 174
Salnave, Silvain, 155
Sam, Tiréas Simon, 155
Sandbrook, Richard, 5, 8

Sandinistas. *See* FSLN
Sandino, Augusto César, 42, 132, 135
Santo Domingo, 15, 91
Santos, Alejo, 226
Santos Zelaya, José
São Tomé e Principe, 38
Sardar As'ad Bakhtiari, Ja'farqoli Khan, 186,
    201
SAVAK, 197–98
Schmitt, Carl, 162
Securitate (Romania), 54, 77–78, 248n. 24,
    253n. 109
Senegal, 38, 240n. 46
Shaba province (Zaire), 32, 66
Shahsavar by-election, 193
Shariati, Ali, 43
Shi'ite clergy of Iran, 43, 185–88
Sin, Jaime (archbishop of Manila), 43, 228, 229
Social Christian parties (Nicaragua), 141, 147,
    150
Somalia, 47
Somoza Debayle, Anastasio: corruption, 138,
    142–43; foreign policy of, 21, 144; and
    National Guard, 133, 135, 139; ouster of, 42,
    59, 148; personality, 37, 136, 144; regime, 17,
    56, 133–34, 137–38, 140–42, 148, 152
Somoza Debayle, Luis, 132, 133, 134
Somoza family, 8, 15, 18, 46, 62, 132, 137
Somoza García, Anastasio, 16, 17, 23, 37,
    assassination, 104, 132, 136; regime, 10, 29,
    56, 133, 135, 137–38, 141
Soulouque, Faustin, 154, 155, 156
sovereignty, crisis of, 28–33, 44. *See also*
    Cuba; Dominican Republic; Haiti; Iran;
    Nicaragua; Philippines; Zaire
Soviet Union, 36, 47, 105, 186, 187, 221, 241n. 57
Spain, 3, 4, 5, 36, 38, 171, 215, 233n. 23
Stalin, Joseph, 15, 16, 24, 241n. 57
Stalinism, 4, 15
Stepan, Alfred, 80, 122, 247n. 12
Stroessner, Alfredo, 8, 71, 252n. 93, 253n. 108
Sudre Dartiguenave, Philippe, 156
sugar, 27, 95, 106, 109, 110, 117, 120, 219–20
sultanism: armed forces under, 53–57, 68;
    breakdown of, 37–45, 51–81; characteris-
    tics of, 10–25; compared to authoritarian-
    ism, 3–4, 24–25; compared to caudillism,
    23; compared to totalitarianism, 23–24,
    160–61; corruption under, 16, 42; defini-
    tion of, 7; dynasticism in, 15–16; econom-
    ics of, 21–23, 26–28; elections under, 18, 39,

sultanism (*cont.*)
  40; genesis of, 26–37; ideology and, 7, 14, 23–24; legacy of, 45–58, 78–81; liberalization in, 38–41; opposition under, 52, 57, 61, 62; origin of term, 4–7; parties under, 13, 18; and place names, 15, 94; and religion, 42–43; and revolutions, 41–45, 49, 56–59; and size, 27; subnational, 47
Syria, 205

Tabatabai, Seyyed Zia, 190, 202
Tabernilla family, 121–22, 130
Tacho, *See* Somoza Debayle, Anastasio
Taiwan, 38
technocrats, 11–12. *See also* Haiti; Iran; Philippines; Zaire
Teimurtash, Abdolhosein, 186, 191–92, 201
Texas, 16
ti legliz (Haiti), 42, 73, 167, 175. *See also* Christian base communities
Timişoara, 78
Titid. *See* Aristide
Tocqueville, Alexis de, 19
Tonton Macoutes (Haiti), 12, 54, 55, 62, 73, 78, 158–59, 162, 163, 164–66, 168, 169, 253[n.] 104
Torrijos Herrera, Omar, 17, 32, 34
totalitarian regimes, 3–4, 23–24, 35. *See also* posttotalitarian regimes
transition to democracy, 38–41, 46, 49–60, 102–3, 226
Troncoso de la Concha, Manuel de Jesús,
Trouillot, Michel-Rolph, 157, 161
Trujillo, Héctor B., 95, 107
Trujillo, Ramfis, 15, 37, 97, 104, 106, 107, 26 42
Trujillo Molina, Rafael Leónidas: and armed forces, 95, 97–98; assassination, 44, 96, 104, 106, 228, 260n. 41; corruption, 93, 95, 99–100, 256–57n. 17; election of, 91, 256n. 14; family background, 16, 90–91, personality cult, 13, 93–94; popularity, 86; regime, 4, 8, 10, 23, 85–87, 93–102, 104, 111; relations with U.S., 21, 91–92, 96, 101–2, 194; seizure of power, 29, 85, 91–92
Tshisekedi, Etienne, 66
Tudeh Party (Iran), 187, 192
Tufanian, Hasan, 195–96
Tunisia, 36–37
Turkey, 38, 233n. 23, 242n. 62
Turkmenistan, 47

Tutsis, 67
tyranny, 163, 234n. 34

UCN (Unión Cívica Nacional [Dominican Republic]), 107

Zahedi, Ardeshir, 196
Zahedi, Fazlollah, 202
Zaydín, Ramón, 116
Zaire, 5, 44, 69–70; armed forces in, 54, 55, 66–67; civil society in, 64; corruption in, 27; crisis of sovereignty in, 31; foreign aid, 28, 64, 66–67; mineral resources, 22, 27, 250n. 59; technocrats in, 11. *See also* Mobutu Sese Seko; Mouvement Populaire de la Révolution; Shaba province

DATE DUE

HIGHSMITH #45115